ADDITIONS AND CORRECTIONS

TO THE
W.P.A.

INVENTORY

OF

CUYAHOGA COUNTY, OHIO:

CLEVELAND

Jana Sloan Broglin

HERITAGE BOOKS
2025

HERITAGE BOOKS

AN IMPRINT OF HERITAGE BOOKS, INC.

Books, CDs, and more—Worldwide

For our listing of thousands of titles see our website
at
www.HeritageBooks.com

Published 2025 by
HERITAGE BOOKS, INC.
Publishing Division
5810 Ruatan Street
Berwyn Heights, MD 20740

(Originally Titled)
INVENTORY OF THE COUNTY ARCHIVES OF OHIO

Prepared by
Cuyahoga County Archives Survey
Division of Women's and Professional Projects
Works Progress Administration

No. 18. CUYAHOGA COUNTY (CLEVELAND)

Cleveland, Ohio
Cuyahoga County Archives Survey
in Cooperation with the
Historical Records Survey
June 1937

International Standard Book Number
Paperbound: 978-0-7884-4849-2

2nd edition

In 1929 after the stock market crash along with the Great Depression, drought of 1930, and crop failures which followed, President Herbert Hoover and his successor Franklin D. Roosevelt formulated relief projects, the most successful was the establishment of the Works Progress Administration (WPA).

Established as the Works Projects Administration in 1935, the WPA was the largest of the many programs developed during Roosevelt's "New Deal." In 1939, the agency's name was changed to Works Progress Administration, and continued as such until its demise in 1943.

The Federal Writers' Project, a division of the WPA (known as Federal Project Number One), created jobs for many unemployed librarians, clerks, researchers, editors, and historians. The workers went to courthouses, town halls, offices in large cities, vital statistics offices and inventoried records. Besides indexing works, many records were transcribed. One of these many projects was the *Inventory of the County Archives* which has benefitted genealogists and historians. The inventories listed the records, either by volumes or file boxes and years per record type, within the office. Although the WPA oversaw this project, the information for each volume of records may differ significantly by the information submitted.

Many of these volumes included in the *Inventory of the County Archives* contain listings of records initiated specifically for the depression era. Records may include volumes for the WPA, CCC (Civilian Conservation Corps), as well as for tuberculosis hospitals. These listings may include the names of the workers.

The information herein is verbatim using the vernacular of the time. Obvious spelling errors have been corrected. Records listed may have met the requirement for retention and have been destroyed as per the records retention act, while other records are considered permanent records. Records once considered "open" to the public, such as lunacy, idiotic, and juvenile cases, or records involving children, such as children's homes, and school records may be "closed" due to a revision of state laws. (*See:* **https://codes.ohio.gov/ohio-revised-code**) Ohio Revised Code, sections 149.31 and 149.34). However, the records may be opened to family members with adequate proof of lineage.

PREFACE
2nd edition

Although this project was to encompass all of Ohio's 88 counties, approximately 30 of these inventories have been located while others may not have been done, lost, or are located in libraries and not known to the general public.

Volumes follow a general format listing the offices. Those for Fulton, Medina, Muskingum, and Wayne include either additional information or may be lacking segments found in other volumes as these were "missing" books.

The addresses and website section of this edition list an up-to-date location guide to each office mentioned. Non-governmental websites may list locations where documentation for the county may be found.

Note: In 1937 when this inventory was done, many records were held off-site (see listing on page xvii and xviii), in basement store rooms or the attic. Each blurb regarding the description of a specific volume gives the location, such as Auditor's office, It is unknown what happened to records listed off-site.

Jana Sloan Broglin
Fellow, Ohio Genealogical Society
Swanton, Ohio
2025

The Cuyahoga County Archives Survey began operation in October 1935, with the Cleveland Public Library as its sponsor. The purpose of the survey was to prepare a descriptive inventory of public records, in order to make such records accessible for local historical research and for the use of government officials and attorneys. Both Donald F. Lybarger, County Recorder, and Mayo Fesler, director of the Citizens League, were actively interested in the planning of this survey, having long felt the need of such an inventory both for reference purposes, and as a means of facilitating the storing and preservation of public records in the county.

This *Guide to the County Archives of Cuyahoga County* contains condensed reports of the inventory of county records, separated as to the county offices with which these records are deposited. Each entry gives the exact title of the record; the limiting dates of the records in existence, noting any missing records; the total volume of the record; a brief description of the contents; the manner of arrangement; the indexing; and the location of the record. In most cases the entries are arranged functionally for each department. A preface to the condensed inventory of each office gives a brief history of the office, based essentially on an analysis of the Ohio statutes. The volume contains an alphabetical index, including cross-references, to the titles of the records. The personnel of the project is entirely responsible for the original inventory, the legal prefaces, the final editing, and the mimeograph work. The volume is mimeographed in an edition of 300 copies.

This volume, number XVIII of the state series, known as the *Guide to County Archives of Ohio,* is the first of a series of volumes to be issued by Project 13692. Further volumes will contain condensed inventories of the records of political subdivisions of the county. They will supplement the inventories of public and semi-public records being compiled by the Historical Records Survey, and by the Survey of Federal Archives in Cuyahoga County. The newspaper digest project is adding to the series of inventories the *Annals of Cleveland,* containing abstracts of local news from Cleveland newspapers since 1818. These enterprises, taken together, are intended to give the community an exhaustive guide to the information about itself, useful for all reference purposes.

Since February 1936, the Cuyahoga County Archives Survey has worked with the technical cooperation of the Historical Records Survey, a Federal project, supervised nationally by Dr. Luther H. Evans, and for the State of Ohio by Dr. William D. Overman and Mr. James J. Dunton. The survey is also indebted to Dr. Robert C. Binkley, Professor of History at Western Reserve University, for technical advice.

Preface
1st edition

Many county officials have aided through their advice and cooperation, particularly Mr. Lybarger, and the County Commissioners, Messers, John F. Curry, James A. Reynolds, and Joseph F. Gorman, who have contributed the working space, and the materials for the mimeographing and the binding of the volumes. The Citizens League has contributed the mimeograph stencils. Col. Joseph H. Alexander, Director of District Four, WPA in Ohio, Mrs. Bess S. Sprague, Supervisor Women's and Professional Projects, and Mr. Forest Barber, Supervisor of Professional and Clerical Projects, have directed operations.

Lillian K. Fuchs, Superintendent
Cuyahoga County Archives Survey
District Four
Cleveland, April 1937.

Record entries

— .... to date
A.P.L. .... Animal Protective League
approx. .... approximately
Bldg. .... Building
CCRA. .... Cuyahoga County Relief Administration
CWA .... Civil Works Administration
I.S. of P.O. .... Inspection and Supervision of Public Offices
no. .... number
pp. .... pages
volume(s) .... volume(s)
SR .... Storeroom

Buildings

C.C. .... County Courthouse
C.H. .... City Hall
Cleve. A. P. L. .... Cleveland Animal Protection League
Cr. Ct. .... Criminal Court
Juv. Ct. .... Juvenile Court
Pub. Sq. .... Public Square
Std. .... Standard

Legal Statements

A.L.R.. .... American Law Report
Art. .... Article
Ass'n .... Association
Capias .... a warrant or order for arrest of a person,
typically issued by the judge or magistrate in a case
Certiorari .... to be more fully informed
Const. .... Constitution
Demurrer .... a legal objection
(Et) passim .... and here and there
Fed. Stat .... Federal Statute
G. C. .... General Code

Legal Statements (continued)

Habeas corpus . . . . protection against illegal imprisonment

H. or H.B. . . . . House Bill

Ibid. . . . . the same reference

Nolle prosequi . . . . notice of abandonment by a
plaintiff or prosecutor of all or part of a suit or action

O. Jur. . . . . Ohio Jurisprudence

O. L. . . . . Ohio Laws

op. cit. . . . . work cited

para. . . . . paragraph

pt. . . . . part

Praecipes . . . . a written request for action

Procedendo . . . . sends case from appellate court to a lower court

Quo warranto. . . . . by what authority or warrant

R.S. . . . . Revised Statute

sec. . . . . section (s)

Ser . . . . Service

Stat. L. . . . . Statutes at Large (Federal)

Supersedeas . . . . . . a stay of enforcement of a judgment pending appeal

U.S.C.A. . . . . United States Code Annotated

Venires . . . . a group of people summoned for jury duty

writ. . . . . a formal, legal document, a decree

The territory comprising Cuyahoga County, and particularly the mouth of the Cuyahoga River, was a focal point in the migration of American Indians. Many of the original paths were used by the white man in the planning of his roads and can be identified today. Title to the land east of the Cuyahoga River was relinquished by the Indians after the Battle of Fallen Timbers in 1735; and title to the land west of the Cuyahoga River was extinguished on July 4, 1805 by the Treaty of Fort Industry.

The territory constituting Cuyahoga County was claimed by Spain, France, and England at various times prior to the Revolutionary War. By his famous lines of Demarcation, Pope Alexander VI, in 1493, gave to Spain all new lands unoccupied by Christian people west of the 38th meridian. Spain never made good by occupancy her title to northeastern Ohio, which was overshadowed by the claims of France and England. English claims date from the voyage of John and Sebastian Cabot in 1497. Virginia claimed title by reason of the charter granted by King James I in 1609, and Connecticut claimed title under the charter granted by Charles II in 1662. The French based their claims upon the exploration, occupancy, and settlement by Le Caron in 1616, by Marquette in 1668; and by La Salle in 1669. By the Treaties of Paris in 1764, France ceded all claims to this territory to England. England, in turn, relinquished title to the Thirteen Colonies and the lands to the west in 1783, following the Revolution. In 1784 Virginia ceded her claims to the United States government, except for a small reservation in the southern part of Ohio. Connecticut ceded her claims in 1786, reserving, however, a strip of land extending westward from the Pennsylvania boundary along Lake Erie. Part of this "Western Reserve" came eventually to be known as Cuyahoga County, going through a long series of changes before emerging as the district we know by that name today.

The whole Ohio country was included in the Territory Northwest of the River of Ohio erected by the Ordinance of 1787 with General St. Clair as governor. The land east of the Cuyahoga River was created as Washington County on July 27, 1788 by a proclamation of the first territorial governor and judges. Marietta was made the county seat of this territory extending from the lake to the Ohio River. The land west of the Cuyahoga River, extending to the headwaters of all streams flowing into Lake Michigan, was created Wayne County by proclamation of August 15, 1796 with Detroit as the county seat.

In 1795 the state of Connecticut sold the fee title to the Western Reserve, except for the Fire Lands, to the Connecticut Land Company, which bought the Indians title in 1796 and 1805. The surveying of the Western Reserve was done under the supervision of Moses Cleaveland, and the land, divided into 100 acre lots and distributed by the classifying and equalizing committee of the Connecticut Land Company, was sold to individual purchasers.

After the creation of the two original counties east and west of the Cuyahoga River there were many changes before Cuyahoga County reached its present form. In 1797 Jefferson County was created out of Washington County. In 1800 the land east and west of the Cuyahoga River was combined in the creation of Trumbull County. From the original Trumbull County in 1807, the state legislature created Geauga County, with Chardon as its county seat, and Cuyahoga County with Cleveland as the county seat. Cuyahoga remained part of Geauga County until June 1, 1810, when it was officially organized. The name Cuyahoga as its origin in the Indian word "cuyahoga" meaning "crooked water."

The first official description of the boundaries of the new county appeared January 22, 1811. Since the sketch contains several errors, the legislature repealed it on February 18, 1812, and substituted a corrected description. However, this soon became obsolete since territory was detached in 1815 to form Huron County, and in 1824 to form Lorain County. This was the last detachment of any great size although subsequent changes in townships affected the county boundary. Townships were detached and annexed to Cuyahoga County affecting its boundaries until 1843. Cuyahoga County, which has an area of 452.58 square miles, is bounded on the north by Lake Erie, on the east by Lake and Geauga counties, on the south by Summit and Medina counties, and on the west by Lorain County.

Cleveland from the time the first surveyors marked the site of the "city" in 1796 was a natural focal point of settlement. In 1809 a commission was appointed to select a location for the seat of justice of Cuyahoga County. The only place besides Cleveland having serious claims to this honor was Newburgh, which had as large a population as Cleveland, or larger, and was a much more healthy and thriving locality. However its position at the mouth of Cuyahoga carried the day and Cleveland was selected. The village of Newburgh bitterly contested this action until 1826 when it was definitely decided that Cleveland remained the county seat.

On May 1, 1810, the first county officers were inaugurated. As provided by the first Constitution of Ohio and ensuing legislation they were the county commissioners, sheriff, and coroner who were elected; the treasurer who was appointed by the commissioners; the judges of the court of common pleas who were appointed by the general assembly; and the surveyor, prosecutor, recorder and the clerk of courts who were appointed by the judges of common pleas court.

The court of common pleas held its opening session in the newly completed frame store building of Eliba and Harvey Murray located on the south side of Superior Avenue between the Public Square and Seneca (now West 3rd) street. This building, which was occupied by county officials for approximately three years, was torn down in 1855.

In two years Cuyahoga County felt the need of a more suitable structure in which its judiciary and executive officers could be properly housed. A contract was therefore made between the county commissioners and Levi Johnson for the erection of the courthouse and jail on the northwest corner of the Public Square facing Superior Street. The work was started in 1812, but was not completed until the summer of the succeeding year. The building, covering a space of 25 by 50 feet, was two stories high, and was built of logs; It cost $700, the lower story was used as a jail and contained two cells, one for criminals and one for debtors, and a living room for the sheriff. An outside stairway led to the courthouse on the second floor. It was in this little building that justice was administered for approximately fifteen years. This first courthouse was torn down in 1830.

With the question as to whether Cleveland remain the county seat permanently settled, a new courthouse was started in 1828 in the southwest section of the square facing Superior Street. It was a two-story brick building costing $8,000. The upper floor contained the court and jury rooms and the lower floor, the county offices. Public meetings ranging in variety from church gatherings to dances were held there and the Cleveland City Council held its first meeting in this courthouse on April 15, 1836. In 1832 a new stone jail was built in the rear of the courthouse. It faced Champlain Street (now Prospect Avenue) and contained the sheriff's residence and several stone cells. In 1841 the county built a new fireproof jail on the site of the old one. The second courthouse was demolished in 1858.

In 1857 it became evident that increased courthouse facilities were needed. The county commissioners thereupon contracted for a new building, to be built at a cost of $152,500, on the north side of the square on Rockwell Avenue just west of where the Cleveland Electric Illuminating Company building now stands.

Construction was begun in 1857 and completed in 1860. The courthouse was built of dressed stone, was three stories high and 80 feet wide by 152 feet long. In the basement were the offices of the coroner and the surveyor; the ground floor housed the offices of the auditor, probate judge, recorder, and treasurer; the second floor contained two courtrooms and offices of the sheriff and clerk; and on the third were two jury rooms, a room for county school examinations, and the criminal courtrooms. In 1884 the building was altered by a $100,000 addition of two stories, making it 110 feet high. This building, for a long time known as the "old courthouse," stood until 1935, when it was demolished; and the space, together with that occupied by the succeeding courthouse facing on Seneca Street, was converted into a parking lot. While this particular courthouse was under construction, the ancient Baptist Church on the corner of Seneca and Champlain streets was used for court purposes.

In 1875 another "new courthouse" was begun on land facing Seneca Street extending to the old courthouse. The new edifice was nearly 70 feet square with rooms in the forepart of the building for various offices and courts. The rear section of the building housed the county jail. It was the most pretentious courthouse yet erected and cost $250,000. Built in renaissance style, it was four stories high and faced with cut stone. This building was one of the first in the city to be entirely constructed of fireproof materials. Upon completion, the probate and criminal courts, offices of the prosecutor, county surveyor, sheriff and the jail were located in this building. Later the juvenile and insolvency courts were also housed there. After the "new courthouse" was constructed, the county treasurer, auditor, recorder, and coroner retained their offices in the "old courthouse;" subsequently offices for the board of education, board of health, soldiers' and sailors' relief commission, juvenile court, mothers' pension bureau, county farm bureau and the citizens' league were established there also. When the new Lakeside Avenue courthouse was completed in 1912, the main branches of the government were moved into it, but the county prosecutor, criminal courts, the jail and the criminal branch of the sheriff's office remained in the Seneca Street courthouse and jail building until 1930, when they were moved to the new criminal court building on East 21st Street. The Seneca Street courthouse and jail were demolished in 1931. Some records were lost, although not a significant amount, when a fire was started in the grand jury room on the third floor of this courthouse early in December 1892.

In 1894 the county built its first morgue on the site where it now stands on Lakeside Avenue and the coroner has since that time maintained his office in this building. It is a two story building substantially constructed of brick and steel. The first floor contains the receiving room, the autopsy room, supply vault and the main office. On the second floor are located the inquest room, laboratory, and additional offices of the coroner and the deputy coroner.

The present county courthouse located on Lakeside Avenue facing Ontario Street was authorized at the election in November 1901, but actual construction was not started until April 8, 1908. The cornerstone was laid May 30, 1908. On July 3, 1909, all exterior work had been completed in 278 working days. Court actions retarded the progress of the work, and the building was not completely finished and dedicated for service until January 2, 1912. The structure overall is 365 feet long, 204 feet wide, and a quarter of a mile in circumference, and has 289,000 feet of floor space. It was constructed at a total cost of $4,706,343.44 exclusive of the land, which amounted to $924,779.71.

The courthouse, which houses most of the county officers, is badly overcrowded, and although the basement, sub-basement, and fourth and fifth floors attics are used to store records, space is rented in other buildings in the city for additional offices and for storage purposes.

In 1930 the new Criminal Court Building, located on East 21st Street between Superior and Payne Avenues, was completed by the county at a cost of approximately $1,250,000. The main structure is four stories high and is surmounted by a tower fourteen stories high. This tower constitutes the county jail and is capable of housing 1,426 inmates. The building, covering a ground area of 196 by 176 feet, is constructed of steel and marble and is entirely fireproof. The following offices are located there: the criminal assignment room, the grand jury room, the criminal branch of the clerk of courts, the criminal record division, the criminal branch of the sheriff's office, the county prosecutor's office, the probation division, and the division of parole of the state welfare department.

The juvenile court was originally organized as a part of the insolvency court in 1902 and its offices and records were maintained in the "old courthouse" on the square. The first detention home for juveniles was established in 1908 on the third floor of the 8th Precinct Police Station at West 29th Street and Detroit Avenue. In 1913 a house on Beech Avenue (now East 43rd Street) near Scovill Avenue was leased as a girls' detention home. A private residence of 2905 Franklin Avenue was acquired by the county the following year, and after extensive repairs and alterations was used as the juvenile detention home. In 1919 the residence to the west was acquired, and in 1924 they purchased the dwelling to the east, to which they added a two story building. The east and west buildings were condemned in 1930. In 1932 these quarters were entirely vacated, and all occupants and records were transferred to the new juvenile court group on East 22nd Street, the construction of which was completed that same year. The group consists of the juvenile court, the detention home, and the county child welfare division. Fronting on East 22nd Street is the juvenile court building, covering an area of 1435 square feet. Facing Cedar Avenue is the Detention Home for Dependent Children which covers an area of about 6,308 square feet.

There is real need at present for another county owned building designed to care for county business other than that of the courts, and for the proper storage of county records. The county at present is renting space in thirteen buildings at a total monthly rental of $4,419.74. The following pages list all county owned buildings, and buildings in which space has been rented by the county.

NAME	LOCATION
County Courthouse	Lakeside Ave. at Ontario St.
Criminal Courts Bldg.	1560 E. 21st Street
Juvenile Courts Bldg. and Detention Home	2163 E. 22nd Street
County Mortgage	712 Lakeside Ave., East
County Relief Administration Bldg.	2905 Franklin Ave.
High Level Garage	2433 Superior Ave., West
Testing Laboratory	2030 West 19th Street
Brook Park Store Yard	4000 Brook Park Rd.
Fitzwater Yard	Fitzwater Rd.
Miles Ave. Yard	Miles Ave.

BUILDING RENTALS

BUILDING	ADDRESS	FLOOR SPACE	MONTHLY RENTAL
Board of Elections	City Hall	7,000 sq. ft.	$1,250.00
Carnegie Bldg.	2341 Carnegie Ave.	2,500 sq. ft.	$250.00
Century Bldg.	414 Superior Ave. N.W.	3,300 sq. ft.	$219.34
Cleveland Animal Protective League Bldg.	1729 Willey Ave.	8,400 sq. ft.	*
County Garage	715 Hamilton Ave.	5,473 sq. ft.	$200.00
Engineer's Bldg.	1365 Ontario St.	3,358 sq. ft.	$282.50
Hart Bldg.	1240 Ontario St.	9,000 sq. ft.	$300.00
Marion Bldg.	1276 West 3rd St.	1,752 sq. ft.	$124.10
Public Square Bldg.	33 Public Square	3,342 sq. ft.	$365.00
Standard Bldg.	1370 Ontario St.	9,827 sq. ft.	$1,351.21
Store Yard Supply Stations	Lyndhurst, Brecksville, Dover Village, Chagrin Falls, West View	-----	$112.50
TOTAL		45,552 sq. ft.	$4, 454.74**

* The building and equipment of the Cleveland Animal Protective League are used without a rental charge.

** This does not include invoices for electric current used.

The county as a unit of government is of English origin, although counties in England were preceded by shires which were governed by an earldermon, as representative of the crown, assisted by a bishop and sheriff. After the Norman Conquest, the shires were replaced by counties and the sheriff became the chief executive of the county. (W. S. Holdsworth, *History of English Law*, Boston, Massachusetts, 1922, I, 6).

The ordinance of 1787 creating the Northwest Territory authorized the governor to lay out sections of the territory in which the Indian title had been extinguished, into counties and townships, subject to such alteration as may thereafter be made by the legislature. (Theodore Calvin Pease, *Laws of the Northwest Territory, 1788-1800*, Springfield, Illinois, 1925, 125-126).

The organization of county government in Ohio is essentially statutory, although some county offices have been affected by provisions of our state constitution of 1802, 1851, and 1912. The county was originally created as an agency of the state for the execution of state policy, and has only such powers as are conferred upon it by constitution or statute, or are necessarily or fairly implied therefrom. State control of county government has been through detailed legislation, rather than administrative supervision. Since the county in Ohio is a quasi-corporation, suits are brought in the name of the county commissioners or individual county offices rather than that in the name of the county. The county is not liable for damages due to negligence of its officers or employees except as provided by statute. (Report of the Governor's Commission, *The Reorganization of County Government in Ohio,* 1934, 28-31).

The tendency, in the last few years, has been away from this accepted theory of the legal status of the county as a pure state agency without local functions of any significance. The change from rural to urban life, with governmental participation in all phases of public service steadily increasing, has made the county more closely resemble a municipal corporation. The Ohio legislature has recognized this tendency by a constitutional amendment of 1933 conferring home rule in the matter of adopting a county charter and by permitting the transfer or vesting of municipal powers in the county under certain specified conditions. (*Ibid.,* 28-31).

The form of county government has not changed fundamentally in the past hundred years, although each of the county offices has assumed more responsibility as we change from an agricultural to an urban community. All county officers were required to be elected by provision of the constitution of 1851 (*Ohio Const.*, Art. 10, sec., 1), and although this provision has been repealed by the county home rule amendment passed in 1933 (116 O. L. 132-133) Cuyahoga County has made no change in organization of county government. Cuyahoga County is governed by elected county officers, and by boards or agencies appointed by these officers. Consequently, there cannot be said to exist an executive head of government, since each elected official derives his authority either from the state constitution or from acts of the state legislature, and is independent within the limits of the law affecting his office.

The board of county commissioners is the central feature of the structure of county government in Ohio, and it is the name of the board that actions for and against the county are brought. The board, which is composed of three members elected for a term of four years, often acts as the legislative and administrative as well as the executive head although it is definitely limited in all three capacities. The functions of the board of commissioners are extremely varied centering mainly in the financial control of county expenditures, and the authorizing of public works and the letting of contracts, and in the planning of many phases of public welfare. The board of commissioners levies taxes and special assessments, adopts the annual tax budget submitted by the county budget commission, and makes the appropriations. It authorizes the borrowing of money, issues bond or notes, and executes loans. The board selects depositories for county funds, authorizes and executes contracts, appraises or makes most county purchases, and authorizes payment of claims. The board of commissioners has general charge of most public improvements undertaking by the county, although in the case of buildings costing in excess of $25,000, control is vested in a building commission. The commissioners authorize improvements, approved plans and specifications and let the contracts. However, the technical operation of such plans is carried out by the county engineer who is an elected official and sanitary engineer who is appointed by the commissioners. The commissioners have wide welfare responsibilities. They provide for and administer practically all county relief. (*Ibid.,* 58-61).

The financial administration of the county is actually carried out by three offices: the board of county commissioners, the auditor, and the treasurer. The principal duties of the auditor are the keeping of accounts, issuance of warrants for payment of obligations, evaluation of real estate for taxation, and preparation of tax lists. The auditor also issues numerous licenses, serving as the county sealer of weights and measures, and serves as a member of the budget commission, board of revision, and sinking fund commission.

The treasurer is a custodian of all county funds, the tax collector, and distributor of county funds upon warrant of the auditor. He also serves as a member of the budget commission the board of revision, and the sinking fund commission.

The offices of recorder, clerk of courts, and the office of probate court are essentially clerical. The office of recorder is concerned chiefly with the protection of property rights and the recorder receives and records deeds, mortgages, leases and liens affecting title to real property. The recorder also accepts and files chattel mortgages, and records many miscellaneous documents entitled to record. However, he is not bound to determine the validity of such instruments.

The clerk of courts is charged with the keeping and supervision of the records of the court of common pleas and of the court of appeals. He files all petitions and other pleadings filed in court cases and is required by statute to keep at least five books known as the appearance docket, trial docket, journal, record, the execution docket, and indexes for each. The clerk also assesses and distributes court cost, collects and pays alimony, keeps naturalization records, issues hunting and fishing licenses, and receives bills of sale for automobiles for filing and indexing. The records for probate court are kept separate since the probate judge is by statute the clerk of his own court.

The chief county agencies concerned with law enforcement, other than the courts, are sheriff, prosecutor, and coroner. The sheriff serves as a peace officer of the county, although in larger counties, such as Cuyahoga, his police duties are taken over by municipalities and villages. The sheriff is also custodian of the county jail and serves as an officer of the courts for the service of process and the execution of court orders. (*Ibid,* 102). The sheriff also cares for the appraisal, advertisement, and sale of property as directed by order of the court.

The prosecuting attorney prosecutes violations of state laws, chiefly involving persons accused of felonies whose cases come before the county or appellate courts. He also serves as a legal advisor of the county commissioners and all other county officers and county boards. It is his duty to prosecute and defend all suits and actions which any such officer or board may direct, or to which it is party. The principal duty of coroner is to determine the cause of death when the death is supposed to have been caused by unlawful or suspicious means.

In addition to these elective county officers are numerous boards and commissions responsible for the administration of various phases of county government. The judicial function of the county rests with the court of common pleas, court of appeals, probate court, and juvenile court. The legal development of these various county offices and agencies are treated in the preface to the inventory of records of each office.

The essential purpose of this survey has been to make public records more usable, particularly for historical purposes, and not to recommend any reorganization of county government. However, for those interested in alternative forms of county government and recommendations for changes within the present forms, we recommend the reading of the Report of the Governor's Commission, *The Reorganization of County Government in Ohio,* 1934. Recommendations for the formation of a record bureau will be found in the section on the housing, care and accessibility of records.

The 1930 census shows the total population of the subdivisions to be 1,201,455, or approximately 18 percent of the total population of the state.

Cities (12)

Bedford
Berea
Cleveland
Cleveland Heights
East Cleveland
Euclid
Garfield Heights
Lakewood
Maple Heights
Parma
Rocky River
Shaker Heights

Townships (6)

Bedford
Chagrin Falls
Olmsted
Orange
River Edge
Warrensville

Villages (42)

Bay
Beachwood
Bentleyville
Bratenahl
Brecksville
Brookview Heights
Brooklyn
Brooklyn Heights
Brook Park

Villages (Continued)

Chagrin Falls
Cuyahoga Heights
Dover
Fairview
Gates Mills
Glen Willow
Highland Heights
Hunting Valley
Independence
Linndale
Lyndhurst
Mayfield
Mayfield Heights
Middleburgh Heights
Moreland Hills
Newburgh Heights
North Olmsted
North Randall
North Royalton
Olmsted Falls
Orange
Parkview
Parma Heights
Pepper Pike
Richmond Heights
Seven Hills
Solon
South Euclid
Strongsville
University Heights
Valley View
Warrensville Heights
West View

In a large urban community the problem of housing and care of its public records demands much more serious consideration than it has been given in the past. Destruction of records can come in many guises. It may come through fire or other upheavals of nature such as flood or hurricane; rodents and vermin are often responsible for partial destruction of records; age, and its accompaniment of dust and dirt can cause serious deterioration; and last but not least, destruction and theft by individuals have often caused significant losses.

Cuyahoga County has at no time suffered serious catastrophes affecting their records. A fire started in the Seneca Street Courthouse in 1892 caused the loss of a few records, but the loss was not great. The county buildings have been well cared for and the only serious problem is that of deterioration in the present attic and basement storerooms because of dust and poor atmospheric conditions. The courthouse sub-basement has fortunately been cleared of records which were deteriorating because of the dampness. In the attics records are exposed to the extremes of heat, if placed near steam pipe lines; and dampness, since they are thrown directly on the floor. There has been an attempt during this past year to remove records from the attic and place them on the wooden shelves in the Hart Building where atmospheric conditions are better but where there is little protection against the hazard of fire.

Practically none of the basement storerooms have windows, and most of them are dusty, have no ventilation at all, and are seriously over-crowded. County officials can improve upon present conditions very slightly unless provision is made for a new county building. Although these records are in constant use by clerks, attorneys, and the general public, accessibility to the older records under such conditions is exceedingly difficult. The following paragraphs describe the record facilities of the individual county departments.

The recorder's office occupies two large rooms on the first floor of the county courthouse, and three rooms in the basement: Room 35 which houses most of the records, Room 41 which contains maps and plats, and Room 73 which is a storeroom for the oldest records and files of the department and also contains the chattel mortgage indexes. Except for Room 73 where wooden shelves and file boxes are used, the records are in excellent condition and are kept on steel roller shelves and in metal files. The accommodations for use are quite good, although there is practically no room for expansion.

The main office of the county commissioners is located on the first floor of the courthouse. Records are kept in metal file boxes, drawers, and shelves. A number of basement rooms are used by the department: Room 47, which is occupied by the budget division; Room 50, which houses the real estate division; Rooms 47 and 50 have metal file cabinets, and the storeroom has metal roller shelving for the bound volumes, and wood shelving and metal and wood file boxes for unbound materials. The storeroom is crowded and the atmospheric conditions are very poor. Two more rooms are occupied on the first floor of the courthouse: Room 135 which houses the blind relief division, and an alcove which is occupied by the purchasing division. Some of the commissioners records are in the courthouse attic and a few are in the Hart Building.

Various branches of the commissioners office occupies space in other buildings. The planning commission and the sanitary engineer's division occupy Room 1113 of the Public Square Building. Steel and wood file cases are used; there is no room for expansion. The soldiers' and sailors' burial division and the soldiers' and sailors' relief commission appointed by the common pleas court, occupy a room in the Century Building. The building itself is frame and the room contains wood shelving and metal file cabinets. The office of dog warden is located in the Cleveland Animal Protective League Building. His records are kept in steel file cabinets and are in excellent condition. The county relief administration and the annat division are housed in office buildings at 2905 Franklin Avenue. Metal boxes and drawers, and wooden shelving are used. The records have recently been rebound and are in good condition, but the rooms are very crowded. The county child welfare board occupies a building of the juvenile court group and Room 305 of the Carnegie Building. Although they are not crowded, their occupancy of the juvenile court building is not a permanent arrangement.

The office of county engineer occupies practically all of the nineteenth floor of the Standard Building. Metal shelving and metal file cabinets are used and the lighting and atmospheric conditions are good. However, most of the rooms are quite crowded and there is little room for expansion.

The office of clerk of courts comprises two large rooms and a private office on the second floor covering a space of approximately 5,432 square feet. All current business is conducted in these rooms. Metal roller shelving and metal file boxes are used, and the rooms are well lighted. However, the office is over-crowded and a space for current records is inadequate.

The clerk also occupies four rooms in the basement, rooms 28, 29, 34, and 71 covering a total floor space of approximately 11,390 feet. Room 29 contains 2,778 metal file boxes and is used exclusively for filing of automobile bills of sale. Room 28 contains 6,826 metal file boxes in which are filed the pleadings in court cases. The room is well lighted but poorly ventilated. Two small tables are provided for persons wishing to consult records. Room 34 contains earlier case files and old records of the common pleas court and court of appeals, as well as records of defunct courts that have been turned over to the custody of the clerk of courts. This room has poor artificial lighting and the records accumulate a great deal of dust from an adjoining room where waste paper is bailed daily. The atmospheric conditions make this room a poor place for consulting records. Room 71 contains naturalization records and other miscellaneous records kept by the clerk. The lighting and atmospheric conditions are poor. One small wall desk serves persons consulting records.

The oldest court records are stored on the second floor of the Hart Building. Although a few metal file boxes are used, the records are almost entirely stored in fibre file boxes and on wooden shelves. Many of these older volumes are badly in need of repair. The oldest criminal records are likewise stored here although the current records are in the Criminal Courts Building where metal shelving is used and atmospheric conditions are good.

The records of domestic relations bureau, jury commission, criminal record room, psychiatric division, and the probation division are kept in the individual offices for each division and are in good condition.

The office and main record room of the probate court occupy the entire east side and one half of the north side of the second floor of the courthouse. Lighting and atmospheric conditions are good and metal file boxes and roller shelves are used. A balcony has been constructed to accommodate the accumulating records and there is practically no room for expansion. Records of the probate court are also stored in Room 27 of the basement which is equipped with shelving of metal roller type. Lighting is poor in this room and the room is crowded with records.

The juvenile court building group comprises three buildings which house the county child welfare board, the juvenile court, the mothers' pension bureau, and the detention home. Lighting and atmospheric conditions are good, and metal shelving and cabinets are used throughout the buildings. There is room for expansion and accommodations for users are good.

The office of the county prosecutor occupies the north half of the first floor of the Criminal Courts Buildings. Metal shelving and cabinets are used, and lighting and atmospheric conditions are good. A vault in the basement houses the files and older records which are not accessible to the public.

The coroner occupies the county morgue which is an old building and needs renovating. The records are stored in a basement vault where metal and wooden file boxes are used, and on the first and second floors. The records are quite accessible.

The civil branch of the sheriff's office occupies one well-lighted room on the second floor of the courthouse, a temporary office just across from the main office, and a storeroom in the basement. Steel shelving is used on the second floor. The rooms are very crowded and there is no room for expansion of records. The basement storeroom has wooden shelving with practically no room for expansion. Lighting and ventilation are very poor.

The criminal branch of the sheriff's office occupies three rooms in the basement of the Criminal Courts Building, the fourth floor where prisoners are booked and released, and the thirteenth or top floor of the jail which houses a few records and is occasionally used for prisoners when the jail is over-crowded. The criminal branch is not crowded. The oldest records of the sheriff's office, both civil and criminal, are kept in the Hart Building.

The office of county auditor occupies a large part of the first floor of the courthouse. In all of these rooms lighting and ventilation are good and although working space is limited in some of the rooms, there are ample accommodations for users. In the basement the auditor uses Room 16 for the building assessing division, Room 17 for the addressograph department, Rooms 30 and 59 to house the property maps, Room 31 for bookkeeping, Room 42 for the filing of tax duplicates, and Rooms 70 and 72 for the storing of old records. All of these basement rooms contain wood and steel shelving and all are crowded. Accommodations for users are fair.

Large sections of both the attic and the Hart Building are used to store records of the auditor's office. A Works Progress Administration project has helped during the past year to arrange the older auditor's records in chronological order.

The treasurer's office occupies Rooms 159 to 162, Rooms A, B, C, and E, and the oval shaped room known as the "race track" on the first floor. In these rooms lighting and ventilation are good and there are sufficient accommodations for users. Records are also kept in Room 74 in the basement, and the fourth and fifth floor attics and in the Hart Building. Old records have recently been moved from the sub-basement where they were quickly deteriorating. Room 74 and the Hart

Building have wooden shelves, and the records in the attics are strewn on the floor.

The office of the board of elections is located on the first floor of the Cleveland City Hall and consists of two large, well-lighted rooms. Room 31 in the basement and a room in the sub-basement are used for storing old records. Steel shelving and cabinets are used, and accommodations for users are good.

The records of the metropolitan park board, county board of health, and county board of education are all well kept, on steel shelving, in the offices of these departments. The accommodations for people wishing to consult their records are good.

Our need in Cuyahoga County at present is a double one - a need for a new building and a need for a central department of records. A new building should be planned as an office structure for the clerical part of the county business and should be well equipped with fireproof vaults for the proper housing of county records. The present county courthouse would then serve essentially as a courthouse, probably housing the municipal courts as well, and thus releasing space at the Cleveland City Hall, which is equally over-crowded. The new building will cause the county to dispense with the exceedingly high outlay in rentals for office and storage space.

Our other need is for a central department of records, or for the vesting in one of the county officers essentially concerned with records, as is the county recorder, with the authority to properly preserve and administer the permanent storing of old records. Steps should be taken not only to store records in conditions that are favorable to the preservation but also to institute a library system that would assure accessibility of the records to the public and responsibility for the proper handling and return of the records. If the storage space and administration were adequate, it might also be advisable to recommend the placing of certain records of political subdivisions in the custody of the county.

American Law Reporter, 106 vols., 1919—, The Lawyers Co-operative Publishing Co., Rochester, N. Y. The Edward Thompson Co., Northport, Long Island, N. Y. Bancroft Whitney Co., San Francisco, Calif. Published periodically.

Armstrong, Barbara Nachrieb, *Insuring the Essentials,* Macmillan and Co. New York City, 1932.

Chase, Salmon P., *The Statutes of Ohio and of the Northwest Territory,* 3 vols., Corey and Fairbank. Cincinnati, Ohio, 1833.

Crabb, George A., *A History of English Law,* Chauncey Goodrich. Burlington, England, 1831.

De Lolme, Jean Louis, *The Constitution of England*, G. G. J. and J. Robinson, and J. Murray. London, England, 1788.

Griffin, Arthur B. and Curtiss, Arthur F., *The Law of Chattel Mortgages and Conditional Sales*, Matthew Bender and Co. Albany, N. Y., 1931.

Holdsworth, W. S., *A History of English Law,* 10 vols., Little, Brown and Co.,Boston, Mass., 1922.

Howe, Henry, *Historical Collections of Ohio,* 2 vols., State of Ohio. Cincinnati, Ohio, 1888.

Johnson, Crisfield, *History of Cuyahoga County, Ohio,* D. W. Ensign and Co. Cleveland, Ohio, 1879.

Kennedy, James Harrison, *A History of the City of Cleveland,* 1796-1896, The Imperial Press. Cleveland, Ohio, 1896.

Kennedy, James Harrison, and Day, Wilson M., *The Bench and Bar of Cleveland,* The Cleveland Printing and Publishing Co. Cleveland, Ohio, 1889.

Niblack, William C., *An Analysis of the Torrens System of Conveying Lands.* Callahan Co. Chicago, Illinois, 1912.

Ohio Constitution, 1802, 1851, 1912.

Ohio Laws, 110 vols., 1802—. Published annually under State authority by various publishers.

Ohio State Reports, 131 vols., 1852—. Published periodically.

Ohio Jurisprudence, 42 vols., The Lawyers Co-operative Publishing Co. Rochester, N. Y., 1930.

Pease, Theodore Calvin, *Laws of the Northwest Territory, 1788-1800,* Trustees of the Illinois State Historical Library. Springfield, Illinois, 1925.

Randall, Emiluis O., and Ryan, Daniel J., *History of Ohio,* 5 vols. The Century History Co. New York City, 1912.

Revised Statutes of Ohio, 3 vols. Published annually by various publishers.

Throckmorton Ohio Code, Annotated, Banks-Baldwin Co. Cleveland, Ohio. Published annually.

United States Code, Annotated, 61 vols., The West Publishing Co. St. Paul, Minn. Edward Thompson Co., Northport, Long Island, N. Y., 1928.

United States Statutes at Large, 49 vols., Edited and published by authority of Congress under the direction of the Secretary of State. United States Government Printing Office. Published periodically, 1776-1859 and published biennially, 1859-1935.

At common law the transfer of title to real property was a public act, making unnecessary any formal public record of transactions. However, the growing need for some guarantee of property rights in Colonial America led to the establishment of the office of recorder.

Under the provisions of an act of 1795 of the Northwest Territory, which bore close resemblance to a prior act of the Territory of Pennsylvania, an office was established in every county to be called the recorder's office, the purpose and function of which was the recording of deeds and mortgages. The recording was required to be done within twelve months after execution of the instrument, and in default of such act, the deed or mortgage was considered fraudulent and void as against any subsequent purchaser for the valuable consideration, unless it had been recorded before the proving and recording of the deed or conveyance by the subsequent purchaser. (Theodore Calvin Pease, *Laws of the Northwest Territory, 1788-1800*, Springfield Illinois, 1925, 197-201).

A statute of January 20, 1802 provided that the deeds and conveyances executed outside the territory be recorded within one year after their execution, and those executed within the territory be recorded within six months from the time of execution. In default of such recording, the deed or mortgage was to be deemed fraudulent against any subsequent bona fide purchaser, without knowledge of the former deed or conveyance. (Salmon P. Chase, *The Statutes of Ohio and of the Northwestern Territory*, Cincinnati, 1833-1861, I, 342-3).

In the year 1803, during the first session of the general assembly of the state of Ohio, a statute was enabled entitled "an act providing for the recording of deeds, mortgages, and other conveyances of land," by which the office of county recorder was established and his duties were defined. His duties were to procure proper books and record therein all deeds, mortgages, leaseholders, and conveyances of lands and tenements lying within the county; to endorse on each instrument the time of filing for record; to record in regular secession according to priority of receipt; and to number the page of the book where recorded. (O. L. 136). The territorial act was but slightly altered by the revised law of 1805. (3 O. L. 348).

The recordation of powers of attorney authorizing the sale of lands, or for the making of any written instrument for the conveyance or encumbrance of land before such sale takes place, was provided for in 1818. (16 O. L. 152-157). The act of 1820 provided that all deeds, mortgages and other instruments, if not recorded, shall be fraudulent against subsequent bona fide purchasers without knowledge of their existence. (18 O. L. 166-170).

The law has remained almost entirely unaltered since 1831, when it was provided that all mortgages shall be recorded in the office of the recorder, and shall take effect from the time of recording. The word "time" was defined as the precise time of day. The stipulations as to deeds and powers of attorney for the sale of land were left unchanged. (29 O. L. 346-349).

The method of choosing the recorder and fixing his term of office has been changed frequently. Until 1829 the office was appointive by authority conferred upon the judges of the common pleas court. By this act it became an elective office for a period of three years, instead of seven, as prescribed by the act of 1803. (27 O. L. 65). The term remained at three years until the constitutional amendment of November 7, 1905, which required county officers to be elected in the even-numbered years and their term to be either two or four years. (Ohio Const. Art. 17, sec. 2). The term of office for the recorder was fixed at two years, and so continued until the amendment of 1933, extending the present existing term of office to January 1937 and providing thereafter for a four-year term. (115 O. L. 192).

Numerous statutes have been enacted affecting the administration and scope of the recorder's office. The recordation of chattel mortgages was provided for in 1846. Such mortgages were filed with the township clerks or the county recorder, depending upon the residence of the mortgagors, and in default thereof, were void as against third parties. (44 O. L. 61-62). In 1906 it was provided that such mortgages be filed with the recorder, exclusively. (98 O. L. 114). Since 1929 it has been permissible to file chattel mortgages given by a railroad or a public utility on its personal property in the office of the secretary of state. (113 O. L. 413). In 1914 the Torrens act was approved, providing for the registration and guarantee of land titles. (103 O. L. 914-960).

Although the recorder necessarily kept certain records in the early days of the office, the language of the statutes as to this duty was vague and ambiguous. The first territorial act which established the office required that the recorder shall provide parchment or good large books of royal or other paper, well bound and covered; wherein he shall record in a fair and legible hand, all deeds and conveyances. In the act of 1803 the wording was changed to read "one book." This clause was not changed in the bill of 1805. At that time, however, he was given the duty of recording maps or plats of new towns, and of the subdivisions thereof. (3 O. L. 213).

He was required to keep three separate sets of record books in 1850. It was stipulated that one of these sets was to be denominated record of deeds, and he was to record therein all deeds, powers of attorney and other written instruments for the unconditional sale or conveyance of lands; in another of these sets, to be denominated record of mortgages, he was to record all mortgages, powers of attorney, and other instruments by which lands may be mortgaged, or otherwise conditionally sold, affected or encumbered; in the third, to be denominated record of plats, he was to record all plats and maps of town lots and the subdivisions thereof. (48 O. L. 65). A separate record of leases was required in 1865 (62 O. L. 170), and daily registers of deeds and mortgages were required in 1896. (92 O. L. 268).

The first mention of a complete general index to all the records in the recorder's office was made in 1835. (33 O. L. 9). This remained the only requirement for indexing until 1896 when the recorder was given the duty of making and keeping up at the beginning of each day's business, general alphabetical indexes of the names of all parties to all instruments received for record by him. (92 O. L. 268). It was directed in 1911 that this index be both direct and reverse, and show the kind of instrument, the date thereof, the range, township and section or the survey number and the number of acres, or the lot and sublot number and the parts thereof, as the case may require, of each tract or a lot of land described in any such instrument of writing. (102 O. L. 288).

With the advent of the Torrens Act in 1913, the recorder was required to keep certain records of registered lands. He must keep signature cards, records of surveys, registers of titles, tract indexes, an alphabetical index of liens and lesser estates, an alphabetical index of owners, a record of leases, records of trust and exceptional estates, and an entry book of documents filed with him. (103 O. L. 945).

Among other documents which the recorder may receive for record are soldiers' discharges; certificates of compliance of foreign corporations and certified copies of renewals granted by such companies to their agents; limited partnership agreements; stallion keepers liens; partition fence records; federal tax liens; contractor's, subcontractors', material man's, laborer's, and mechanic's liens; liens of mutual fire insurance companies; liens on public works; grants of right of way to railroads; leases of natural gas and oil lands; and certificates, assignments or conveyances executed by the state superintendent of insurance. (62 O. L. 79; 69 O. L. 32; 78 O. L. 248; 81 O. L. 179; 97 O. L. 140; 110 O. L. 252; 75 O. L. 48, 514 and 103 O. L. 168; 69 O. L. 640; 95 O. L. 609; 72 O. L. 71; 85 O. L. 179; 69 O. L. 32).

Cashier's Division

1. DAILY REGISTER
1899—. 54 volumes; 2 bundles.

A daily listing of all instruments filed for record, giving date and exact time of receipt, document number, name of grantee, and type of instrument. In order of instrument numbers. Handwritten on printed forms. Volumes average 350 pages. 16 x 11.25 x 2. 1899-1932, 52 volumes, 2 bundles, Room 73; 1933—, 2 volumes, Room 144, County courthouse.

2. RECORD OF FEES
1907—. 3 volumes.

A daily record of fees received, listing dates of filing, recording or cancellation; recorder's serial number; quantity of papers listed under each type of instrument, such as deeds, mortgages, leases, liens, maps, power of attorney, releases, chattel mortgages attested, cancellation and assignment of mortgages, insurance certificates, court bonds, soldiers' discharges, probate court certificate of devise, and discharges of personal and excise liens. A daily analysis is also made showing the total fees collected for each of these classifications. In chronological order. Handwritten on printed forms. Volumes average 200 pages. 16 x 13 x 1. Room 144, County courthouse.

3. CASH BOOK AND RECORD OF FEES
1892—. 112 volumes, 1-110; 2 volumes, not numbered.

A daily cash record listing consecutive number of instrument, kind of instrument or service, amounts collected for recording, filing, cancellation and miscellaneous charges. A daily and monthly analysis is made of instruments and fees collected; also a monthly statement of accrued interest, witness or court fees received, and other cash receipts is shown. In chronological order. Handwritten on printed forms. Volumes 1892-1934, 1-110, average250 pages. 18.5 x 12.5 x 2.25. Balance average 630 pages. 17 x 14 x 4. 1892-Dec. 1935, 111 volumes, Room 73; 1936—, 1 volume, Room 144, County courthouse.

4. LAND CONVEYANCE STATISTICS
1892—. 3 volumes, 2-4. (Volume 1 missing).
An analysis of land convenience showing, daily, under deeds recorded, mortgages recorded, mortgages cancelled, and leases, the number of city lots or farms, and the amount of money involved. The record is totaled monthly. In chronological order. Handwritten on printed forms. Volumes average 200 pages. 14.5 x 11 x 1.5. Room 144, County courthouse.

5. RECORDER'S RECEIPTS
November 1921—. Approximately 1,235,000 in 1235 file drawers.
Receipts for all documents filed and delivered, listing file number, date and exact time document was filed for record, and amount of fee. In order of file numbers. Handwritten on printed forms. Each file drawer 4 x 12 x 3.5. November 3, 1921— May 8, 1929, 871 file drawers, Room 35; May 9, 1929—, 364 file drawers, Room 144, County courthouse.

6. GENERAL COURT BONDS
1929—. Approximately 2800 in 4 file boxes.
An alphabetical index to general court bonds, arranged by names of sureties, listing file number, date and exact time of filing, name of defendant, amount of recognizance, and description of the real estate. Handwritten on printed forms. 350 pages. 16 x 17 x 2. Room 144, County courthouse.

7. INDEX TO NOTICES OF LIENS SURETY TO RECOGNIZANCES
1929—. 1 volume, A-Z.
An alphabetical index to general court bonds, arranged by names of sureties, listing file number, date and exact time of filing, name of defendant, amount of recognizance, and description of real estate. Handwritten on printed forms. 350 pages. 16 x 17 x 2. Room 144, County courthouse.

8. CERTIFICATES OF RELEASE OF DELINQUENT PERSONAL TAX LIENS
1933—. Approximately 372 in 1 file box.
List name of party against whom the lien was placed, date filed, fee for filing, volume and page of the personal tax lien record, and amount of the lien. In chronological order. For index see number 9. Typed on printed forms. File box 10.25 x 20 x 4.5. Room 144, County courthouse.

9. COUNTY RECORDER'S PERSONAL TAX LIEN RECORD
1933—. 8 loose-leaf volumes, 1-8.

Lists delinquent personal tax liens amounting to one hundred dollars or more, and shows name and address of taxpayer, date of entry, book and page number of personal property tax duplicate, number of certification, amount of delinquent tax, the ten percent penalty, total amount due, the discharge of the lien, dates, and certificate number. In alphabetical order. Typed on printed forms. Average 400 pages. 19.5 x 19.5 x 2.5. Room on 144, County courthouse.

10. FEDERAL TAX LIEN NOTICES
Oct. 1923—. Approximately 262 in 2 file boxes.

List of taxpayer, residence or place of business, nature of tax, the taxable period, amount of tax assessed, the additional penalty, and date on which assessment list was received. Filed numerically. For index see number 11. Handwritten on printed forms. Each file box 11 x 5 x 27. Room 144, County courthouse.

11. FEDERAL TAX LIEN INDEX
1923—. 2 loose-leaf volumes.

A record listing date of filing, notice number, name and address of taxpayer, total tax, the penalty, and date of discharge. Arranged alphabetically. Handwritten on printed forms. Volumes average 500 pages. 14.5 x 18 x 4. Room at 144, County courthouse.

12. DEEDS AND MORTGAGES (recorded but not called for)
March 1874—. Approximately 1500 in 68 file boxes.

Arranged in order of instrument numbers. Handwritten and typed on printed forms. Each file box 10.25 x 20 x 4.5. 1874-1924, 58 file boxes, Room 73; 1924—, 10 file boxes, Room 144, County courthouse.

13. MISCELLANEOUS INSTRUMENTS (recorded but not called for)
19, 000 in 58 file boxes and 13 file drawers.

Deeds, mortgages, leases, insurance papers, satisfactions, mechanics' liens, and all other instruments filed for record but not claimed. Arranged numerically. Handwritten and typed on printed forms. 1873-1903, 1 file drawer, Room 73; 1904-1925, 58 file boxes, Room 35; 1884—, 12 file drawers, Room 144, County courthouse.

13a. MORTGAGE CANCELLATION (Work Sheets)
January 1921—. 4 file drawers, 32 envelopes.
Daily list of mortgage cancellations, showing names of mortgagor and mortgagee; volume and page number of mortgage record, and amount of mortgage. Arranged chronologically. Handwritten on printed forms. Each file drawer 27 x 16 x 11.5; each envelope 13 x 10 x 1. 32 envelopes, 4 file drawers, Room 73; current records, Room 144, County courthouse.

14. SOLDIERS' DISCHARGES (recorded but not called for)
1919—. Approximately 69 in 1 file box.
Original discharges issued to soldiers and sailors on release from the Army and the Navy. Arranged chronologically. Handwritten and typed on printed forms. File box 10.25 x 20 x 4.5. Room 144, County courthouse.

15. MISCELLANEOUS FILES
1922—. 4 file boxes.
Miscellaneous correspondence; opinions of the county prosecutor pertaining to the recorder's office; reports and correspondence concerning the Civil Service Commission, the Home Owners' Loan Corporation, and the Civil Works Administration; matters pertaining to general departmental statistics, payrolls, and budgets; general legislation affecting the recorder's office; the personnel file; and annual reports of land conveyance statistics, which are copies of such summaries sent at the end of each fiscal year to the secretary of state. Handwritten and typed. Each file box 13 x 11 x 18. Room 144, County courthouse.

Record and Index Division

16. COPY ROOM DAY BOOK
1894—. 38 loose-leaf volumes.
A daily record of all instruments recorded, listing document number, kind of record, and the volume number checked out. The only permanent value of this "checking out" is that it discloses the volume in which an instrument is recorded but only the serial or instrument number is known. In chronological order. Handwritten on printed forms. Each volume 8.5 x 11 x 8. 1894-1935, 37 volumes, Room 35; current volume, Room 142, County courthouse.

17. DEEDS AND MORTGAGES

November 1800—. 4687 volumes, (November 1800-September 1810 8 volumes, A-H, Trumbull; April 1806- August 1818, 4 volumes, A-E, Geauga; July 1810-June 1838, 24 volumes, A1-Z24, Cuyahoga; July 1838—, 4651 volumes, 25-4675, Cuyahoga).

Exact copies of all deeds and mortgages recorded in Cuyahoga County, and a transcription of such portions of the records of Trumbull and Geauga Counties as affect lands in Cuyahoga County. The Deeds include warranty, limited warranty, quit claim, sheriff's and administrator's deeds. In chronological order. For indexes see numbers. 18, 19, 20, 21, and 22. 1800-1910, handwritten; 1910-1930, typed; 1930—, photostat. Volumes average 680 pages. 18.5 x 13 x 2.25. 4687 volumes, Room 35; 83 original volumes, Room 73, County courthouse.

18. INDEX TO DEEDS AND MORTGAGES

1800-1913. 160 volumes (1800-1806, 1vol. A-Z, Trumbull; 1806-1801, 1 volume, A-Z, Geauga; 1810-1854, 6 volumes, A-Z, Cuyahoga; 1855-1912, 79 volumes, 7-85; 1850-1913, 73 volumes, 88-160).

An alphabetical index of mortgagors and mortgagees Handwritten on printed forms. and grantees and grantors, listing date of filing, and the volume and page number of the record. Handwritten on printed forms. Volumes average 350 pages. 15 x 12 x 6. 35, County courthouse.

19. DEED GRANTORS INDEX

1913—. 68 volumes (1913-1914,1 volume, A-Z; 1914-1923, 18 volumes, A-Z, 1924-1926, 19 volumes, 1-19; 1927-1930, 12 volumes, A-Z; 1931-1934, 11 volumes, A-Z; 1931-1934, 1 volume.; Sheriff's Volume; 1935—, 6 volumes, A-Z).

An alphabetical index of grantors, listing date of filing, name of grantee, file number, volume and page of the record, sublot, allotment, name of township, tract, original lot, volume and page of the map record and name of street, road, or area. 1913-1924, typed on printed forms; 1925—, handwritten on printed forms. Volumes average 640 pages. 15 x 14 x 3.25. Room 35, County courthouse.

20. DEED GRANTEES INDEX

1913—. 56 volumes (1913-1914, 1 volume, A-Z; 1914-1923, 19 volumes, A-Z; 1924-1926, 14 volumes, 1-14; 1927-1930, 9 volumes, A-Z; 1931-1934, 7 volumes, A-Z, 1935—, 6 volumes, A-Z).

An alphabetical index of grantees, listing date of filing, name of grantor, file number, volume and page of the record, sublot, allotment, name of township, tract, original lot, volume and page of the map record, and name of street, road or area. 1913-1924, typed on printed forms; 1925—, handwritten on printed forms. Volumes average 200 pages. 14 x 15.5 x 2.25. Room 35, County courthouse.

21. INDEX TO MORTGAGES–MORTGAGORS

65 volumes (1914-1923, 20 volumes, A-Z; 1924-1926, 19 volumes, A-Z; 1927-1930, 11 volumes, A-Z; 1931-1934, 9 volumes, A-Z; 1935—, 6 volumes, A-Z).

An alphabetical index of mortgagors, listing date of filing, name of mortgagee, file number, volume and page of the record, sublot, allotment, name of township, tract, original lot, volume and page of the map record and name of street, road, or area. 1914-1923, typed on printed forms; 1924—, handwritten on printed forms. Volumes average 200 pages. 14 x 15 x 2.25. Room 35, County courthouse.

22. INDEX TO MORTGAGES–MORTGAGEES

1914—. 42 volumes (1914-1923, 12 volumes, A-Z; 1924-1926, 12 volumes, A-Z; 1927-1930, 6 volumes, A-Z; 1931-1934, 6 volumes, A-Z; 1935—, 6 volumes, A-Z).

An alphabetical index of mortgagees, listing date of filing, name and mortgagor, file number, volume and page of the record, sublot, allotment, name of township, original lot, volume and page of the map record, and name of street, road or area. 1914-1923, typed on printed forms; 1924—, handwritten on printed forms. Volumes average 200 pages. 14 x 15 x 2.25. Room 35, County courthouse.

23. RECORD OF LEASES

April 22, 1865—. 209 volumes, 1-209. (Short-term leases, 161 volumes; long-term leases, 29 volumes; gas and oil well leases, 17 volumes).

Exact copies of all leases filed for record. In chronological order. For index see number 24. 1865-1905, handwritten; 1905-1930, typed; 1930—, photostat. Volumes average 650 pages. 18.5 x 12 x 2.5. Room 35, County courthouse.

24. INDEX TO LEASES
April 22, 1865—. 18 volumes (1865-1914, 7 volumes, 1-7; 1914-1919, 3 volumes, A-Z; 1920-1923, 3 volumes, A-Z; 1924-1926, 2 volumes, A-Z; 1929-1934, 2 volumes, A-Z; 1935—, 1 volume., A-Z).

An alphabetical index of lessors and lessees, listings for 1865-1914, date of filing and volume and page of the record. The new index, 1914—, lists file number, volume and page of the record, sublot, allotment, name of township, tract, original lot, volume and page of the map record, and name of street road or area. Handwritten on printed forms. Volumes average 672 pages. 14.25 x 15 x 3. Room 35, County courthouse.

25. RECORD OF RELEASES
1891—. 145 volumes, 1-145.

Exact copies of releases, assignments, waivers notices to foreclosed mechanics' liens, satisfaction of liens, and cancellations of mortgages. In chronological order. For index see number 26. 1891-1912, handwritten; 1912-1930, typed; 1930—, photostat. Volumes average 652 pages. 18.5 x 12 x 2.5. Room 35, County courthouse.

26. INDEX TO RELEASES
1891—. 19 volumes (1891-1894, 2 volumes, 1-2; 1894-1913, 7 volumes, 3-7; 1914-1919, 3 volumes, A-Z; 1920-1928, 3 volumes, A-Z; 1929—, 4 volumes, A-Z).

An alphabetical index of both parties, listing for 1891-1894, date of entry, instrument number, and record volume and page. The new index, 1914—, lists date of entry, file number, volume and page of the record, sublot, allotment, name of township, tract, original lot number, volume and page of the map record, and name of street, road, or area. Handwritten on printed forms. Volumes average 300 pages. 14 x 15 x 2.5. Room 35, County courthouse.

27. MECHANICS' LIENS
1843—. 94 volumes, 1-94.

Exact copies of mechanics' liens filed for record. In chronological order. Releases are recorded in the left-hand margin. 1843-1876, Alphabetical index of property owners in each volume. For index, 1876—, see number 28. 1843-1912, handwritten; 1912-1931, typed; 1932—, photostat. Volumes average 630 pages. 18.5 x 13 x 2.25. Room 35, County courthouse.

28. INDEX TO MECHANICS' LIENS
1876—. 14 volumes (1876-1913, 4 volumes, 1-4; 1914-1919, 3 volumes, A-Z; 1920-1923, 3 volumes, A-Z; 1924-1928, 2 volumes, A-Z; 1929—, 2 volumes, A-Z).

An alphabetical index of property owners, listing name of holder of mechanic's lien, and volume and page of the record. The new index, 1914—, list date of entry, name of parties to lien, file number, volume and page of the record, sublot number, allotment number, township, tract, original lot, volume and page of the map record, and name of street, road, or area. Handwritten on printed forms. Volume average 250 pages. 17.5 x 14.5 x 2.25. Room 35, County courthouse.

29. RAILROAD MECHANICS' LIENS
1892-1911. 1 volume. 1.

Exact copies of railroad mechanics' liens. Releases, satisfactions, and cancellations are recorded in the left-hand margin. Arranged chronologically. Handwritten. 640 pages. 18 x 13 x 3. Room 73, County courthouse.

30. EMPLOYEES' LIENS
1894-1905. 1 volume.

Exact copies of employees' liens. Arranged chronologically. Contains an alphabetical index of property owners, listing name of holder of employee's lien, and volume and page of the record. Handwritten. 640 pages. 18 x 13 x 3. Room 73, County courthouse.

31. MISCELLANEOUS RECORD
January 1873—. 37 volumes, 1-37.

Exact copies of all documents which have been accepted for record and do not belong in any of the records provided by statute. The following is a partial list of the instruments recorded: contracts, agreements, affidavits, copyrights, dissolution of corporations and partnerships, cemetery deeds, land contracts, nuptial agreements, notes, receipts, sales of leases, divorce and alimony decrees, party walls, appointments of trustees and administrators, bonds, bills of sale, appointments of guardians, options, releases of damages, apprenticeships, cancellations of leases, injunctions, notices to commence suit, appraisals, releases of sick benefits, permits to build fences, leases of machinery, settlements of contracts, claims for damages, releases of claims for damages, insurance policies, confirmations of appointments, permits, releases of conditions, and petitions for distribution of estates. In chronological order. 1873-1920 an alphabetical index in each volume. For index, 1920—, see number 32. 1873-1912, handwritten; 1912—, typed. Volumes average 640 pages. 18.5 x 12 x 3. Room 35, County courthouse.

32. INDEX TO MISCELLANEOUS RECORD
1920—. 4 loose-leaf volumes (1920-1928, 2 volumes, A-Z; 1928—, 2 volumes, A-Z).

An alphabetical index of all parties to the instrument, listing date of filing, file number, volume and page of the record, sublot, allotment, name of township, tract, original lot, volume and page of the map record, and name of street, road, or area. Handwritten on printed forms. Volumes average 300 pages. 17.5 x 14.5 x 3. Room 35, County courthouse.

33. RECORD OF BONDS
January 1897—. 2 volumes, 1-2.

Exact copies of bonds, other than court bonds, that have been accepted for record. Contains an alphabetical index of sureties. Handwritten. Volumes average 640 pages. 18.5 x 13 x 2.25. Room 35, County courthouse.

34. MUNICIPAL COURT BOND RECORD
July 1919—. 54 volumes, 1-54.

Exact copies of municipal court bonds, discharges of which are recorded on the margin. In chronological order. For index see number 35. 1919-1932, typed; 1932—, photostat. Volumes average 660 pages. 18.5 x 12.5 x 3. Room 35, County courthouse.

35. MUNICIPAL COURT BOND INDEX
1919—. 3 loose-leaf volumes, A-Z.

An alphabetical index of sureties, listing bond number, date received for record, and volume and page of the record. Handwritten on printed forms. Volumes average 300 pages. 18 x 13 x 3.25. Room 35, County courthouse.

36. POWER OF ATTORNEY
February 1858—. 14 volumes, 1-14.

Exact copies of instruments conferring power of attorney. In chronological order.

For index see number 37. 1858-1914, handwritten; 1914-1932, typed; 1932—, photostat. Volumes average 590 pages. 18.25 x 13 x 3.25. 12 volumes, Room 35; 2 volumes, Room 142, County courthouse.

37. INDEX TO POWER OF ATTORNEY
February 1858—. 2 loose-leaf volumes, A-Z.

An alphabetical index of names of principals, listing names of agents, date received for record, and volume and page of the record. 1858-1917, typed on printed forms; 1918—, handwritten on printed forms. Volumes average 200 pages. 18.25 x 12.25 x 2.25. Room 35, County courthouse.

38. RECORD OF SOLDIERS' DISCHARGES
1865—. 16 volumes, 1-16.

Exact copies of official discharges from the Army and the Navy. Chronological. For index see number 39. 1865-1918, handwritten; 1918—, typed on printed forms. Volumes average 300 pages. 18.5 x 12.5 x 3.25. Room 142, County courthouse.

39. SOLDIERS' DISCHARGE INDEX
1865—. 1 loose-leaf volume., A-Z.

An alphabetical index to the record of soldiers' discharges, listing date received for record, docket number, and volume and page of the record. Handwritten on printed forms. 300 pages. 17.5 x 14.25 x 2.25. Room 35, County courthouse.

40. AUTHORITY TO PAY TAXES
1904—. 2 volumes, 1-2.

Exact copies of certificates of authority from owners of real property to individuals or corporations to pay taxes and thereby obtain a lien on the property. Alphabetical index in each volume. Handwritten. Volumes average 600 pages. 18.5 x 13 x 3. Room 35, County courthouse.

41. CEMETERY DEED RECORD
1849—. 3 volumes, 1-3.

Exact copies of deeds to cemetery lots accepted for record. Arranged chronologically. Each volume contains an alphabetical index. Handwritten. Volume 1 is marked "Cemetery Records;" volume 2, "Cemetery Associations;" and volume 3, "Cemetery Deed Record." Volumes average 300 pages. 18.5 x 12 x 1. Room 35, County courthouse.

42. PARTITION FENCE RECORD
September 1904-1924. 1 volume, 1.

Exact copies of partition fence agreements. In chronological order. Contains an alphabetical index to parties to the agreements. Handwritten. 150 pages. 18.5 x 14 x 2. Room 35, County courthouse.

43. NOTARY PROTEST RECORD
1911-1912. 1 volume, 1.

Exact copies of protest notices to drawers, markers, and endorses, of notes, checks, and drafts, showing name and address, date of presentation or mailing, name of notary, and a copy of the instrument protested. Typed on printed forms. Volumes average 250 pages. 8 x 5 x 1. Room 73, County courthouse.

44. INSURANCE AGENTS' AND SOLICITORS' LICENSE CERTIFICATES
1929—. Approximately 75,000 in file boxes and 3 drawers.

Copies of original card certificates, listing name of insurance company, city and state where company is located, county where agents certificate is recorded, name and residence of agent, and date of filing. In numerical order. For index see number 45. Typed on printed forms. Each file box 10.25 x 20 x 4.5; each drawer 18 x 24 x 10. Room on 73, County courthouse.

45. INSURANCE RECORD
1897—. 9 loose-leaf volumes, 2-10.

An alphabetical index of all insurance company agents and their solicitors doing business in Cuyahoga County. It lists certificate number, name and address of company, agent, or solicitor, date of filing, and remarks. Typed. Volumes average 700 pages. 18.5 x 14 x 5. Room 73, County courthouse.

46. SOCIETIES-RELIGIOUS, FRATERNAL, ETC.
1845-1924. 2 volumes, 1-2.

Copies of articles of incorporation, charters, etc. of religious and fraternal societies, cemetery associations, etc. Chronologically arranged. For partial index see number 51. Handwritten. Volumes average 250 pages. 18.5 x 12.5 x 2. Room 35, County courthouse.

47. MANUFACTURER'S RECORD
1847-1911. 1 volumes, 1-2.

Contains articles of incorporation, amendments thereto, change of name, etc. of corporations; also shows date received and recorded; and serial number. For partial index see number 51. Volumes average 300 pages. 18.5 x 12 x 3. Room 35, County courthouse.

48. INCORPORATED COMPANIES
1870-1897. 1 volume, 1.

Copies of articles of incorporation, amendments thereto etc, of companies, principally insurance companies. Contains an alphabetical index; for separate index see number 51. Handwritten. 64 pages. 18.5 x 12 x 2. Room 35, County courthouse.

49. RECORDS OF PARTNERSHIPS
January 1850—. 3 volumes, 1-3.

Contains copies of partnership agreements, notices of dissolution, articles of co-partnership, certificates of special and limited partnerships, etc. Each volume contains an alphabetical index. 1850-1917 handwritten; 1918—, typed. Volumes average 300 pages. 18.25 x 11.25 x 1.5. Room 35, County courthouse

50. CORPORATION RECORD
1911—. 9 volumes, 1-9.

Exact copies of articles of incorporation, amendments thereto, agreements and declarations, agreement on mergers, articles of trust, charters, notices of payments of franchise or excise tax, discharges of liens therefor, certificates of reinstatement, etc. Volumes 5 to 9 contain only copies of notices from the Tax Commission of Ohio, dating from 1932, certifying that certain companies have failed to pay the franchise tax. Notices show amount of tax, penalty and total, instrument number, date received and date recorded. Volume 1 contains an alphabetical index; for complete index see number 51. 1911-1917, handwritten; 1918—, typed on printed forms. Volumes average 640 pages. 18.5 x 12.5 x 3.25. Room 35, County courthouse.

51. CORPORATION INDEX
1845—. 2 volumes, A-Z.

An alphabetical index of corporations, listing the name, date filed, type of instrument and the file, volume and page numbers. This record serves as an index to the Corporation Record, and all records of incorporation contained in the Manufacturer's Record; Incorporated Companies Record; Record of Societies - Religious, Fraternal, etc.; Record of Partnerships and the Miscellaneous Record. Handwritten and typed. Volumes average 1000 pages. 18.5 x 16 x 5. Room 35, County courthouse.

52. WESTERN RESERVE DRAFT BOOK OF THE CONNECTICUT LAND COMPANY
September 7, 1795- January 5, 1809. 1 volume.

A photostatic copy of the original draft book now in the possession of the recorder of Trumbull County. Contains the resolutions of the general assembly of the State of Connecticut; names of original purchasers and copies of deeds made to them; the deed to John Caldwell, John Morgan, and Jonathan Brace, trustees for the Connecticut Land Company; the articles of association, proceedings, and the appointment of directors of the Connecticut Land Company, the mode of partitions of the Western Reserve; descriptions of the various townships in the Western Reserve, including the equalization of townships; a description of the Salt Spring Reservation; the grants of land to the first settlers in Cleveland; proceedings relating to the extinguishing of the Indian title; draft of the various townships; and the report of the classifying committee on the partition of the lands of the Connecticut Land Company. Contains an alphabetical index as to the proprietors and the various drafts. 500 pages. 13.5 x 18.5 x 2.25. Room 144, County courthouse.

Chattel Mortgage Division

The word "mortgage" is one of Norman-French adoption, meaning a "dead"pledge." Chattel mortgages are liens on any species of property, movable or immovable, which is less than a freehold. (Austin B. Griffin and Arthur F. Curtis, *The Law of Chattel Mortgages and Conditional Sales*, 1931, 1).

On February 24, 1846, it was provided that all chattel mortgages were to be void as against creditors of the mortgagors, or subsequent purchasers and mortgagees, unless the mortgage was deposited with the clerk of the township where the mortgagor resided at the time of execution of the mortgage. Otherwise, if the mortgagor was not a resident, he was required to file the mortgage with the clerk of the township where the property was located. The clerk had to endorse thereon the time of filing. The instrument then remained in force for one year unless re-filed within thirty days of the expiration of the year. The act also provided that in any township in which the office of county recorder is located such instruments shall be deposited with him for recordation and filing. (44 O. L. 61-62).

Two years later, an amendment was passed providing that every instrument filed with the county recorder shall be numbered consecutively, and that the names of all parties to such instruments shall be entered alphabetically in a book provided by the recorder, with the number of the instrument opposite each name. (46 O. L. 103). This statute was again amended in 1869, making it compulsory that the instrument, when executed, show the actual amount of money loaned, and be verified before some justice of the peace or other officer authorized to administer oaths. (66 O. L. 345).

In 1877 the original act was again amended providing for the filing of chattel mortgages or bills of sale with the township clerk or recorder, changing the fees for filing, and providing for the cancellation of the mortgage when such mortgage or bill of sale shall have been satisfied. (74 O. L. 149). The provision as to numbering these instruments and entering the same names of all parties alphabetically, which formerly applied only to the recorder, was now made to apply to township clerks as well. (75 O. L. 519).

In 1906 an act was passed which required the filing of chattel mortgages with the county recorder exclusively. (98 O. L. 114). Two years later an act was passed providing that the chattel mortgages were to remain in force for three years, instead of one year, after filing, unless re-filed within thirty days. (99 O. L. 230).

Since 1927 the sections of the General Code required the re-filing of chattel mortgages have not been applicable to such mortgages filed by corporations. It was stipulated that they continue to be a lien on the personal property therein described until discharged or released. (112 O. L. 39).

Since 1929 it has been permissible to file mortgages executed by a railroad or other public utility corporation and covering or including rolling or movable stock, such as cars, locomotives, motor vehicles, or machines for aerial transportation, in the office of the secretary of state. If so filed they have the same effect as though filed in the office of the recorder of the county in which such rolling stock, movable equipment or machines, may be situated or employed. (113 O. L. 413).

In 1935 a statute provided that chattel mortgages, six years after re-filing, are void as to third parties and may be destroyed. In Cuyahoga County, however, it has been customary to keep all such instruments at least ten years. (116 O. L. 324).

53. GENERAL CHATTEL FILE
1925—. Approximately 1,500,000 in 1455 file boxes and 31 file drawers. Contains duplicate or originals of chattel mortgages, bills of sale, conditional bills of sale, trust receipts, assignments of wages, cancellation orders, and attested accounts. Attested accounts are numbered consecutively with chattel mortgages, but are separately indexed. For index see numbers 55, 56, and 57. Arranged in order of instrument numbers. Typed and handwritten on printed forms. File box 10.25 x 20 x 4.5; file drawer 11 x 14 x 24. 783 file boxes, Room 35; 672 file boxes, Room 141; releases filed separately in 31 file drawers, Room 73, County courthouse.

54. CHATTEL MORTGAGE RECORD
1877—. 7 volumes, 1-7. (1877-1878, 3 volumes, 1-3; 1891—, 4 volumes, 4-7.
Copies of chattel mortgages filed for record in the chattel mortgage department. For index see numbers 55, 56, and 57. 1877-1913, handwritten; 1914—, typed. Volumes average 640 pages. 18 x 3 x 13. 1875-1928, 6 volumes, 1-6, Room 73; 1928—, 1 volume, Room 142, County courthouse.

55. INDEX TO CHATTEL-MORTGAGES
1903—. 120 volumes; 153 file boxes. (1903-1913, 21 volumes, 47-57; 1913-1914, 4 volumes, A-Z; 1915-1919, 10 volumes, A-Z; 1920-1922, 9 volumes, A-Z; 1923-1925, 15 volumes, A-Z; 1926-1928, 16 volumes, A-Z; 1929-1931, 25 volumes, A-Z; 1932-1934, 20 volumes, A-Z; 1935—, 153 file boxes, A-Z).
An alphabetical index of mortgagors, listing name of mortgagee, date of instrument, date of filing, amount secured, instrument number, cancellations, and various remarks. 1903-1934, handwritten; 1935—, typed. Volumes average 640 pages. 16.5 x 14.25 x 4.25. 1903-1928, 75 volumes, Room 73; 1929—, 45 volumes, 153 file boxes, Room 144, County courthouse.

56. CHATTEL INDEX- MORTGAGEES
1914—. 20 volumes; 153 file boxes. (1914-1916, 1 volume, A-Z; 1917-1920, 2 volumes, A-Z; 1921-1922, 2 volumes, A-Z; 1923-1924, 2 volumes, A-Z; 1925-1926, 2 volumes, A-Z; 1927-1928, 2 volumes, A-Z; 1929-1930, 3 volumes, A-Z; 1931-1933, 4 volumes, A-Z; 1934, 2 volumes, A-Z; 1935—, 153 file boxes). (No separate index to mortgagees prior to 1914).
An alphabetical index of mortgagees, listing instrument number, date of filing, and

amount. The record, 1935—, lists date of filing; date of instrument; amount; and name of mortgagee, mortgagor, and assignee.1914-1934, handwritten on printed forms; 1935—, typed. Volumes average 800 pages. 18.5 x 16 x 5. 1914-1930 , 14 volumes, Room 73; 1931-1933, 4 volumes, Room 35; 1934—, 2 volumes, 153 file boxes, Room 144, County courthouse.

57. INDEX TO ATTESTED ACCOUNTS
July 1884—. 1 volume.

An alphabetical index to attested accounts listing name of contractor; number of instrument; date of filing; source of material; name of sub-contractor, man, mechanic, or laborer; amount due; and remarks. Handwritten on printed forms. 300 pages. 17.25 x 13 x 3. Room 144, County courthouse.

Map Division

58. MAPS
May 1836—. Approximately 5200 maps in 130 volumes, 1-130.

Original ink drawings with copies of statements of officials and property owners dedicating lands, and officials' approvals and acceptance of plats. In chronological order. For index see numbers 59 and 60. Volumes average 40 pages. 28 x 27 x 2. 1836-1934, India ink drawings; February 1934—, Photostats. Room 41, County courthouse.

59. ALPHABETICAL INDEX TO RECORDED MAPS
May 1836—. 1 volume.

An alphabetical index of property owners, listing volume and page of the recorded map, the locality, and remarks. Typed on printed forms. Approximately 500 pages. 14 x 14 x 5. Room 41, County courthouse.

60. LOCALITY INDEX TO RECORDED MAPS
1917—. 1 volume.

Lists name of subdivision, the volume and page of the record, the original lot number and remarks. Arranged according to two-acres, ten-acre, and one hundred-acre lots in Cleveland, and then according to townships. Townships arranged alphabetically. Handwritten and typed on printed forms. 474 pages. 14 x 14 x 3. Room 41, County courthouse.

61. ANNEXATION AND INCORPORATIONS
1867—. 5 file boxes. (1867-1932, 1 file box, Annexations and Incorporations, Cleveland City; 1867-1933, 1 file box, Annexations and Incorporation, West; 1873-1927, 2 file boxes, Annexations and Incorporations, East; 1926-1932, 1 file box, Incorporation of Villages, West).

Proposals, maps, information, and transcripts of the proceedings of the county commissioners relating to incorporations, annexations and detachments of cities, villages and townships in Cuyahoga County. Typed, handwritten, printed, and drawings of various types. Chronologically arranged. Each file box 6 x 10 x 24. Room 35, County courthouse.

62. VILLAGE INCORPORATIONS, ANNEXATIONS ETC.
1856—. 3 volumes, 1-3.

Transcripts of proceedings of township trustees; election proceedings; plats of territory involved; petitions to county commissioners; commissioners' resolution as to detachment or attachment of certain territory; and incorporation proceedings. Each transcript shows date received by recorder, date recorded, fee for record, and recorders instrument number. Chronological order. For index see number 64. 1856-1913—, typed. Volumes average 320 pages. 19 x 12 x 3. Room 41, County courthouse.

63. VILLAGES AND HAMLETS, MAPS
1866-1903. Approximately 300 maps in 6 volumes, 1-6.

Original ink drawings and descriptions of proceedings concerning annexations, incorporations, and detachments of township and villages, or parts thereof, and properties of private owners. Arranged chronologically. For index see number 64. Volumes average 50 pages. 28 x 25 x 2. Room 41, County courthouse.

64. INDEX TO RECORD OF INCORPORATED VILLAGES AND HAMLETS
1856—. 1 volume.

An alphabetical index of property owners, listing description of proceedings, and the volume and page of the map record. Alphabetically arranged. Handwritten on printed forms. 156 pages. 16 x 10 x 2. Room 41, County courthouse.

65. ATLAS OF CUYAHOGA COUNTY AND CLEVELAND CITY
1892. 116 maps in 1 volume.

Shows sections of the city, streets, lots, buildings, allotments, communications, waterways, house numbers, and names of property owners. An index map in front gives the location of census tracts on maps. Scale, 200 and 300 feet to the inch. 24 x 27 x 2. Publishers, G. M. Hopkins Company, Philadelphia, Pennsylvania, Room 41, County courthouse.

66. ATLAS OF THE CITY OF CLEVELAND
1898. 44 maps in 1 volume.

Shows sections of the city, streets, lots, buildings, allotments, communications, waterways, house numbers, and names of property owners. An index map in front gives the location of census tracts on maps. Scale, 200 and 300 feet to the inch. 23 x 27 x 3. Publishers, G. M. Hopkins Company, Philadelphia, Pennsylvania, Room 41, County courthouse.

67. ATLAS OF THE SUBURBS OF CLEVELAND, MAPS
1898. 28 maps in 1 volume.

Shows sections of the suburbs, streets, lots, buildings, allotments, communications, waterways, house numbers, and names of property owners. An index map in front gives the location of census tracts on map. Scale, 200 and 300 feet to the inch. 22 x 17 x 1.5. Publishers, G. M. Hopkins Company, Philadelphia, Pennsylvania, Room 41, County courthouse.

68. ATLAS OF CUYAHOGA COUNTY
1920. 55 maps in 1 volume.

Shows sections of the county, streets, lots, buildings, allotments, communications, waterways, house numbers, and names of property owners. An index map in front gives the location of census tracts on maps. Scale, 200 and 300 feet to the inch. 23 x 16 x 2. Publishers, G. M. Hopkins Company, Philadelphia, Pennsylvania, Room 41, County courthouse.

69. PLAT BOOK OF CLEVELAND, OHIO
1921-1922. Approximately 78 maps in 2 volumes.

A plat book comprising The eastern section of Cleveland, showing streets, lots, buildings, allotments, communications, waterways, house numbers, and names of property owners. An index map in front gives the location of census tracts on maps.

Scale, 200 and 300 feet to the inch. 25 x 21 x 1. Publishers, G. M. Hopkins Company, Philadelphia, Pennsylvania, Room 41, County courthouse.

70. PLAT BOOK OF CUYAHOGA COUNTY
1927. Approximately 110 maps in 2 volumes (Volume 5, County East of River; volume. 6, County West of River, West Park).

Shows streets, lots, buildings, allotments, communications, waterways, house numbers, and names of property owners. An index map in front gives the location of census tracts on maps. Scale, 200 and 300 feet to the inch. 24 x 18 x 2.5. Publishers, G. M. Hopkins Company, Philadelphia, Pennsylvania, Room 41, County courthouse.

71. CLEVELAND OHIO, OHIO, MAPS
Approximately 172 maps in 4 volumes (Volume 1, 1932; volume. 2, 1922; volume. 3, 1933; volume. 4, 1932).

Shows streets, lots, buildings, allotments, communications, waterways, house numbers, and names of property owners. An index map in front gives the location of census tracts on maps. Scale, 200 and 300 feet to the inch. 24 x 18 x 2.5. Publishers, G. M. Hopkins Company, Philadelphia, Pennsylvania, Room 41, County courthouse.

Torrens Division

The registration of lands in England can be traced to the 16th century, during the reign of Queen Elizabeth, when a law was passed requiring sales of land to be enrolled in certain counties. This law was loosely drawn and soon became inoperative. From that time on various bills for registration of land titles were introduced, some of which were passed by Parliament. However, few became effective.

In 1857 Sir Robert Torrens, a member of the first colonial ministry of the Province of Australia, introduced a bill in Parliament for registration of land titles, which, with various changes, was passed and became effective in 1858.

The first Torrens law in the United States was passed in 1895, in the state of Illinois, but was declared unconstitutional by the Supreme Court of that state. Another law, which was passed in Illinois and 1897, is still in effect. (William C. Niblack, *An Analysis of the Torrens System of Conveying Land*, 1912, 1, 7-8).

An act to provide for the registration of land titles in Ohio was passed by the general assembly on April 27, 1896, but was declared unconstitutional by the Supreme Court of Ohio on June 22, 1897, as being repugnant to Sec. 16 of the Bill of Rights of the state constitution. (92 O. L. 220; 56 O. S. 575).

On September 3, 1912, the Ohio constitution was amended to the effect that laws may be passed providing for a system of registering, transferring and guaranteeing of land titles, and for the creation of guarantee funds by fees assessed against lands, the titles to which are registered. Judicial powers with rights of appeal may, by law, be conferred upon county recorders or other officers in matters arising under the operation of such a system. (Ohio Const., Art. 2, sec. 40).

The present act, which was passed April 18, 1913, comprehensively delineated the powers, duties and mode of procedure for the Torrens system in the office of the county recorder. The Torrens system is one under which the title itself is recorded and guaranteed by the state - a public title system operated at cost. The registration of land titles is perfected by the filing of an application with the court of common pleas or probate court, a memorandum of which is filed with the recorder, and the submission of a certified copy of the decree of registration by the clerk of courts to the recorder. The recorder then issues a certificate of title to the person named in the decree as the owner, and enters a duplicate thereof in a book kept in his office for that purpose. The land then becomes registered land and the owner named therein holds it free from every claim, except those named in the certificate. Subsequent transfers of registered lands, and all claims operating as liens upon the land must be entered on the certificate of title. (103 O. L. 945).

An amendment passed March 8, 1915, provided that any person owning real estate, the title of which is registered, may surrender the certificate to the county recorder, who can then cancel the certificate of record. (106 O. L. 25). Additional amendments, past June 8, 1933, affected the entering of transfers of registered land in the auditor's office, the holding of mortgages or liens on registered property, and the liability of registered land for assessments for public improvements. A change was also made regarding the schedule of fees. (115 O. L. 455-447).

72. RECEPTION BOOK - DAILY RECEIPTS OF DOCUMENTS AFFECTING REGISTERED LANDS
1914—. 7 volumes, 1-7.
A record listing date of filing, document number, kind of instrument, date of instrument, names of parties, description of land, and certificate number. In

chronological order. Handwritten on printed form. Volumes average 400 pages. 20.5 x 18.5 x 2.5. Room 144, County courthouse

73. REGISTER OF TITLES; REGISTERED LANDS
1914——. 157 loose-leaf volumes, 1-157.

Shows ownership of the fee and the memorials of all lesser estates and liens with name and address of owner. It also shows document number, certificate number, date of original registration, reference to the volume and page of the register showing previous registered titles, and the date of certificate. Small drawings show the location and boundaries of each property. For index see number 74. Typed on printed forms. Volumes average 200 pages. 19 x 15 x 2.75. Room 144, County courthouse.

74. INDEX TO OWNERS OF REGISTERED LANDS
1914——. 2 loose-leaf volumes.

An alphabetical index of owners, listing certificate number, document number, date of entry, book and page number of the register, location of registered land, indicating tract and lot number, and date of cancellation. Handwritten on printed forms. Volumes average 200 pages. 21 x 16 x 4. Room 144, County courthouse.

75. RECORD OF TRUST AND EXCEPTIONAL ESTATES
1914——. 1 loose-leaf volume.

A record of trust and exceptional estates registered in the Torrens department. In chronological order. Typed. 600 pages. 18.5 x 12.5 x 3. Room 144, County courthouse.

76. RECORD OF LIENS ON REGISTERED LANDS
1914——. 2 volumes, 1-2.

A record of liens placed against registered lands, when such record has been requested. These liens may be traced through number 73. In chronological order. Typed. Volumes average 600 pages. 18.5 x 12.5 x 3. Room 144, County courthouse.

77. RECORD OF LEASES ON REGISTERED LANDS
1914——. 1 loose-leaf volume.

A record of all leases on registered lands, where such record has been requested. These leases may be traced through number 73. In chronological order. Typed. 600 pages. 18.5 x 12.5 x 3. Room 144, County courthouse.

78. INDEX TO HOLDERS OF LIENS AND LESSER ESTATES
1914——. 2 loose-leaf volumes, A-Z.

Lists names of holders of liens and lesser estates, kind of instrument, amount of instrument, document number, date of instrument, and book and page number of the register. It gives a description of the registered lands affected, and shows whether assigned or cancelled. Handwritten on printed forms. Volumes average 400 pages. 21 x 16 x 4. Room 144, County courthouse.

79. SIGNATURE CARDS
1914——. Approximately 35,000 in 33 file boxes, A-Z.

Cards kept for owners of land, lesser estates, and liens, listing address, age, certificate of title number, and date of signature. Alphabetical as to owners. Typed and handwritten. Each file box 3 x 5 x 20. Room 144, County courthouse.

80. TORRENS DOCUMENTS
1914——. Approximately 83,300 in 419 file boxes.

Original deeds, mortgages, leases, liens, and other documents filed with the Torrens department, including all files in all Torrens cases in common pleas court. In order of Torrens document numbers. Typed in handwritten. Each file box 10.5 x 4.5. Room 144, County courthouse.

81. ABSTRACTS OF TITLE
1914——. Approximately 186 in 20 file drawers.

Filed with the county clerk as evidence of title. These abstracts, are held by the recorder until called for by the owners. Filed numerically. Typed. Each file drawer 11 x 16 x 4. Room 73, County courthouse.

82. RECEIPTS FOR DOCUMENTS AND CERTIFICATES DELIVERED
1914——. Approximately 31,500 in 31 file boxes.

Lists certificate number, date received, certificate of title number, to whom delivered, and amount of fee received. In order of certificate numbers. Typed and handwritten. Each file box 4 x 6 x 20. Room 144, County Courthouse.

83. RECORD OF SURVEYS OF REGISTERED LANDS
1915. 1 volume.
Survey made by the county surveyor upon order of the court. One map made May 8, 1915. Scale, 200 feet to the inch. 19 x 23.5. Room 41, County Courthouse.

84. TORRENS PLATS
130 maps in 5 file drawers.
Individual maps of subdivisions of registered land. They are also recorded in the recorder's map records. Various scale. Black-and-white and shaded. Arranged in order of Torrens document numbers. Each file drawer 45 x 16.5 x 4.5. Room 41, County courthouse.

The office of county commissioners, at its inception, involved little power or responsibility. It was created in 1792, by an act of the Northwest Territory which provided for the erection in each county of a courthouse, a pillory whipping post, and several stocks. The judges of the court of common pleas were empowered to appoint two commissioners who were to draft plans for, and supervise the construction of such buildings and apparatus. Three years later their duties were enlarged to include the assessment of moneys for the building and repair of public works, the levying of taxes and the auditing of county accounts. At the same time a third commissioner was provided for. (Theodore Calvin Pease. *op. cit.,* 1, 78, 203).

When the first Ohio constitution was adopted in 1802, no mention was made of the office of commissioners. This, however, was remedied by the general assembly in 1804, when the office was re-created, its tenure made three years, and the number of commissioners set at three. They were required to keep a record of their corporate proceedings and for that purpose to appoint a clerk; appointed a county treasurer who had to settle his accounts with them annually; assessed taxes; constructed and repaired courthouses, prisons, and bridges; were required to make a financial report annually to the court of common pleas; and were empowered to do any act or perform any duty enjoined by law. They were paid on a per diem basis. The county auditor acted as clerk to the commissioners in 1821, and served in that capacity until 1908 when it was provided that whenever the commissioners found it necessary for the clerk to devote his entire time to his duties, they appointed a clerk in place of the auditor, and such assistance as they deem necessary. (2 O. L. 150; 19 O. L. 147; 99 O. L. 337).

The commissioners were divested of the power to appoint a county treasurer in 1827, when that office was made elective. At that time the treasurer also took over the duties of tax collector which had formerly been fulfilled by an appointee of the county commissioners. (25 O. L. 25; 8 O. L. 219).

The commissioners were authorized in 1815 to discharge from imprisonment persons confined to jail with non-payment of fines or cost. This authority was transferred to the county auditor in 1833. The power to regulate weights and measures was also taken from the commissioners in 1846 and given to the auditor. (O. L. reprint of 1816, 52; 31 O. L. 18; 44 O. L. 56; 22 O. L. 465).

They were given the duty, in 1824, of examining all suspected lunatics and, whenever necessary, could employ a physician to aid them in the discharge of their duties. They were relieved of this task in 1853. Since 1831 the commissioners have been capable of suing and being sued, and of pleading and being impleaded, in any court; and of asking, demanding and recovering by suit or otherwise, any real estate or interest therein, belonging to their county, or other property or money due the county. The money so recovered must be paid into the county treasury. (Chase, *op. cit.*, II, 1319; 51 O. L. 422-426; 29 O. L. 268).

In 1865 the commissioners were given the authority to alter or change the boundaries of any township within the county, by either attaching one township to another, or by laying off and designating a new township from the territory of one or more townships, whenever petitioned by a majority of the householders residing within the territory affected. (62 O. L. 18). Since 1869 the inhabitants residing in territory adjacent to any city or incorporated village, have had the right to petition the commissioners for annexation to such city or village. (66 O. L. 264).

Bridges were an absolute necessity in this state almost from the beginning, but many decades passed before anything was done about roads. In 1846 the commissioners were given the duty of laying out and establishing state roads, and of converting free turnpikes into such roads. At the same time private companies were being authorized by the legislature to construct plank roads. In 1857 these companies found themselves in financial difficulties and the county commissioners were authorized to take over their roads, provided the transfer was made without consideration. It was not until 1873 that they were authorized to make such purchases. In 1869 they were empowered to levy taxes for the repair or reconstruction of roads. Two years later the commissioners of Cuyahoga and Hamilton Counties were authorized to levy taxes for roads and bridges. In 1906 the county surveyor (now the county engineer) was placed in charge of construction, reconstruction, improvement, maintenance and repair of roads. An even more expert handling of road matters was presaged, when in 1920 the county surveyor was empowered to appoint one of his deputies as a county road maintenance engineer. He was also directed, with the consent of the commissioners to appoint a road maintenance supervisor. (44 O. L. 74; 44 O. L. 126-127; 54 O. L. 198; 70 O. L. 255; 66 O. L. 60; 68 O. L. 117; 98 O. L. 245; 108 O. L. pt. 1, 497).

During the 19th century and the early part of the 20th, county sanitation was badly neglected. In 1917 the commissioners were authorized to lay out, establish and maintain one or more sewer districts within the county, and to construct and maintain such sewers within the district as would be necessary. They were also empowered to employ a competent sanitary engineer for the purpose of aiding them in the performance of these duties, and, in counties having a population exceeding 100,000, they could create and maintain a sanitary engineering department. Another important health measure was promulgated when in 1913 the commissioners were authorized, with the approval of the state department of health, to appoint one or more visiting nurses to visit homes or places in the county wherein there were cases of tuberculosis. Since 1917 the commissioners have been empowered to establish and maintain tuberculosis dispensaries and to provide the necessary funds by tax levies. However, in Cuyahoga County the commissioners co-operate with the Visiting Nurses' Association and have financial agreement with the Anti-Tuberculosis League and the various hospitals aided by the Community Fund. (107 O. L. 440-452; 10. O. L. 261; 107 O. L. 498).

Since the days of the Northwest Territory counties have provided for the relief of the poor. Three years after Ohio's admission to statehood the general assembly met this responsibility and re-enacted a poor relief law. In 1816 the first poorhouses were established by the county commissioners, and since 1913 the commissioners have been empowered, by any county containing a city which has an infirmary, to contract with the proper city officials for the care of the county indigent. Since 1908 the commissioners have had the duty of providing for the relief of the needy blind. In 1933 they were constituted a board to administer aid for the needy aged; and were required to provide direct housing relief to indigent persons. (Pease, *op. cit.,* 217; 3 O. L. 273; 14 O. L. 576; 99 O. L. 256; 115 O. L. pt. 2, 431-439 ; 115 O. L. 194).

The commissioners also have numerous duties in respect to veterans. In 1886 they were authorized to levy a tax for the relief of indigent soldiers, sailors, and marines of the Civil War, or if such veterans are deceased, for their dependents. The original provisions of the act were amended in 1919 to include all veterans. Since 1884, the commissioners have also been empowered to defray the funeral expenses of any honorably discharged soldier, sailor, or marine who dies indigent. Ten years later the provisions of the act were amended to include any army nurse, or the mother, wife or widow of any soldier, sailor, or marine.

In April 1935 the commissioners were authorized to provide non-institutional assistance to needy persons, and the following month they were given all poor relief powers which have formally been vested in the state relief commission. They were relieved of the latter responsibility in July 1936 when the state relief commission was re-invested with its old powers, and the commissioners given the alternative of either administering the advances of poor relief funds made by the commission, or of re-allocating such funds, on a basis of need, to the officials of the various political subdivisions. In Cuyahoga County, the commissioners have chosen to administer the funds through the Cuyahoga County Relief Administration. (116 O. L. 134; 116 O. L. 571; 116 O. L. pt. 2, H. 663).

The commissioners have been delegated certain duties regarding child welfare. In 1908 they were authorized upon the recommendation of the judge of ,juvenile court, either to purchase or lease a place to be known as a "detention home," for the housing of delinquent, dependent, or neglected minors under the age of eighteen. In 1927 they were empowered to build such a home. Since 1921 they have been authorized, with the aid of the child welfare board, to care for all dependent and neglected children by placing them in private homes or public institutions. Since 1913 they have been empowered to levy a tax for the payment of pensions to mothers with children under the age of sixteen years, whose husbands have either deserted them or are dead, permanently disabled, or imprisoned. (99 O. L. 166; 112 O. L. 381; 109 O. L. 566; 103 O. L. 878).

The commissioners have also certain powers in respect to finance. In 1853 they were given the authority to empower the auditor to contract for the making of all repairs and improvements on public buildings and grounds, providing the cost in no instance exceeded $50. Since 1859 claims against the county have been paid by the county treasurer upon allowance of the commissioners and upon warrant of the auditor, except in cases where the amount is fixed by law. In 1894 they were authorized to designate the banks or trust companies which were to act as depositories of the county funds. Such banks were required, however, to post adequate collateral. Since 1927 they have appointed a budget commissioner for the purpose of checking the departmental budgets and bringing about possible economies. The annual budget for the county is submitted to the commissioners for approval by the county budget commission. (51 O. L. 422-424; 56 O. L. 130; 91 O. L. 403; 112 O. L. 399).

The commissioners have been given various powers regarding taxation other than those already enumerated. In 1814 they were given the authority to make a special real property levy at any time, when after paying for the usual expenses of the county, the ordinary revenue was found to be insufficient to pay for the erection or repair of suitable public buildings. Since 1878, however, they have been forbidden to levy any tax for building purposes without submitting the question to a vote. A capitation tax on all doctors and lawyers were authorized in 1830, but was abolished in 1853. In 1859 they were given the duty of causing a list of persons delinquent in the payment of personal property tax to be read publicly each year. This requirement was abolished in 1931. (12 O. L. 298; 75 O. L. 31; 29 O. L. 304; 51 O. L. 422-426; 56 O. L. 210; 114 O. L. 832).

The commissioners have in some instances, acted in a supervisory capacity over other county officers and over certain institutions in the county. The prosecutor, clerk of common pleas court, sheriff and treasurer have, since 1850 been required to report to the commissioners annually. These reports are filed with the county auditor, and are then submitted to the commissioners who must scrutinize them and place the results of the examination on their journal. Since 1896 it has also been their duty to visit semi-annually each private or public hospital, reformatory, detention home, and private asylum within the county for the purpose of noting sanitary conditions and the treatment of inmates. They must file with the county prosecutor a complete report of the investigations of such institutions. These reports are open to the inspection of the public. Since 1904 that has been the duty of the county auditor to submit a monthly statement of the county's finances to the commissioners who places them in a file and post one copy in the auditor's office for public inspection. (48 O. L. 66; 92 O. L. 212; 97 O. L. 457).

Although the commissioners have had little to do with the administration of criminal justice they have at times been invested with certain powers regarding it. In 1839 they were authorized to employ persons confined in the county jail on any road or in any stone quarry in the county. This power was broadened in 1852 to include work on the erection of public buildings and the construction of other public works. Both acts applied only to Hamilton and Cuyahoga Counties and repealed in 1853. Since 1843 they have provided for equipment, furnishings, fixtures, fuel, and repairs for the county jail, as well as food and bed clothing for persons imprisoned therein. Since 1890 they have also appointed a jail physician. In 1845 it became their duty to mutilate confiscated counterfeiting instruments, melt counterfeit coin, and to sell both, together with all unclaimed stolen property, for the benefit of the common schools of the county. In 1865 they were authorized to offer and pay out rewards for the apprehension of persons guilty of murder and four years later this authority was widened to include all felons. Since 1929 the county commissioners and the county prosecutor have been empowered, with the consent of the court of common pleas, to contract with radio stations for the broadcasting of information concerning any violent felony, when the perpetrator therefore has escaped. Since 1929 it has also been competent for the commissioners of any county which has no workhouse, but contains a city which has one, to make arrangements for the maintenance therein, at the expense of the county, of all persons convicted a violation of any law in the of the state. Since 1935 they have been allowed to provide for the relief of all persons disabled by reason of their automobile being commandeered by any police officer in the discharge of his duty. (37 O. L. 54; 50 O. L. 3-4; 53 O. L. 422; 41 O. L. 74; 87 O. L. 186; 42 O. L. 16; 62 O. L. 4; 113 O. L. 139, 200; 116 O. L. 405).

From 1917 to 1927 the sheriff was authorized to impound all dogs found in the county not wearing registration tags. In 1927 an act authorized the county commissioners to appoint a county dog warden who was made responsible to the commissioners for the conduct of his office. (112 O. L. 348; 107 O. L. 735).

The county commissioners have often served as members of various county boards and commissions. The first of these boards was a board of equalization conceived in 1831 to hear complaints regarding real and personal property assessments. They also became members of a separate board of equalization in 1859 which met every six years to pass on the returns of the district assessors. The president of the board of county commissioners is now a member of the board of revision. Since 1884 the commissioners have appointed three persons in each township to supervise the interment of veterans who die indigent. Since 1921 they have been authorized to appoint the four members of the child welfare board, two of whom must be women. They also appoint the eight members of the county planning commission which was created in 1923. In 1921 they were empowered to appoint three of the five members of the county library board. When the board was enlarged in 1931 the commissioners were authorized to appoint four of the seven members. (29 O. L. 272; 56 O. L. 193; 109 O. L. 533; 81 O. L. 146; 110 O. L. 311; 109 O. L. 351; 114 O. L. 56).

The commissioners have at various times been given authority in connection with libraries and civic centers. Since 1898 they have been authorized to receive bequests and gifts of books, buildings for the use of county public library, or money for such purposes. Since 1923 they have been empowered, upon the approval of the voters, to issue bonds for the construction and furnishing of public library buildings. In 1913 they were authorized to provide and maintain civic and social centers throughout the county, and to employ expert directors to superintend them. (93 O. L. 355; 110 O. L. 242; 103 O. L. 830).

Various duties have been given the commissioners relating to archives. In 1850 they were authorized to subscribe for one copy of each issue of the leading newspapers of each political party, published in the county, and cause them to be bound and filed in the county auditor's office as public archives. An amendment in 1923 provided that after such newspapers have been kept on file ten years, they were to be transferred to the custody of the Ohio State Archaeological and Historical Society. They were empowered in 1913 to annually expend a sum not to exceed $100 to defray the expenses of county historical or pioneer associations in collecting, compiling and publishing historical data. (48 O. L. 65; 110 O. L. 4; 103 O. L. 755).

In 1906 the commissioner's tenure of office was reduced from three to two years. Since 1920 it has remained at four years. (98 O. L. 272; 108 O. L. pt. 2, 1300).

The legislature which passed the original act creating the board of county commissioners in 1804 could not have anticipated the present scope of the office. Successive legislatures have so added to the duties and powers of the commissioners that today we have a unique office, one which has both legislative and executive, as well as quasi-judicial functions.

Executive Division

85. COMMISSIONERS' JOURNAL

January 1810—. 93 volumes, (January 1810- December 1872, 3 volumes, 1-3; December 4, 1872-February 1881, 1 volume, 4; March1881- March 1883, 1 volume; March 19-October 11, 1883, 1 volume; March 1881-October 11, 1883, 1 volume, 5; October 12, 1883-July 1926, 60 volumes; August 1926, 26 volumes, 66-91).

A record of the proceedings of the board of county commissioners. Contains copies of resolutions relating to bonds, road legislation, and miscellaneous matters; and copies of agreements, leases, and village and city ordinance. It also contains a list of communications, vouchers, and requisitions. The file numbers of all underlying documents are indicated. Volume 5 is a handwritten copy of the two unencumbered volumes of the same years. For index (1883—) see number 86. 1810-1906, handwritten; 1906—, typed. Volumes average 700 pages. 14 x 17 x 3.5. 1810-1872, 3 volumes, 1-3; 1926—, 26 volumes, 66-91, Room 135; 1872-1926, 64 volumes, Basement storeroom, County courthouse.

86. MISCELLANEOUS INDEX

1883—. 18 volumes, 1-18.

An alphabetical index to the commissioners' journal, listing date of proceedings, and journal and page numbers. Volumes 1-10 (1883-1921), handwritten; volumes 11-18 (1922—), typed. Volumes average 200 pages. 14 x 17 x 1. 1883-1925, 13 volumes, Basement storeroom; 1926—, 5 volumes, Room 135, County courthouse.

87. MEETING NOTES
1925—. 1 file box; 2 bundles.
Memoranda of meetings of the board of commissioners. 1925-1929, handwritten; 1930—, typed. File box 14 x 9 x 4.75; each bundle 11 x 9 x 5.5. 1925-1930, 2 bundles, Basement storeroom; 1930—, 1 file box, Room 135, County courthouse.

88. COMMISSIONERS' CORRESPONDENCE FILES
1910—. 28 bundles; 8 letter boxes; 8 file drawers.
Communications and responses pertaining to the proceedings of the board. Arranged alphabetically. Typed. Each file drawer 24 x 15 x 11.5; each letter box 13 x 10 x 4; each bundle 9 x 12 x 14. 28 bundles, 8 letter boxes, 5 file drawers, Basement storeroom; 3 file drawers, Room 135, County courthouse.

Resolutions

89. MISCELLANEOUS RESOLUTIONS
1914—. 70 file boxes; 11 bundles.
All resolutions pertaining to matters other than road legislation. Filed numerically. For index see number 90. Typed. 1914-1928, 52 file boxes, 4 x 10 x 20, Room 135, County courthouse.

90. INDEX TO MISCELLANEOUS RESOLUTIONS
1926—. 2 volumes
An alphabetical index showing date of proceedings, resolution number, and general remarks. Typed on printed forms. Volumes average 1,000 pages. 18 x 13 x 3. 135, County courthouse.

91. MISCELLANEOUS RECORDS
1909-1921. 1 file box.
Resolutions of the county commissioners pertaining to miscellaneous taxes and levies, 1913; transfer of funds, 1919; transfer of appropriations, 1916, 1917; resolutions to borrow money,1917; allowances for county offices, 1909-1921; and allowances for the sheriff in municipal court, 1909-1919. Typed and handwritten on printed forms. File box 10.5 x 4.5 x 14. Basement storeroom, County courthouse.

92. RESOLUTIONS ON LORAIN-CARNEGIE BRIDGE
1927-1930. 1 volume.

A record of various resolutions pertaining to the Lorain-Carnegie Bridge. Gives number and page of the commissioners' journal, and dates of the resolution. Arranged chronologically. Typed. 150 pages. 14.5 x 11.75 x 1.5. Basement storeroom, County courthouse.

93. FUND TRANSFERS
1930-1933. Approximately 28 folders in 4 file boxes.

Resolutions for the transfers of funds and miscellaneous communications covering these transfers. In chronological order. Typed. Each file box 10.5 x 14 x 4.75. Basement storeroom, County courthouse.

94. MISCELLANEOUS FILE, SANITARY ENGINEER'S RESOLUTIONS
1922-1930. Approximately 350 in 7 bundles. (1922-1927, 5 bundles; 1929-1930, 2 bundles).

Resolutions pertaining to the work of the sanitary engineer, such as sewer construction, repairs, and sewage disposal. Typed. Each bundle 15 x 9.5 x 1. Basement storeroom, County courthouse.

95. APPROPRIATIONS
1922-1927. 2 file boxes.

Resolutions for the appropriation of funds approved by the county commissioners for the conduct of public works and services. In chronological order. Handwritten and typed. Each file box 14 x 10.5 x 4.5. Basement storeroom, County courthouse.

Deeds, Releases, Agreements, and Franchises

96. DEEDS AND ABSTRACTS
1903-1928. Approximately 325 in 12 file boxes.

Deeds, abstracts, resolutions for appropriating funds, warranty deeds, petitions for appropriations, and miscellaneous notes. Filed numerically. For index to deeds and abstracts see number 98. Typed. Each file box 10 x 15 x 4. Room 135, County courthouse.

97. DEEDS AND RELEASES
1928—. 760 in 9 file boxes.

Deeds and releases to property appropriated by the county for the building of public highways, bridges and sanitary drainage. Filed numerically. For index see number 98. Typed on printed form. Each file box 10 x 15 x 4. Room 135, County courthouse.

98. RECORD OF DEEDS, APPROPRIATIONS, AGREEMENTS OF COUNTY PROPERTY
1902—. 1 volume.

Copies of deeds, appropriations, and agreements of county property. Contains an alphabetical index. Typed. 1,000 pages. 3 x 12 x 18. Room 135, County courthouse.

99. DEEDS FOR THE COUNTY DETENTION HOME AND JUVENILE COURT BUILDING SITE
1931. 15 abstracts and deeds in 1 file box.

Abstracts, warranty deeds, and quit claim deeds, for property appropriated by county commissioners for erection of the Juvenile Court Child Welfare Building. Handwritten and typed on printed forms; photostats. File box 10.5 x 14 x 4.5. Room 135, County courthouse.

100. WARRANTY DEEDS
1832-1902. 1 volume.

A record of warranty deeds showing grantors, grantees and conditions of the transfer of real property for the county. Alphabetical as to grantors. For separate index see number 101. Handwritten and typed on printed forms. 600 pages. 8.5 x 14 x 1.75. Basement storage room, County courthouse.

101. INDEX TO DEED RECORDS
1832-1932. 1 volume.

An alphabetical index to "Warranty Deeds," listing names of grantors. Handwritten. 100 pages. 13.75 x 8.5 x .25. Basement storeroom, County courthouse.

102. DEEDS, EASEMENTS, RELEASES, AGREEMENTS, ON ALL PROPERTY FOR WEST APPROACH TO LORAIN-CENTRAL BRIDGE ETC.

1931. 2 file boxes.

Handwritten and typed. File box 13.25 x 10.5 x 1.75. Room 135, County courthouse.

103. AGREEMENTS

1903—. 10 file boxes.

Official copies of all agreements between the commissioners and county units, corporations, banks, etc. Filed numerically. For index see number 104. Handwritten and typed. Each file box 14 x 10.5 x 4.5. 1903-1929, 7 file boxes, Basement store room; 1931—, 3 file boxes, Room 135, County courthouse.

104. COMMISSIONERS RECORD OF MISCELLANEOUS AGREEMENTS, LEASES, ETC.

April 1903—. 2 volumes.

A record containing copies of agreements and leases. Volume contains an alphabetical index. Typed. 1000 pages. 3 x 12 x 18. Room 135, County courthouse.

105. FRANCHISES

1907—. 129 in 8 file boxes.

Documents relating to purchases of property, bonds issued, resolutions submitting proposals to issue bonds to the electors, and original petitions. Filed numerically. For index see number 106. Typed on printed forms. Each file box 10 x 15 x 4. Room 135, County courthouse.

106. COMMISSIONERS' RECORD OF MISCELLANEOUS FRANCHISES AND GRANTS

October 1898—. 1 volume.

Copies of all grants and franchises between the board of county commissioners and various railroads, townships, and public utilities. Contains an alphabetical index. Typed. Approximately 200 pages. 3 x 12 x 18. Room 135, County courthouse.

Bank Depositories

107. BANK STATEMENTS
1927—. Approximately 58 and 1 file box.

Comparative statements of banks regarding security given for the county funds. Arranged as to names of banks. Typed. File box 4 x 4 x 10. Room 135, County courthouse.

108. DEPOSITORIES AND BANKS QUALIFIED
1918—. Approximately 84 in 14 file boxes. (1918-1924, 4 file boxes; 1926-1927, 1 file box; 1928-1933, 8 file boxes; 1934—, 1 file box).

Copies of releases of the mortgagor, listing amount of first mortgage, amount of bonds posted as security, and journal volume and page. In chronological order. Each file box 14 x 10.5 x 4.75. 1918-1924, 1928—, 13 file boxes, Basement storeroom; 1926-1927, 1 file box, Room 135, County courthouse.

109. GUARANTY FUNDS
1930—. Approximately 50 in 1 file box.

Insurance and bonds put up as security to guarantee county funds. Arranged as to names of companies. Typed on printed forms. File box 4 x 4 x 10. Room 135, County courthouse.

110. THE CAPITAL BANK; LAKE ERIE TRUST COMPANY
1927-1933. 10 receipts in 1 file box.

Receipts for interest coupons on county bonds refunded to banks. Arranged as to names of banks. Typed on printed forms. File box 4 x 4 x 10. Room 135, County courthouse.

111. SCHEDULE OF MORTGAGES FOR HYPOTHECATION AS SECURITY FOR COUNTY DEPOSITS
1931-1932. 1 volume.

A record of mortgages given by banks as security for deposits of the county. Typed. 150 pages. 14.5 x 13.5 x 1.25. Basement storeroom, County courthouse.

112. COUNTY DEPOSITORIES
1925-1926. 1 file box.
Releases and memoranda regarding security given by banks. Filed numerically. Typed on printed forms. File box 4 x 10 x 20. Room 135, County courthouse.

113-114. HYPOTHECATION AND SUBSTITUTION OF SECURITIES, BONDS ON COUNTY DEPOSITORIES
1919-1923. 4 file boxes; 1 bundle.
Agreements between the commissioners and various banks guaranteeing substitutions of securities deposited against county funds; also, receipts for bonds accepted as security. Filed alphabetically. Handwritten and typed. Each file box 4.5 x 10.5 x 14. Basement storeroom, County courthouse.

115. WARRANTS OUTSTANDING
1914-1921. 1 volume.
A record of warrants outstanding, listing date, depository number, person to whom the warrant is issued, warrant number, and amount. In order of depository numbers. Typed. 700 pages. 13.5 x 9 x 1.75. Basement storeroom, County courthouse.

116. CORRESPONDENCE, BIDS ON BONDS
1923-1924. 1 bundle.
Correspondence pertaining to bids on county bonds offered by the county commissioners on collateral securities, giving name of bank, name of bidder, amount of bond, and interest due. Typed. Bundle 13 x 10 x 3. Basement storeroom, County courthouse.

Notes and Bonds

117. RECORD OF BONDS
1912—. 1 file box; 12 bundles.
Files contained petitions and certificates for publication of the notice of the bonds; shows coupon number, amount involved, the interest and the name of the bond issued. Typed. File box 13.25 x 10.5 x 1.25; each bundle 15 x 9.5 x 2.5. 12 bundles, Basement storeroom; 1912—, 1 file box, Room 135, County courthouse.

118. TAX ANTICIPATION ON SCRIPT AND INTEREST-BEARING NOTES
1933—. 1 file box.

A record of notes issued by the commissioner for funds to secure script issues and to meet interest payments on notes outstanding or public works.   Handwritten and typed. File box 14 x 10.5 x 4.5. Basement storeroom, County courthouse.

119. RECORD OF LOAN IMPROVEMENT NOTES
1925—. 1 loose leaf volume.

Lists date of issue of notes, date delivered, amount authorized, village or township, amount of loan, name of road issued for, callable certificates, serial number, interest accrued, total amount due, and date payable. Handwritten and typed on printed forms. 350 pages. 20 x 15 x 3. Room 135, County courthouse.

120. CORRESPONDENCE AND MISCELLANEOUS PAPERS ON MAINTENANCE OF OLD COURTHOUSE
1910-1914. Approximately 12 folders in 1 file box.

General correspondence, estimates, bids, payrolls, etc. pertaining to the old courthouse. Typed. File box 15.25 x 10.5 x 5. Basement storeroom, County courthouse.

121. REDEEMED BOND COUPONS
1923-1928. Approximately 33,000 in 132 file boxes.

Bond certificates with coupons attached. The certificates are for $1,000 each and show the date issued and number. In order of certificate numbers. Typed. Each file box 12 x 11 x 5.5. Attic storeroom, fourth floor, County courthouse.

Proposals, Contracts, Bids on Bonds, and Attested Accounts

122. PROPOSALS, BIDS
1894—. 6 volumes; 6 file boxes; 16 bundles. (1904-1925, 6 volumes; 1894-1932, 5 file boxes, 16 bundles; 1932—, 1 file box).

Show date of advertisement, how proposal was received, record volume and page, engineer's and contractor's estimate, estimated quantities of material, total estimate, and name of person to whom contract was awarded. Handwritten and typed on printed forms. Volumes average 240 pages. 23.25 x 15.25 x 1.25. Each file box

14 x 14 x 1. 1904-1925, 6 volumes; 1894-1932, 5 file boxes, 16 bundles, Basement storeroom; 1932—, Room 135, County courthouse.

123. PROPOSALS AND MAINTENANCE REPORTS
1933—. (1933-1934, 2 bundles; 1934—, 1 file box).

Proposals for county improvements, and maintenance reports, stating estimates of the unit cost and total cost, the unit price, total amount of the bid, name of job, and date of report. In order of contract numbers. Handwritten and typed on printed forms. Each bundle 15 x 9 x 3; file box 14 x 10 x 24. 1933-1934, 2 bundles, Basement storeroom; 1934—, 1 file box, Room 135, County courthouse.

124. PROPOSALS FOR DETROIT- SUPERIOR BRIDGE
1912. 1 bundle.

Proposal for the building of the Detroit-Superior Bridge, showing estimated cost and quantity of material, cost of labor and a specified time for completion. Handwritten. Bundle 15 x 9 x 1.5. Basement storeroom, County courthouse.

125. CONTRACT BOOK-COUNTY BUILDING COMMISSION OF 1898
1902-1908. 1 volume.

A record of contracts authorized by the county building commission of 1898, listing the name of the person to whom each contract was let, consideration in each instance, and description of work or service. In order of contract numbers. Handwritten on printed forms. Volumes average 250 pages. 15.25 x 11.25 x 1.75. Basement storeroom, County courthouse.

126. CONTRACTS
1895—. Approximately 8470 in 242 file boxes.

Contracts issued by the county commissioners, giving in each instance name of contractor, location of work, and estimated cost of job. Arranged as to contract numbers. Handwritten and typed on printed forms. Each file box 4.5 x 10.5 x 14. 1895-1929, 208 file boxes, Basement storeroom; 1929—, 34 file boxes, Room 135, County courthouse.

127. CONTRACT BOOKS
1891—. 17 volumes (1891-1899, 2 volumes; 1893—, 15 volumes, 1-15).
A record of the contracts let by the commissioners, listing name of person to whom each contract was let, consideration in each instance, and description of work or service. Arranged numerically as to contract numbers. 1893—, 15 volumes, contain an alphabetical index of contractors in each volume. Handwritten on printed forms. Volumes average 230 pages. 15.25 x 11.5 x 1.25. 1891-1899, 2 volumes, 1893-1926, 11 volumes, Basement storeroom; 1927—, 4 volumes, 12-15, Room 135, County courthouse.

128. MISCELLANEOUS BROKERAGE HOUSES
1936. 3 bids in 1 file box.
Bids on bonds offered by county commissioners. Arranged as to brokerage houses. Typed on printed forms. File box 4 x 4 x 10. Room 135, County courthouse.

129. MISCELLANEOUS DOCUMENTS AND COUPON RECEIPTS ON BONDS HELD AS SECURITY FOR DEPOSITORIES
30 file drawers.
Contain resolutions calling for proposals; resolutions accepting proposals submitted for the deposit of public money; resolutions for change of rate of interest; receipts given by depository banks for coupons surrendered by the county commissioners on bonds hypothecated as security for county funds; bids and proposals submitted by various banks in response to resolutions of the county commissioners to provide depositories for county funds; depository bonds of various banks approved by county commissioners; powers of attorney of various surety companies; legal opinion submitted by depository banks; certificate of compliance of the state surety department; hypothecation and substitution of securities; county employees' surety bonds; fire insurance policies for the county fairgrounds in Berea, and the C.C.R.A. building on Franklin Avenue; bills of sale and certificates of registration for county owned motor vehicles; miscellaneous treasurer's receipts; resolutions granting permission for street openings and the transportation of heavy machinery over county highways. Typed and handwritten on printed forms. Each file drawer 4 x 4 x 10. In safe, Room 135, County courthouse.

130. ATTESTED ACCOUNTS
1917—. 5 file boxes.

Gives name of company or person to whom material was sold, an itemized record of all material purchased, date of purchase, sworn statement as to purchase of material by company furnishing it, and name of job for which material was purchased. Chronological. Handwritten and typed on printed forms. Each file box 14 x 10.5 x 4.5. 1917-1927, 3 file boxes, Basement storeroom, 1927—, 2 file boxes, Room 135, County courthouse.

131. RELEASED ATTESTED ACCOUNTS
1917-1928. Approximately 70 folders in 2 file boxes.

Correspondence covering payments of attested accounts; and affidavits of accounts for material furnished and labor performed for contractors of county improvements and repairs showing name of contractor, names of parties performing labor or furnishing material, and the amount due and unpaid. No arrangement. Accompanying the affidavit is a copy of the account. Typed and handwritten. Each file box 15.25 x 10.25 x 5. Basement storeroom, County courthouse.

132. LEGAL ADVERTISEMENTS
1912—. 20 volumes; 5 file boxes.

Published advertisements giving notice of projected public works and inviting bids and proposals on the materials and the execution thereof, with the date of publication. In chronological order. Newsprint clippings. Volumes average 200 pages. 12 x 15 x 4. Each file box 5 x 10.5 x 14. 1912-1931, 19 volumes, Basement storage room; 1932—, 1 volume, 1927—, 5 file boxes, Room 135, County courthouse.

Establishment of Townships and Villages, and Annexations

133. ESTABLISHMENT OF TOWNSHIPS AND VILLAGES, AND ANNEXATIONS
1911—. Approximately 210 folders in six file boxes.

Official copies of resolutions regarding the erection of townships out of villages, listing date of petition, date of adoption of resolution, and clerk's file number. Filed numerically. For index see number 134. Handwritten and typed. Each file box 14 x 10.5 x 4.5. Room 135, County courthouse.

134. COUNTY COMMISSIONERS' RECORD OF ESTABLISHMENTS OF VILLAGES AND TOWNSHIPS
1911—. 1 volume.

An alphabetical index of villages and townships giving a complete record of the proceedings. Typed on printed forms, 200 pages. 15 x 12 x 2. Room 135, County courthouse.

135. ANNEXATIONS
1920-1933. Approximately 132 folders in 11 file boxes.

Resolutions and all papers pertaining to the annexation of territory to political subdivisions in the county. On the outside of the folder is listed the date of the filing of the petition and of the map, the date of the resolution, the date of hearing, and the date of adoption. Filed numerically. Typed and handwritten. Each file box 4.5 x 10 x 14. 10 file boxes, Room 135; 1 file box, Basement storeroom, County courthouse.

136. INTER-COUNTY HIGHWAY RECEIPTS, OLD ANNEXATIONS
1909-1917. 1 file box.

Resolutions on the transfer of roads and the annexation of political subdivisions to Cuyahoga County. Handwritten and typed. File box 4.5 x 10.5 x 14. Basement storeroom, County courthouse.

Roads and Road Repairs

137. ACTIVE ROADS
1925—. 8 file drawers.

Contain proposals for new roads, general correspondence, tabulations, and information pertaining to maps, plats, approaches, appraisals, widening, extensions, establishment of settlements, intersections, relocations, vacations and ditches. Arranged numerically. For index see number 138. Handwritten and typed. Each file drawer 24 x 12 x 10. Room 135, County courthouse.

138. INDEX TO ACTIVE ROAD FILE
1925—. 300 cards in 1 file box.

A card index listing name of road, village or township, resolution declaring necessity, date of adoption, date of notice, dates published, date of view, date of hearing, continuing dates, file number, and journal volume and page. Alphabetical as to names of roads. Typed. File box 24 x 12 x 10. Room 135, County courthouse.

139. CLOSED ROADS
1914—. 28 file boxes; 3 letter boxes; 6 file drawers.
Correspondence and proceedings pertaining to complete road work. Arranged numerically. For index see number 140. Typed. Each file drawer 24.5 x 16.25 x 11.25; each file box 14 x 10.75 x 4.75; each letter box 12.75 x 11 x 3. 1914-1926, 3 letter boxes, 6 file drawers, basement storage room; 1917—, 28 file boxes, Room 135, County courthouse.

140. INDEX TO CLOSED ROADS FILE
1926—. 1000 cards in 1 file box.
A card index listing name of road, village or township, resolution declaring necessity, date of adoption, date of notice, date published, date of view, date of hearing, continuing dates, file number, date disposed, and journal volume and page. Alphabetical as to names of roads. Typed. File box 24 x 12 x 10. Room 135, County courthouse.

141. RESCINDED ROADS CORRESPONDENCE
1916-1934. 6 file drawers.
Correspondence covering contemplated road work that has been cancelled. Arranged numerically. For index see number 142. Typed. Each file drawer 23.5 x 16.5 x 12. Basement storeroom, County courthouse.

142. INDEX TO RESCINDED ROAD FILE
1916-1934. 400 cards in 2 file boxes.
A card index listing name of road, village or township, resolution declaring necessity, date of adoption, date of notice, date published, date of view, date of hearing, continuing dates, file number, date rescinded, and journal volume and page number. Alphabetical as to names of roads, Typed. Each File box 4.75 10.5 x 14. Room 135, County courthouse.

143. ROADS WHICH ARE DEAD OR DISPOSED OF, AND REJECTED ROAD PETITIONS
1914-1918. 2 file boxes.
General files on the disposition of road work, listing date, location of work, and the journal page where the commissioners' resolutions are recorded. Arranged alphabetically. Handwritten and typed. Each file box 14 x 10.5 x 4.5. Basement storeroom, County courthouse.

144. INACTIVE ROADS
1898-1913. 27 file boxes.
Files cover roads on which work was suspended. Alphabetical as to names of roads. Handwritten and typed. Each file box 14 x 10.5 x 4.5. Basement storeroom, County courthouse.

145. ROAD PETITIONS
1891-1918. 77 bundles.
Petitions of property owners for or against the construction of proposed roads. Handwritten and typed on printed forms. Basement storeroom, County courthouse.

146. MISCELLANEOUS ROAD RECORDS
1898-1914. Approximately 25 folders in 1 file box.
Folders contain general data on roads; and copies of commissioners' resolutions for road work, and for the changes of road names. Arranged chronologically. Handwritten. File box 14 x 10.5 x 2. Basement storeroom, County courthouse.

147. INTER-COUNTY HIGHWAY RECEIPTS; OLD ANNEXATIONS
1917—. 9 folders in 1 file box.
Folders contain grants, resolutions, and ordinances to repair county roads and bridges in political subdivisions of the county. Handwritten. File box 4 x 10 x 20. Room 135, County courthouse.

148. STATE AND COUNTY IMPROVEMENT FUND
1901-1908. 1 volume.
Lists name of road, name of political subdivision, number and page of the commissioners' journal and date of improvement. Alphabetical as to political subdivisions. Handwritten. 410 pages. 18.25 x 12.25 x 2.25. Basement storeroom, County courthouse.

149. MISCELLANEOUS COMMUNICATIONS FROM COUNTY SURVEYOR (Personal Receipts)
1913. 1 letter box.
Miscellaneous letters and notes on various matters relating to road works. Typed and handwritten. Letterbox 11 x 12 x 3. Basement storeroom, County courthouse.

150. COUNTY EMPLOYEES' PAPERS PERTAINING TO ROAD WORK DEPARTMENT
1913. 1 file box.

Alphabetical as to names of roads. Handwritten and typed. File box 14 x 14.5 x 4.5. Basement storeroom, County courthouse.

151. ROAD REPAIR REPORTS
1924. Approximately 200 sheets in 1 bundle.

List report number, job number, number of road, and estimated cost. Handwritten on printed forms. Bundles 14.5 x 9.5 x 2. Basement storeroom, County courthouse.

152. BULLETIN NUMBER 11 HIGHWAY MAP OF THE COUNTIES OF OHIO
1909. 1 volume.

An atlas of county roads showing mileage in each county, and total mileage for the state; also shows data used in preparation of the maps. Arranged alphabetically as to counties. 90 pages. 17 x 13.5 x .75. Printed by State Highway Department of Ohio. Basement storeroom, County courthouse.

153. PROFILE SPECIFICATIONS AND MAP OF DOVER CENTER DITCH
1885. 1 volume.

Shows profile specifications, property owners and proposed work. A printed map shows location of ditch. Arranged as to profile specification numbers. Handwritten. 27 pages. 22.5 x 18 x .5. Basement storeroom, County courthouse.

154. TURNPIKE TRANSFER
1828-1867. 1 volume.

A record of turnpike transfers which were under franchise to individuals to collect tolls, showing date of transfer, to whom transferred, and name of turnpike. Alphabetical as to individuals to whom franchise was issued. Handwritten. 500 pages. 13 x 8.5 x 2. Basement storeroom, County courthouse.

155. PLANK ROAD RECORD
1854-1883. 1 volume.

Record of toll roads, constructed of planks, which were purchased by the commissioners, showing name of road, location, and name of owner. Alphabetically arranged as to roads. Handwritten. 50 pages. 13 x 8.5 x 2. Basement storeroom, County courthouse.

156. LORAIN-HURON HIGH LEVEL BRIDGE
1914-1920. 1 volume.
Copies of communications to the county commissioners, resolutions, and valuations of property pertaining to the Lorain-Huron High Level Bridge. In chronological order. Typed. 38 pages. 11 x 13 x 2. Basement storeroom, County courthouse.

157. BROOKLYN BRIGHTON BRIDGE
1912-1917. 20 folders in 2 file boxes.
Papers pertaining to the construction of this bridge, bids for bonds and a record of proceedings pertaining to the issuance of bonds. Typed. Arranged as to subject. Each file box 14 x 10.5 x 4.5. Basement storeroom, County courthouse.

158. REPORTS OF HIGHWAY BRIDGES
1903. 1 volume.
Reports of iron and wood truss bridges of all kinds, submitted by the county surveyor, showing condition of bridge; location; measurements of span and roadway; kind of arch; date bridge was built and by whom. Also contains a map published by Whitworth Brothers Company, 1899, on which is indicated the location of each bridge. Reports are alphabetically arranged as to taxing districts. Typed. 150 pages. 13 x 19.5 x 1. Basement storeroom, County courthouse.

Pay Rolls and Budget Requests

159. PAY ROLL, MISCELLANEOUS
July 1936—. 4 loose-leaf volume; 8 bundles. (1897-1903, 1 volume; 1912-1913, 2 volumes, 1-2; 1914-1934, 8 bundles; 1935—, 1 volume).
Semi-monthly payroll ledger sheets of employees of the commissioners' office. Chronologically arranged as to divisions. Typed. Volumes average 480 pages. 20 x 18 x 1. 1897-1934, 3 volumes, 8 bundles, Basement storeroom, 1935—, 1 volume., Room 135, County courthouse.

160. PAY ROLL BOOKS
July 1936—. 1 loose-leaf volume.
Gives name of employees, nature of employment, date, total days worked, rate of

pay, total wages, and signature of employee. Arranged chronologically, and alphabetically for each pay period. Typed on printed forms. 150 pages. 20 x 17 x 1. Room 135, County courthouse.

161. BUDGET REQUEST FOR SALARIES
1926-1928. 1 volume.

Lists all budgeted amounts approved by the commissioners for the county workers' salaries. Typed. 300 pages. 14.5 x 14.5 x 3. Basement storeroom, County courthouse.

162. PAYROLL BOOKS
1912-1914. 2 volumes.

A record of all persons employed by the county commissioners, amounts of their salaries, and their positions. Typed. Volumes average 600 pages. 18.5 x 15 x 2. Basement storeroom, County courthouse.

Employees and Employees' Bonds

163. SURETY BONDS OF COUNTY EMPLOYEES
1922—. Approximately 250 in 1 file box.

Bonds given by county employees to the county commissioners to insure the faithful performance of their duties to the county. Arranged as to employees' names. Typed on printed forms. File box 10 x 12 x 3. Basement storeroom, County courthouse.

164. COUNTY COMMISSIONERS' APPLICATIONS
1921-1925, 1 file box; 1926, 1 bundle.

Applications filed with the commissioners for employment in the county service. Handwritten and typed. File box 10 x 12 x 3. Basement storeroom, County courthouse.

165. RECORD OF COUNTY EMPLOYEES
January 1910- September 1914. 1 volume.

Gives name and address of employee, occupation, amount of salary, and journal volume and page. Alphabetical as to name of employees. Handwritten. 800 pages. 11.5 x 16.25 x 2. Basement storeroom, County courthouse.

166. EMPLOYMENT BOOK
1897-1900. 1 volume.

Lists name of employee, kind of employment, and rate of pay. In chronological order. Handwritten. 400 pages. 10 x 14.5 x 1.75. Basement storeroom, County courthouse.

Miscellaneous Expenditures

167. RECEIPTS AND DISBURSEMENTS
1935—. 1 bundle; 20 sheets.

Monthly reports of the county auditor of receipts, disbursements, and balance of county funds and accounts, including the balance in the hands of the county treasurer and of special depositories. They list names of funds, and receipts and disbursements for each. 1935-1936, 1 bundle, Basement storeroom; January 1936, sheets on wall in Room 135, County courthouse.

168. TREASURER'S RECEIPTS
1930—. Approximately 150 in 2 file boxes.

Receipts of the county treasurer for various amounts paid for commissioners requisitions. Typed. Each file box 4 x 4 x 10. Room 135, County courthouse.

169. CASH BOOK
1925—. 1 volume.

Gives date, township or village, and amount paid on account to the credit of the board of elections. In chronological order. Handwritten on printed forms. 150 pages. 20 x 12 x 1.5. Room 135, County courthouse.

170. DISBURSEMENTS, COUNTY BUILDING FUND
1902-1908. 1 volume.

An account of the payments from the county building fund for the erection, maintenance, and repair of county buildings. Arranged as to names of building funds. Handwritten. 400 pages. 18.5 x 18.5 x 2. Basement storeroom, County courthouse.

171. PAROLE RECEIPTS
1926-1931. 1 volume.

Receipts and duplicates giving name of payee, amount, date, purpose of payment and signature of the receiving official. In order of receipt numbers. Handwritten on printed forms. 150 pages. 15 x 12 x 1. Room 135, County courthouse.

172. STATEMENT OF COST DUE THE COUNTY CLERK'S OFFICE
1911-1921. 2 volumes; 1 bundle. (1911-1913, 2 volumes; 1916-1921, 1 bundle).

A statement of costs due the clerk's office. Typed. Volumes average 150 pages. 13 x 8.5 x .5. Basement storeroom, County courthouse.

173. STATEMENT OF COST, PENALTIES, ETC., DUE PROBATE JUDGE
1930. 1 volume.; 1932, 1 bundle.

Lists charges against the commissioner's office for services rendered by the probate court. Typed. Volume average 150 pages. 13.75 x 13 x .5. Basement storeroom, County courthouse.

174. SPECIAL FUNDS
1893-1896. 1 volume.

A record of funds not otherwise accounted for in the regular budget and for special purposes. Handwritten. 504 pages. 14.5 x 9 x 1. Basement storeroom, County courthouse.

175. VOUCHERS
1917-1922. 1 bundle.

Vouchers, retained as receipts for miscellaneous bills paid.. Handwritten on printed forms. Bundle 12 x 9 x 4. Basement storeroom, County courthouse.

176. OLD BILLS
1922. 1 letter file box.

Old commercial bills that were paid by the commissioners. Handwritten and typed on printed forms. Letter box 11 x 12 x 3. Basement storeroom, County courthouse.

177. MISCELLANEOUS PAPERS
1917. 1 file box.

Resolutions of the county commissioners authorizing the payment of fees to the coroner, the sheriff, and for miscellaneous purposes. Handwritten and typed on printed forms. File box 4.5 x 10 x 14. Basement storeroom, County courthouse.

178. INDEX TO CLAIMS AGAINST COUNTY.
1880-1882. 1 volume.

An index of claimants, giving volume and page of the record, date on which claim was approved and ordered paid, and amount of the claim. Handwritten. 450 pages. 18.5 x 14.5 x 1.5. Basement storeroom, County courthouse.

Miscellaneous

179. LEGAL OPINIONS
1907—. 18 file boxes.

Legal opinions rendered by the prosecuting attorney and courts on the legal aspects of the public works and acts of the commissioners. Filed by document number. Typed. Each file box 4.5 x 10.5 x 14. 1907-1926, 7 file boxes, Basement storeroom; 1926—, 11 file boxes, room 135, County courthouse.

180. PERMITS
1922—. 142 in 3 file boxes.

Permits allowing contractors the right to proceed on certain work. Arranged as to names of contractors. Typed on printed forms. Each file box 4 x 4 x 10. Room 135, County courthouse.

181. JOURNAL, COUNTY BUILDING COMMISSION
1896-1899. 1 volume.

A record of activities of the county building commission showing the purchase of land, the approval of building plans, the sale of bonds, etc. Typed. 60 pages. 18.5 x 12.75 x 1.5.

182. RECORD OF VILLAGE AND TOWNSHIP OFFICERS
1902-1912. 1 volume.

Lists the names and tenure of office of village and township officers. In alphabetical order. Handwritten on printed forms. 48 pages. 16 x 11 x 1.5. Basement storeroom, County courthouse.

183. ANNUAL REPORT OF COUNTY COMMISSIONER AND AUDITOR
1890-1901. 12 volumes

A detailed summary of the receipts and disbursements of county funds showing the county commissioners' budget and tax levy; and funds necessary for the year. For detailed description see number 1086. Handwritten and typed. Volume to average 108 pages. 18 x 11 x .5. Basement storeroom, County courthouse.

184. TRANSMISSION RECORD, ENGINEER, AUDITOR, TREASURER, AND MISCELLANEOUS
1910-1924. 4 volumes
Lists all documents transferred, or loaned to other county departments. Arranged chronologically. Handwritten on printed forms. Volumes average 700 pages. 15 x 14.5 x 2. Basement storeroom, County courthouse.

185. FEDERAL ROAD SURVEY VOUCHERS
1927. Approximately 50 folders in 1 file box.
Give number and amount of voucher, date of filing, voucher number, journal page, and name of treasurer. Handwritten on printed forms. File box 12.25 x 10.75 x 5.5. Attic storeroom, fourth floor, County courthouse.

186. AGRICULTURAL SOCIETY (Miscellaneous Papers)
1910-1924. Approximately 7folders in 1 bundle.
Papers pertaining to the construction of Central and Berea Armories, the county agricultural society, the society for prevention of cruelty to animals, the quadriennial appraisement, and the fairground. Typed. Bundle 10 x 8.5 x 5.5. Room 135, County courthouse.

187. LIQUOR PAROLE RECORD
1922-1931. Approximately 375 sheets in 5 bundles.
Contains the names of all liquor law violators paroled from justice of peace courts by the commissioners, stating the nature of arrest and appeal. Arranged chronologically. Each bundle 15.5 x 9 x .5. Basement storeroom, County courthouse.

188. WARRENSVILLE PRISONER RECORDS
1919-1925. 23 bundles.
Card listing date of commitment, term of imprisonment, and name and age of prisoner. Handwritten on printed forms. Each bundle 4 x 6 x 6. Basement storeroom, County courthouse.

189. OLD INSURANCE POLICIES
1920-1921. 3 file boxes.

Cancelled and expired insurance policies covering county property. In chronological order. Typed and handwritten on printed forms. Each file box 14 x 10.5 x 4.5. Basement storeroom, County courthouse.

190. MUNICIPAL ELECTION RETURNS
1935. 1 loose-leaf volume.

Lists election returns for the mayor, council, judge of municipal court, board of education, charter amendment, school district tax levy, county home rural charter, and relief and welfare bonds. In order of ward numbers. Photostat. 150 pages. 20 x 12 x 1.5. Room 135, County courthouse.

191. CEMENT AND BRICK TESTS
1907-1908. Approximately 9 folders in 1 file box.

Reports of cement and brick test showing quality of material and tensile strength. Typed. Arranged chronologically. File box 14 x 10.25 x 4.75. Basement store room, County courthouse.

192. SOLDIERS' AND SAILORS' RELIEF COMMISSION, GRAND JURY REPORTS; REPORTS OF COUNTY OFFICERS
1910-1918. 1 file box.

Correspondence relating to the burial of soldiers and sailors, communications from the grand jury to presiding criminal court judges as to their findings, reports of the county prosecutor, statements of fees due and unpaid, etc. Arranged alphabetically as to subject matters. Typed. File box 10.5 x 5 x 15.75. Basement storeroom, County courthouse.

193. MISCELLANEOUS REPORTS
1913-1918. 1 file box.

Contains papers of the soldiers' and sailors' relief commission on the Memorial Day Commission on the appointment of the burial commission; annual reports of the county officers; and grand jury reports and recommendations on the county jail and the criminal court housing conditions. Handwritten and typed. File box 14 x 10.5 x 4.5. Basement storeroom, County courthouse.

194. COMMUNICATIONS FROM CIVIL SERVICE COMMISSION
1916-1921. 3 letter boxes.

Communications on the appointments to personnel in the commissioners' office. Typed and handwritten. Arranged alphabetically as to name of appointee. Each letter box 11 x 12 x 3. Basement storeroom, County courthouse.

195. COMMUNICATION in re TELEPHONE
1 letter box.

Correspondence between the telephone companies and the county commissioners on the installation of telephones in various county departments. Also statements from the commissioners to the various departments authorizing payment. Typed and handwritten. Arranged alphabetically as to county departments. Letterbox 11.5 x 12 x 3. Basement storeroom, County courthouse.

196. COMMISSIONERS' SCRAP BOOK
1935. 1 volume.

Contains newspaper clippings pertaining to Cuyahoga County. Printed. 26 pages. 18 x 13.75 x 1. Room 135, County courthouse.

197. BLANK FORMS
21 scrap books.

Specimens of the forms used in county office transactions, such as those for the use of the auditor, assessor, treasurer, recorder, sheriff, surveyor, commissioners, jury commission, and prosecutor; the departments of engineering, road repairing, assignments, purchasing, and probation; the common pleas court, insolvency court, probate court, clerk of courts, Animal Protective League, and bureau of domestic relations. Printed forms. Books average 50 pages. 16 x 20 x .5. Basement storeroom, County courthouse.

198. RECORD OF UNFINISHED BUSINESS
1911-1912. 1 volume.

A listing of damage claims filed against the county that have not been settled. In order of file numbers. Handwritten. 600 pages. 14 x 11 x 1. Basement storeroom, County courthouse.

Purchasing Division

The board of county commissioners, since its organization in 1810, has had, in addition to statutory powers, a certain implied authority to purchase equipment, material, and furnishings necessary to the effective performance of its duties. (8 O. L. 358).

The purchasing division of the commissioners' office takes certain preliminary steps before purchases are made by the board. The department advertises for competitive bids on everything purchased and never acts on less than three bids. However, when the estimated cost of a public building, bridge, or bridge substructure, or additions or repairs does not exceed two hundred dollars, the job may be let at private contract without publication for notice. (68 O. L. 103). Nor are the commissioners required to invite bids before contracting for the furnishing of medical relief or medicines, or for the construction, reconstruction or repair of roads where the total estimated cost of the work does not exceed $3,000 per mile. (1933, O. A. G., number 1988; 111 O. L. 103).

After the purchasing division has arranged for a purchase and it has been approved by the board of commissioners as a condition precedent to the making of any contract or the giving of any order requiring the expenditure of money, the county auditor must certify that the amount of money required has been lawfully appropriated and is in the treasury or in process of collection. (112 O. L. 406).

The purchasing agent arranges for the purchase of supplies, equipment, motor vehicles, and all other purchases except land and county buildings. Special provision is made for the purchase of land costing over $1000 (63 O. L. 32), and of a courthouse or other county buildings. If the latter purchase is in excess of 25,000, the commissioners submit the question of issuing bonds to a vote of the electors. (98 O. L. 53).

199. PURCHASING RECORD
1913—. 35 volumes.

A daily record of all purchases, listing order number, requisition number, quantity and description of items, amount received, vendors invoice number, gross amount of invoice, cash discount, date of payment, and name of the department receiving material. Each volume contains an alphabetical index of firms. Handwritten on printed forms. Volumes average 3000 pages. 16.25 x 12.5 x 3.5. 1913-1932, 31 volumes, second floor, Hart Building; 1933—, 4 volumes, first floor, County courthouse.

200. GENERAL INQUIRIES
1934—. 5 volumes.

Gives date of communications, name of vendor, quantity needed, and inquiry as to price of goods. Arranged as to serial numbers. Typed. Volumes average 1000 pages. 11.75 x 9 x 5. First floor, County courthouse.

201. PURCHASE ORDERS
January 1918—. 47 volumes.

Give name and address of vendor, purchase order number, description and quantity of items ordered, purchase price, date of order, and auditor's voucher number. Arranged as to order numbers. Typed on printed forms. Volumes average 1200 pages. 12.5 x 9.25 x 6.5. 1918-1931, 31 volumes, second floor, Hart Building; 1932—, 16 volumes, first floor, County courthouse.

202. REQUISITIONS
1925—. 12 bundles; 13 volumes.

Requisitions for materials and supplies purchased by the county. Typed on printed forms. Volumes average 2000 pages. 8.5 x 11 x 5. 1925-1931, 12 bundles, Basement storeroom; 1932—, 13 volumes, first floor, County courthouse.

203. INQUIRY FOR PRICE
January 1925–May 1934. 19 loose-leaf volumes.

Lists addressee, date of closing quotation, requisition number, quantity wanted, description of material, net price delivered, and terms of payment. Arranged chronologically. Typed on printed forms. Volumes average 1600 pages. 11.5 x 9 x 7. Second floor, Hart Building.

204. OFFICIAL REQUISITIONS
January 1912—. 38 loose-leaf volumes.

List date of entry, cost per unit, order number, total cost of material, quantity ordered, date on which received, date on which bill was received, date bill was approved, and name of vendor. In order of requisition numbers. Typed on printed forms. Volumes average 900 pages. 13.5 x 11 x 6. 1912-1933, 34 volumes, second floor, Hart Building; 1934—, 4 volumes, first floor, County courthouse.

205. COUNTY RECORD OF SUPPLIES PURCHASED
February 1912-1919. 2 volumes.

Lists date of entry, requisition number, quantity and description of material ordered and received, date of receipt, and name of person receiving material. Alphabetical as to firms. Handwritten. Volumes average 300 pages. 14 x 9 x .5. Fourth floor, County courthouse.

206. SPECIAL REQUISITIONS
1936. 2 volumes.

Commissioners' requisitions, listing date, quantity of material, unit cost, total cost, order number, name of vendor, and kind of material. Arranged as to order numbers. Typed. Volumes average 150 pages. 13.25 x 10 x .75. First floor, County courthouse.

207. EMERGENCY REQUISITIONS
1931. 1 volume.

Requisitions for road repair material, giving in each instance the item wanted, the quantity, description of job, date of order, and signature. In order of requisition numbers. Handwritten or printed forms. 50 pages. 11 x 8 x .25. Fourth floor, County courthouse.

208. DEPARTMENT RECORDS
1936. 1 volume.

Purchase requisitions, giving a description of the material, date of entry, unit cost, total cost, order number, and name of vendor. Arranged alphabetically as to departments. Typed. 1280 pages. 12.75 x 10.25 x 2.75. First floor, County courthouse.

209. ANIMAL PROTECTIVE LEAGUE REQUISITIONS
1932—. 2 volumes.

Show date of requisition, quantity of material ordered, unit cost, total cost, order number, name of vendor, and date of approval. Arranged as to order numbers. Typed. Volumes average 300 pages. 14.5 x 9.25 x .75. First floor, County courthouse.

210. ANIMAL PROTECTIVE LEAGUE PURCHASE ORDERS
1935—. 1 volume.

List unit price, total price, material and amount ordered, number of order, and name of vendor. Arranged as to order numbers. Typed. 1000 pages. 11.5 x 9.25 x 2.25. First floor, County courthouse.

211. ANIMAL PROTECTIVE LEAGUE INQUIRY BLANKS
1933—. 1 volume.

A record of inquiries, listing requisition number, name of vendor, date, and quantity of material needed. In order of requisition numbers. Typed. 700 pages. 11.75 x 9.75 x 2.25. First floor, County courthouse.

212. GENERAL CORRESPONDENCE
1933—. 4 file drawers.

Miscellaneous letters and correspondence covering all outstanding bills of county departments. Arranged alphabetically as to correspondence and departments. Typed. Each file drawer 25.5 x 12 x 11. First floor, County courthouse.

Real Estate Division

The county commissioners were authorized in 1894, to designate in each county the bank or banks to be the depositories of county funds. (91 O. L. 403). Such bank or banks were required to give a bond, signed by six resident freeholders or sureties, or by a fidelity or indemnity insurance company, for the faithful performance of all duties imposed by law upon depositories of county funds. (99 O. L. 465).

The Standard Trust Bank of Cleveland, designated as a depository for county funds, pledged real estate as security for the safekeeping of such funds. When the bank failed in 1931, the property pledged was taken over by the county commissioners, who created the real estate division for the maintenance and supervision of such property, with authority to rent and sell the property for the purpose of reimbursing the county.

213. LIQUIDATION SECURITIES OF STANDARD TRUST COMPANY
1931—. Approximately 194 in 5 file boxes.

Mortgages on properties which were pledged to secure county deposits, showing name of grantor, location and description of property, and terms and conditions of mortgage. In chronological order. For index see number 214. Typed on printed forms. Each file box 5 x 10 x 18. Room 50, County courthouse.

214. INDEX TO MORTGAGES
1931. 1 card file.

An alphabetical card index of grantors, listing address, dates, amount of mortgage, payments made, and amount due, together with the recorder's file number. Handwritten and typed. Each card 10 x 8. Room 50, County courthouse.

Soldiers' and Sailors' Burial Division

An enactment by the general assembly of April 11, 1884, provided that the county commissioners appoint suitable persons in each township in their respective counties, whose duty it was to cause to be interred, in a decent and respectable manner, any honorably discharged soldier, sailor or marine having at any time served in the Army or Navy of the United States, who dies, not having the means to defray funeral expenses. (81 O. L. 146).

The act of 1884 was amended in 1893 to include the internment of the mother, wife, or widow of any honorably discharged soldier, sailor, or marine or any army nurse who did service at any time in the army of the United States. Another amendment in 1908 provided for only two commissioners, and the amount of money allowed was increased from thirty-five to seventy-five dollars. In 1919 the expenses for burial were increased to one hundred dollars. The present law, amended in 1921, prescribes that the county commissioners shall not contribute an amount in excess of one hundred dollars toward the cost of such funeral, and that any remaining costs shall be paid by the family or friends of the deceased. (90 O. L. 177; 99 O. L. 99; 108 O. L. pt. 1, 34; 109 O. L. 212).

215. RECORD OF SOLDIERS' AND SAILORS' BURIAL BY THE COUNTY
1914—. 7 volumes.

Lists name of decedent, members of the committee, undertaker, and the cemetery; cost of funeral; and amount awarded by the committee. In chronological order. Handwritten on printed forms. Volumes average 1000 pages. 15 x 8.5 x 2.5. Room 204, Century Building.

216. REPORTS OF BURIAL CLAIMS OF SOLDIERS' AND SAILORS' RELIEF COMMISSION

1934—. 1 folder.

Monthly reports listing name of decedent and of undertaker, amount of burial claim, and date of approval or rejection. In chronological order. Typed on printed forms. Folder 8.5 x 11.5 x 2. Room 204, Century Building.

Blind Relief Division

Blind relief was first provided for in 1898 and the administration of the law was vested in the township trustees. Both this act and an act passed in 1904 was declared unconstitutional. In 1908 relief was extended to all needy blind persons who were residents of the state, or became blind while residents thereof, and who were residents of the county for one year. The law was administered by a county blind relief commission composed of three members, each of whom was appointed for a term of three years by the judge of the probate court. The amount of relief was not specified. In 1913 this commission was abolished and its duties conferred upon the board of county commissioners. The annual amount of each relief for each person was set at $150; the board given the duty of annually examining each recipient, with the authority to either increase or decrease the allowance; and they were also empowered, upon finding that anyone applying for or receiving an allowance could be benefitted by a surgical operation, to spend all or part of the year's allowance for that purpose. In 1919 the maximum annual amount of relief for each person was raised to $200, and in 1927 it became $400. When a husband and wife were both blind and both had made application for relief, the maximum annual amount was $600. (93 O. L. 270; 97 O. L. 392; 99 O. L. 56-58; 103 O. L. 60; 108 O. L. pt. 1, 421; 112 O. L. 108).

The law was changed in 1936 in order to comply with the Federal Social Security Act of 1935. The revised state statute provides for relief to any needy blind person who is not less than 18 nor more than 65 years of age; and lost his eyesight while a resident of the state or shall have resided in the state for a period of five years during the nine years immediately proceeding the filing of the application for assistance. Any person whose application has been denied by the county commissioners has the right to have a fair hearing before the Ohio Commission for the Blind. (49 Stat. L. 645 U. S. C. A 1201-1305; 116 O. L. pt. 2, 195-200).

217. ACTIVE BLIND RELIEF APPLICATIONS
1918—. 2 file drawers.

Applications and correspondence of person seeking blind relief, giving name and address, date of application, and a complete history of the applicant. Arranged as to names of applicants. For index see number 218. Handwritten and typed. Each file drawer 10.5 x 16 x 30. Room 135, County courthouse.

218. INDEX TO ACTIVE BLIND RELIEF APPLICATIONS
1918—. 1 wooden file box.

An alphabetical card index of blind relief applicants, showing name, address, total amount of relief allowed, name of person to whom paid, date on which the claim was allowed, date of coming quarterly payment, and date of the discontinuance. Handwritten and typed on printed forms. File box 4 x 6 x 16. Room 135, County courthouse.

219. INACTIVE BLIND RELIEF APPLICATIONS
1918—. 2 metal file drawers.

Applications and correspondence giving name and address of applicant, and a complete history of each. Alphabetical as to names of applicants. For index see number 220. Handwritten and typed. Each file drawer 10.5 x 16 x 20. Room 135, County courthouse.

220. INDEX TO INACTIVE BLIND RELIEF APPLICATIONS
1918—. 3 wooden file boxes.

An alphabetical card index of blind relief applicants, showing name and address, total amount of relief allowed, name of person to whom paid, date on which claim was allowed, date of coming quarterly payment, and date of discontinuance. Typed and handwritten on printed forms. Each file box 4 x 6 x 16. Room 135, County courthouse.

221. BLIND RELIEF CORRESPONDENCE
1916-1917. 1 letter box.

Letters between the Associated Charities and the commissioners relative to blind relief. In alphabetical order. Typed. Letter box 12 x 11.5 x 2.75. Basement storeroom, County courthouse.

222. BLIND RELIEF COMMISSION
1908-1909. 1 volume.

A record listing name and address of client; number of his certificate of award; his state, county, and country; age at which he became blind; cause of blindness; amount of relief given him; and date of approval. Alphabetical as to clients. Typed. 500 pages. 11 x 11 x 2. Basement storeroom, County courthouse.

Division of Dog Warden

The duties of the dog warden previous to 1917 were under the supervision of the sheriff's office. At that time, the county commissioners took over direct supervision, and immediately appointed a dog warden, whose duties are specifically described by statute.

It is the duty of the dog warden to keep a record of all dogs owned, kept and harbored in his respective county. He patrols the county, seizes and impounds on sight all dogs more than three months of age found not wearing a valid registration tag, except dogs kept constantly confined in a registered dog kennel. He investigates all claims for damage to livestock inflicted by dogs. A weekly report and writing is made to the county commissioners of all dogs seized, impounded, redeemed, and destroyed; also of all claims for damage to live stock inflected by dogs. Upon seizure of any dog running at large, it is the duty of the dog warden to give notice to the owner, if known, or by posting a notice in the county courthouse describing the dog and place where seized, advising the owner of the dog will be sold or destroyed within three days.

The warden has the same police powers as are conferred upon sheriffs and police officers in the performance of his duty. He has the authority to summon the assistance of bystanders, to serve writs and other legal proceedings issued by any court in the county with reference to enforcing the provisions of the act. (G. C. secs. 5652 to 5652-7A; 107 v. 735).

223. DOG LICENSES
1925—. Approximately 1,100,000 in 220 cardboard file boxes.

List name and address of owner of dog; age, sex, color, and breed of dog; and fee paid for license. In order of license numbers. For index see number 224. Handwritten on printed forms. Each file box 4 x 8 x 12. First floor, Cleveland A. P. L. Building.

224. INDEX TO DOG LICENSES
1925—. 1 Acme card system stand.

An alphabetical index of owners, listing address of owner and license number of dog. The sex of the dogs is indicated by cards of different color. Typed. Each card 7 x 12. First floor, Cleveland A. P. L. Building.

225. OFFICIAL DOG LICENSE NOTICES
1932—. 3 bundles.

Notices of failure to renew licenses, giving name and address of owner; age, sex, color, breed of dog; and amount of the license fee. Handwritten on printed forms. Each bundle 14 x 8 x 8. Basement storeroom, Cleveland A. P. L. Building.

226. PICK-UP SHEETS
1933—. Approximately 11,000 in 36 bundles.

Gives name and address of owner of dog; description, weight, and measurement of dog; and the number of the cage where impounded. In chronological order. Typed. Each bundle 6 x 9 x 1. First floor, Cleveland A. P. L. Building.

227. KENNEL RECORD OF DOGS IMPOUNDED
1933—. 1 loose-leaf volume.

Lists number of dog, date impounded, name of agent who brought in the animal, name and address of person who had it impounded, sex, description, reason for impounding, number of days impounded, number of days charged for housing and feeding, date and matter of disposal, and the total cost. In chronological order. Handwritten on printed forms. 1000 pages. 11.75 x 18.75 x 4. First floor, Cleveland A. P. L. Building.

228. KENNEL RECORD
1933—. Approximately 10,800 in 36 packages.

Gives name and address of person at whose house the dog was picked up, date, number of entry, description of the animal, cage number, and manner of disposal. In chronological order. Typed. Each package 5.25 x 2.5 x 6. First floor, Cleveland A. P. L. Building.

229. RECEIPTS FOR DOGS SOLD OR RETURNED TO OWNER
1934—. 40 volumes.

List age, sex, color, and breed of the dog, and name and address of person receiving it. In order of receipt numbers. Handwritten on printed forms. Volumes average 96 pages. 9 x 3 x .5. First floor, Cleveland A. P. L. Building.

230. KENNEL RECORD OF DOGS DISPOSED OF
1933——. 1 volume.

Lists receipt number, number of the dog, date it was received, name of agent who picked up the animal, name and address of person receiving it, sex of dog, whether a stray or an owner's dog, description, reason for obtaining, date and manner of disposition, number of days in kennels, number of days charged for board, license number, affidavit for seizure notice, cost of housing and feeding the dog, and the selling price. In chronological order. Typed on printed forms. 300 pages. 11.75 x 18.25 x 1. First floor, Cleveland A. P. L. Building.

231. OFFICIAL REQUISITIONS
1933——. 1 volume.

In order of requisition numbers. Typed on printed forms. 940 pages. 14.75 x 8.25 x 4. First floor, Cleveland A. P. L. Building.

232. PURCHASE ORDERS
1933——. 1 loose-leaf volume.

List name of firm to whom order is issued, order number, quantity and description of items ordered, date of order, and name of the department for which order is issued. Arranged as to order numbers. Typed on printed forms. 2522 pages. 9.5 x 11.5 x 4. First floor, Cleveland A. P. L. Building.

Planning Commission

A statute passed June 1, 1916 provided that the county commissioners of any county in which a municipality is located, and those of an adjoining county, may co-operate in the creation of a regional planning commission for any region, exclusive of territory within the limits of a municipal corporation which already has a city planning commission. The number of members of the regional planning commission, their method of appointment, and the proportion of the costs of the commission to be borne by the various municipalities were to be determined by the planning commission and the county commissioners.

A county planning commission was provided for in an act effective July 15, 1923. The commissioners representing the county, and the city council representing the municipality were authorized to appropriate their respective shares of expense. The sums are paid into the treasury of the county and disbursed on the certificate of the planning commission and the warrant of the auditor. The commission consists of eight citizens of the county appointed by the county commissioners, together with the board of county commissioners. If the population of any city in the county exceeds fifty percent of the county's population, then at least three of the appointed members are selected from persons nominated by the city planning commission of the city. The board of county commissioners, as members of this commission, are appointed for a term of three years. Of the other eight members the first three are appointed for a term of two years, two for a term of three years, and two for a term by one year. The members serve without pay. (110 O. L. 310).

The county planning commission is authorized to employ such engineers, accountants, and other employees as may be necessary, who are paid from appropriations made by the county commissioners. (G. C. sec. 4366-14). The duties imposed upon the planning commission are to make plans and maps of the region or county respectively, showing the commission's recommendations for systems of transportation, highways, parks and recreational facilities, water supply, sewerage and sewage disposal, garbage disposal, civic center, and all other improvements. (110 O. L. 310).

233. COUNTY PLANNING COMMISSION
1930—. Approximately 15 folders in 1 file cabinet.
Office correspondence, reports, letters to members, contemplated project data, and data on the sewerage of Rocky River Valley. Handwritten, typed, and printed. File cabinet 15 x 24 x 11.5. Room 1118, Public Square Building.

234. SEWER AND WATER MAPS, AVON TO WILLOUGHBY
1930—. 13 maps.
These maps show sewer, water, and pumping stations in Cuyahoga County. Proposed developments are designated by shading. Printed, black-and-white, and colored. Scale, 1 inch to the mile. Each map 36 x 36. Room 1113, Public Square Building.

Sanitary Engineer Division

Prior to 1924, at which time the department of sanitary engineer was created, the functions of this department were performed under the supervision of the county surveyor. (G. C. sec. 2792). A statute was then passed providing that in any county having a population exceeding 100,000 the board of county commissioners may create and maintain a sanitary engineering department, to be under their supervision and in charge of a competent engineer who shall be appointed by the board of county commissioners for the purpose of aiding them in the performance of the duties under this act, or their duties regarding sanitation provided by law. (G. C. sec. 6602-1). For the purpose of preserving and promoting the public health, the board of county commissioners is empowered by resolution to lay out, establish, and maintain one or more sewer districts within the county outside of the municipalities. They may acquire, construct, maintain, and operate main branch intercepting, or local sewers and outlet sewers, sewage treatment, or disposal works within these limits. No sewer or sewage treatment works can be constructed in the county outside of incorporated municipalities by any firm or corporation unless the plans and specifications are approved by the county commissioners, and the construction is supervised by the county sanitary engineer, the person or firm shall pay to the county all expenses incurred by the commissioners. (G. C. secs. 6602-1-a to 6602-14).

Improvements and Assessments

235. RECORD OF NOTES AND BONDS ISSUED
1925—. 1 volume.
Lists name of bank, amount of note, date of issue, district number, number of improvement, bid, price, and amount of interest. In order of improvement numbers. Handwritten. 200 pages. 14 x 9 x .75. Room 1113, Public Square Building.

236. ASSESSMENT DATA WATER SUPPLY IMPROVEMENT
July 16, 1921—. 1 volume.
A record listing date, improvement number, name of contractor, amount of bid, and name of improvement. In order of improvement number. Typed. 700 pages. 14.25 x 12.5 x 2.75. Room 1113, Public Square Building.

237. MAINTENANCE AND IMPROVEMENT ASSESSMENT CARDS
1928—. Approximately 7500 cards in 128 file boxes.
List name and address of owner, zone number, units established, and revised assessments. Alphabetical as to names a property owners. Handwritten on printed forms. Each file box 18 x 5.5 x 6.5. Room 1113, Public Square Building.

238. WATER IMPROVEMENTS, CORRESPONDENCE, AND PAPERS.

1923—. 5 file drawers.

Folders containing correspondence, resolutions, and other papers pertaining to water improvements. Filed numerically. Typed. 26.75 x 16.75 x 5.25. Room 1113, Public Square Building.

239. ASSESSMENT CARDS

1932—. Approximately 3500 cards in 1 file box.

List name of road, the units, estimated assessment, revised assessment, local district number, and total amount of assessment. Alphabetical as to roads. File box 27 x 13 x 4.25. Room 1113, Public Square Building.

240. COLLECTION RECORD OF SEWER AND WATER ASSESSMENTS

1922—. 1 volume.

Lists name of improvement, total assessments on property, years assessment are to run, and district number. Arranged as to townships and districts. Handwritten. 250 pages. 17.5 x 11.75 x 1.75. Room 1113, Public Square Building.

241. ASSESSMENT RECORD, S and W

1923—. 12 volumes.

Lists name of owner, original lot number, sublot number, name of street, local district number, total amount of assessment, improvement number, and rate of interest. In order of improvement numbers. Handwritten and typed. Volumes average 100 pages. 10 x 11.5 x 1.5. Room 1113, Public Square Building.

242. AUDITOR'S CERTIFIED COPIES OF SURVEY DISTRICT MAINTENANCE ASSESSMENT

1932—. 3 volumes.

A record listing name of owner, name of subdivision, sublot number, name of street, description of property, local assessment, district number, and total assessments. Alphabetical as to names of townships. Typed. Volumes average 1000 pages. 20 x 16.5 x 3.25. Room 1113, Public Square Building.

243. IMPROVEMENTS, ASSESSMENTS
1921—. 12 loose-leaf volumes. Approximately 150,000 cards in 100 file drawers. (1921-1930, 12 volumes, Old System; 1930—, 100 file drawers, New System).

Gives name of owner, original lot or block number, name of subdivision, sublot number, name of street, description of property, sewer and water assessment, and total assessment. Arranged as to improvement numbers. Typed. Volumes average 1300 pages. 16 x 19 x 2.5; each file drawer 5 x 4 x 17. Room 1113, Public Square Building.

244. GENERAL ASSESSMENT CORRESPONDENCE
Approximately 2500 copies in 1 file drawer.

Letters bearing on assessment levies, and complaints on sewerage and water improvements. Arranged alphabetically. Typed and handwritten. File drawer 8.5 x 11 x 15. Room 1113, Public Square Building.

245. IMPROVEMENT RECORD, RESOLUTIONS, ETC.
1925—. 1 volume.

Lists proposals received, engineer's estimate, cost of improvement, date of entry, the items, and number of each item. In order of improvement numbers. Typed on printed forms. 700 pages. 21.25 x 14.5 x 3.25. Room 1113, Public Square Building.

246. DELINQUENT RECORD OF SUBDIVISIONS
1926-1932. 200 loose-leaf sheets in 1 bundle.

Record of gross assessment delinquencies of county subdivisions, giving amount and date of entry. Handwritten and typed. Bundle 8.5 x 11 x 1.25. Room 1113, Public Square Building.

247. INDEX OF SUBDIVISIONS
1 volume., A-Z.

Lists name and location of allotment, name of owner, and number of the file drawer containing blueprints of allotments. Alphabetical as to townships. Handwritten. 50 pages. 11.5 x 9.5 x .5. Room 1113, Public Square Building.

248. CONTRACTS, TABULATIONS OF BIDS FOR SEWERAGE IMPROVEMENTS; PROGRESS, ETC.

1925-1926. 1 volume.

A tabulation of contractors' responses to the call for bids for sewer improvements. Chronological. Typed. 500 pages. 12 x 9 x 2. Room 1113, Public Square Building.

249. CONTRACTS, TABULATION OF BIDS, PROGRESS RECORD, ETC.

1925. 1 volume.

A record of the conduct of various sewer and water improvements, giving cost of material per unit, total cost of material, name of contractor, and date on which job was completed. Arranged as to bidders. Typed and handwritten. 500 pages. 9 x 12 x 2. Room 1113, Public Square Building.

250. CONTRACTS, S and W

1921—. Approximately 300 folders in 1 file drawer.

Shows specifications for the construction of sewers, and amount of contractor's bond. Arranged as to contract numbers. Handwritten and typed. File drawer 22 x 16.5 x 11. Room 1113, Public Square Building.

251. RECORD OF ESTIMATES FILED

1921—. 1 volume.

Lists date received and filed, improvement number, estimates, and principal and interest. In order of file number. Handwritten. 100 pages. 14.75 x 9 x .75. Room 1113, Public Square Building.

252. RECORDS, ESTIMATES, CONTRACTS, SCHEDULES, ETC.

November 14, 1921-1923. 1 volume.

A record of the inception and progress of sewer and water projects. Typed and handwritten. 500 pages. 9 x 12 x 2. Room 1113, Public Square Building.

253. BALANCE SHEET, SEWERAGE IMPROVEMENT

1923-1933. 2 volumes.

Lists receipts, expenditures, payrolls, estimates, transfers, supplies, and interest on certificates. Handwritten. Volumes average 700 pages. 18 x 11.75 x 2.5. Room 1113, Public Square Building.

254. INDEX OF SEWERAGE AND WATER IMPROVEMENTS
1922—. 2 pamphlets.

A numerical index of improvements, listing name of township, year certified, and number of years improvement has been installed. Typed. Pamphlets average 50 pages. 8.5 x 11 x .5. Room 1113, Public Square Building.

255. SEWER IMPROVEMENTS, CORRESPONDENCE, AND PAPERS
1922—. Approximately 315 folders in 7 file drawers.

Folders containing correspondence, resolutions, and other papers relating to sewer improvements. On the outside of folder is listed number of improvement, location of work, dates of resolution and noticed of adoption. Arranged as to improvement numbers. Typed. Each file drawer 26.75 x 16.75 x 5.75. Room 1113, Public Square Building.

256. INDEX OF SEWER AND WATER CONNECTIONS BY STREETS,
No dates. 1 card file.

An alphabetical index of streets, listing size of street and section of sewer district. Handwritten and typed. File box 6 x 5 x 12. Room 1113, Public Square Building.

257. APPLICATIONS FOR LOANS
1933-1934. 1 volume.

Copies of application for loans by Cuyahoga County to the Federal Emergency Administration of Public Works submitted to the state advisory board at Columbus, Ohio. Typed and handwritten. 100 pages. 2 x 10 x 1. Room 1113, Public Square Building.

258. INDEX OF CONTRACTORS AND IMPROVEMENTS
Approximately 50 cards in 1 file box.

Gives name of contractor, name of title, and number of jobs. Alphabetical as to names of contractors. Handwritten on printed forms. File box 18 x 5.5 x 6.5. Room 1113, Public Square Building.

259. SEWER DISTRICTS' MAINTENANCE CONTRACTS
1921-1932. 57 folders in 2 file drawers, 1-17.

Contracts, agreements, memoranda, resolutions, and miscellaneous correspondence. Alphabetical as to names of districts. Each file drawer 24.25 x 11.25 x 16.75. Room 1113, Public Square Building.

Engineering Records

260. PERMIT LIST BOOKS
1924——. 2 volumes.

Sewer permits for house and building connections. Show permit number, sublot number, date of permit, date of sealing, date of connection, and name of road. Alphabetical as to names of roads. Handwritten. Volumes average 250 pages. 11.5 x 10.5 x 2. Room 1113, Public Square Building.

261. PERMITS FOR SEWER CONNECTIONS
1922——. 66 volumes, 1-66.

List date, sublot number, frontage, and name of property owner. Arranged as to permit numbers. Handwritten on printed forms. Volumes average 80 pages. 7 x 14 x 1. Room 1113, Public Square Building

262. PERMITS FOR SEWER CONNECTIONS
1927——. Approximately 5300 in 1 file drawer.

List date and number of permit, sublot number, name of street, and size of sewer. In order of permit numbers. File drawers 32 x 24 x 6. Room 1113, Public Square Building.

263. INSPECTOR'S RECORD
1924——. 500 volumes.

List improvement number, book number, section number, location, description of sewer, street address, sublot number, and date of connection. In order of improvement numbers. Handwritten. Volumes average 24 pages. 6.5 x 4 x .125. Room 1113, Public Square Building.

264. IMPROVEMENT FILE
1928——. 3 file boxes. 1-1700.

Engineer's survey data, listing the name of township, number of district, benchmark levels, data on pump stations, and information as to motor trucks. In order of improvement numbers. Each file box 12.5 x 12.5 x 12. Room 1113, Public Square Building.

265. FIELD RECORD
No dates. Approximately 90 folders in 3 file drawers.
Maintenance contracts, benchmark level notes, traverse notes, and topographical notes. Alphabetical as to districts. Handwritten and typed. Each file drawer 12.25 x 9.5 x 5. Room 1113, Public Square Building.

266. ESTIMATES
1927-1929. Approximately 75 in 1 file drawer.
Estimates on the field of work, giving name of employee, description of work, name of contractor, amount of material contracted for, and amount of estimate. In order of estimate numbers. Handwritten and typed. File drawer 26 x 16.5 x 5.5. Room 1113, Public Square Building.

267. SEWERAGE RECORD
1921—, 2 volumes.
A record of improvements constructed by the sanitary engineering department showing location of Y connections. List sublot number, side of street, size of sanitary Y, size of storm Y, distance along curb from manhole to curb Y connections, depth at curb, distance from center line of street, and permit number. Arranged alphabetically as to street names. 800 pages. 3 x 17.5 x 13.34. Room 1113, Public Square Building.

268. SEWER BUILDERS' LICENSE
No dates. 1 volume.
Records name and address of builder, location of work, sublot number, name of street, size and kind of sewer, permit number, and improvement number. Alphabetical as to roads. Handwritten. 750 pages. 17 x 14 x 4. Room 1113, Public Square Building.

269. WATER COMPUTATIONS
1921-1923. 1 volume.
Computations of measurements, costs, etc., of projected water improvements. Handwritten and typed. 150 pages. 9 x 11 x 2. Room 1113, Public Square Building.

Bookkeeping Records

270. MISCELLANEOUS TRUCK RECORD
1925—. Approximately 65 pages in 1 folder.
Shows distribution of operating costs, together with bills of sale, applications for licenses, and general correspondence. Handwritten and typed. Folders 8.5 x 11 x .25. Room 1113, Public Square Building.

271. RECORD OF GAS AND OIL USED
1932—. 400 bills in 1 letter file box.
Miscellaneous bills covering cost of gasoline and oil. Arranged chronologically. Handwritten and typed. Letter box 11.5 x 12 x 3. Room 1113, Public Square Building.

272. EMPLOYEES' RECORD
1921—. Approximately 200 cards in 2 file boxes.
Name and address of employee, position, pay rate, date of appointment, and dates of increases in salary. Alphabetical as to names of employees. Handwritten and typed. Each file box 7 x 5 x 4; each card 4 x 6. Room 1113, Public Square Building.

273. CWA PAYROLLS
1933-1934. Approximately 375 sheets in 5 folders. (Also see number 430).
Payrolls covering sewer and water work done by CWA workers showing names of employees, dates, and location of work. Typed and handwritten. Each folder 8.5 x 11 x .5. Room 1113, Public Square Building.

274. PAYROLLS
1932—. 15 folders in 1 file box.
Payroll sheets, listing name of employee, kind of employment, rate per diem, and total amount of wages. Chronological. Typed. File box 22 x 16.5 x 11. Room 1113, Public Square Building.

275. PAYROLL DISTRIBUTION SHEETS
1921—. Approximately 54 folders in 1 file drawer.
Payroll sheets of the road maintenance department listing date of entry, sewer district, name of employee, nature of employment, total number of days worked,

rate of pay, and total wages. In chronological order. Handwritten and typed. File drawer 16.5 x 26 x 5.5. Room 1113, Public Square Building.

276. PAID VOUCHERS
1930—. Approximately 1500 in 1 file box.

Cancelled vouchers, listing number of voucher, date of filing, date of payment, and amount paid. In chronological order. Typed. File box 22 x 16.5 x 11. Room 1113, Public Square Building.

277. DISTRIBUTION AND COST RECORD
1921—. 3 volumes.

A record of sanitary fund showing the distribution of funds for sewer and water maintenance, giving amounts appropriated and all expenditures. Arranged according to sewer and water districts. Volumes average 150 pages. 11.5 x 9.5 x 1.5. Room 1113, Public Square Building.

278. DEPARTMENT FUND
1921-1925. 1 volume.

A record listing date of entry, cost of transportation of workers, supplies required, miscellaneous expenses, loans from other funds, and salaries of department employees. Arranged chronologically. Handwritten. 100 pages. 19 x 11.5 x .75. Room 1113, Public Square Building.

279. BUDGET REQUEST
1925-1935. Approximately 110 pages in 1 folder.

A schedule of annual cost estimates for the operation of sanitary engineering department. Handwritten and typed. Folder 8.5 x 11 x .5. Room 1113, Public Square Building.

280. REPORTS ON OPERATIONS OF THE SANITARY ENGINEER
December 31, 1924—. Approximately 1600 pages in 40 folders.

A brief account of the activities of this department, listing name of contractor, kind of work, date started, and date completed. Typed. Each folder 8.5 x 11 x .25. Room 1113, Public Square Building.

281. ANNUAL REPORTS ON OPERATIONS OF COUNTY SANITARY ENGINEER
December 31, 1924—. Approximately 10,000 sheets in 40 folders.
Reports on sewer water operations, listing names of all the contractors, kind of work, and dates when started and completed. Filed chronologically. Typed. Each folder 8.5 x 11. Room 1113, Public Square Building.

282. AUDITOR'S MONTHLY STATEMENTS
1934—. 24 statements in 2 folders.
A record of operating costs for the sanitary engineering department. Handwritten and typed. Folder 18 x 20. Room 1113, Public Square Building.

283. DAILY WORK REPORTS
June 1925—. Approximately 2000 cards in 2 file drawers.
List name of employee, name of street, date of report, district number, hours worked each day, kind of work done, and name of foreman. In chronological order. Each file drawer 18 x 5.5 x 6.5. Room 1113, Public Square Building.

284. OFFICIAL REQUISITIONS
January 6, 1930—. 1 volume.
List quantity and description of material, total cost, order number and date of requisition, from whom purchased, name of department receiving material, and purpose for which material was ordered. In order of requisition numbers. Typed on printed forms. 500 pages. 12.25 x 10.75 x 2.5. Room 1113, Public Square Building.

Maps

285. DRAWINGS (Maps), CUYAHOGA COUNTY
1916—. Approximately 2000 maps in 45 file drawers.
Blueprints, tracings, and white prints, mainly allotment maps. For index see number 286. Scale, 50 feet, 400 feet, and 1 mile to the inch. Drawn by county engineer. File drawer 44 x 25 x 2.25. Maps approximately 30 x 22. File room, 11th floor, Public Square Building.

   a.   Township Property Maps; Railroad Property Maps; Private Property Maps; Sewer District Maps; Drainage Maps etc., 9 file drawers, 1-1799.Township property maps include topographical lines.

b.   Village and City Plans. 1 file drawer. Sewer and improvement maps.

c.   Profiles S. D., 1-16. 5 file drawers. Shows profiles of roads of the respective sewer districts.

d.   Test boring record; Bench Mark Index; Triangulation Maps. 1 file drawer.

e.   Incomplete. 1 file drawer. Tracing of incompleted improvements on sewer and appurtenances and water mains.

f.   Unfiled. 1 file drawer. (Pertain to "e").

g.   City-Village Sewer and Water Plans. 1 file drawer.

h.   Extra prints on existing contracts. 1 file drawer. (Pertain to "g").

i.   W. P. A. Plans. 1 file drawer. Tracings of landscaping, roads, sanitary sewers, and water main plans.

j.   State and City Approved. 4 file drawers. Sewer plans, water mains, and appurtenances.

k.   Location Plans, 1 file drawer. Show improvements and locations of service and water mains.

l.   Planning Commission. 1 file drawer. Contain street and road maps.

m.   Assessment Maps. 2 file drawers. Show streets, roads, and boundaries of zones, buildings, lots, owner's names, and areas not served by sewer or water.

n.   Record Field Notes. 1 file drawer. Contain blueprints, giving all information of the county survey on sewer and water.

o.   X 1-100; X 101-200. 2 file drawers. Contain blueprints of dedication and allotment maps, Cuyahoga County.

p.   W1-68; W69-179. 2 file drawers. Allotment maps, Cuyahoga County.

q.   M1-50; 01-50; G1-100. 2 file drawers. Allotment and dedication maps, Cuyahoga County.

r.   B-D-s. 1 file drawer. Plats showing dedications by private owners in Berea, Bay Village, Dover, and Solon.

s.   (Not marked). 1 file drawer. Contains tracings on improvements of water mains and appurtenances.

t.   Miscellaneous. 2 file drawers. Physical and topographical maps pertaining to subjects shown above.

u.   Easements. 1 file drawer. Zoning, sewer and water maps of community served with water by the city of Cleveland.

v.   (Not marked). 4 file drawers. Contain blueprints on all subjects
          shown above.

286. INDEX TO DRAWING MAPS OF SEWER DISTRICT IMPROVEMENTS
1916—. 1 volume.

Alphabetically arranged as to names of townships and as to improvement numbers,
listing drawing number, name of the allotment, name of owner and of township, and
sewer district number. Handwritten. 60 pages. 12 x 8 x .5. File room, 11th floor,
Public Square Building.

287. MAPS OF TOWNSHIPS OF CUYAHOGA COUNTY
September 1921-May 1923. Approximately 450 maps in 9 file drawers.

Lithographed topographical sheets, showing contours lines, elevations, and
boundaries of sewer districts. Each file drawer 34 x 27 x 2.5. Each map 31 x 24.
Scale, 400 feet to the inch. File room, 11th floor, Public Square Building.

288. CUYAHOGA COUNTY: "Original Topographical Sheets"
1931-1935. 75 maps in 5 file drawers.

Show topographical features of parts of Cuyahoga County. Each file drawer 34 x
27 x 2.5. Pen-and-ink drawings. Scale, 50 feet, 200 feet, and 400 feet to the inch.
File room, 11th floor, Public Square Building.

289. ATLAS, "PLAT BOOK OF CUYAHOGA COUNTY, OHIO, EAST AND WEST OF RIVER"
1927- 2 volumes, 5-6.

Shows cities, townships, and villages, and their boundaries and allotments. Printed
and colored. Scale, 300-400 feet to the inch. Each volume 24 x 18 x 2.5. G. M.
Hopkins Company, Philadelphia, Pennsylvania, publishers. File room, 11th floor,
Public Square Building.

290. CUYAHOGA COUNTY: U.S. TOPOGRAPHICAL MAPS
No dates. 1 map.

Shows boundaries of sewer districts in different colors, with the district names and
numbers. Map 3' 10" x 3' 6". Drawn by government engineer. Assessment room,
Public Square Building.

291. CUYAHOGA COUNTY; "BLUEPRINTS ON SEWER CONNECTIONS"

No dates. 2 volumes (1 volume. Parma; 1 volume, Mayfield Heights).
Blueprints and drawings on sewer connections, giving improvement number, location, and section of the county. Scale, 50 feet to the inch. Volumes average 50 pages. 36 x 18 x 1.5. Drawn by sanitary engineer. File room, 11th floor, Public Square Building.

292. MAPS OF CUYAHOGA COUNTY

December 1935. 1 map.
Shows the location and corresponding numbers of all W. P. A. Projects of the sanitary engineer's department, with a description of each project. Colored. Map 2' x 2' 8". Drawn by county engineer. File room, Public Square Building.

293. "MAP OF CUYAHOGA COUNTY"

No dates. 1 map.
Shows boundary lines of townships, villages, and school district in colors. Scale, 1 mile to 2 inches. Map 4' 3" x 5' 5". Drawn by county engineer. File room, Public Square Building.

294. MAPS OF NO PARTICULAR DISTRICT, CUYAHOGA COUNTY

No dates. Approximately 150 maps.
Extra copies of blueprints covering county improvements. Scale, 50 feet to 1 mile to the inch. In the steel cabinets in file room, 11th floor, Public Square Building.

Miscellaneous

295. GENERAL CORRESPONDENCE FILE

1921—. 2 file drawers.
Correspondence, miscellaneous reports and statements. Filed as to subjects. Typed. File drawer 26 x 16.5 x 5.5. Room 1113, Public Square Building.

296. PROSECUTOR'S OPINIONS; COURT DECISIONS

1925-1926. 1 volume.
Legal decisions on sewer and water projects; and general correspondence. Typed. 300 pages. 9 x 12 x 2. Room 1113, Public Square Building.

297. INDEX TO RESOLUTIONS
1919—. 2 volumes.

An index to resolutions recorded in the county commissioners' journal pertaining to the sanitary engineering department. Lists date, name of sanitary engineer, description of resolution, and name of contractor. Alphabetical as to contractors. Typed. Volumes average 700 pages. 17.75 x 14 x 2.5. Room 1113, Public Square Building.

Budget Division

The county budget commission is appointed by the county commissioners to assist in preparing the annual appropriation measure to be adopted each year by the county commissioners to meet the fiscal expenditures of the county. It is his duty, after receiving the budget request for the different county offices, to consult with the county budget commission, composed of the county auditor, the county treasurer, and the county prosecutor, to determine the amount necessary to meet the county budget estimate and amount of revenue which the county shall receive for various sources, and to ascertain and advise economics pertinent to all county expenditures. The budget is balanced on the basis of the total tax collection of the last fiscal year, and the divisional amount requested by each office.

His appointment is permitted by implied authority of the board of commissioners to appoint assistants, and not by direct statute.

298. RECORD AND CORRESPONDENCE FILES OF BUDGET COMMISSION
1928—. 10 file drawers.

Financial reports, financial statements, budget reports, and related correspondence on all offices of the county. Alphabetical as to names of offices. Typed. Each drawer 16 x 11.75 x 28. Room 145, County courthouse.

Child Welfare Division

The first agency to care for children in this county was the Cleveland Humane Society. Originally organized in 1873 for the prevention of cruelty to animals, it modified its program in 1876 to include the prevention of cruelty to children. Major emphasis was soon laid on the latter problem, and the society began to place children in free homes.

In 1921 the commissioners were authorized to appoint a county welfare board to consist of four members, two of whom shall be women. This board has full powers in respect to the care of neglected and dependent children. The act further provided that the children be placed in the care of private families within the county, and that the commissioners pay not only for the children's board, clothing, and personal necessities, but also for their medical, dental, and optical care. (109 O. L. 533). Although the bill was passed in 1921, the child welfare board was not established until 1929. In the meantime, the Humane Society took care of the county's wards.

Since its inception, the board has steadily increased its activities. Two departments in particular have been added; one for the orthopedic care of crippled children, and another for vocational guidance of all its wards.

These records are not open to the public, and will be shown at the discretion of the director in charge.

Records

299. ACTIVE FAMILY CASES

1930—. Approximately 2100 folders in 21 file cases.
A complete record of each case, listing date of entry; family case number; names of the child's parents and their address if known; their birthplace, age, nationality, religion, etc.; names of all other minor children and their ages, ward numbers, and birthplaces; and names of all their relatives. The record includes all related correspondence, medical reports, prior agencies reports, visitors' and investigators' reports, commitments, etc. In order of case numbers, for index see number 300. Handwritten and typed on printed forms. Each file case 11 x 13 x 27. First floor, Juvenile Court Building.

300. FAMILY INDEX

1930—. Approximately 3000 cards in 1 file drawer, A-Z.
An alphabetical card index of active families, listing addresses of parents, family case number, and names and ward numbers of the children. Typed on printed forms. File drawer 13 x 5.5 x 25. First floor, Juvenile Court Building.

301. CHILD'S PLACING FILE

1930—. Approximately 2800 cards in 3 file cabinets.
A record of the children's present boarding homes, listing name of each child,

family case number and ward number, name and address of foster home, date of placement, type of home, and name of visitor. Alphabetical as to children. For index see number 302. Typed and handwritten on printed forms. Each file cabinet 6 x 16 x 16. First floor, Juvenile Court Building.

302. CHILDREN'S INDEX
1930—. Approximately 2200 cards in 1 file drawer, A-Z.
An alphabetical index of children, listing child's ward and family case number, date of birth, date received by the board, names and addresses of child's parents, nationality of parents, and child's recommitments. Typed on printed forms. File drawer 13 x 5.5 x 25. First floor, Juvenile Court Building.

303. CLOSED STATE CASES
1930—. Approximately 200 folders in 1 file drawer.
A complete history of each case, and all correspondence pertaining to it. Arranged as to family case numbers. For index see number 304. Typed and handwritten on printed forms. File drawer 11 x 13 x 27. First floor, Juvenile Court Building.

304. INDEX TO CHILDREN'S CLOSED CASES
1930—. Approximately 700 cards in 1 file drawer.
An alphabetical card index of children, listing ward and family case number of child, date of acceptance by the child welfare board, name and address of child's parents, nationality of parents, and the child's recommitments Typed on printed form. File drawer 13 x 5.5 x 25. First floor, Juvenile Court Building.

305. CLOSED FAMILY CASES
1930—. Approximately 1000 folders in 4 file cases.
A complete history of each case and all correspondence pertaining to it. Filed by case number. Handwritten and typed on printed forms. Each file case 11 x 13 x 27. First floor, Juvenile Court Building.

306. PENDING FAMILY APPLICATIONS
1930—. Approximately 250 in 1 file.
Applications which have not yet been accepted by the child welfare board; and correspondence referring to each case. Arranged as to family case numbers. Handwritten and typed on printed forms. Drawer 11 x 13 x 27. First floor, Juvenile Court Building.

307. CHILDREN'S STATISTICAL CARDS
1935—. Approximately 3000 in 1 file drawer.
Show family case number, children's ward number, date on which family was referred to welfare board, and name of person who referred them; and data as to parents' nationality, date of birth, whether native born or nationalized citizens, education, health, and present address. This information is given for all children and the family. Typed on printed forms. File drawer 11 x 13 x 27. First floor, Juvenile Court Building.

308. ASSIGNMENT CHILDREN RECORD CARDS
February 1930—, 1 file box.
List name of child assigned, name of person to whom assigned, date of assignment, family and ward numbers. In order of ward numbers. Typed on printed forms. File box 5 x 11 x 24. First floor, Juvenile Court Building.

309. ASSIGNMENT FAMILY RECORD CARDS
February 1930—. 1 file box.
List person or persons to whom child is assigned, child's ward number, family number, and date of assignment. In order of ward numbers. Typed on printed forms. File box 5 x 11 x 24. First floor, Juvenile Court Building.

310. TRANSFER CARDS
1930—. Approximately 2500 cards in 1 file drawer.
A record of dates of transfer of children from one home to another, listing child's family, case, and ward numbers; nationality, birth date, and religion; old and new foster homes; date of the child's transfer; rate of board; and name of person paying for board. Arranged alphabetically for each month. Handwritten and printed on forms. File drawer 13 x 5.5 x 25. First floor, Juvenile Court Building.

311. FOSTER HOME LEADS APPROVED
1930—. 1 file box.
Lists name and address of each foster home, source of information, date of interview, sex and name of child, and name of foster parents. In order of foster homes. For index see number 312. Handwritten and typed on printed forms. File box 6 x 11 x 24. First floor, Juvenile Court Building.

312. INDEX TO FOSTER HOME PENDING AND APPROVED
1930—. 1 file drawer, A-Z.

An alphabetical index of the names of boarding mothers, listing address; nativity, race, and religion; date of application for boarding homes; date of approval of application; date license was issued; number and sex of children boarding; and record number of foster home. Typed on printed forms. File drawer 13 x 5.25 x 25. First floor, Juvenile Court Building.

313. ACTIVE FOSTER HOMES
1930—. Approximately 2100 folders in 9 file cases, 1-3251.

Reports and correspondence, giving name and address of foster parents, record number of foster home, data relative to the history of each child; ward number of child, and date placed in home. In order of foster homes numbers. Handwritten and typed on printed forms. Each file case 11 x 13 x 27. First floor, Juvenile Court Building.

314. FOSTER HOMES IN USE
1930—. Approximately 1700 folders in 2 file cabinets.

Show name of child and family case number, name of visitor, date of placement in home, rate for boarding, names and addresses of foster parents, and record number of foster home. Alphabetical as to foster homes. Handwritten and typed on printed forms. Each file cabinet 6 x 16 x 16. First floor, Juvenile Court Building.

315. WITHDRAWN FOSTER HOMES
1930—. Approximately 1400 folders in 6 file boxes.

A record of foster homes from which children have been withdrawn. Arranged numerically. For index see number 316. Handwritten and typed on printed forms. Each file box 11 x 13 x 27. First floor, Juvenile Court Building.

316. INDEX TO FOSTER HOMES WITHDRAWN AND REJECTED
Approximately 1500 in 1 file drawer, A-Z.

An alphabetical card index of foster homes which have been withdrawn or rejected. Handwritten and typed on printed forms. File drawer 13 x 5.5 x 25. First floor, Juvenile Court Building.

317. FOSTER HOME LEADS WITHDRAWN

1930—. Approximately 1800 cards in 1 file box.

Lists name and address of foster home, source of information upon which interviews were granted, date of each interview, type of child, name of child, and names of foster parents. Alphabetical as to foster homes. Handwritten and typed on printed forms. File box 5 x 11 x 24. First floor, Juvenile Court Building.

318. FOSTER HOME GEOGRAPHICAL FILE

1930—. Approximately 1000 cards in 1 file drawer.

Shows exact locations of the foster homes in use, listing name of avenue, street, or road; house number and record number of home; and names of foster parents. Arranged for the city according to streets and avenues; for the county alphabetically as to cities, townships, and villages; and for the State of Ohio as to cities, townships, and villages, typed on printed forms. Drawer 13 x 5.5 x 25. First floor, Juvenile Court Building.

319. RECORD OF RE-LICENSES

1930—. Approximately 1200 in 1 file drawer.

Gives record number of each foster home, its name and address, date on which license was first issued, and dates of renewals. Arranged first by months, and then as to names of foster homes. Typed on printed forms. File drawer 13.5 x 5.5 x 25. First floor, Juvenile Court Building.

320. RECORD OF CHILDREN PLACED OUTSIDE OF CLEVELAND SCHOOL DISTRICT

1930—. Approximately 900 in 1 file drawer, A-Z.

Cards list name, ward number, names of parents, child's birth date, name and address of present boarding home, date of placing, name of school attended, remarks, and dates of correspondence. Alphabetical. Typed and handwritten on printed forms. File drawer 13 x 5.5 x 25. First floor, Juvenile Court Building.

321. ACTIVE SUPPLEMENTARY JEWISH CASES

1930—. Approximately 500 in 2 drawers.

A complete record, giving name of child, name of parents if known, addresses of all parties involved, domestic record of parents, habits of child, doctor's reports, etc. Arranged as to case numbers. Each drawer 11 x 13 x 27. Basement, Juvenile Court Building.

322. ACTIVE FAMILY CASES
1930—. Approximately 1600 in 8 file cases.
All reports and records (except correspondence) concerning the case of crippled children and those outside the city limits. In order of family case numbers. Typed and handwritten on printed forms. Each file case 11 x 13 x 27. Room 305, Carnegie Building.

323. CRIPPLED CHILDREN'S INDEX AND ADOPTION
1930—. Approximately 1300 cards in 1 file box.
Cards list name of each child, its ward number, family case number, date of birth, and date received by the child welfare board; names, addresses, and nationality of parents; addresses of husband and wife who adopted child, and date of adoption. Alphabetical as to names of children; adoption cards as to names of foster parents. Typed on printed forms. File box 6 x 10 x 6. First floor, Juvenile Court Building.

324. SUPPLEMENTARY CLOSED CRIPPLED CHILDREN CASES (ROTARY CLUB RECORDS)
1931. Approximately 500 in 2 file drawers.
Gives name of child, name of parents if known, addresses of all parties involved, domestic record of parents, habits of child, doctor's reports, etc. In order of family case numbers. Each drawer 11 x 13 x 27. First floor, Juvenile Court Building.

325. CLOTHING RECORD
1930—. 2 file boxes.
Cards list date on which boy or girl is accepted for care, name, date of birth, case number, types of garments or necessities given to child, cost of each, and total to date. In order of case numbers. Each file box 11 x 13 x 27. First floor, Juvenile Court Building.

326. CHILD WELFARE, CLOTHING ISSUED
1930—. 2 file boxes.
Requisitions show date of issue, number of articles issued, cost of articles, name of child who received clothing, and name of person who issued order. Alphabetical as to names of children. Handwritten on printed forms. Each file box 20 x 14 x 14. Fourth floor, County courthouse.

327. SUPPLEMENTARY HUMANE SOCIETY RECORDS
No dates. Approximately 900 in 2 file boxes.
A complete record of each case, giving name of child, name of parents if known, addresses of all parties involved, domestic record of parents, habits of child, doctor's reports, etc. In order of case numbers. Each file box 11 x 13 x 27. First floor, Juvenile Court Building.

Accounts

328. GENERAL LEDGER
1930—. 1 loose-leaf ledger; 1 envelope; 2 bundles.
Contains all the accounts of the child welfare board, listing dates of debts and credits, amounts, and titles. The recapitulation sheets give the monthly and yearly totals. A marginal index of accounts is arranged by a special code system. Typed on printed forms. Loose-leaf ledger 10 x 12 x 1.75; envelopes 10 x 12 x 1; each bundle 10 x 12 x 4. 1933—, 1 volume., 1 envelope, Room 126; 1930-1932, 2 bundles, Room 7, Juvenile Court Building.

329. CHILD'S LEDGER
1930—. Approximately 2400 cards in 2 file drawers.
A record of the cost of boarding at all homes, listing name of child and of boarding mother, period of time for which child is boarded, amount of board, and incidental expenses if any. Alphabetical as to names of children. Typed on printed forms. Each file drawer 10 x 10 x 18. Room 126, Juvenile Court Building.

330. CASH BOOK
1935—. 1 loose-leaf ledger; 3 bundles.
A record in five sections, of all money paid and received by the child welfare board. The first section is called the "journal," and lists the journal entries which give a description of the items for which money is received and paid. The second section is called "cash disbursements register," listing names of persons to whom money is paid, voucher number, date of payment, and amount. The third section is called "voucher register." These vouchers are for children's clothing only, and are kept separate from the other accounts. The fourth section is called "requisition register." It lists date of requisition, name of child, and amount of requisition charged to the child's account. The fifth section is called "cash received register." It lists name of person paying money to the welfare board, name of child whose account is credited,

and amount and date of payment. The money received is mostly from parents whose children are being cared for by the board. Arranged chronologically. Typed on printed forms. Ledger 15 x 18 x 2; each bundle 15 x 18 x 3. 1930-1934, 3 bundles, Room 7; 1935—, 1 volume, Room 126, Juvenile Court Building.

331. RECEIPT BOOK
1930—. 2 volumes.
Lists receipt number, amount received, name of person from whom money is received, and name of child. In order of receipt numbers. Typed on printed forms. Volumes average 250 pages. 12 x 10 x 1.5. Room 126, Juvenile Court Building.

332. TRIAL BALANCE
February 1930—. 2 volumes.
A record of balances of accounts, taken monthly and yearly from the general ledger. Lists titles of the accounts and shows whether the balance is a credit or debit. Chronological. Handwritten. Volumes average 100 pages. 10.75 x 14.5 x .5. Room 126, Juvenile Court Building.

333. BOARDING MOTHERS' CARDS FOR CRIPPLED CHILDREN
1930—. Approximately 350 in 1 file drawer.
Give name and address of boarding mother, amount due her each month, name of child, and date of placement. Alphabetical as to mothers. Typed on printed forms. File drawer 6 x 4 x 17. Room 126, Juvenile Court Building.

334. BOARDING MOTHERS' PAYROLL
1930—. 2 loose-leaf ledgers; 5 bundles.
Lists name and address of mother receiving pay, name of child, rate per week or month, other expenses if any, total amount of check, and check number. Arranged by months; the record of each month is in order of the names of the mothers. Typed on printed forms. Each ledger 15 x 18 x 4; each bundle 15 x 18 x 3. 1930-1934, 4 bundles, Room 7; 1935—, 2 ledgers, Room 126, Juvenile Court Building.

335. CLOTHING REQUISITIONS
1930—. Approximately 15,000 in 4 file boxes.
Give order number, family case number, child's name and age, name of visitor, names and addresses of foster parents, and names and cost of articles requisitioned. Arranged according to months and which issued. Handwritten and typed on printed

forms. Each file box 8 x 12 x 18. 1930-1934, 3 boxes, Room 7; 1935—, 1 file box, Room 126, Juvenile Court Building.

336. VOUCHERS
1930—. Approximately 7000 in 2 drawers, 7 file boxes; 3 bundles.
Vouchers are in jacket form and list the amounts paid for merchandise or for service rendered. The outside of the voucher jacket lists voucher number, name and address of firm or person to whom voucher is made out, and amount of money paid. Enclosed within the voucher are itemized statements from the merchant or firm for merchandise sold or for service rendered. Filed by voucher number. Typed and handwritten on printed forms. Each drawer 4.5 x 11.5 x 17; each file box 5 x 10 x 12; each bundle 6 x 12 x 4. 1930-1934, 2 drawers, Room 126; 1935—, 7 file boxes, 3 bundles, Room 7, Juvenile Court Building.

337. CHILD WELFARE CANCELLED CHECKS
1930. 1 cardboard file box.
Typed. File box 24 x 9.5 x 3.5. Fourth floor, County courthouse.

Annat Division

The necessity for providing direct housing relief became manifest in 1932 and 1933, and the legislature on March 22, 1933 passed an emergency measure to provide direct relief to meet the problem of both the relief client and the landlord.

The act authorizes the county commissioners, in addition to providing for all other forms of relief, to appropriate the sum they decide is necessary for the purpose of direct housing relief for indigent persons. The commissioners may appoint the clerk of their board to investigate the claim for such relief, and may issue a voucher to the auditor of the county for each month's rent. Such vouchers must, in no case, exceed one-twelfth of the tax for the calendar year immediately preceding the issuance thereof, and in no event must the vouchers exceed the sum of ten dollars without including special assessments upon the premises, or a portion of the premises occupied by the indigent person. Upon receipt of a voucher the auditor shall issue a warrant. The warrants are not negotiable, nor can they be applied to any other property but that before mentioned. At each semi-annual settlement between the treasurer and the auditor, the warrants that were presented for payment of taxes are entered in a book supplied by the auditor, who deducts from each taxing subdivision the portion of the tax represented by the warrants; and in making the settlement with each taxing subdivision he enters the amounts deducted as taxes with-held for direct housing relief.

Any municipality, by its council, or any township, by its trustees, is authorized to appoint one or more officials, individual persons, or corporations not for profit, to secure applications, and make investigation of persons applying for direct housing relief. The commissioners deputized and authorized such persons for corporations to appointed to represent the commissioners to make investigations subject to the approval of the commissioners, and to issue the vouchers before mentioned.

The owner of real estate, according to the provisions of the act, is not required to accept these vouchers for rent unless he shall so elect; the voucher will not be honored by the auditor unless it is endorsed by the first mortgagee; and an agreement must be given not to foreclose the property as long as it is occupied. (115 O. L. 194-195). This law has been extended to March 1, 1937, without an interm. (116 O. L. 39).

338. ORIGINAL APPLICATIONS FOR HOUSING RELIEF
July 1933. 8 file boxes.

Gives date of application; name and address of owner; description of lot; taxing district; book number; the item; tax-list year date; total number of suites on property; number of rooms occupied by tenant; amount of rent to be paid each month; amount of rent paid with money, goods, or services; the agency; date of receipt; and signature of landlord and of tenant. It also contains a report of the relief agency investigation and a certification of the county auditor. Handwritten on printed forms. Each file box 15 x 10 x 20. Sixth floor, National Building.

339. DIRECT HOUSING RELIEF INVESTIGATION
July 1933—. 11 bins.

Lists name of district, month, book, and item; amount of annual tax; application number; amount of rent; name and address of owner, agent, and tenant; and location of property. Handwritten on printed forms. Each bin 30 x 12 x 20. Sixth floor, National Building.

340. MASTER CARDS
July 1933—. 16 metal file boxes; 4 wooden file boxes.

A record listing name and address of owner of property; year date of duplicate; valuation; full account of general tax; one-half of general tax; amount of rent; taxes paid; taxes delinquent; name of district; name, address, and case number of tenant; and date of entry. The other side of the card list land contract; name of lease holder, receiver, administrator, executor, agent, and former owner; amount they would allow for the rent; and date of entry. In order of tax book numbers. Handwritten on printed forms. Each file box 15 x 20 x 12; each metal file box 19 x 10 x 4.5. Sixth floor, National Building.

341. TENANT CARDS
July 1933——. 6 metal file boxes.
Show name and address of tenant and of owner, thereby serving as a double check on the master cards. Typed. Each file box 5.5 x 18 x 5. Sixth floor, National Building.

Cuyahoga County Relief Administration

Poor relief, as well as work relief, is an ancient problem. A statute adopted in the Northwest Territory in 1795 provided for a tax to be paid for the relief of the poor, not only by those who had real property, but by those who had none. Those of the poor who were physically able were put to work with hemp, flax, and thread. Nothing, however, was expected of the disabled, the old, and the blind. (Pease, *op. cit.,* 217).

The first act passed for the relief of the poor after Ohio's admission to statehood was in 1810, and provided for a poor tax and an overseer for each township. The overseers were obliged to supply relief to all who were in need of it. (8 O. L. 220).

Prior to August 1, 1933, relief in Cuyahoga County was administered chiefly by the Associated Charities and the Jewish Social Service Bureau, both private agencies under the jurisdiction of the Community Fund. The funds for emergency relief, however, came from the Federal Government through the Reconstruction Finance Corporation. Direct grants were made to the State, which in turn allocated funds to the two agencies mentioned. The joint relief committee existed at the time which had little authority, and both agencies were represented on this committee. This situation existed despite the fact that the county, the cities, and the villages within the county are required by statute to care for all paupers. (G. C. sec. 3480).

On August 1, 1933, the Government promulgated a new ruling to the effect that Federal funds would thereafter be distributed by official bodies only. The Cuyahoga County Relief Administration then came into being, and the joint relief committee became the county relief committee. This committee functioned as a county relief agency until March 1935, when the Government took over the direct control of relief for Ohio. County relief then was put under the Federal Emergency Relief Administration with the Cuyahoga County relief committees as an advisory commission.

On November 1, 1935, the Government, upon the creation of the Works Progress Administration, again relegated direct relief to the county commission, and the citizen's advisory committee again became the relief committee.

In the same year a statute was enacted, vesting in the commissioners and imposing upon them all poor-relief powers which had been vested in and imposed upon the State Relief Commission. (116 O. L. 571). This was superseded by an act carried in 1936, which again vested the power and the State Relief Commission, and imposed upon the commissioners merely the duty of cooperating with all Federal, State, and county agencies engaged in the administration of relief. Since then, most of the funds raised for relief have come from the State, with a supplement from the county, and the cities and the villages within the county.

General Records

342. CASE INDEX FILES
August 1, 1933—. 86 metal file boxes.

An alphabetical card index of relief clients, giving address; first name and birth year; names and birth years of the children; race and social status, and relationships to others; physical defects if any; case number; date case was opened; district in which located; date closed. The file also includes cross-reference cards for other members of the family. The index to Central Bureau cases was incorporated in this file on August 1, 1934, and is complete from August 1, 1933 to date. The index to Transient Bureau Cases was incorporated December 1, 1935. It is not yet completed. Typed on printed forms. Each file box 4 x 5.5 x 20. Room 228, Center Building, 2905 Franklin Avenue.

343. RECORD FILES - MAJOR CASES
August 1, 1933—. 456 metal file drawers.

Closed cases, with face card, relief record, financial sheets, interviewer's reports, visitor's reports, and general correspondence on each case. All active cases are kept at the district offices. Central Bureau keeps the record files of its own active and inactive cases. Transient Bureau (now Central Bureau for homeless and transients) keeps all active and inactive transient case records; inactive records on the homeless are sent to Central Office record department. In order of case numbers. Typed and handwritten. Each file drawer 13.5 x 11.25 x 24.75. Room 228, Center Building, 2905 Franklin Avenue.

344. RECORD FILES - MINOR CASES
August 1, 1933—. 46 metal file drawers.

Closed cases, with application blank and financial report of each client, report of interviewer, and all correspondence on the case. All active minor-service cases are kept at the district office. After no contact for three months, minor-service cases are sent to Central Office. Transient Bureau keeps its own active and inactive cases. Central Bureau was discontinued in March 1936, and the active cases were transferred to the district and to Transient Bureau. All minor cases are sent to the Central Office record department. In order of case numbers. Typed and handwritten. Each file drawer 13.5 x 11.25 x 24.75. Room 228, Center Building, 2905 Franklin Avenue.

345. NUMERICAL REGISTER - MAJOR CASES
August 1, 1933—. 3 volumes.

Lists case number, name, and address of client; district office; date of registration; and classification of client. In order of case numbers. Typed on printed forms. Volumes average 700 pages. 9 x 12 x 4. Room 228, Center Building, 2905 Franklin Avenue.

346. NUMERICAL REGISTER AND DAY BOOK - MINOR CASES
August 1, 1933—. 2 volumes.

Gives case number, name, and address of client; date of registration; and district office. This register includes the day book for inter-city minor service. In order of case numbers. Typed on printed forms. Volumes average 800 pages. 9 x 12 x 4. Room 228, Center Building, 2905 Franklin Avenue.

347. CASE COUNT CONTROL
1935—. 36 cardboard file boxes.

A card record, listing name of each client, case number, day book and page number, date of entry, and district. Alphabetical as to clients in each district. Typed. Each file box 5.5 x 4 x 20.75. Room 228, Center Building, 2905 Franklin Avenue.

348. DAY BOOK
August 1, 1935—. 3 loose-leaf volumes.

A daily record of cases received, listing date of entry, district or division, classification, case number, and name and address of client. In chronological order. Typed on printed forms. Volumes average 700 pages. 9 x 12 x 4. Room 228, Center Building, 2905 Franklin Avenue.

349. STREET INDEX, FILES
August 1, 1933—. 100 file boxes.

An alphabetical card index of relief clients, listing address, case number, and date of entry. In order of street numbers. Typed on printed forms. Each file box 4 x 5.5 x 20. Room 228, Center Building, 2905 Franklin Avenue.

350. W .P. A. CERTIFICATION FILE
July 1935—. 43 cardboard file boxes.

Each card gives name, address, and case number of clients. The number 600 form and all succeeding forms, such as 601, 602, 325, 360, 402, 403, and 340, are stapled to this card. Alphabetical as to names of clients. Handwritten and typed. Each file box 8.5 x 5.75 x 16.5. Room 228, Center Building, 2905 Franklin Avenue.

Accounting Records

351. CASH DISBURSEMENT AND RECEIPT LEDGER
August 1, 1933—. 10 volumes.

Gives date of entry, invoice number, name and address of vendor, account number, and amount of disbursement or receipt. In order of account numbers. Handwritten on printed forms. Volumes average 350 pages. 14.5 x 17.5 x 1. Room 106, Center Building, 2905 Franklin Avenue.

352. INVOICE REGISTER
August 1, 1933- April 1, 1935; December 1, 1935—. 3 volumes.
Lists number of entry, name of vendor, date received, period covered, gross amount of invoice, political distribution, and amount of voucher. Chronological. Handwritten on printed forms. Volumes average 1200 pages. 11.5 x 18 x 4.5. Room 106, Center Building, 2905 Franklin Avenue.

353. COMMODITY ORDER CARDS
August 1, 1933—. 1700 cardboard boxes.
List name, address, and case number of relief client; commodities given; and signature of client receiving the commodities. In order of case numbers. Handwritten on printed forms. Each box 4 x 6 x 26. Basement storeroom, Center Building, 2905 Franklin Avenue.

354. COAL PURCHASES
October 1, 1933—. 3 volumes.
Show name of shipper, date and number of order, number of tons specified on order, date of shipment, name of railroad, car number, railroad rates, dealer's weight, date of bill, total tonnage, and amount of invoice. Arranged as to order numbers. Handwritten on printed forms. Volumes average 200 pages. 14.5 x 17.5 x 1. Room 106, Center Building, 2905 Franklin Avenue.

355. GAS STATEMENTS
January 1, 1934- April 1, 1935; December 1, 1935—. 28 bundles.
Statements of payments of gas and light bills, listing date and number of requisition, name and address of client, date bill is due, and amount due. In order of requisition numbers. Typed. Each bundle 8.5 x 14 x 4. Basement storeroom, Center Building, 2905 Franklin Avenue.

356. VENDOR'S INDEX FOR ADMINISTRATION PURCHASES
December 15, 1934—. 5 cardboard file boxes.
An alphabetical index of vendors, listing address, date of invoice, voucher number, and schedule number. Typed and handwritten on printed forms. Each file box 4.5 x 6 x 16. Room 106, Center Building, 2905 Franklin Avenue.

357. CROSS FILE OF LANDLORDS AND CLIENTS
1933—. 38 cardboard file drawers.
An alphabetical card index of clients, listing name of landlord, location of property, date and number of order, period covered, and amount of order. Handwritten on printed forms. Each file drawer 4 x 6 x 18. Room 106, Center Building, 2905 Franklin Avenue.

358. VENDORS' INDEX ON GROCERS' AND MEAT DEALERS' ASSOCIATION.
August 1, 1933—. 2 cardboard file boxes.
An alphabetical index of grocers and meat dealers, listing address, date and number of entry, amount of order, voucher number, schedule number, and net amount of invoice. Typed and handwritten. Each cardboard file 4 x 6 x 20. Basement storage room, West Building, 2905 Franklin Avenue.

359. CORRESPONDENCE FILES
August 1, 1933—. 8 file drawers.
General correspondence on accounts receivable and accounts payable. Arranged alphabetically. Typed. Each file drawer 11 x 14 x 28. Room 106, Center Building, 2905 Franklin Avenue.

360. CARD INDEX - EMPLOYEES
August 1, 1933—. 10 cardboard file boxes.
An alphabetical index of employees, listing address and phone number of employee; amount of starting salary; classification and change of classification; and amount of salary paid semi-monthly. Typed. Each file box 4 x 6 x 20. Room 106, Center Building, 2905 Franklin Avenue.

361. PAYROLL AND RECEIPT OF EMPLOYEES
1933—. 12 volumes.
Lists name of employees, nature of employment, and total amount of salary. In alphabetical order. Handwritten and typed. Volumes average 2000 pages. 16 x 11 x 14. Room 106, Center Building, 2905 Franklin Avenue.

362. CARD INDEX - EMPLOYEES MILEAGE
August 1, 1933—. 4 file boxes.

An alphabetical index of employees, giving date of entry, district in which employed; make, model, and year of car; number and amount of check; and an itemized statement of expense. Typed and handwritten. Each file box 4 x 6 x 18. Room 106, Center Building, 2905 Franklin Avenue.

Purchasing Records

363. PURCHASE ORDERS
August 1, 1933—. 12 bundles.

List order number, name and address of firm ordered from, and description and quantity of the item ordered. Arranged as to order numbers. Typed. Each bundle 6 x 9 x 12. Second floor, West Building, 2905 Franklin Avenue.

364. REQUISITION BOOKS
August 1, 1933—. 320 cardboard cartons.

List name, address, and case number of client; the item requisitioned; amount of requisition; and signature of client. In order of requisition numbers. Handwritten. Each cardboard carton 20 x 20 x 18. Room 106, Center Building, 2905 Franklin Avenue.

365. SCHEDULE AND RELIEF ORDERS
August 1, 1933—. 1034 bundles.

Give case record number, date of issue, name and address of person to whom issued, amount of order, name and address of client to whom order is to be furnished, order number, class of relief, and an itemized list of the commodities furnished. In order of schedule numbers. Handwritten and typed on printed forms. Each bundle 24 x 15 x 8. Basement storeroom, West Building, 2905 Franklin Avenue.

366. GENERAL CORRESPONDENCE
August 1, 1933—. 4 file drawers.

General correspondence on items that were to be purchased. In alphabetical order. Typed. Each file drawer 11 x 14 x 28. Second floor, West Building, 2905 Franklin Avenue.

Statistical Records

367. MINUTES OF RELIEF COMMITTEE MEETINGS
August 1, 1933——. 4 loose-leaf volumes.

A record of all matters discussed at relief committee meetings, giving a complete analysis of all expenditures for previous months. It also gives an accurately estimated budget for the following month. In chronological order. For index see number 368. Typed. Volumes average 2500 pages. 8.5 x 11 x 7. Room 211, Center Building, 2905 Franklin Avenue.

368. INDEX TO MINUTES OF COMMITTEE MEETINGS
August 1, 1933——. 1 file box.

An alphabetical card index of subjects, listing subject under consideration, date referred to committee, and date taken up at meeting. Typed. File box 3.5 x 5.5 x 10. Room 211, Center Building, 2905 Franklin Avenue.

369. CUYAHOGA COUNTY RELIEF ADMINISTRATION STATISTICAL REPORTS
August 1933——. 1 volume.

Statistical charts of cases divided as to districts and divisions of districts, listing number of case under care; of intake cases; new cases; old cases; recurrent cases; number exchanged within district offices; total number open during current month; total number lost; cases transferred to other offices; cases exchanged within offices; cases closed; number carried forward to next month; number of active cases; cases receiving relief; work-relief cases not supplemented; cases receiving service only; total number of active cases; number needing attention; number of inactive cases according to plans; and number waiting to be closed. 80 pages. 8.5 x 14 x .75. Room 211, Center Building, 2905 Franklin Avenue.

Recreation Division

The recreation department was not created by statute. It was formed by the commissioners to see that the sponsor funds and the Federal funds were distributed to the best advantage on work relief projects of the recreation type. This department sponsors playground, music, and theatrical projects.

370. WELFARE FINANCIAL RECORD
1934—. 49 folders.
Lists the distribution of finances furnished through the welfare federation. In chronological order. Handwritten. Each folder 8.5 x 11 x .5. Second floor, 1555 West 29th Street.

371. PROJECTS' WEEKLY REPORTS
July 1934—. 77 folders.
Accounts of the activities of various recreational projects, giving names of public and private institutions served by the projects; number of employees, both male and female; and total attendance in recreational activities. In chronological order. Typed and handwritten. Each folder 8.25 x 11 x .5. Second floor, 1555 West 29th Street.

372. PROJECT RECORDS
July 1934—. 49 folders.
Contain applications, correspondence, cost reports, etc. for six Federal music projects, two Federal drama projects, and five recreational projects. In chronological order. Typed and handwritten. Each folder 8.5 x 11 x .5. Second floor, 1555 West 29th Street.

The General Assembly, in 1886, provided for the appointment by any judge of the court of common pleas of a soldiers' relief commission, for each township, composed of three resident persons of the respective townships, and who should be honorably discharged Union soldiers, sailors, or marines. The duties of the commission were to recommend to any county commissioners the names of any indigent Union soldiers, sailors, or marines or of the indigent parents, wives, widows, and minor children of Union veterans who were entitled to relief under this act. The commissioners were authorized to make such levies as were necessary to raise funds for the required relief. (83 O.L. 232).

An amendment in 1917 to the act of 1886 provided for the appointment of the soldiers' relief commission in each county, one member of the commission to be the wife or the widow of an honorably discharged soldier, sailor, or marine of the Civil War or Spanish-American War. Two other persons so appointed shall be honorably discharged soldiers, sailors, or marines of the United States. (107 O. L. 26). The commission shall prepare a list of application for relief of all indigent soldiers, sailors, and marines, their widows, wives, and minor children, and shall determine the monthly amount payable to them. The list shall be certified by the county commissioners and then sent to the auditor who shall draw a warrant on the county treasurer for payment. (107 O. L. 26).

By the provisions of amendment in 1919, relief was extended to the indigent veterans of the World War and to indigent parents, wives, widows, or minor children of such veterans. (108 O. L. pt. 1, 633). (G. C. secs. 2930-2942).

373. ACTIVE RELIEF CASES
1928—. 7 metal file drawers.
A record giving name and address of relief client, case number, and a complete history of the case. In order of case numbers. For index (1934—) see number 374. Typed and handwritten on printed forms. Each file drawer 11 x 13 x 26.5. Room 204, Century Building.

374. INDEX TO ACTIVE RELIEF CASES
July 1934—. 8 metal file boxes.
An alphabetical card index of relief clients, listing address, age, case number, and complete past employment record. Typed on printed forms. Each file box 9 x 6 x 11. Room 204, Century Building.

375. INACTIVE RELIEF CASES
1928—. 32 metal file drawers.

A card record giving name and address of relief client, case number, and a complete history of the case. In order of case numbers. Typed and handwritten. Each file drawer 13 x 11 x 26. Room 204, Century Building.

376. MINUTES OF MEETINGS HELD BY SOLDIERS' AND SAILORS' RELIEF COMMISSION
1901-1919. 5 volumes.

Minutes of all subjects and cases discussed at the meeting of the Soldiers' and Sailors' Relief Commission. In chronological order. Handwritten. Volumes average 500 pages. 9 x 14.25 x 1. 1901-1908, 3 volumes, Sub-basement, County courthouse; 1908-1919, 2 volumes, second floor, Hart Building.

377. ROSTER OF OHIO SOLDIERS
1861-1866. 12 volumes.

Lists name of soldier, rank, and period of service. Arranged alphabetically. Printed. Volumes average 800 pages. 7 x 11.5 x 1.5. Room 204, Century Building.

378. ROSTER OF OHIO SOLDIERS
1898-1899. 2 volumes.

Lists name of soldier, rank, and period of service. In alphabetical order. Printed. Volumes average 800 pages. 7 x 11.5 x 1.5. Room 204, Century Building.

379. ROSTER OF OHIO SOLDIERS', SAILORS', AND MARINES
1917-1918. 22 volumes.

Lists name of soldier, rank, and period of service. Arranged alphabetically as to names of soldiers, sailors, and marines. Printed. Volumes average 800 pages. 7 x 11.5 x 1.5. Room 204, Century Building.

380. PAYROLL WARD RECORD
1928-1934. 7 loose-leaf volumes.

Lists name and address of each client, case number, and amount awarded for each month of relief. In order of case numbers. Handwritten on printed forms. Volumes average 500 pages. 17 x 27 x 3. Room 204, Century Building.

381. SOLDIERS' AND SAILORS' RELIEF RECORD
1901-1925. 25 volumes.

Lists case number, name and address of client, and amount awarded for each month of relief. In order of case numbers. Handwritten on printed forms. Volumes average 200 pages. 13 x 18 x 1. Fourth floor, County courthouse.

382. CANCELLED VOUCHERS AND MISCELLANEOUS DOCUMENTS ON RELIEF PAYMENTS TO SOLDIERS' AND SAILORS'
1916-1928. 19 metal file boxes.

A record listing name of client, case number, and amount of voucher. In chronological order. Typed. Each file box 10.5 x 5 x 12. Fourth floor, County courthouse.

383. CANCELLED CHECKS, SOLDIERS' AND SAILORS' RELIEF
1912-1928. 2 bundles; 17 file boxes.

Checks issued to soldiers and sailors for relief, listing name, check number, date of issue, and amount. In order of check number. Typed printed forms. Each bundle 10.25 x 8.5 x 3.5; each file box 11.75 x 11 x 3.5. Fourth floor, County courthouse.

The office of surveyor in England can be traced to the 16th century when the church parishes had charge of the building and maintenance of roads. The laborers were recruited from the poor, and the surveyor was the supervisor of works. He was appointed by the church wardens and constables. (W. S. Holdsworth, *A History of English Law,* IV, 56).

The first surveys of government lands in Ohio were begun in 1786, under the management of Thomas Hutchins, the geographer of the United States. The Western Reserve, of which the present county was a part, was first surveyed by General Moses Cleaveland in 1796. In 1799 all the surveys in the Northwest Territory were placed in charge of a special officer, with the title of surveyor-general. General Rufus Putnam was appointed to the place, which he held until the State of Ohio was admitted to the Union. In 1802 the township trustees made a map of the city. The lands of the Western Reserve were surveyed five times, the last survey being made of Brooklyn in 1807. In 1803 the Ohio legislature created the office county surveyor, and authorized the appointment of a suitable person to such office. (1 O. L. 90). In the summer of 1806, as a preliminary to the creation of the county, townships were laid out by the Federal Government. This was done under the direction of Seth Pease, then assistant postmaster-general of the United States, who had previously surveyed a limited survey here in 1797. (Henry Howe, *Historical Collections of Ohio* and Crisfield Johnson, *History of Cuyahoga County, Ohio*).

The next act of the legislature pertaining to the office of surveyor, passed in 1816, provided that the person appointed to be a resident of the county, give bond, and take an oath of office. He was to serve for a term of five years, and could appoint three deputies. The county surveyor under the statute did not receive any specified salary, but retained all fees collected by him in the operation of his office. His duties were to lay off all land to be sold for taxes and to keep a record of all surveys. (14 O. L. 424).

In 1831 the office was made elective for a term of three years, the remuneration still being by fees. The authority of the surveyor, however was increased in that he was given limited judicial powers in respect to real estate. He also was given the duty of inspecting public improvements and making records and surveys of such works. (29 O. L. 299). In 1842 the duties of ascertaining and reporting trespasses on public lands were added. (40 O. L. 57). In 1867 the making, correcting, and the keeping up to date of a complete set of tax maps of the county was made incumbent upon him. (64 O. L. 216). In 1881 the duty of procuring field notes was laid upon him. (78 O. L. 285).

In 1906 the term of office was changed to two years. By the same act the surveyor was put in charge of the construction, reconstruction, improvement, maintenance, and repairing of all bridges and highways in the county. He was also authorized to prepare all plans, specifications, and estimates of cost, and to submit forms of contracts for the repair of all culverts, roads, drains, ditches, and other public improvements, except buildings, constructed under the authority of any board within and for the county. He was authorized to perform all necessary services required of a surveyor or a civil engineer in connection with the construction, repair, inspection, or opening of all county roads, turnpikes and ditches authorized by the board of county commissioners, and to perform such other duties as the board may require. The county engineer was also made responsible for the inspection of all public improvements made under authority of the board of county commissioners. He was to keep a complete record of all estimates, summaries of bids received, and of contracts for the various improvements. He was to make all surveys as required by law. (98 O. L. 245-246).

In March 1917 the general assembly enacted a statute giving the county surveyor general charge of the construction, reconstruction, improvements, maintenance, and repair of all bridges and highways within the county. (107 O. L. 111). The enactment further provided that his compensation was not to exceed $6000 per year. (107 O. L. 111). In 1919 another act provided that the county surveyor, when authorized by the county commissioners, appoint a maintenance supervisor, to have charge of the maintenance of improved highways within a district or districts established by the commissioners and surveyor, and containing not less than ten miles of improved county roads. (108 O. L. pt. 1, 197).

In 1923 the county auditor was delegated to assist the county planning commission. (110 O. L. 312). The term of office was again changed in 1927, when it was increased to four years. (112 O. L. 179). This became effective in 1928. The last three laws applicable to the surveyor's office were passed in 1935 and 1936. In the former year the title of the office was changed to that of "county engineer," and eligibility to the office was restricted to one who is a "professional engineer and registered surveyor." (116 O. L. 283-284). This was amended in 1936 so as to permit any person who now holds the office to continue therein upon re-election despite lacked of these qualifications. (116 O. L. pt. 2, 1st special session, 333).

Although the engineer's office is an independent elective office, all authority for work carried out by the department must come from the commissioners. The development of duties and scope of this department presents an interesting picture of change from a simple agricultural society responsible for the clearing of ditches and making of plank roads to a highly urbanized center responsible for intricate road building, bridge building and other construction.

Road Division

General Records

384. ROAD RECORD

1802—. 20 volumes, (1802-1811, 1 volume, Trumbull County Road Record; 1826-1842, 1 volume, State Road Record; 1812-1933, 16 volumes, A-Q; 1894—, 2 volumes, R-S).

A complete record of all road work, including copies of resolutions, proceedings, and the final date of establishment. For index see number 285. Handwritten and typed. Volumes average 1050 pages. 13 x 19 x 2.5. In addition to the 20 volumes that are duplicates of the Trumbull County record and of D and E; there are triplicates of the State Road record and of A, B, and C. Room 1904, Standard Building.

385. INDEX TO ROAD RECORD

1802—. 1 drawer.

An alphabetical index of roads listing the location of the road; the original township in which the road was located; all proceedings to establish, alter, or vacate; the date of road was ordered established; the volume and page of the road record; and general remarks. Typed on printed forms. Drawer 11.5 x 16.5 x 9. Room 1904, Standard Building.

386. COUNTY SURVEYOR'S RECORD

1823—. Approximately 1300 maps in 26 volumes (1823-1893, 3 volumes, 3, 4, 5; 1881, 2 volumes, 1, 2; 1882-1885, 5 volumes, 6, 7, 8, 10, 11; 1888-1913, 15 volumes, 12-26; 1913—, loose-leaf sheets.

The maps show road and street sections with adjoining allotments (water-colored). Distance and figures of field surveys are indicated. In the more recent volumes a front index gives a list of roads and the corresponding numbers. Volumes 3, 4, and

5 contain much handwritten information but few map drawings. Volumes 7 and 8 (1883-1886) are specified as "Canal Boundary Commissioners' Records." Contain colored and pen-and-ink drawings. Scale, 50-200 feet to the inch. Each map 26 x 19. Drawn by the county engineer. For index see number 387. Room 1904, Standard Building.

387. INDEX TO SURVEYOR'S RECORD
1824-1899, 1 volume.; 1824——, 18 file boxes.

An alphabetical index of tracts or subdivisions, listing original lot number, sublot number, name of county surveyor, date of survey, name of person the survey was made for, and the record volume and page.760 pages. 15 x 18 x 2; Each file box 6.5 x 5 x 16. Room 1904, Standard Building.

388. TRANSIT BOOKS
1906——. 401 volumes.

Street diagrams and complete technical data on surveys of land and earthwork. For index see number 390. Handwritten. Volumes average 200 pages. 5 x 8 x .75. Room 1904, Standard Building.

389. LEVEL BOOKS
1907——. 429 volumes.

A record of elevations, together with the surveyor's computations of road measurements. For index see number 390. Handwritten. Volumes average 120 pages. 5 x 8 x .75. Room 1904, Standard Building.

390. INDEX TO TRANSIT AND LEVEL BOOKS
1906——. 1 volume.

An alphabetical index of roads, giving number of book, location of road, name of township, and name of engineer. Handwritten. 200 pages. 5 x 8 x .75. Room 1904, Standard Building.

391. CONSTRUCTION NOTES
1905——. 316 volumes.

A survey of road construction showing sketches of jobs, with the number and location of each job. For index see number 392. Handwritten on printed forms. Volumes average 150 pages. 7.5 x 4.75. .5. 1905-1910, 54 volumes, second floor, Hart. Building; 1910——, 262 volumes, Room 1904, Standard Building.

392. INDEX TO CONSTRUCTION NOTES
1910—. 1 volume.

An alphabetical index of streets, giving number of book containing notes on construction. Handwritten. 150 pages. 7 x 4.25 x .5. Room 1904, Standard Building.

393. MISCELLANEOUS FIELD NOTES
1934. Approximately 35 envelopes in 1 file box.

Diagrams of roads, with field notes of surveyors and jottings by field men on road work, listing name of each road. Alphabetical as to roads. Handwritten. File box 5 x 10 x 15. Room 1904, Standard Building.

394. BENCH MARKS OF CUYAHOGA COUNTY
1925. 1 volume.

Gives name of road and location of bench mark. Contains an alphabetical index of roads. Handwritten. 500 pages. 12.5 x 11.25 x 2.25. Room 1904, Standard Building.

395. RECORD OF DITCHES
1869—. 2 volumes.

Concerns certificates for the opening of ditches, and lists name of township, cost of work, and date on which work was completed. Arranged alphabetically as to roads. Typed. Volumes average 840 pages. 13 x 19 x 2.5. Room 1904, Standard Building.

396. RECORD OF SURVEYS BY COUNTY SURVEYOR
1849—. Approximately 6300 in 18 file boxes.

Surveys of property in Cuyahoga County, giving name of township, location, date of survey, and name of surveyor. In order of lot numbers. For index see number 397. Each file box 13 x 5.25 x 4. Room 1904, Standard Building.

397. INDEX TO RECORD OF SURVEYS BY COUNTY SURVEYORS
1849—. 1 volume.

An index of surveys taken in the county, listing original lot number, name of subdivision, volume and page number and date of deed. Arranged chronologically for cities, villages, and townships, which are arranged alphabetically. Handwritten. 1,000 pages. 15 x 14 x 3. Room 1904, Standard Building.

398. COMMISSIONERS' ROAD AND SECTION RECORD
No dates. 1 volume.

A road cost record listing patrol number, location of road, kind of paving, estimated cost, job number, name of road, and estimated yardage. In order of control numbers. Handwritten on printed forms. 600 pages. 18.5 x 14.25 x 2. Second floor, Hart Building.

399. RECORD OF ASSESSMENTS
1907—. 6 volumes, 1-6.

A cost record of road improvements listing the assessments on property for roads and construction improvements. Arranged chronologically. Handwritten. For index see number 400. Volume average 566 pages. 15 x 15 x 4. Room 1904, Standard Building.

400. INDEX TO ASSESSMENTS
1915—. 500 cards in 1 file box.

An index to assessments listing the assessments levied on properties for road improvements. Arranged chronologically for cities, villages, and townships, which are arranged alphabetically. Handwritten on typed forms. File box 10 x 5 x 15. Room 1904, Standard Building.

401. STATE AND COUNTY CONTRACTS
1924—. 6 file drawers; 180 steel drawers.

Contracts for state and county roads and road work. Filed alphabetically. 6 file drawers 10 x 16 x 24. Room 1904; 180 steel drawers, 9 x 14 x .75. Room 1904, Standard Building.

402. RECORD OF STATE ROADS
1929-1932. 1 volume.

Gives description of work, name of road, location and number of job, estimated cost of material, estimated yardage, and cost of labor. Alphabetical as to roads. Handwritten on printed forms. 900 pages. 25 x 16 x 4. Fourth floor, County courthouse.

403. ROAD ESTIMATES
1915-1918. 4 volumes, 1-4.
Gives name of road, cost of paving, name of contractor, description of job, and kind of material used. Handwritten. Volumes average 600 pages. 12 x 9.75 x .75. Room 1904, Standard Building.

404. OFFICIAL COUNTY PLANS
1936—. 1 volume.
Photostatic copies of plans for county roads. Approximately 50 photostats. In alphabetical order. Room 1904, Standard Building.

405. OFFICIAL STATE PLANS
1926—. 5 volumes.
Photostatic copies of original plans for state roads under county supervision, including a bridge and culvert record. They give a complete sketch showing location of the road, dates of approval, and signatures of various officials of the State Highway Department and of the county commissioners. In order of state route numbers. Volumes average 600 pages. 21 x 14 x 5. Room 1904, Standard Building.

406. UNOFFICIAL STATE PLANS
No dates. 5 volumes.
Photostats of plans for State roads, bridges, and culverts submitted to the State Highway Department. In order of road numbers. Volumes average 600 pages. 21 x 14 x 5. Room 1904, Standard Building.

407. ALLOTMENT PLATS
1849—. Approximately 6300 in 87 file boxes.
Drawings of allotment plats, contained in folders which list name of subdivision, record volume and page, and the original lot number. In order of lot number. For index see number 408. Each file box 15.25 x 4.25 x 12.5. Room 1904, Standard Building.

408. COUNTY DRAFTSMAN'S INDEX
1849—. 2 volumes.

An alphabetical index of townships and villages in the county, showing original lot number, subdivision record volume and page, and file number. Handwritten. One volume is obsolete. Volumes average 514 pages. 15 x 14.5 x 2.75. Room 1904, Standard Building.

409. ESTIMATE WORK SHEETS
1920—. 24 file drawers, A-Z.

Draftsmens' calculations estimating construction cost of proposed roads. Also diagram of street intersections and assessment calculations. Alphabetical to names of roads. Blueprint. Each file drawer 29 x 14.5 x 3. Room 1904, Standard Building.

410. STORM SEWER DESIGN
1930-1931. Approximately 12 folders in 1 file box.

An outline of sewer construction, showing diagram of sewer, date of recommendation, date approved, and name of road. Arranged alphabetically as to roads. File box 5 x 10 x 14. Room 1904, Standard Building.

411. DRAWINGS (Proposed Cross-sections of Roads)
1905—. Approximately 1200 in 24 file drawers.

The drawings show cross-sections of roads, their construction, the kind of paving, curbs, sidewalks, etc. Alphabetical as to road names. Pen-and-ink tracings. Scale, 3/8 inch to the foot. Each drawing 32 x 10; each file drawing 29 x 15 x 2.5. Drawn by county engineer. Room 1904, Standard Building.

412. ROAD MAPS AND PROFILES
1905—. Approximately 650 drawings in 45 drawers, A-W.

The drawings show layout plan and elevation profiles, figures of surveys on elevations, grading, sloping, dimensions of roads, sidewalks, etc. Arranged alphabetically as to roads. Ink tracings. Scales; profile, 1 inch to 10 feet; plan, 1 inch to 50 feet. Drawn by county engineer. For index see number 414. Each file drawer 29 x 25 x 2.5. Room 1904, Standard Building.

413. TRACINGS AND BLUEPRINTS OF ROAD MAPS

1922—. Approximately 5200 ink drawings, tracings, and blueprints in 88 file drawers.

For index see numbers 414 and 415. Drawn by county engineer. Room 1904, Standard Building.

a. Road Maps and Survey. Approximately 240 ink tracings in 6 file drawers, 200-999. Pertain to roads of townships of Cuyahoga County, scale in majority. 50 feet to the inch. Tracings approximately 35 x 25. Each file drawer 13 x 32 x 4.

b. Ditch Profiles. Approximately 105 ink drawings in 3 file drawers. Survey maps pertaining to ditches excavated in township and village of Cuyahoga County. Scale, horizontal, 1 inch to 50 feet; vertical, 1 inch to 10 feet. Sizes vary.

c. Road Cross-sections. Approximately 180 ink drawings in 6 file drawers, 1500-1700. Pertain to roads in Cuyahoga County. Average scale, horizontal, 1 inch to 5 feet; vertical, 1 inch to 5 feet. Drawings of average size, 22 x different lengths. Each file drawer 28 x 32 x 4.

d. Profile Drawings. Approximately 300 ink drawings of various sizes and scales in 4 file drawers. Profiles A-Y now obsolete. Pertain to the territory of Cleveland and are similar to those in 'c'. The obsolete file contains drawings and blueprints of all items listed above. For index see number 415.

e. Property Maps, Bridge Approaches, Road Maps. Approximately 1000 drawings and ink tracings in 4 file drawers, 255-3100. Scale varies. Each file drawer 57 x 32 x 4.

f. Allotment Maps and Road and Ditch Maps. Approximately 1000 maps, ink tracings 10 file drawers, A-J. Pertain to townships and cities of Cuyahoga County. Scale varies. Each file drawer 57 x 32 x 4.

g. Road Establishment and Improvement. 43 file drawers, 1000-3500. Approximately 2000 maps.

h. Construction Maps of County Roads. Approximately 600 ink tracings in 12 file drawers, A-Z. Scale varies. Each file drawer 22 x 26 x 2.5.

414. INDEX TO MAPS, CROSS-SECTIONS, AND PROFILES
1896—. 33 drawers in 1 cardex cabinet.

List number to profiles, cross-sections, and maps, and limits of improvements. Alphabetical as to roads. 27 x 24 x 7. Room 1904, Standard Building.

415. MISCELLANEOUS INDEX
1898-1914. Approximately 300 cards in 1 file box, A-Z.

An alphabetical card index of roads, inactive profiles, old profiles, intersections, ditch maps, and ditch profiles. Handwritten on printed forms. File box 16.5 x 6.25 x 5.25. Room 1904, Standard Building.

416. GEOLOGICAL ATLAS OF THE STATE OF OHIO
1879. 7 maps in 1 volume.

Published by authority of the Ohio Legislature in 1879. The maps indicate the rock formations and layers of deposits of the geological ages. Shows sections of shafts and slopes in the Mahoning Valley Coal Field, originally drawn by E. R. Mathews, Youngstown, Ohio. An indefinite number of maps appear to be missing. J. S. Newberry, Chief Geologist, author; Julius Bien, New York, engraver. Scale, 4 miles to the inch. Each map 37 x 26. Room 1904, Standard Building.

417. ATLAS, CLEVELAND
1898. 28 maps in 1 volume.

Communication and allotment maps of the city of Cleveland, surrounding villages, hamlets, and townships. Printed. Colored. Scale, 300 feet to the inch. 1 general map, 1790 feet to the inch. Each map 32 x 22. Flynn Barthel, Bunning, Hassan, authors. A. H. Mueller and Company, Philadelphia, Pennsylvania, publishers. In steel file cabinet in Room 1904, Standard Building.

418. ATLAS
1892. Approximately 116 maps.

The atlas contains one map of the U. S. (no scale given); one map of Ohio (3/4" to 10 miles); one map of Cuyahoga County (3/4" to 1 mile). All other maps show part of the city of Cleveland and townships (1700 and 200 feet to 1 inch), indicating communications, wards, precincts, original lots, allotments, public buildings, and paving of streets. Printed. Colored. Each map 26 x 23. Copyright, George F. Cram and Company. Room 1904, Standard Building.

419. ATLAS, "CUYAHOGA COUNTY OUTSIDE OF CLEVELAND"
1903. 79 maps in 1 volume.

These maps show, by means of various colors, the types of material used in buildings. It also shows allotments and railroads. Contains an index map indicating townships by numbers. Printed, colored. Scale, 400 feet to the inch. Each map 28 x 17. H. B. Stranahan and Company, Cleveland, Ohio, publishers. Room 1904, Standard Building.

420. PLAT BOOKS
1922-1927. Approximately 300 maps in 6 plat books, 1-6.

The maps show allotments, location of railroads, wards, and the materials of which buildings are constructed. Each volume contains an index to streets and allotments. Printed and colored. Scale 100, 150 and 200 feet to the inch. Map 33 x 24. G. M. Hopkins Company, Philadelphia, Pennsylvania, publishers. Room 1904, Standard Building.

Accounting Records

421. SEMI-MONTHLY TIME BOOKS
September 1, 1906—. 14 volumes.

Lists the name of the employee, his position, and amount paid. Arranged chronologically. Handwritten on printed forms. 10 volumes, 1906-1924, 8.5 x 14 x 2; 4 volumes, 1924—, 9 x 15 x 2.5, Room 1904, Standard Building.

422. PAYROLLS
July 1, 1926-July 1, 1928. 6 volumes.

A record listing name and number of each employee, date, total number of hours, rate of pay, and total amount of wages. Arranged alphabetically. Typed. Volumes average 1000 pages. 17 x 14.5 x 2. Second floor, Hart Building.

423. RECORD OF REQUISITIONS
January, 1934—. 1 volume.

Copies of requisitions for supplies for the road and bridge division, showing material requisitioned, the unit and total cost, the amount, the order number, and the name of the vendor. Chronologically arranged. Typed on printed forms. 10 x 13 x 2. Room 1904, Standard Building.

425. AUTOMOBILE EXPENSE ACCOUNT
1935. Approximately 300 cards in 1 file box.
Lists month, rate, mileage, and name of driver. Alphabetical as to names of drivers.
Typed. File box 12 x 6.5 x 5. Each card 4 x 6. Room 1904, Standard Building.

426. ENGINEER'S TIME RECORDS
July 16, 1930- March 20, 1932. 20 volumes.
Lists type of work, number of hours spent on project, and cost data for
miscellaneous highway work. In order of contract numbers. Handwritten on printed
forms. Volumes average 100 pages. 7.5 x 5 x .5. Second floor, Hart Building.

427. DRAFTSMENS' TIME SHEETS
1920-1932. Approximately 150 in 1 file box.
Engineer's time reports, giving name of improvement, name of employee, and date
of work. In chronological order. Handwritten. File box 5 x 10 x 14. Room 1904,
Standard Building.

428. ENGINEERS' AND INSPECTORS' REPORTS
January 1, 1932—. 4 file drawers; 1 cardboard box.
Reports on material and time, listing, according to job number, the names of the
contractor, engineer, and inspector on all road, ditch, bridge, earthwork, and
highway jobs. Arranged numerically as to job numbers. Handwritten on printed
forms. January 1932- December, 1936, box 12 x 6.5 x 3.5, second floor, Hart
Building; 1933—, 4 steel file drawers, 14 x 24 x 5, Room 1904, Standard Building.

429. CWA COUNTY REPORTS
1933-1934. 1 metal file drawer.
Material reports on CWA projects doing county road work. Alphabetical as to
roads. Handwritten and typed. Each metal drawer 14 x 11.5 x 25. Room 1904,
Standard Building.

430. CWA PAYROLLS
1933-1834. 1 bundle. (Also see number 273).
Payroll sheets for road work done by the CWA giving name of employee, date, and
location of work. Arranged in order of project numbers. Handwritten and typed.
Each sheet 15 x 15. Room 1904, Standard Building.

431. PERMITS AND APPLICATIONS FOR PERMITS
1918-1926. 8 volumes.

Lists date and number of permit, to whom issued, name of applicant, location of job, and name of road or highway. In the order of permit numbers. Handwritten on printed forms. Volumes average 500 pages. 15.5 x 11.5 x 2. Second floor, Hart Building.

432. PROPOSALS FOR COUNTY WORK
1904-1909. 1 volume.

Lists the date of advertisement, the date of opening of the bid, the engineer's estimate, the bids submitted by contractors on various improvements, the award to the successful bidder, and the contract number. Listed chronologically. 100 pages. 8 x 14 x .5. Room 1904, Standard Building.

433. ROAD IMPROVEMENT RECORD
1916-1919. 4 volumes.

A record of road improvements showing costs, contracts number, date contract was awarded, and date of completion of work. Alphabetical as to improvements. Handwritten on printed forms. Volumes average 100 pages. 23 x 13 x 2.5. Fourth floor, County courthouse.

Maintenance Division

Contract Records

434-435. MAINTENANCE CONTRACTS
1913—. 35 file boxes; 175 steel file drawers; 15 bundles.

Copies of contracts for the road maintenance and repair departments. Show date of contract; location of road, ditch, or earthwork; name of contractor; specifications for the work; and dates bid was received, posted, and let. Filed numerically as to contract numbers. Handwritten and typed on printed forms. 1913-1924, 15 bundles, 14 x 12 x 6, second floor, Hart Building; 1925—, 25 file boxes, 10 x 16 x 24, Room 1939; 175 file drawers, 9 x 14 x .75, Room 1906, Standard Building.

436. BILL BOOK ON CONTRACTS
1929—. 2 volumes.

A record of maintenance contracts, listing name of contractor, contract number, engineer's estimate, price bid, date of answering bid, date awarded, date work was started, and date of completion of work. Arranged as to contract numbers. Handwritten on printed forms. Volumes average 150 pages. 14.5 x 12.5 x 1.25. 1 volume, 1929-1932, Room 1939; 1 volume, 1932—, Room 1906, Standard Building.

437. CONTRACT BIDS
1935—. 5000 in 3 file drawers.

Give kind of material, report number, total estimate, date, and name of person from whom purchased. Typed. Filed chronologically. Each file drawer 25 x 16.5 x 10.5. Room 1933, Standard Building.

438. ENGINEER'S MAINTENANCE REPORTS
1927—. 9 bundles; 1 file drawer.

Contain proposals, instructions to bidders, resolutions, and material specifications on the maintenance of roads. In alphabetical order. Typed on printed forms and handwritten. File drawer 14.5 x 11 x 28. 1927-1932, 9 bundles, commissioners' Basement storeroom, County courthouse; 1933—, 1 file drawer, Room 1933, Standard Building.

439. APPROVALS
1917—. Approximately 300 folders in 2 file boxes.

Approvals for road repair contracts, listing contract number, report number, name of contractor, class of work, and location of work. In order of contract numbers. Typed. Each file box 13.5 x 10.5 x 5. Room 1933, Standard Building.

440. PERMIT LEDGER (Roads)
1932—. 1 volume.

A record of water permits, showing amount of material and labor, total cost, amount deposited, and date of completion. In order of permit numbers. Handwritten on printed forms. 350 pages. 12.5 x 8.75 x 2.25. Room 1933, Standard Building.

441. EXPENDITURES AND BALANCE OF ROAD DEPARTMENT
1930-1933. 1 volume.

A journal covering road repair work, giving voucher number, name of road, date on which road was completed, data on sale of old bricks, and description of warrant. Chronological. Handwritten on printed forms. 500 pages. 15.5 x 14.75 x 1.25. Fourth floor, County courthouse.

442. SPECIAL ROAD REPAIR FUND
1925-1926. 20 folders.

Shows name of company furnishing material, quantity and quality of material, date of contract, order number, and name and location of road. Handwritten on printed forms. No arrangements. Each folder 14.5 x 9 x .5. Fourth floor, County courthouse.

443. MAINTENANCE BID FORMS ON MATERIALS
1932-1933. 1 file drawer.

A record of bids received on materials for road maintenance jobs. Alphabetical as to names of roads. Handwritten and typed on printed forms. File drawer 14.5 x 11 x 28. Room 1933, Standard Building.

444. GENERAL COUNTY ROAD SPECIFICATIONS
1928-1930. 12 folders and 30 bundles.

Lists name of road, number of contract, name of contractor, name of street, amount of material, additional quantities of material required for natural variations and work, and unstable condition of subgrade. Typed on printed forms. Each bundle 13.5 x 8.5 x 7. Fourth floor, County courthouse.

Equipment, Materials, and Miscellaneous Service

445. DAMAGE TO EQUIPMENT AND COLLISIONS
1933—. 2500 copies in 1 file drawer.

Reports of damages, accidents, and collisions in the course of road maintenance work. Alphabetical as to roads. Handwritten and typed on printed forms. File drawer 14.5 x 11 x 28. Room 1933, Standard Building.

446. INVENTORIES OF EQUIPMENT AND MATERIALS
1930—. Approximately 5000 in 2 file drawers.

Complete inventories of all store yards of the county engineer's office, listing road maintenance properties, and all materials used by the department. Arranged alphabetically as to store yards. Handwritten and typed on printed forms. Each file drawer 14.5 x 11 x 28. Room 1933, Standard Building.

447. COUNTY YARD RECORDS
1934—.

Duplicates of road maintenance, equipment, gas, and disbursement records are located at five county yards of the department. They are known as; Yard 1, Westview; Yard 2, Brookpark; Yard 3, Fitzwater; Yard 4, Miles Avenue; and Yard 5, Mayfield and Brainard Roads.

448. YARD ORDERS
1934—. 1500 copies in 1 file drawer.

Orders for work equipment and material issued for the five county store yards. Arranged alphabetically as to names of yards. Handwritten and typed on printed forms. File drawer 14.5 x 11 x 28. Room 1933, Standard Building.

449. YARD ORDERS
1935—. 3000 copies in 2 file drawers.

Purchase requisitions for the county yards, giving date, order number, name of yard, date order was delivered, and name of person from whom purchased. Alphabetical as to yards. Handwritten and typed on printed forms. Each file drawer 25 x 16.5 x 10.5 Room 1933, Standard Building.

450. REQUISITION BILL BOOK
1929—. 2 volumes.

A record of all material purchased for road work, listing date, requisition number, the items, ticket number, date received, by whom received, unit price, amount, and date paid. Alphabetical as to name of firms. Handwritten on printed forms. Volumes average 600 pages. 14.5 x 12.5 x 2.75. Room 1933, Standard Building.

451. ACCOUNTS RECEIVABLE BOOK
1934—. 1 volume.

A record of materials used for road repair, listing labor and material required, number of invoice, date, name of department requiring service, and cost of material. In order of invoice numbers. Typed. 100 pages. 9.75 x 10 x 1.25. Room 1933, Standard Building.

452. OPERATION COST JOURNAL
1935—. 2 volumes.

A road cost journal, listing date, the items, reference number, amount of material, and distribution of costs. Handwritten. 150 pages. 24.25 x 15.75 x 1.75. Room 1933, Standard Building.

453. NET COST DISTRIBUTION, SECTIONAL COST JOURNAL
1935. 2 volumes (1935, 1 volume, East Side; 1935, 1 volume, West Side). Shows the distribution of cost items for road maintenance. Arranged alphabetically as to roads. Handwritten on printed forms. Volumes average 500 pages. 24 x 15 x 2.5. Room 1933, Standard Building.

454. RECORD OF MAINTENANCE EXPENDITURES
1935. 1 volume.

Lists road name; county road number; section of road; type of road repaired; description of work done; length in miles; width of metal; width of roadway; cost distribution according to maintenance; and repair, additions, and improvements for roadway surface, bridges, and culverts, and traffic control; and amount paid. 35 pages. 24 x 15.5 x 1. Arranged alphabetically as to roads. Room 1933, Standard Building.

455. GAS, OIL, ALCOHOL REQUISITIONS
1934. Approximately 9000 in 3 bundles.

Give amount of time required, truck number, name of yard, requisition number, and signature of person using supplies. Handwritten on printed forms. Each bundle 15 x 7 x 5. Attic storeroom, fourth floor, County courthouse.

456-457. DAILY TRUCK REPORT
1929-1933. 25 volumes.

Lists date of trip, destination of truck, time of arrival, job number, mileage, weight, load capacity, quantity of supplies, name of company from whom purchased, the price, various remarks, and driver's signature. Arranged chronologically. Handwritten on printed forms. Volumes average 300 pages. 8.5 x 3 x 5.5. Attic storeroom, fourth floor, County courthouse.

458. GASOLINE SLIPS FOR WEST SIDE
1934. 1 volume.

Request slips for gasoline, showing number of slip, date of request, name of department, signature of truck driver, number of truck, and name of road being repaired. Handwritten on printed forms. 500 pages. 8.5 x 5.75 x 1.5. Attic storeroom, fourth floor, County courthouse.

459. AUTOMOBILE EXPENSE
1930-1932. 7 cardboard file boxes.

Gives name of driver, date of entry, amount of expenditure, signature of driver, and name of person who approved the expense account. Handwritten on printed forms. Attic storeroom, fourth floor, County courthouse.

460. STORE YARD MATERIAL REPORT
1932. 1 volume.

Lists material requisitioned at store yard showing report number, date, quantity of material, to whom delivered and name of storekeeper. Handwritten on printed forms. Chronologically arranged. 500 pages. 8.75 x 5.75 x 2. Attic storeroom, fourth floor, County courthouse.

461. ROAD REQUISITIONS, MATERIALS, AND SUPPLIES
1922-1926. 4 volumes.

A record of requisitions for materials and supplies for road maintenance, giving date and number of each requisition. Arranged as to names of roads. Handwritten on printed forms. Volumes average 900 pages. 12.5 x 10 x 5.5. Attic storeroom, fourth floor, County courthouse.

462. INVENTORY OF MILES AVENUE STOREROOM
1931. 1 folder.

A complete inventory of all materials stored at the Miles Avenue store yard. Typed. Folder 14 x 9 x .25. Attic storeroom, fourth floor, County courthouse.

463. INVENTORY OF BROOKPARK STORE YARD
1931. 1 folder.

A record of buildings, equipment, furniture, fixtures, materials and supplies of the Brookpark store yard. Typed. Folder 14 x 9 x .25. Attic storeroom, fourth floor, County courthouse.

464. STOREHOUSE TOOL REPORT
1929-1932. 2 volumes.

A record of the quantity, kind, and condition of tools kept in the storehouse. Handwritten on printed forms. Volumes average 816 pages. 8.5 x 5.75 x 2. Attic storeroom, fourth floor, County courthouse.

465-466. DRAY TICKETS
1926-1930, 6 bundles; 6 folders.

List materials delivered to store yards of the road maintenance and repair departments, giving date, ticket number, project number, materials delivered, place of delivery and signature of person receiving material. Chronologically arranged. Each bundle 13 x 9 x 6; each folder 14 x 9 x 2. Attic storeroom, fourth floor, County courthouse.

467. INVENTORY OF GARAGE
1931. Approximately 10 in 1 folder.

Lists conveyors, cranes, graders, trailers, trucks, road maintainers, and equipment stored in the county garage. Typed. Folder 14 x 9 x .25. Attic storeroom, fourth floor, County courthouse.

468. MATERIALS AND SUPPLIES
January 1919- December 1921. 3 volumes.

A purchase record of all material and supplies used on miscellaneous highway jobs. Alphabetical as to roads. Handwritten. Volumes average 600 pages. 14 x 12.5 x 3. Second floor, Hart Building.

469. MAINTENANCE COST SHEETS
1920-1929. Approximately 3000 in 10 bundles.

Cost sheets of road repair work, listing name of road, location of job, estimated cost, dates, and cost of hauling and unloading the material. Handwritten on printed forms. Each bundle 15.5 x 23 x 3. Attic storeroom, fourth floor, County courthouse.

470. PURCHASE RECORD
January 1, 1926- July 3, 1929. 4 volumes.

Copies of requisitions, giving date ordered, active number, purchase number, quantity and kind of material used, estimated cost, and auditor's certificate. In chronological order. Handwritten on printed forms. Volumes average 500 pages. 24 x 15 x 2. Second floor, Hart Building.

471. PURCHASE RECORD
1931. 3 volumes.

Lists date of order, job number, quantity and kind of material, requisition number, purchase order number, name of person who gave order, estimated cost, and total expenditures. Alphabetical as to roads. Handwritten on printed forms. Volumes average 700 pages. 23 x 15.5 x 2. Attic storeroom, fourth floor, County courthouse.

472. MAINTENANCE COST SHEETS OF ROADS
1931. 3 volumes.

Shows date of order, job number, kind and quantity of material, number of requisition, purchase order number, for whom ordered, estimated cost, name of firm, and total expenditures. Arranged alphabetically as to road names. Handwritten on printed forms. Volumes average 700 pages. 23 x 15.5 x 2. Attic storeroom, fourth floor, County courthouse.

473. INVOICE RECORDS - ROAD MAINTENANCE AND REPAIR DEPARTMENT
1929-1930. Approximately 1000 in 2 bundles.

Lists date and number of requisition, the materials invoiced, number of ticket, date on which material was received, name of person receiving material, unit price, total amount, and date of payment. Arranged chronologically. Handwritten on printed forms. Each bundle 14 x 12.5 x 3.5. Attic storeroom, fourth floor, County courthouse.

474. FILE OF MATERIAL USED
1935. 1 file drawer.

Lists date of order, kind of material required, material used, and name of firm from whom purchased. Alphabetical as to roads. Handwritten on printed forms. File drawer 14.5 x 11 x 28. Room 1933, Standard Building.

475. STOREROOM MATERIAL AND SUPPLIES RECORD
1922. 1 volume.

Lists name of company supplying material, date and number of requisition, materials ordered, date ordered and received, purchase order number, and name of person receiving material. Arranged alphabetically as to companies. Handwritten on printed forms. 500 pages. 14 x 12.75 x 2.25. Attic storeroom, fourth floor, County courthouse.

476-477. ROAD REPORT, ROAD WEST OF RIVER, INCLUDING PATROL WORK, PAVEMENT OPENINGS, STATE ROADS, STATE MAINTENANCE
1933-1931. 7 volumes.

A record of road cost, showing name of road, cost of labor, the cost and amount of material, overhead cost, and total cost. Alphabetically arranged as to roads. Typed on printed forms. Volumes average 250 pages. 15 x 11 x 1. Attic storeroom, fourth floor, County courthouse.

Employee Records and Payrolls

478. EMPLOYEES' RECORD
1890—. 1 card cabinet.

A card file of employees of the engineer's office showing vital statistics, service history, and efficiency record of all employees, where employed and type of work to which assigned. Alphabetical as to employees. Handwritten on printed forms. Cabinet 16 x 20 x 20; each card 8 x 5. Room 1933, Standard Building.

479. FILE OF MAINTENANCE EMPLOYEES
1933—. 5000 cards in 1 file cabinet.

Cards give name and address, rate of pay, kind of work, location of job, and a health report for each employee. Alphabetical as to names of employees. Handwritten and typed. Cabinet 3.25 x 5.5 x 28; each card 3 x 5. Room 1933, Standard Building.

480. MAINTENANCE PAYROLLS
1928—. 10 volumes.

Payroll records of employees listing name of employee, position held, hours worked, hourly rate of pay, and amount earned for each pay period. Alphabetical as to names of employees. Typed. Volumes average 600 pages. 17 x 14 x 2.5. Room 1933, Standard Building.

481. TIME SHEETS, MISCELLANEOUS ENGINEERS
1933-1934. 1 volume.

A monthly time record listing date, name of road, number of hours, rate of pay, name of supervisor, total amount of pay, and daily time record. Arranged alphabetically as to roads. Handwritten on printed forms. 300 pages. 8.75 x 5.75 x 2. Attic storeroom, fourth floor, County courthouse.

482. RECORD OF C.W.A. EMPLOYEES
1933-1934. 5000 cards in 1 card file.

A record of C.W.A. road work, giving name, address, and rate of pay of each employee. Alphabetical as to names of employees. Handwritten and typed. Card cabinet 3 x 5 x 28; each card 3 x 5. Room 1933, Standard Building.

483. EMPLOYEES' PAY RATE AND TIME BOOKS
January 31, 1931- November 30, 1932. 25 volumes.

List name of employee, rate of pay, daily job and time reports, and name of road where employed. In chronological order. Handwritten. Volumes average 100 pages. 7.5 x 5 x .5. Second floor, Hart Building.

484. ORIGINAL TIME SHEETS FOR PAYROLL, ROAD REPAIR DEPARTMENT
1916-1924. 11 volumes.

List name of each laborer, occupation, number of hours worked, wage rate, date of payroll, name of foreman, and signature of employee. In chronological order. Typed. Volumes average 700 pages. 17.5 x 14.5 x 3.5. Attic storeroom, Fourth floor, County courthouse.

485. PAYROLLS
1914-1934. 384 volumes; 400 folders in 8 file boxes.

List name of road, date of entry, number of employee, job number, number of hours worked, rate of pay, and name of truck driver. Handwritten on printed forms. Volumes average 650 pages. 9 x 5.5 x 2.5; each file box 12.25 x 10 x 5. Attic storeroom, fourth floor, County courthouse.

486. ROAD MAINTENANCE AND REPAIR DEPARTMENT, LABOR COST SHEET
1932- January 1, 1936. Approximately 1500 in 5 bundles; 1 loose-leaf binder.

Gives a description of all work being done, location of each job, name of road, date, estimated yardage, and estimated cost. Handwritten on printed forms. Each bundle 24 x 15 x 2.5. Attic storeroom, fourth floor, County courthouse.

487. MAINTENANCE TIME CARDS
1933—. 10,000 cards in 1 file case.

Employees' time cards, giving name and number of employee, and a daily time report. Handwritten on printed forms. Card case 73 x 45 x 6.5. Room 1933, Standard Building.

488. WEST SIDE TIME RECORDS
1933. 3 volumes.

Give name of store yard, date, name of employee, number of hours worked, rate of pay, amount of pay, and signature of timekeeper. Chronological. Volumes average 500 pages. 8.5 x 5.75 x 1.5. Attic storeroom, fourth floor, County courthouse.

489. ROAD REPAIR TIME SLIPS
June 1934- July 1935. Approximately 5000 in 1 bundle.

Shows name of laborer, position, number of hours worked, rate of pay, amount of pay, name of road, cost of job, name of foreman, and certifications of work performed. Handwritten. Bundle 20 x 16 x 10. Attic storage room, fourth floor, County courthouse.

490. WORK CARDS–DITCH WORK, ROAD REPAIR
1932. Approximately 5000 in 1 bundle.

Shows date of entry, signature of employee, name of foreman, kind of work, name of road, and name and address of worker. Handwritten on printed forms. Bundles 15 x 10 x 7. Attic storeroom, fourth floor, County courthouse.

491. TRANSPORTATION PASS RECORD
No dates. Approximately 1500 cards in 9 cardboard boxes.

Lists number of pass, and name and address of holder. Typed. Each box 11 x 5.75 x 3.75. Second floor, Hart Building.

492. TIME SLIPS
June 16, 1928-July 2, 1930. 3 volumes.

A charge record listing number of workers on each job; name of highway; date; location of job; condition of weather; and charges for both labor and material. Handwritten. Volumes average 100 pages. 5 x 7.5 x .5. Second floor, Hart Building.

Miscellaneous

493. MISCELLANEOUS MAINTENANCE FILE
1934—, 2500 copies in 1 file drawer.

Contains interdepartmental correspondence and miscellaneous papers on road maintenance. Arranged alphabetically as to road names. Handwritten and typed. File drawer 14.5 x 11 x 28. Room 1933, Standard Building.

494. MAINTENANCE CIVIL SERVICE FILE
1933—. 3000 sheets in 2 file drawers.

List appointments, discharges, and transfers of civil service employees in the engineer's department. Handwritten on printed forms. Each file drawer 14.5 x 11 x 28. Room 1933, Standard Building.

495. INDUSTRIAL COMMISSION REPORTS
1924—. Approximately 4500 in 3 file drawers.

Reports relative to the industrial compensation records for personnel injured on road maintenance jobs. Alphabetical as to names of persons injured. Handwritten and typed on printed forms. Each file drawer 14.5 x 11 x 28. Room 1933, Standard Building.

496. COMPLAINTS OF ROAD CONDITIONS
1934—. Approximately 250 in 1 file drawer.
Give name and location of road, date of complaint, by whom made, nature of complaint, and date of repair. Arranged as to names of roads. File drawer 20 x 13 x 10.5. Room 1933, Standard Building.

497. WORK ORDER
1933. Approximately 400 in 1 bundle.
Work orders, giving rate of pay, name and address of worker, kind of work, and location of job. Handwritten. Bundle 12 x 12 x 2.5. Attic storeroom, fourth floor, County courthouse.

498. TRAFFIC CENSUS, ROAD AND REPAIR
1924-1925. Approximately 1500 in 1 bundle.
Lists name of road, location of job, date, condition of weather, name of handyman, and number of hours worked. Handwritten on printed forms. Bundle 12 x 12 x 6.5. Attic storeroom, fourth floor, County courthouse.

499. MAINTENANCE REPORTS
1930-1931. Approximately 36,000 in 240 folders.
Reports on roads and public works, specifications for improvements, etc. Handwritten and typed on printed forms. Each folder 15 x 9.5 x .25. Second floor, Hart Building.

500. BLUEPRINTS ON GENERAL REPAIR, CUYAHOGA COUNTY
1933—. 150 maps in 1 file drawer.
Contains blueprints of storm sewers and culverts showing necessary repairs. Drawn by county engineer. Scale varies. File drawer 20 x 13 x 10.5. Room 1933, Standard Building.

County Testing Laboratory

501. COUNTY CONTRACT JOBS AND MAINTENANCE REPORTS ON TESTS OF MATERIALS
1927—. 4 file boxes; 12 file drawers.

Information covering kinds of materials used in maintenance repair work, copies of contracts, and general reports of materials to be used. In order of job numbers. Typed. Each file box 10.5 x 4.5 x 14; each file drawer 11 x 13 x 24. Second floor, 2039 West 19th Street.

502. STATE HIGHWAY REPORTS ON TEST OF MATERIALS
1928—. 3 file drawers.

Reports on tests of materials used in the maintenance and repair of state highways. In order of job numbers. Typed. Each file drawer 11 x 13 x 24. Second floor, 2039 West 19th Street.

503. C.W.A. REPORTS ON TESTS OF MATERIALS
1934—. 2 file drawers.

Reports of materials used on C.W.A. projects, giving formulas for mixing of concrete materials, strength test of materials, etc. In order of job numbers. Typed. Each file drawer 11 x 13 x 24. Second floor, 2039 West 19th Street.

504. PROCEEDINGS AND STANDARD SPECIFICATIONS OF THE AMERICAN SOCIETY FOR TESTING MATERIALS
1924-1935. 24 volumes.

Printed forms on the proceedings and standards specifications covering material tested. Alphabetical as to names of materials. Volumes average 1,000 pages. 6 x 9 x 2. Second floor, 2039 West 19th Street.

505. GENERAL CORRESPONDENCE
1933—. 1 file drawer.

Departmental correspondence with the bureau of public roads, and material producers. Alphabetical as names of correspondence. Typed. File drawer 11 x 13 x 24. Second floor, 2039 West 19th Street.

506. PAVEMENT TEST
1927. Approximately 1500 cards in 1 file box.
Gives data concerning pavement tests, name of subdivision, and name of street.
Handwritten on printed forms, typed, and sketched. File box 4 x 9 x 14. Second
floor, Hart Building.

County Bridge Garage

507. TIME BOOK
March 1933—. 40 volumes.
Daily time reports, listing time card number, name of employee, classification,
number of hours worked, rate per hour, amount earned, and location of work. In
chronological order. Handwritten on printed forms. Volumes average 50 pages. 14
x 8.5 x .75. Bridge garage at west end of old Superior Viaduct Road.

508. PURCHASE REQUISITIONS
March 1933—. 5 volumes.
Give date and number of requisition, the quantity, a description of the material, and
place of delivery. In chronological order. Handwritten on printed forms. Volumes
average 130 pages. 10.5 x 8 x .75. Bridge garage at west end of old Superior
Viaduct Road.

509. REPORT OF MATERIAL RECEIVED
March 1933—. 1 volume.
List date ordered, date received, from whom received, amount received, kind of
material, county order number, bill number, by whom received, and the cost. In
chronological order. Handwritten on printed forms. Volumes average 100 pages. 23
x 16 x 1.5. Bridge garage at west end of old Superior Viaduct Road.

510. MATERIAL AND EQUIPMENT RECEIVED AND DISBURSED
January 1934. Approximately 300 cards in 1 cardboard file box.
Lists date received or disbursed, requisition number, name of person from whom
received and person to whom delivered, quantity, and amount on hand. Alphabetical
as to names of items. Handwritten on printed forms. File box 11 x 8.75 x 6. Bridge
garage at west end of old Superior Viaduct Road.

Right of Way and Planning Division

511. ACTIVE AND DISPOSED FILES
1926—. 7 file boxes.
Papers pertaining to claims arising from improvements on county roads. Filed numerically by road numbers. Handwritten and typed; photostats, blueprints. File box 13 x 12 x 28. Room 1918, Standard Building.

512. CLAIM BOOK
1926—. 1 volume.
Cclaims and legislation instituted and connection therewith. Lists plat number, file number, road, owner, village legislation, amount of claims and award, journal page and date of award, voucher date, date payable, title ordered, statement of title, release of mortgage, claim release, and date claim was paid. Alphabetical by road names. 200 pages. 20 x 13 x 1.5. Room 1918, Standard Building.

513. VOUCHER RECORD
1926—. 1 volume.
A record of awards paid to claimants. It lists name of road or improvement, of person who receives award in connection with the improvement, date of granting award by resolution of the county commissioners, the journal volume and page, and the voucher date and number. Arranged alphabetically as to road names. Typed. 11.5 x 10.5 x 1. 150 pages. Room 1918, Standard Building.

514. TRAFFIC SURVEY
1927—. 6 file drawers; 1 bundle.
A record giving an actual account of auto traffic from 7 A.M. to 7 P.M. by fifteen-minute periods at given road points. The survey is usually made at the same season of the year. 1930-1931, 1 bundle, commissioners' Basement storeroom, County courthouse; 1927—, 6 file drawers, 13 x 12 x 28. Room 1918, Standard Building.

515. FLOW MAP OF TRAFFIC DENSITY, CUYAHOGA COUNTY
1934. 1 map.
A descriptive map showing traffic density on all county thoroughfares, as compiled from the annual traffic survey data. Printed, colored, and mounted. Drawn by county engineer. 10,000 to 40.000 cars to the inch. Map 30 x 36. Room 1918, Standard Building.

516. ESTABLISHMENT, VACATION, AND DEDICATION MAPS
1928—. 8 file drawers.
Also calculations pertaining to the procuring of right of way. Filed alphabetically as to names. Drawer 9.5 x 16 x 28. Room 1914, Standard Building.

517. MISCELLANEOUS MAPS AND SURVEYS
1928—. 15 steel file drawers.
Bridge plans, surveys, and topographical maps. Blueprints, Photostats, and Van Dykes. Filed by subject matter. Drawn by engineering department and private engineers. Drawer 34 x 44 x 2. Room 1914, Standard Building.

Bridge Division

518. CONTRACT FILE
1930—. 102 file drawers.
Contracts for completed and current projects for improvements, also a file of rescinded contracts. Index as to original townships. Old contracts are returned to the county commissioners. Drawer 4 x 10 x 13. Room 1944, Standard Building.

519. BRIDGE DEPARTMENT CONTRACT BOOK
18 volumes, (1891-1906, 7 volumes, 1-7, Bridge Department Contract Book; 1906, 11 volumes, 1-11, Record of Bridges).
A record of all contracts let out by the bridge department, listing kind of work, name of contract, location of job, the original estimated cost and the final estimate, the contract number, the report number, the date work was started, and the date of completion. Alphabetical under original townships. Handwritten on printed forms. Volumes average 750 pages. 16 x 14 x 2. Room 1944, Standard Building.

520. ESTIMATE BOOKS
1906—. 75 volumes.
Contain calculations showing the amount of concrete, steel, and other materials required, and estimates for each. Each volume is separately indexed. Handwritten. Volumes average 300 pages. 12.5 x 10.25 x .5. Room 1944, Standard Building.

521. TOPOGRAPHICAL MAPS
1920—. Approximately 600 maps in 1 steel cabinet.
Topographical maps made up from field surveys used and the preparation of plans
for new structures. Filed numerically and pigeon-holes, 2 x 2. For index see number
524. Room 1944, Standard Building.

522. MISCELLANEOUS BRIDGE FILE
1910—. 36 file drawers.
a. 12 drawers contain plans and tracings for the Detroit-Superior bridge.
b. 12 drawers contain plans for other bridges such as the Lorraine- Carnegie
and Main Avenue bridges.
c. 12 drawers contain plans for completed and current work for 1933—. For
index see number 524. Drawer 45 x 30 x 2. Room 1944, Standard Building.

523. BRIDGE AND CONSTRUCTION PLANS
1895-1933. 40 file drawers.
Tracings, maps, and blueprints of bridge and culvert work. Also data pertaining to
bridge and culvert construction. Ink drawings. For index see number 524. File
drawer 45 x 30 x 2. Room 1944, Standard Building.

524. INDEX TO BRIDGE PLANS AND TRACINGS
1895—. 4 drawers. (1900-1933, old system, 3 drawers; 1933—, new
system, 1 drawer).
The old system identified plans as to size of sheet (W, X, Y, and Z) as to type of
improvement (C for culvert, B for bridge, etc.), and then numerically. It lists letters,
number, reports number, and location. The new system list the number of the road,
the kind of work, report number, contract number, drawing number, and location.
Handwritten on printed forms. File box 6 x 4 x 13. Room 1944, Standard Building.

525. BRIDGE SURVEY BOOKS
1893—. 400 volumes.
Contain field notes for all improvements for which plans are prepared in the Bridge
Department. For index see number 526. Handwritten. Volumes average 200 pages.
7.5 x 5 x .5. Room 1944, Standard Building.

526. INDEX TO BRIDGE SURVEY BOOKS
1893—. 2 file drawers.

An alphabetical card index of roads, listing the kind of work, report number, the field book volume and page, location, and job number. File drawer 6 x 4 x 13. Room 1944, Standard Building.

527. FIELD ENGINEER'S REPORT CARDS
1934-1935. 5 file drawers.

A card record of all bridges and culverts in the county, showing location, type, material, size when built, and the condition of each at the time of inspection. A similar inspection was made in 1916. Filed alphabetically as to roads. Handwritten on printed forms. File drawer 13 x 6 x 4. Room 1944, Standard Building.

528. BRIDGE RECORD
1908—. 1 volume.

A record of contract work let by the bridge department, giving name of road, bridge number, report number, contract number, drawing number, description of work, location, and date of repair. Alphabetical as to names of roads. Handwritten. 700 pages. 21.5 x 13.5 x 1.5. Room 1944, Standard Building.

529. REPORT OF HIGHWAY BRIDGES
1896-1903. 2 volumes.

Reports made by the county surveyor on all iron and wood truss bridges in the county, giving name of township, kind of bridge, location of bridge, and date of completion. Arranged as to original townships. Typed. Volumes average 300 pages. 13 x 10.25 x 1. Room 1933, Standard Building.

530. PAID VOUCHERS
1917—. 10 file boxes.

Vouchers list name of road of township, report number, estimate number, to whom voucher was paid, name of inspector, contract number, and estimated cost. Filed numerically. Typed. Each file box 13.5 x 10.5 x 5. Room 1944, Standard Building.

531. BRIDGE DEPARTMENT FILES
1911-1915. 14 file boxes.

Bridge reports, contracts, and miscellaneous communications. Handwritten on printed forms and typed. File box 16 x 9 x 4. Fourth floor, County courthouse.

532. MAP OF CUYAHOGA COUNTY
1934. Shows cities and villages; county and state roads; number and location of the culverts and bridges on county roads. Lithographed, colored. 30 x 26. On the wall in Room 1944, Standard Building.

General Office Records

533. LEGISLATION FILE
1923—. 24 file drawers.
General correspondence and legislation pertaining to road improvements. Filed alphabetically. For index see number 534. Handwritten and typed. File drawer 28 x 14 x 11. Room 1904, Standard Building.

534. INDEX TO LEGISLATION FILE
1923—. 2 file cabinets (Cardex system).
Card index to general legislation and correspondence regarding road work. Handwritten and typed. Alphabetical by road name. Cabinet drawers 23 x 12 x 1.5. Room 1904, Standard Building.

535. GENERAL FILES
1933—. 2 file drawers.
Miscellaneous papers and reports pertaining to the activities, finances, and legal status of county engineering department; general correspondence, resolutions, transcripts of proceedings of commissioners and state highway department etc. Filed by subject. Handwritten, typed, and photostats. File drawer 28 x 12 x 10.5. Room 1918, Standard Building.

536. CIVIL SERVICE CLASSIFIED POSITIONS
1935. Approximately 300 folders in 1 file drawer.
Record of civil service personnel in engineer's department. Alphabetical by classified positions. Typed on printed forms. Drawer 10.5 x 12 x 28. Room 1918, Standard Building.

537. MISCELLANEOUS FILE
1927-1932. 11 file drawer.
Certified resolutions of auditor pertaining to funds expended on road improvements, receipts for requisitions, and reports of the Cuyahoga Abstract Title Company. File

drawer 10.5 x 12 x 28. Room 1918, Standard Building.

538. PERSONNEL RECORD
1910—. 1 steel file cabinet.

A card record of the personnel of the county engineer's department excepting laborers. Shows the date of appointment; effective day of layoff; title of position; rate of pay; organization unit; name of department head; date appointment was approved by the civil service commission; and the type of appointment. Arranged alphabetically as to names of employees. Cabinet 16 x 10.5 x 23.5. Room 1918, Standard Building.

539. GENERAL CORRESPONDENCE
1934—. 4 file drawers.

Files contain reports of the County Charter Commission, Cleveland Engineering Society, Cleveland Road Builders' Association, and the Ohio Council for Roadside Improvements. Also contains correspondence, applications, appointments, and construction reports of a general character pertaining to business of the department. Road correspondence is arranged alphabetically as to road names; the other correspondence and reports are arranged as to subjects. Typed, Handwritten and printed. File drawer 15 x 10 x 26. Room 1926, Standard Building.

540. COPIES OF DEEDS
9 file boxes.

Copies of deeds used in the preparation of tax maps. Handwritten and typed. Each file box 5 x 10 x 14. Room 1904, Standard Building.

541. MAP OF CUYAHOGA COUNTY
1933. 1 map.

Shows road numbers and road sections, U.S. highway numbers, railroads, villages, and townships. Scale, 1 inch to the mile. Map 34 x 26. On wall, engineer's office, 19th floor, Standard Building.

542. MAP OF CUYAHOGA COUNTY
Shows city, township and village boundary lines; highways; main streets; route numbers. The kind of paving and service covering of roads is also indicated. Lithographed. Colored. Framed. 62 x 48. On wall, engineer's office, 19th floor, Standard Building.

The office of clerk had its inception in England before the Norman Conquest. The appointment of clerks was the judges' patronage, and was regarded as a property right. Each writ was issued by a different clerk, all of whom were compensated by fees. (Holdsworth, *op. cit.,* I, 19, 403-441).

The ordinance of 1787 for the Northwest Territory authorized the judges of the common pleas court to appoint a clerk of court to serve indefinitely subject to good behavior. (Chase, *Statutes of Ohio*, I, 66).

The Ohio Constitution of 1802 creating the Supreme Court and the court of common pleas, provided for the appointment of a clerk of courts for the respective courts, to be chosen by the judges thereof for a term of seven years. After the clerk had qualified, he was removable doing his term only for a breach of good behavior. (Ohio Const., Art. 3, sec. 9).

The first general assembly, that of 1803, authorized the clerk to issue all writs and process of the court of common pleas and select jurors from names of electors submitted to him by the trustees of each township. It also provided that he be commissioned to take bail and administer oaths. He was required to give bond and take oath and was paid by way of fees collected in his office. In addition he had to perform certain duties regarding elections. He received one of the poll books thereof, opened the returns with the assistance of one or two judges, or justice of the peace, and made two abstracts of the votes. (10 O. L. 44-47). This was changed to four abstracts in 1852. (50 O. L. 311-325).

Inasmuch as the lower court did not at that time try capital offenses unless the accused so desired, it was the further duty of the clerk by an act of 1807 to deliver to the clerk of the supreme court a certified copy of each indictment charging such an offense. He also had to issue executions of the latter court's judgments to the sheriff, returnable to the next court of common pleas. (5 O. L. 98-103).

A bill carried In 1810 empowered him to issue marriage licenses. (8 O. L. 121). An act of 1816 authorized him to take bonds on writs of error. (14 O. L. 218). Various bills passed in 1823 added to his duties. He was required to keep a trial and execution docket (22 O. L. 68), take depositions (22 O. L. 51), issue subpoenas for witnesses (22 O. L. 52), make up and post list of stray animals (22 O. L. 346), and grant licenses to tavern keepers, peddlers, ferry operators (22 O. L. 377-381), and auctioneers. (22 O. L. 424). He was also empowered to appoint a deputy. (22 O. L. 47).

By the provisions of the Ohio Constitution of 1851, the office of clerk of common pleas court was made an elected one for term of three years, and the incumbent thereof was made the clerk of all other courts of record held in the county. By re-creating the probate court it also abolished the clerk's duties of issuing marriage licenses. (Art. 4 sec. 16; Art. 4, sec. 7-8).

The next year bills were passed which provided that the transcripts of judgments from justice of peace courts be filed with the clerk, that he accept payments of all judgments and make disbursements of the money in is custody to the proper persons. (50 O. L. 222; 50 O. L. 21).

In 1853 he was given the duty of keeping an accurate record of the business and proceedings of both the civil and criminal branches of the court, posting all documents received by him in the court docket, recording all entries, material acts, and proceedings made in various courtrooms in the court journal, endorsing the date of filing on each petition, answer, summons, return, pleadings subsequent thereto, records, verdicts, orders, judgment and all docket and journal entries. He was required to keep at least five books to be called appearance docket, trial docket and printed duplicate thereof, journal, record and the execution docket together with indexes or them. It was also specified that he keep an alphabetical index, direct and inverse, of the plaintiffs' and defendants' names distinctively numbering each case. (51 O. L. 57; O. L. 158; 51 O. L. 159).

In 1858 the duty of recording notary commissions was given to him. (55 O. L. 13). In 1859 he was empowered to tax and collect all court costs and receive deposits. (56 O. L. 21). In 1861 he was authorized to appoint sufficient deputies, subject to the approval of the court, to assist him in the conduct of his office. (58 O. L. 13). In 1867 the recording of special police commissions was placed in his hands. In 1886, the city board of elections was created, the clerk of courts was relieved of the duty of abstracting the votes cast in the general elections. In 1892, after the setting up of a county board of elections, the clerk received one poll book which he was required to preserve for one year for public inspection. (89 O. L. 430). In 1894 his recording duties were extended to include partnership agreements. (91 O. L. 357).

In 1905 the constitution was amended by a provision that the term of all elective county officers be for an even number of years not exceeding four. Therefore, the General Assembly of 1906 fixed the clerk's term at two years. In the same session his prerequisite of being compensated exclusively by fees was abolished and it was provided that he received a salary in proportion to the population of his county. In 1906 a federal statute was enacted which extended the power of naturalization to all state courts of record. This caused a department of naturalization to be set up in the clerk's office for the purpose of keeping the necessary records and the giving of information thereto upon order or decree of court. (Ohio Const., Art. 17, sec. 2; 98 O. L. 273; 98 O. L. 117; 34 Fed. Stat. 596).

In 1911 the clerk was given the duty of recording trade marks. (102 O. L. 512). A measure was adopted in 1921 which provided for the compulsory filing with the clerk of courts in the county where the sale of a motor vehicle is consummated, of a copy of the bill of sale, within three days after such transfer of title. (109 O. L. 330-334).

A bill was carried in 1931 which stipulated that the clerk verify the names of jurors drawn from the jury wheel, prepare a list in the order in which they are drawn for submission to the jury commission, and pay the jurors. (114 O. L. 199-200).

A measure was enacted in 1935 which specifies that in order for a judgment or decree of court to operate as a lien on real estate located in the state, there must be filed with clerk of the court of common pleas a certificate of such judgment or decree, which shall be recorded by the clerk in a book kept by him for that purpose. (116 O. L. 273-278).

An act carried in 1936 provided that the clerk's term of office be four years. (116 O. L. pt. 21st special session H. 603).

A clerk of courts, popularly known as the county clerk, is the ministerial officer of court, who has charge of the clerical part of its business, with power to certify the correctness of its transcripts and other records. In Cuyahoga County he has supervision of the records of the court of common pleas and of the court of appeals, as well as other duties which have been given him by statute. The records of defunct courts are also in his custody.

COURT OF COMMON PLEAS

The year 1187 marked the creation of the common pleas court in England when King Henry II selected five men, two clerks and three laymen, all members of his household, whom he authorized to hear and adjudicate all suits of the realm. However, the provision was made that should any question arise which they could not solve, it should be reserved for the King's hearing, where it would be settled by him and the wiser men of the realm. (Holdsworth, *op. cit.,* I, 3).

Following this precedent in the Northwest Territory a law of 1788 provided that a number of suitable persons not exceeding five, nor less than three, shall be appointed and commissioned by the governor, under the seal of the territory, to hold and keep a court of record, to be styled by the County Court of Common Pleas. The persons appointed were commissioned during good behavior and had jurisdiction in all civil and criminal matters extending over the whole of the Northwest Territory. The court thus constituted was fixed at no certain place, and its process, civil and criminal, was returnable wheresoever it might be in the territory. (Pease, *op. cit.,* 7).

The Ohio Constitution of 1802 provided for a court of common pleas of general original jurisdiction in each county in Ohio. (Ohio Const., Art. 3, sec. 3). No jurisdiction was conferred upon this court in civil or criminal cases, but merely being given the capacity to receive jurisdiction which was to be fixed by law. (Ohio Cont., Art. 3, sec. 4). It did, however, give the court jurisdiction in probate and testamentary matters. (Ohio Const., Art. 3, sec. 5). The court was also given jurisdiction on appeal from decision of the county commissioners, justices of peace, and other inferior courts in all civil cases. (Ohio Const., Art. 3, sec. 6). It also prescribed that the court was to consist of a president and three associate judges, that they were to be chosen by a joint ballot of both houses of the General Assembly and were to hold office for a term of seven years. (Ohio Const., Art. 3, sec. 8). The judges so chosen were authorized to appoint a clerk of courts. (Ohio Const., Art 3, sec. 9).

By enactment in 1803, jurisdiction was conferred on the court of common pleas in all civil cases, both in law and equity, where the matter in dispute exceeded the jurisdiction of the justice of the peace, and in all criminal cases, except in cases of capital punishment. (1 O. L. 40).

In the same year, a bill was carried authorizing the court to appoint a county prosecutor, who was to be paid by fees. (1 O. L. 50). In 1824 the Chancery Act conferred general chancery powers on the court. (22 O. L. 75).

In 1833 a bill was passed taking away from the court the power to appoint the county prosecutor and the office was made elective. (31 O. L. 13). The constitution of 1851 made many significant changes. For the purpose of electing judges the state was divided into nine districts. Each district in turn was to be subdivided into three or more counties, in each of which one common pleas judge was to be elected. (Ohio Const., Art. 4, sec. 3, 4). The same article took the probate and testamentary jurisdictions away from the court and invested such jurisdiction in the recreated probate court. (Ohio Const., Art. 4, sec. 7, 8). The office of judge of common pleas court was made elective for a term of five years. (Ohio Const., Art. 4, sec. 12). On March 14, 1853, jurisdiction in criminal cases was given to the Supreme Court and the court of common pleas. (51 O. L. 475). In 1906 a statute was enacted changing the term of office to six years. (98 O. L. 119).

A bill was voted in 1915 establishing a jury commission in each county, which was to be appointed by the court. (106 O. L. 106). A Jury Code was adopted in 1931 providing for a permanent jury commission. (114 O. L. 213). In 1917 a bill was passed making it necessary for a common pleas judge to be an attorney who shall have been admitted to practice for a period of six years preceding his election. (107 O. L. 164). The bureau of domestic relations was created in 1923 by virtue of an enactment authorizing the chief justice of common pleas court to classify and distribute the business of the court. (110 O. L. 52).

The office of chief justice of the court of common pleas is based on an act of March 13, 1923. This act provided that in each county having two or more common pleas judges the judges may designate one of their number as chief justice, to continue as such until the end of his term, after which time the office was to be elective. (109 O. L. 230). By an act of 1925 the judges of the court of common pleas were authorized to establish a county department of probation. Such department to consist of a chief probation officer, and such assistance as may be fixed by the judges. (111 O. L. 423). An amendment of February 15, 1927 eliminated the elective feature of the office of chief justice, following the decision of the Supreme Court of February 12, 1924, declaring the creation of such a new elective office unconstitutional. The chief justice has general superintendence of the business of the court, classifying and distributing it among the judges, and fixing vacations of the judges. In January of each year, he files a complete annual report with the clerk of the court covering the preceding calendar year, showing the work performed by the court and by each of the judges thereof, and such other data as the chief justice of the Supreme Court shall require. (113 O. L. 467).

By the same act the judges of the court of common pleas in counties having a population in excess of 300,000 were authorized to appoint one or more psychiatrists, psychologists or other examiners or investigators, whose duty it was to inquire into the mental condition of a person convicted of a felony. (113 O. L. 467).

An act of 1931 provided that the judges of the court of common pleas of any county having two or more judges may appoint assignment commissioners to attend the assignment of all cases for trial and to discharge such other duties as the court may require. (114 O. L. 212). The tremendous increase in the number of cases heard and the ever-changing character of civil and criminal offenses makes the history of this court an interesting reflection of our social and economic development.

Civil Branch

Preliminary Court Records (Not kept by the Clerk of Courts)

543. CASE CARDS
1931—. Approximately 25,000 cards in 125 file boxes.
A record of all pending cases. Each card lists the number and classification of the case; the names of plaintiffs, defendants, and attorneys; and the history of the case from the filing date to its final disposition. Filed numerically. Handwritten on printed forms. File box 4.5 x 13.5 x 11. All jury cases are filed in 50 file boxes in the assignment room, third floor; all cases not triable by jury, in 75 file boxes. Room 259, County courthouse.

544. ASSIGNMENT ROOM TICKLERS
September 1900—. 77 volumes.
List name of plaintiffs and defendants, dates of hearings, courtroom number, docket number, case number, and verdict rendered in the case. In order of case numbers. Handwritten and typed on printed forms. Volumes average 200 pages. 1901-1923, 63 volumes, 15 x 9 x 1.25, second floor, Hart Building; 1923—, 10 volumes, 15 x 12 x 3.5, assignment room, third floor, County courthouse.

545. COURTROOM CALENDARS
January 1873—. 1821 volumes.
List names of plaintiffs and defendants, lawyers representing each, cause of action, case number, disposition of case, and date. In chronological order. Handwritten. Volumes average 200 pages. 16 x 11 x .5. 1873-1931, 1549 volumes, second floor, Hart Building; 1931-1936, 272 volumes, assignment room, third floor, County courthouse. The current calendars are in the individual courtrooms.

546. CALENDAR, SETTLEMENT COURT, COURTROOM 8
1931—. 38 volumes.

A list of causes prepared by the clerk of courts, showing title of each cause, nature of the action, date of issue, names of attorneys, case number, and final entry. In chronological order as to terms of court. For index see number 547. Handwritten. Volumes average 200 pages. 18 x 12 x .5. 1931-1935 and January term, 1936, assignment room, third floor; May term, 1936, courtroom 8, County courthouse.

547. INDEX TO CALENDAR, SETTLEMENT COURT
1931—. Approximately 1000 cards in 1 file box.

An alphabetical card index of plaintiffs and defendants, showing the court clerk's notations on the whether passed, settled, or returned to the assignment room for trial. Handwritten. File box 24 x 5 x 8. Room 8, County courthouse.

548. TRIAL DOCKET
1900—. 175 volumes.

A list of all cases pending at the beginning of the court term, and all cases filed subsequent thereto. Shows number of the case, actions taken by the court, names of plaintiffs and defendants, and classification of case. In order of case number. Handwritten and handwritten on printed forms. Volumes average 1,000 pages. 17 x 13 x 4.5. 1900-1910, dockets 13-44, sub-basement; 1910-1917, dockets 46-64, attic storeroom, fourth floor; 1917-1933, 82 volumes, Room 34; 1933—, 25 volumes, Room 359, County courthouse.

549. SPECIAL DOCKET
November 1855—. 49 volumes, 1-49.

Contains entries made subsequent to the disposition of the original case. Lists name of plaintiff and defendant, case number, docket number, cause of action, and disposition of case. Alphabetical index of plaintiffs and defendants in each volume. Handwritten. Volumes average 400 pages. 14.5 x 11 x 2. 1855-1923, 36 volumes, second floor, Hart Building; 1923-1925, 5 volumes, Room 34; 1930—, 8 volumes, Room 259, County courthouse.

550. RECEIVERSHIP DOCKET
1921—. 13 volumes, 1-13.
Lists case number, names of plaintiffs and defendants, and final reports of the court including date of decision. In order of case numbers. Contains an alphabetical index of plaintiffs. Handwritten and typed on printed forms. Volumes average 400 pages. 15 x 12.5 x 3.5. 1921-1932, 8 volumes, Room 34; 1932—, 5 volumes, Room 259, County courthouse.

551. MOTION AND DEMURRER DOCKET
1874—. 148 volumes, 1-148.
Contains motions and *demurrers* pertaining to pleadings previously filed. Lists name of plaintiff and defendant, case number, appearance docket number, cause of action, and disposition of case. In chronological order. Alphabetical index of plaintiffs and defendants in each volume. 1874-1922, handwritten; 1922—, typed. Volumes 1-105 average 400 pages. 14 x 9 x 2; volumes 106-148 average 600 pages. 14.5 x 12.5 x 3.5. 1874-1929, 129 volumes, 1-129, second floor, Hart Building; 1929-1931, 12 volumes, 130-141, Room 34; 1931—, 7 volumes, 142-148, Room 254, County courthouse.

552. ORDERS OF SALE
1932—. 4 volumes.
Lists names of plaintiffs and defendants, the case number, and the order of confirmation of sale to the purchaser. Typed on printed forms. In order of case numbers. Volumes average 700 pages. 14 x 8.5 x 1.5. Room 259, County courthouse.

553. CARD INDEX TO PENDING AND DISPOSED-OF RECEIVERSHIPS
1924—. 15 file drawers.
Each card lists number of case, classification of case, date, names of plaintiffs and defendants, names of receivers and attorneys, amount of bond, date report was filed, objections, when approved, fees of receiver, fees of attorney, amount of collections, expenses, and balance. Filed numerically. File box 8.5 x 16 x 6. Room 259, County courthouse.

General Records

554. ANNUAL REPORT OF HONORABLE HOMER G. POWELL, CHIEF JUSTICE, COURT OF COMMON PLEAS
1924, 1925, 1926, 1928, 1930, 1931, 1936. 7 reports.

Annual statistical reports of the following departments of the common pleas court; civil and criminal assignment rooms, criminal records department, domestic relations division, grand jury, jury commission, probation division, and psychiatric clinic. The reports also contain summaries of the work of the judges of the common pleas court. The 1936 volume contains an alphabetical index of names of bureaus. Assignment at room, third floor, County courthouse.

555. COMMON PLEAS JOURNAL
1810—. 366 volumes, A-Z, 26-277.

Contains entries of all courts proceedings in the civil branch of common pleas court. Each entry list the case number. In chronological order. 1810-1906, handwritten; 1907—, typed. Volumes average 300 pages. Volumes A-Z, 13.25 x 8.5 x 2.5; volumes 27-277, 16 x 12.5 x 3.5. Volumes A-Z, 27-265, Room 34; volumes 266-277, Room 254, County courthouse.

556. COMMON PLEAS RECORD
February 1810—. 1557 volumes, 1-1557.

A complete record of all cases in the civil and criminal branches of the court of common pleas. Shows names of plaintiffs and defendants, case number, execution docket number, petitions, and answers, various exhibits, journal entries, term of court, amount involved, and disposition of the case. In order of case numbers. Each volume contains an alphabetical index of plaintiffs and defendants. Volumes from 1810-1882 combine civil and criminal cases. From 1883—, civil and criminal cases are entered in separate volumes. 1810-1897 handwritten; 1897—, typed. Volumes average 640 pages. 18.75 x 12.75 x 3.75. 499 volumes, second floor, Hart Building; 1031 volumes, 500-1530, Room 71; 27 volumes, 1531-1557, Room 354, County courthouse.

557. EXECUTION AND LEVY DOCKET
August 1848—. 93 volumes, 1-93.

Lists name of plaintiff and defendant, case number, appearance docket number, amount of sheriff's fee, and date on which judgment was ordered effective. In order of case numbers. 1848-1913, handwritten; September 1913—, typed. Volumes average 600 pages. 17.5 x 12 x 3. 87 volumes, Room 34; 6 volumes, Room 254, County courthouse.

558. EXECUTION DOCKET
1810—. 140 volumes, 1-140.

Contains transcripts from other courts and list name of plaintiff and defendant, cost assessed to plaintiff or defendant, statement of proceedings, and case number. For index see number 559. Handwritten. Volumes average 650 pages. 18 x 12.75 x 3.5. 126 volumes, 1-126, Room 34; 14 volumes, 127-140, Room 254, County courthouse.

559. INDEX TO PENDING SUITS AND LIVING JUDGMENTS AND EXECUTIONS
1890—. 55 volumes, 1-55.

An alphabetical index of all parties to suits filed in common pleas court. Lists case numbers, and execution docket number and page. Banks and corporations are separately indexed. From 1922—, there are separate indexes for each six months period. Prior to that time each index covered one or more years. Handwritten. Volumes average 200 pages. 18 x 12 x 2. Volumes 1-24, Room 34; Volumes 25-55, Room 254, County courthouse.

560. CIVIL APPEARANCE AND EXECUTION DOCKET
November 1810—. 864 volumes (1810-1932, 742 volumes, 1-742; 1932—, 122 volumes, 373B-435B).

Lists name of plaintiff and defendant, names of attorneys, statement of proceedings, date summons is returnable, date of answer, and date on which petition on transcript is due. In order of case numbers. For index see number 561. Handwritten, typed, and handwritten on printed forms. Volumes average 552 pages. 18 x 12.5 x 2.25. Volumes 1-130, Room 34; volumes 373B-435B, 391-742, Room 254, County courthouse.

561. GENERAL INDEX - APPEARANCE DOCKET
1810—. 40 volumes, 1-40.

An alphabetical index of plaintiffs and defendants, listing case number and appearance docket number. Handwritten. Volumes average 520 pages. 18.25 x 12.5 x 2.75. Room 254, County courthouse.

562. INDEX TO PENDING CASES
May 1861—. 44 volumes, 3-46. (Missing, volumes 1-2).

An alphabetical index of plaintiffs and defendants in all pending cases in the civil branch of the common pleas court, listing docket number and case number. An alphabetical index for each year. Handwritten. Volumes average 780 pages. 14 x 10 x 4. 33 volumes, second floor, Hart Building; 11 volumes, Room 254, County courthouse.

563. JUDGMENT LIEN DOCKET
1935—. 5 volumes, 1-5.

Record of liens on judgment, showing name of property owner, location of property, date of original filing, date of judgment, filing date of lien, and amount of lien. Alphabetical index of plaintiffs and defendants, arranged chronologically as to date of filing of judgment liens. For separate index see number 564. Typed on printed forms. Volumes average 400 pages. 15 x 12 x 3. Room 254, County courthouse.

564. GENERAL INDEX TO JUDGMENT DOCKET
4 volumes, A-Z.

Alphabetical index of persons against whom there are judgments. Lists names of creditor and debtor, and volume and page of judgment lien docket. Handwritten on printed forms. Average 400 pages. 15 x 12 x 3. Room 254, County courthouse.

565. COPY ORDER BOOK
1855—. 183 volumes.

Contains orders for copies of journal entries and other court records. In chronological order. Handwritten on printed forms. Volumes average 200 pages. 11 x 8 x .5. 1855-1928, 122 volumes, second floor, Hart Building; 1929-1932, 26 volumes, Room 34; 1927, 1 volume, attic storeroom, fourth floor; 1932—, 34 volumes, Room 254, County courthouse.

566. *PRECIPE* BOOK
1856—. 32 volumes

Lists date the sale is ordered, number and classification of case, and names of attorneys. Executions and orders of sale are now separated. Handwritten. Volumes average 440 pages. 14 x 9 x 2. 1856-1922, 21 volume, second floor, Hart Building; 1923-1929, 6 volumes, Room 71; 1930—, 5 volumes, Room 254, County courthouse.

567. LAND DOCKET
1914—. 2 volumes

Lists all action pertaining to torrenized property. Shows name of plaintiffs and defendants, dates of filing pleadings, and file number of each case. Typed on printed forms. Volumes average 500 pages. 18 x 13 x 3. Room 254, County courthouse.

568. RELEASE ORDERS
1929—. 9 volumes

A record showing name of plaintiff and defendant, case number, date of issue, and copy of the order for release. In chronological order. Handwritten. Volumes average 600 pages. 18 x 12.5 x 3. Room 254, County courthouse.

569. COMMON PLEAS LIEN DOCKET
1856-1881. 4 volumes, 1-4.

Lists name of plaintiff and defendant, names of attorneys, case number, and statement of proceedings in each case. Transcripts to liens filed before and after the period covered by above dockets are in the civil execution docket. Chronological order. Alphabetical index of plaintiffs and defendants in each volume. Handwritten, Volumes average 600 pages. 18 x 13.25 x 2. Room 34, County courthouse.

570. COMMON PLEAS COURT DOCKET
1850-1881. 10 volumes.

Lists docket number, case number, name of plaintiff and defendant, cause of action, and disposition of the case. In order of case numbers. Handwritten. Volumes average 300 pages. 14 x 9.25 x 1.75. 1850-1875, 7 volumes, second floor, Hart Building; 1873-1881, 3 volumes, Room 34, County courthouse.

571. INDEX TO EXECUTION DOCKETS
7 volumes, 1-4.

An alphabetical index of plaintiffs and defendants, listing case number and cause of action. Handwritten. Volumes average 400 pages. 16.5 x 11.75 x 2. Room 34, County courthouse.

Files and Special Appointments

572. COMMON PLEAS FILES
1810——. 1665 bundles; 13,247 file boxes. (1-450,000).

Contains petitions, answers, motions, *demurrers*, and all other pleadings filed in the case. In order of case numbers. Bundle and file box, each 13.5 x 4.5 x 11. 1810-1865, 1665 bundles, second floor, Hart Building; 1866-1927, 4950 file boxes, Room 34; 1928-1936, 6622 file boxes, Room 28 ; 1928——, 1575 file boxes, Room 254; 100 file boxes, assignment room, third floor, County courthouse.

573. BILLS OF EXCEPTION
1810——. 127 bins; 22 file boxes.

Written narratives of testimony in all cases appealed from the court of common pleas. Until 1888 filed as pleadings in the case files. From 1888— filed as separate transcripts. Lists name of plaintiff and defendant, case number, date filed, names of attorneys, judge, and witnesses, the court's charge to the jury, testimony in the case, and mandate of the court hearing the charge. In order of case numbers. Handwritten and typed. Occasionally includes an index of witnesses. Each bin 36 x 27 x 10; file box 20 x 30 x 8. 1888-1920 114 bins, second floor, Hart Building; 1920——, 13 bins, Room 71; 22 final boxes, active cases, Room 254, County courthouse.

574. DEPOSITIONS
1836——. 41 bins; 8 file drawers.

Transcripts of evidence presented to the court by absentee witnesses. Handwritten and typed. In order of case numbers. Each bin 36 x 27 x 10; each file drawer 25 x 13 x 5.5. 1836-1911, 17 bins, second floor, Hart Building; 1911-1934, 24 bins, Room 71; 1934——, 8 file drawers, Room 254, County courthouse.

575. RELEASES AND ASSIGNMENTS
1923——. 31 file boxes.

Releases of liens and judgments, and assignments of judgments from one party to another. In order of case numbers. 1923——, 30 file boxes, Room 34; current file, 1 file box, Room 254, County courthouse.

576. SPECIAL DOCKET FILES
February 1868—. 374 file boxes.
Executions and other pleadings filed after the case has been disposed. In order of
case numbers. 1868-1926, 192 file boxes, Room 34; 1926-1936, 176 file boxes,
Room 28; 1936—, 6 file boxes, Room 254, County courthouse.

577. INDUSTRIAL COMMISSION TRANSCRIPTS
1911—. 2 final drawers; 9 bins.
Transcripts of evidence gathered by the State Industrial Commission prior to the
filing of the case in the common pleas court. Arranged in order of case numbers.
Handwritten and typed. Each file drawer 24 x 22 x 12; each bin 36 x 27 x 10. 1911-
1930, 3 bins, second floor, Hart Building; 1930—, 6 bins, Room 71; 1931—, 2 file
drawers, Room 254, County courthouse.

578. CIVIL BONDS
1810—. 149 file boxes.
Receivers' bonds, injunction bonds, attachment bonds, trustees' bonds, etc., filed
with civil cases. In order of case numbers. Handwritten and typed on printed forms.
Each file box 12 x 6 x 18. 1810-1899, 15 file boxes, second floor, Hart Building;
1899-1929, 105 file boxes, Room 34; 1929—, 29 file boxes in bond safe in Room
254, County courthouse.

579. PARTNERSHIPS AND FICTITIOUS NAMES
1894—. 9 file drawers.
Registration of fictitious names and partnerships filed with the clerk of courts. Filed
chronologically. For index see number 580. Each file drawer 13.5 x 4.5 x 11.
1894—, 7 file drawers, Room 34; 2 file drawers, Room 254, County courthouse.

580. INDEX TO REGISTER OF PARTNERSHIPS
1894—. 3 volumes.
An alphabetical index of partners and companies, listing their residence, the filing
date, and the certificate number. Handwritten on printed forms. Volumes average
500 pages. 19 x 12 x 4. Room 254, County courthouse.

581. MARKS OF OWNERSHIP
August 1915——. 2 file boxes.

Registration of trade names. For index see number 582. Each file box 13.5 x 4.5 x 11. Room 254, County courthouse.

582. INDEX TO MARKS OF OWNERSHIP
1915——. 1 volume.

An alphabetical index listing the name of the company, the city or town, the date of filing, and the certificate number. 150 pages. 9 x 14 x 1. Room 254, County courthouse.

583. AUCTIONEER APPLICATIONS
July 1914——. 1 file box.

Applications for license to auctioneer in the State of Ohio. For index see number 584. File box 13.5 x 4.5 x 11. Room 254, County courthouse.

584. INDEX TO AUCTIONEER'S APPLICATIONS
1900——. 1 volume.

An alphabetical index listing the name of the auctioneer, his address, date qualified, expiration date, and certificate number. 250 pages. 8 x 13.5 x .5. Room 254, County courthouse.

585. PRELIMINARY LETTERS OF APPRAISAL
1921-1931. Approximately 3000 in 2 file boxes.

Abstracts of the property involved in foreclosure actions. Filed as to case numbers. Each file box 13.5 x 4.5 x 11. Second floor, Hart Building. After 1931 they are filed with the pleadings in the case files.

586. OATHS OF OFFICE
1924——. 4 file boxes.

Copies of oaths administered to office-holders in the county courts. Filed chronologically. Each file box 13.5 x 4.5 x 11. 2 file boxes, Room 28; 2 file boxes, Room 254, County courthouse.

587. SPECIAL POLICE BONDS
1900—. 10 file boxes.
Bonds for special police and watchmen for banks and railroads. For indexes see numbers 588 and 589. Handwritten and typed on printed forms. Each file box 13.5 x 4.5 x 11. 1900-1931, 6 file boxes, Room 34; 1932—, 4 file boxes, county clerk's office, Room 254, County courthouse.

588. POLICE RECORD
1900—. 9 volumes
A record of special police commissions. An alphabetical index in each volume. Typed on printed forms. Volumes average 270 pages. Room 254, County courthouse.

589. INDEX OF SPECIAL POLICE BONDS
December 1904- January 1921. 1 volume.
An alphabetical index of special policeman, listing dates on which bond was approved and cancelled. Handwritten on printed forms. 300 pages. 10 x 8.25 x .75. Room 71, County courthouse.

590. RECORD OF APPOINTMENTS
1876-1930. 7 volumes, 1-7.
Lists appointments, name of auctioneer, commissioner's office, names of railroad police, miscellaneous appointments, and names of special police commissioned by the governor. In chronological order. Handwritten on printed forms. Volumes average 350 pages. 18.5 x 13.5 x 2. Room 34, County courthouse.

591. OFFICIAL REGISTER OF ATTORNEYS
1882—. 1 volume.
An alphabetical index of attorneys, listing the attorney's name, address, telephone number, and date of certificate, and by whom issued. In chronological order under each letter. Records previous to 1900 in back part of book. Handwritten on printed forms. 400 pages. 17 x 10 x 3. Room 254, County courthouse.

Cashier's Records

592. CASH BOOKS (Incoming Receipts)
April 1898—. 63 volumes

List date of entry, case number, names of plaintiff and defendants, cause of action, and amount paid. In chronological order. Handwritten. Volumes average 400 pages. 24 x 18 x 3. 1890-1928, 25 volumes, Room 34; 1929—, 25 volumes, Room 254, County courthouse.

593. CASHIER'S RECEIPTS
1856—. 261 volumes.

List name of payer, case number and amount paid. In order of receipt numbers. Handwritten on printed forms. Volumes average 200 pages. 11 x 8 x .5. 1856-1924, 35 volumes, second floor, Hart Building; 1925-1930, 96 volumes, Room 34; 1930-1933, 115 volumes, Room 71; 1936—, 15 volumes, Room 254, County courthouse.

594. DISBURSEMENT BOOK
1910—. 30 volumes.

List all checks drawn, name of payee, title of the case, case number, and cash book number. Handwritten on printed forms. In chronological order. Volumes 1-25, Room 34; volumes 26-30, Room 254, County courthouse.

595. BANK STATEMENTS
1929—. 8 bundles.

Monthly bank statements, such as alimony accounts, general fund and notary accounts, showing checks issued, deposits, and balances. In chronological order. Each bundle 12 x 4 x 4. 1929-1932, 8 bundles, Room 71; current statements in safe, cashier's window, Room 254, County courthouse.

596. CASHIER'S CHECKBOOK STUBS
1925—. 299 books.

List check number, name of party issued to, case number, cash book number, and amount for which drawn. In order of check numbers. Handwritten on printed forms. Volumes average 200 pages. 16 x 5.5 x .75. 1925-1930, 167 books, Room 34; 1930-1935, 97 books, Room 71; 1936—, 35 books, Room 254, County courthouse.

597. CHECK STUBS

1930-1932. Approximately 100,000 in 2 bins.

Show docket number, number in cash book, name of payee, and amount. In chronological order. Typed on printed forms. Each bin 7 x 14 x .75. Room 71, County courthouse.

598. CANCELLED CHECKS

1913—. 89 bundles; 285 file boxes.

In order of check numbers. Handwritten on printed forms. 89 bundles 13.5 x 10.5 x 4.75, second floor, Building; 260 file boxes, 15 x 10.5 x 5. Room 71; January 1935—, 25 file boxes, Room 254, County courthouse.

599. LIST OF UNCLAIMED MONIES, FEES, ETC., PAID TO THE COUNTY TREASURER

1890—. 5 volumes.

A record of unclaimed money. A duplicate is filed with a county auditor. Lists name of party to whom money is due, amount, check or case number, date of payment, and warrant number. Contains an alphabetical index. Handwritten on printed forms. 1890-1917, 2 volumes, Room 71; 1918—, 3 volumes, Room 254, County courthouse.

600. UNCLAIMED FEE WARRANTS

1931—. 1 volume.

Warrants for unclaimed money turned in to county auditor. In order of voucher numbers. Handwritten on printed forms. 150 pages. 12 x 9 x 2. Room 254, County courthouse.

601. NOTARY CHECK STUBS

1923—. 215 volumes.

List check number, name of party issued to, certificate number, cash book number, amount of check, and date of issue. In order of check numbers. Handwritten on printed forms. Volumes average 400 pages. 16 x 5.5 x 1. 1923-1930, 118 volumes, Room 34; 1930-1935, 85 volumes, Room 71; 1936—, 12 volumes, Room 254, County courthouse.

602. WITNESS FEE BOOK
1930—. 26 volumes.

A record giving name and address of witness, number of days served, case number, and amount of fees paid. Each volume arranged alphabetically as to witnesses. Handwritten on printed forms. Volumes average 250 pages. 17.5 x 13.5 x 2. 25 volumes, Room 34; 1 volume, Room 254, County courthouse.

603. MISCELLANEOUS RECEIPTS
1897—. 145 volumes.

Journals recording the daily cash receipts of the office of the clerk of courts, and listing name of payee, case number, reason for payment, and amount of payment. In order of receipt numbers. Handwritten on printed forms. Volumes average 400 pages. 8.5 x 11 x .75. 1897-1928, 50 volumes, Room 34; 1910-1911, 5 volumes, attic storeroom, fourth floor; 1929-1932, 86 volumes, Room 71; 1932—, 4 volumes, Room 254, County courthouse.

604. CORRESPONDENCE PERTAINING TO COST OF CASES
1927—. 2 file boxes.

Letters received and answered by the clerk of courts. Most refer to cases on which cost remain unpaid. Arranged alphabetically to correspondence. Typed. Each file box 11.5 x 12 x 3. 1927-1932, 1 file box, Room 71; 1932—, 1 file box, Room 254, County courthouse.

605. FEES DUE EX-CLERKS, EX-SHERIFF'S, AND FORMER CORONERS
1884-1897. 7 volumes.

List date of entry; volume and page of record; names of parties from whom fees are due; names of ex-sheriff's, ex-clerks, and former coroners. In chronological order. Handwritten on printed forms. Volumes average 250 pages. 17 x 12 x 1.5. Second floor, Hart Building.

606. PAYROLLS
1924—. 4 loose-leaf volumes.

Lists name of employee, position held, amount of salary, and date of payment. In chronological order. Typed on printed forms. Volumes average 200 pages. 15 x 9 x 1. 1924-1930, 3 volumes, Room 71; 1930—, 1 volume, Room 254, County courthouse.

607. FEE BOOK

February 20, 1856- February 8, 1861. 1 volume.

A record of fees collected and paid by the clerk to authorize agents appointed by business concerns and individual persons, showing date and amount of fees collected, docket volume and page, names of parties involved, and name of authorized agent. Chronological. Handwritten. 500 pages. 16 x 10 x 1. Second floor, Hart Building.

608. CLERK"S RECORD OF ACCRUED FEES

September 1914- April 1917. 3 volumes, 1-3.

Lists case number, cause of action, party to whom charged, total cost incurred, cost to each party in case, civil or criminal causes, amount due from county, cost of transcripts and copies, cost of certificates, sundry cost, amount paid, line and page number in cash book, and date of payment. In chronological order. Handwritten on printed forms. Average 500 pages. 18.5 x 18 x 2.5. Second floor, Hart Building.

609. CLEVELAND FEES RECORD, RECEIVED BY CLERK, JOHN BARR

1855-1858. 1 volume.

Gives name of clerk, case number, disposition of case, and amount of fees paid to clerk for his services. Contains an alphabetical index of plaintiffs and defendants. Handwritten on printed forms. 250 pages. 17 x 12.5 x 1.5. Second floor, Hart Building.

610. POLICE COURT WITNESS FEES

1900-1907. 3 volumes.

Contains title of case, names of witnesses, number of days, miles traveled, voucher number, date voucher was issued, and case number. Alphabetical index of witnesses in each volume. Handwritten. Volumes average 520 pages. 16.25 x 11.5 x 2.5. Second floor, Hart Building.

611. DEPOSITS, TENDERS, PROCEEDS, ETC., RECEIVED

1895-1917. 1 volume.

Lists date of entry, volume and page number, names of plaintiffs and defendants, purpose of payment, amount, and date of payment. In chronological order. Handwritten on printed forms. 202 pages. 1.5 x 9.5 x 1.5. Second floor, Hart Building.

Alimony Records

612. ALIMONY RECORD
1912—. 15 volumes, 1-15.
Shows date of entry, amount of payment, and names of payer and payee. In chronological order. Each volume contains an alphabetical index. Handwritten. Volumes average 400 pages. 12 x 10 x 2. Volumes 1-6, Room 34; Volumes 7-15, Room 254, County courthouse.

613. RECEIPTS AND DISBURSEMENTS
1912—. 15 volumes, 1-15.
Shows date of entry, amount of payments, and name of payer and payee. Arranged chronologically. Handwritten. Volumes average 200 pages. 18 x 15 x 1. Volumes 1-9, Room 34; Volumes 10-15, Room 254, County courthouse.

614. ALIMONY RECEIPT BOOKS
1928—. 186 volumes.
Lists amount of alimony, names of parties, case number, date and manner of payment, and name of payer. In order of receipt numbers. Volumes average 250 pages. 12 x 10 x 1. Handwritten on printed forms. 1928-1935, 163 volumes, Room 34; 1930-1932, 14 volumes, State Examiner's cage, Room 71; 1935—, 9 volumes, Room 254, County courthouse.

615. CANCELLED CHECKS
1925—. 91 file boxes.
Cancelled checks covering alimony payments. Filed numerically. Each file box 13.5 x 4.5 x 11. 1925-1930, 45 boxes, second floor, Hart Building; 1931-1935, 36 file boxes, Room 71; 1936—, 10 file boxes, Room 254, County courthouse.

616. ALIMONY CHECK BOOK STUBS
1925. 140 books.
List name of party receiving alimony, amount, case number, and name of payer. In order of check numbers. Handwritten on printed forms. Volumes average 400 pages. 16 x 6.5 x .75. Prior to 1925 alimony accounts were included with the general accounts. 130 books, Room 34; 10 books, Room 254, County courthouse.

617. ALIMONY BOOKS AND ACCOUNTS
1903-1912. 3 volumes.
Lists case number, amount received by the court, and signature of the recipient. Alphabetical index of plaintiffs and defendants in each volume. Handwritten on printed forms. Volumes average 500 pages. 17 x 15 x 2.5. Second floor, Hart Building.

618. DIVORCE DEPOSITS
1906-1917. 1 volume.
Lists date of deposit, case number, name of parties, amount, and the date of disbursement. In chronological order. Handwritten. 400 pages. 11.5 x 9.75 x 2. Second floor, Hart Building.

Cost Records

619. COST CARD FILES
1810—. Approximately 1,170,000 in 94 file boxes; 93 bundles.
List names of plaintiffs and defendants, cause of action, case number, and date of entry. In order of case numbers. Handwritten and typed on printed forms. Each file box 10.25 x 20 x 4.5. 1810-1928, 93 bundles, second floor, Hart Building; 1928—, 164 file boxes, Room 28; current cards, 35 boxes, Room 254, County courthouse.

620. COST CARDS
1926—. 85 file boxes.
A record of all unpaid court costs. Lists case number, names of plaintiff, defendant, and plaintiff's attorney, and the total court cost. Typed on printed forms. In order of case numbers. Each file box 10.25 x 20 x 4.5. Room 254, County courthouse.

621. APPLICATIONS FOR RESIDENT HUNTERS' AND FISHERS' LICENSES, WITH AFFIDAVITS
1925—. Approximately 70,000 in 2 burlap bags; 1 file box.
List names, addresses and application numbers. Affidavits are attached. Arranged alphabetically. Handwritten on printed forms. 1925-1936, 2 bags, second floor, Hart Building; current applications, 1 file box, Room 254, County courthouse.

622. RESIDENT HUNTERS' AND TRAPPERS' LICENSE STUBS
1925-1928. Approximately 70,000 in 2 burlap bags.
List names and addresses of hunters and trappers, and the license numbers issued. Handwritten on printed forms. Second floor, Hart Building.

623. RECORD OF HUNTERS' LICENSES
1914-1933. 19 volumes. (Missing, January 1915- January 1919).
List name and addresses of applicant for license, date issued, and license number. Contains an alphabetical index. Handwritten. Volumes average 300 pages. 14 x 12 x 1.25. Second floor, Hart Building. (This record was discontinued, as licenses are now issued by hardware and sporting goods merchants as well as the clerk of courts).

Notaries' Records

624. RECORD OF NOTARIES
January 1858—. 81 volumes, 1-81.
A record of notaries' commissions signed by the secretary of state, showing dates of issue and names of notaries. Alphabetical index of notaries in each volume. For separate index see number 625. Handwritten on printed forms. Volumes 1-16 average 240 pages. 14 x 9 x 2; volumes 17-81, 500 pages. 18.5 x 12.5 x 2.75. 53 volumes, second floor, Hart Building; 21 volumes, 61-81, Room 254; 7 volumes, Room 34, County courthouse.

625. INDEX TO NOTARIES
March 1858—. 5 volumes, 1-5.
An alphabetical index of notaries, listing record volume and page, and date on which commission expires. Handwritten on printed forms. Volumes average 400 pages. 18.5 x 13 x 2.25. Room 254, County courthouse.

626. LETTERS PERTAINING TO IDENTIFICATION OF NOTARIES
1920-1929. Approximately 200 in 1 letter file box.
Letters received by the clerk of courts from corporations and individuals asking for certificates of identification of notaries. Arranged alphabetically as to names of notaries. Typed. File box 12 x 11 x 3. Room 71, County courthouse.

627. NOTARY RECEIPTS
1934—. 1 bin; 1 file box.
Cash receipts for the recording of notary commissions showing name of notary, date of entry, amount of fee, and certificate number. In order of receipt numbers. Handwritten on printed forms. Bin 15 x 7 x 1; file box 12 x 18 x 6. 1934-1935, 1 bin, Room 34; current receipts, 1 file box, Room 254, County courthouse.

628. NOTARY FEE BOOKS
1858-1920. 16 volumes, 1-16.
Show name of notary and the fee charged for recording of commission. Entries in chronological order. Alphabetical index of notaries in each volume. Handwritten. Volumes average 390 pages. 16.5 x 12.75 x 2.25. Second floor, Hart Building.

Jury Records

629. ORDERS FOR PETIT JURORS (Jury Venire)
1915—. 32 volumes.
List name and address of juror, number of days served, amount paid for services, and date voucher was issued. Contain alphabetical indexes for each period of service. Handwritten. Volumes average 250 pages. 18.5 x 13 x 2. 1915-1924, 23 volumes, second floor, Hart Building; 1924-1936, 8 volumes, Room 71; 1936—, 1 volume, Room 254, County courthouse.

630. PETIT JURY CERTIFICATES OF FEES
1931—. 4 volumes.
Lists name and address of juror, number of days served, and amount paid for services. In chronological order. Handwritten on printed forms. Volumes average 250 pages. 16.25 x 9 x 1.5. 1931-1933, 2 volumes, Room 34; 1933—, 2 volumes, Room 254, County courthouse.

631. OHIO NATIONAL GUARD JURY ROSTER
1930—. 4 loose-leaf volumes.
Lists name and address of members of the Ohio National Guard, and date of entry. In chronological order. Typed. Volumes average 100 pages. 14.75 x 9.5 x 1. 1930-1934, 2 volumes, Room 71; 1934—, 2 volumes, Room 254, County courthouse.

632. JURORS' TIME BOOK RECORD
April 1918- September 1928. 4 loose-leaf volumes.

Lists name and address of juror, date summoned for duty, mileage covered, number of days served, and certificate number. In alphabetical order for each term of court. Handwritten. Volumes average 500 pages. 16.75 z 14 z 2. Room 71, County courthouse.

633. JURY REPORT
1933-1935. 6 Loose-leaf volumes.

Lists name and address of juror, date of jury service, number of days served, mileage coverage, and amount of money received for jury duty. In chronological order. Typed. Volumes average 100 pages. 14.75 x 9.5 x 1. Room 71, County courthouse.

634. LIST OF CONTRIBUTING MEMBERS, OHIO NATIONAL GUARD
1922—. 14 volumes.

Gives name and address of officers, enlisted men, and contributing members of the Ohio National Guard. In chronological order. Typed. Volumes average 200 pages. 15 x 9.5 x 1.75. 13 volumes, Room 71; 1 volume, Room 254, County courthouse.

635. JURY SUMMONS
1932-1935. 2 loose-leaf volumes.

Lists name and address of each person summoned for jury duty. In chronological order. Typed. Volumes average 100 pages. 14.5 x 9 x 1. Room 71, County courthouse.

Justice of Peace Records

636. JUSTICE OF PEACE RECORD (Justices' Commissions)
April 1839—. 5 volumes.

Contains original oath of office administered to each justice of the peace before the clerk of courts, name of the justice, township or village in his jurisdiction, and name of county. In chronological order. An alphabetical index in each volume. Handwritten on printed forms. Volumes average 400 pages. 12.25 x 8.5 x 2. 4 volumes, Room 34; 1 volume, Room 254, County courthouse.

637. JUSTICE OF PEACE FILES
1923-1931. Approximately 14,000 in 1 basket; 4 cartons; and 1 bundle.
Contains writs; summonses; and bills of particulars, listing name of plaintiff and defendant, names of attorneys, case number, and amount of cost and fees. Chronological order. Handwritten and typed on printed forms. Attic storeroom, fourth floor, County courthouse.

638. MISCELLANEOUS CRIMINAL DOCKET, JUSTICE OF PEACE DOCKETS
1919-1931, 11 Loose-leaf volumes.
Lists name of defendant, names of attorneys, crime charged, final termination of case, court costs, and justice of peace fees. Alphabetical index of defendants in each volume. Handwritten on printed forms. Volumes average 600 pages. 18 x 12 x 2. Attic storeroom, fourth floor, County courthouse.

639. JUSTICE OF PEACE CASH BOOKS
January 1922- December 1929. 12 volumes.
List date of entry, case number, payee or recipient, purpose of payment, distribution and disbursement of receipts, and name of the justice of peace. Alphabetical index of payees and recipients in each volume. Handwritten on printed forms. Volumes average 500 pages. 12 x 12 x .5. Attic storeroom, fourth floor, County courthouse.

640. CIVIL DOCKET, JUSTICE OF PEACE COURT
July 1916-December 1930. 3 loose-leaf volumes. (July 1916-January 1917, 1 volume, East Cleveland; February 1924-December 1929, 1 volume, Parma; February 1925-December 1930, 1 volume, Goldwood Township).
Lists name of plaintiff and of defendant, names of attorneys, court case, justice of peace fees, and final disposition of case. Alphabetical index of plaintiffs and defendants in each volume. Handwritten on printed forms. Volumes average 500 pages. 18 x 12 x 1.5. Attic storeroom, fourth floor, County courthouse.

641. JUSTICE COURT PROCEEDINGS
1885-1892. 1 volume.
List name of plaintiff, of defendant, and of justice; amount claimed; amount of justice fees; and costs involved. Contains an alphabetical index of plaintiffs and defendants. Handwritten on printed forms. 600 pages. 16 x 11 x 2.25. Second floor, Hart Building.

642. TRAFFIC CRIMINAL DOCKET, JUSTICE OF PEACE COURT
January 1924 - November 1924. 1 volume, Parma.

Lists names of defendants and attorney; felony or misdemeanor charged; court costs; justice of peace fee; and final disposition of case. In chronological order. Handwritten. 300 pages. 18 x 12 x 2.75. Attic storeroom, fourth floor, County courthouse.

643. CRIMINAL DOCKET, JUSTICE OF PEACE W. K. SMITH
1879. 1 volume, 3.

Gives name of defendant, name and address of prosecuting witness, charge against defendant, date, amount of justice court fees, complete history, and disposition of case. Contains alphabetical index of defendants. Handwritten on printed forms. 358 pages. 14.25 x 9.5 x 3. Second floor, Hart Building.

644. CLAIMS OF JUSTICES AND CONSTABLES FOR ALLOWANCE FROM COUNTY TREASURER IN LIEU OF FEES
1885-1894. 1 volume.

A record of mileage claims, justice costs, and constable fees. Contains alphabetical index of justices and constables. Handwritten. 300 pages. 14 x 9 x 2. Second floor, Hart Building.

Automobile Bills of Sale

645. AUTOMOBILE BILLS OF SALE DUPLICATES
1921—. Approximately 1,440,800 in 4084 file boxes.

List name of grantee and grantor; make, year, and model of car; and date issued. In order of instrument numbers. For index see numbers 646 and 647. Handwritten and typed on printed forms. Each file box 10.25 x 20 x 4.5. 1921-1925, 1169 file boxes, second floor, Hart Building; 1926, 16 file boxes and 1927-1934, 2688 file boxes, Room 29; 1935—, 211 file boxes, Room 254, County courthouse.

646. AUTOMOBILE INDEX, GRANTEE - GRANTOR
1921—. 52 loose-leaf volumes.
An alphabetical index of grantees, listing name of grantor, the serial number, date of filing, and name of manufacturer. Handwritten on printed forms. Volumes average 800 pages. 16 x 14.5 x 5. 1921-1925, 26 volumes, Room 71; 1926—, 26 volumes, Room 254, County courthouse.

647. AUTOMOBILE INDEX, GRANTOR - GRANTEE
1921—. 52 loose-leaf volumes.
An alphabetical index of grantors, listing name of grantee, original number, serial number, make of car, and date of filing. Handwritten on printed forms. Volumes average 800 pages. 16 x 14.5 x 5. 1921-1925, 10 volumes, Room 71; 1926—, 42 volumes, Room 254, County courthouse.

648. CLERK CERTIFICATES
1934—. 1010 volumes.
A record listing name and address of the person applying for the certificate, the name of the person from whom the car has been acquired, date of filing, name of car, horsepower, type, engine number, bill of sale number, manufacturer's number and date of issue. In order of certificate numbers. Handwritten on printed forms. Volumes average 100 pages. 15 x 8 x .5. Room 71, County courthouse.

649. APPLICATIONS FOR NOTATION ON CANCELLATION OF LIEN AND NOTICE TO COMMISSIONER OF MOTOR VEHICLES
1931. Approximately 5000 in 1 bin.
List amount of the chattel mortgage, make of car, name and address of owner, and date of application. In chronological order. Typed on printed forms. Each bin 7 x 14 x .75. Second floor, Hart Building.

650. CERTIFICATES OF TITLE
1913. Approximately 2000 in 2 cardboard boxes.
Lists names and addresses of grantees and grantors; make, year, and model of car; engine number; certificate number; and date of issue. In chronological order. Handwritten. Each box 10.25 x 20 x 26. Second floor, Hart Building.

651. AUTOMOBILE RECORD, CERTIFICATE OF TITLE INDEX
July 31, 1931- September 30, 1931.1 volume.
Lists the names of grantee and grantor, make of car, type of body, and motor and serial numbers of car. (Automobile bills of sale were not required between July 31, 1931 and September 30, 1931). Arranged as to name of grantee. Handwritten. 500 pages. 18 x 12.5 x 2. Room 71, County courthouse.

652. AUTOMOBILE RECEIPTS
1921—. 4007 volumes.
Receipts for bills of sale filed with the clerk of courts. In order of receipt numbers. Handwritten on printed forms. Volumes average 240 pages. 15.5 x 9.5 x 1. 1921-1931, 3042 volumes, second floor, Hart Building; 1932—, 945 volumes, Room 71; 20 current volumes, Room 254, County courthouse.

Naturalization Records

653. INDEX OF CITIZENSHIP
1810—. 14 file drawers.
A complete alphabetical card index of naturalized citizens, listing name, date of naturalization, date petition was filed, native country, certificate number, and volume and page of the record. Drawer 36 x 15 x 3. Room 254, County courthouse.

654. DECLARATION OF INTENTION
1906—. 172 volumes, 1-172.
Original copies of declarations of intention, of which the duplicate is sent to the district office of naturalization, and the triplicate is returned to the individual. The certificates list the applicant's name, residence, occupation, age, sex, color, complexion, color of eyes, color of a hair, height, weight, race, nationality, and date of birth. It also lists date of entrance to the United States, residences of children, place of immigration, declaration number, vessel of crossing, and date of filing a declaration. An alphabetical index in each volume. Volumes average 800 pages. 9 x 10.5 x 3. Volumes 1-146, Room 71; volumes 147-172, Room 254, County courthouse.

655. NATURALIZATION INDEX OF DECLARATION OF INTENTION
1906—. 5 volumes.

Lists name of individual, and volume and page of the record. Alphabetical for periods of varying lengths. Volumes average 550 pages. 18.25 x 13 x 3. Room 254, County courthouse.

656. PETITIONS AND RECORD FOR NATURALIZATION
1906—. 91 volumes, 1-91.

Copies of petitions for naturalization to which are attached the declaration of intention and the certificates of arrival. The petitions list the name, residence, occupation, port of emigration, vessel, date of declaration of the applicant, date and place of birth, present address, and date of entrance to the United States. It also lists the name of witnesses and the signature of the judge. Cancellations and all court actions are attached to the petition. Each volume contains an alphabetical index. In order of filing date. Handwritten on printed forms. Volumes average 450 pages. 18 x 11 x 4. Volumes 1-84, Room 71; volumes 85-91, Room 254, County courthouse.

657. DECLARATIONS OF ALIENS
October 1878 - September 1906. 25 volumes, 8-32.

Copies of declarations showing certificate number, name of applicant, date of arrival, oath renouncing old allegiance, and date of declaration. In order of certificate numbers. Handwritten on printed forms. Volumes average 400 pages. 14 x 9.5 x 2. Room 71, County courthouse.

658. PRELIMINARY FORMS FOR PETITIONS FOR NATURALIZATION
1923—. Approximately 5500 in 55 folders.

List date of application; name, address, occupation, and birth date of applicant; date of arrival in country; name of boat or train on which applicant arrived; name of each member of family; where ticket was purchased; present residence; and references. In chronological order. Handwritten on printed forms. Each folder 10 x 12 x .5. Room 71, County courthouse.

659. NATURALIZATION RECORD AND JOURNAL
1903 - September 1906. 11 volumes.

Contains petitions and affidavits of witnesses. Petitions list name, occupation, address, date of entrance to the United States, and date of declaration. In order of certificate numbers. Handwritten on printed forms. The volumes average 3200 pages. 16 x 18 x 3.25. Room 71, County courthouse.

660. DECLARATION OF ALIENS UNDER 18
1888 - 1906. 11 volumes.

Lists name of applicant, native country, date of arrival in the United States, renunciation of former allegiance, and date of declaration. In order of certificate numbers. Handwritten on printed forms. Volumes average 500 pages. 10 x 14 x 2.25. Room 71, County courthouse.

661. ALIEN INDEX
1838-1903. 6 volumes, 1-6.

Lists name of alien, place of birth, date of naturalization, when and where declaration was filed, when naturalized, and journal volume and page. Handwritten. Volumes average 500 pages. 12.5 x 18 x 2.5. Room 71, County courthouse.

662. ALIEN DOCKET, DISTRICT COURT
1818 - 1882. 1 volume.

Lists name of alien, date declaration was filed, and date certificate of naturalization was granted. In order of certificate number. Contains an alphabetical index. Handwritten and handwritten on printed forms. Volume average 300 pages. 13.5 9 2. Room 71, County courthouse.

663. ALIEN APPEARANCE DOCKET
1883-1895. 4 volumes.

Lists name of person applying for citizenship, date petition was filed, date of affidavit of witness, term of court, whether petition was granted, and the journal volume and page. Volumes average 228 pages. 14 x 9 x 1.25. Room 71, County courthouse.

664. ALIEN DOCKET
1842-1854. 7 volumes.

Lists name, country of birth, court with which the petition was filed, and the term of court. In order of certificate numbers. Each volume contains an alphabetical index. Handwritten. Volumes average 300 pages. 13.5 x 9 x 2.25. Room 71, County courthouse.

665. ALIEN WITNESSES
October 1878-1883. 2 volumes.
Copies of affidavits of witnesses listing name of witness; name, nativity, and residence of applicant; and oath of witness. Each volume contains an alphabetical index. Volumes average 600 pages. 14 x 9.25 x 2.25. Room 71, County courthouse.

666. ALIEN CALENDAR
1894-1904. 7 volumes.
Lists name of alien and date citizenship was granted. Handwritten. In order of certificate numbers. Volumes average 450 pages. 14.25 x 9.5 x 2. Room 71, County courthouse.

667. GENERAL INDEX
November 6, 1810-December 3, 1841. 1 volume.
Lists surname, Christian name, and volume and page of the docket. Alphabetical as to names of aliens. 500 pages. 26 x 16 x 4. Room 71, County courthouse.

668. LETTERS FROM U. S. DEPARTMENT OF LABOR, BUREAU OF NATURALIZATION
1921-1926. Approximately 5500 in 1 bundle.
Letters authorizing the clerk of courts to issue certificates of citizenship to persons of the names and addresses given in the letters. Handwritten and typed. Bundle 8.5 x 11 x 8. Second floor, Hart Building.

669. NOTICES OF APPLICATIONS FOR ADMISSION TO CITIZENSHIP
1917-1923. 1 volume.
List name and addresses of persons making applications for citizenship and length of time they have resided in the country. In chronological order. Handwritten on printed forms. 600 pages. 18.5 x 12.5 x 2. Second floor, Hart Building.

Miscellaneous

670. HABEAS CORPUS RECORD AND DOCKET
1849-1878. 2 volumes, 1-2.
Lists name of plaintiff and of defendant, case number, appearance docket number, journal volume and page, date writ was issued, date application of writ was

returned, a brief statement of the hearing on the writ, and disposition of the case. In chronological order. Handwritten. Volumes average 968 pages. 14 x 9.25 x 2. Second floor, Hart Building.

671. COPY OF PLEADING
February 1888-September 1895. 5 volumes, 1-5.
Lists date of entry, name of plaintiff and of defendant, case number, petition and answer, and amount of cost. Alphabetical index of plaintiffs and defendants in each volume. Volumes average 300 pages. 15.25 x 10.25 x 2. Second floor, Hart Building.

672. REPORT OF JUDICIAL STATISTICS
1878-1888. 11 volumes.
Annual statistical reports of findings in all branches of the court of common pleas. In chronological order. Handwritten on printed forms. Volumes average 10 pages. 21.25 x 15.5 x .25. Second floor, Hart Building.

673. NOTICED CASES
November 1876-January 1892. 27 volumes.
Contain journal entries of all cases about which notice has been published in the official court paper, the Daily Legal News. In order of case numbers. Handwritten. Volumes average 256 pages. 14 x 9 x 1. Second floor, Hart Building.

674. DOCKET INDEX
(Dates cannot be determined). 4 volumes.
Lists case number, and name and address of plaintiff and defendant. In order of case numbers. Handwritten. Volumes average 400 pages. 16 x 11 x 2. Second floor, Hart Building.

675. MINUTE BOOK OF COURT PROCEEDINGS
November 21, 1831-March 26, 1836. 1 volume.
A record of all cases tried before the common pleas and supreme courts, giving name of plaintiffs, defendants, and jurors; number of days served by each juror; a complete list of the grand and petit jurors for each term; names of administrators appointed; licenses issued, to whom, and for what purpose; and a general summary of all matters submitted to the court. In chronological order. Handwritten. 250 pages. 15 x 7 x 1. Second floor, Hart Building.

676. RAILROAD RECORDS
1849-1853. 1 volume.

Exact copies of petitions for appraisal of lands, giving names of parties, and location, description, and valuation of property. Each volume contains an alphabetical index. In chronological order. Handwritten. 500 pages. 17 x 12 x 2.5. Room 254, County courthouse.

677. RECORD OF RAILROAD APPRAISALS
December 1849-June 1853. 1 volume.

Gives names of parties involved, names of attorneys, amount of appraisal, and description of property. In chronological order. Handwritten. 420 pages. 13.5 x 9.25 x 1.75. Room 254, County courthouse.

678. MEMORANDUM BOOKS
1875-1927. 35 volumes.

List case number, execution docket, name of plaintiff and defendant, names of witnesses, the verdict of the jury or judge, and name of presiding judge. Contains an alphabetical index of plaintiffs and defendants in each volume. In chronological order. Handwritten. Volumes average 400 pages. 14 x 9.5 x 2. Second floor, Hart Building.

679. EXECUTIONS
1923. Approximately 1000 in 1 bundle.

Executions issued by the clerk and returned by the sheriff. Typed on printed forms. Executions are ordinarily placed with the case files. Bundles 12.5 x 10.5 x 8. Second floor, Hart Building.

680. DIVORCE EXECUTION DOCKET
1876-1882. 2 volumes, 1-2.

Lists name of plaintiff and defendant, case number, appearance docket number, date order of execution was issued, and a copy of the execution. Alphabetical index of plaintiffs and defendants in each volume. Handwritten. Volumes average 300 pages. 16 x 12 x 1.5. Second floor, Hart Building.

681. DIVORCE JOURNAL
1876-1882. 2 volumes, 1-2.
Journal entries pertaining to divorce actions, listing name of plaintiff and defendant, and case number. Journal entries can be traced by case number from the divorce execution docket. Handwritten. Volumes average 320 pages. 12.5 x 8.25 x 1.25. Second floor, Hart Building.

682. DIVORCE APPEARANCE DOCKET
1876-1882. 2 volumes, 1-2.
Lists name of plaintiff and defendant, case number, cause of action, and various court entries. In order of case numbers. For index see number 638. Handwritten. Volumes average 568 pages. 12.5 x 8.25 x 2.5. Second floor, Hart Building.

683. DIVORCE INDEX
1876-1882. 1 volume.
An alphabetical index of plaintiffs and defendants, listing case number and name of attorneys. Handwritten, 256 pages. 14 x 9.25 x 1.5. Second floor, Hart Building.

684. BOARD OF ELECTORS' TALLY SHEETS
1904-1934. Approximately 3950 in 393 bundles.
List name and address of voter, ward number, and precinct letter. Alphabetical as to names of voters in each ward. Handwritten on printed forms. Each bundle 11 x 16.5 x .25. Second floor, Hart Building.

685. STRAY AND DRIFT RECORD
1885-1921. 1 volume, 2.
A record listing property that was lost, found, or has drifted away; and giving a complete description of the property and the name and address of the person who has either found the property or reported it strayed. In chronological order. Handwritten on printed forms. 400 pages. 17 x 12.5 x 1.5. Room 34, County courthouse.

686. COMMON PLEAS BAR AND COURT LIST
1852-1875. 12 volumes.
Lists case number, name of plaintiff and defendant, names of attorneys, and cause of action. Arranged as to terms of court. Handwritten. Volumes average 200 pages. 14.5 x 9 x 1.75. Second floor, Hart Building.

Criminal Branch

687. CRIMINAL COURTROOM CALENDARS
1899—. 140 volumes.
List name of defendant, the crime, case number, and judge's entry. Handwritten on printed forms. In chronological order. Volumes average 150 pages. 16 x 11 x .5. 1899-1935, 115 volumes, second floor, Hart Building; 1935—, 25 volumes, Clerk's office, first floor, Criminal Court Building.

688. CRIMINAL ASSIGNMENT INDEX
1920—. 3 volumes.
Lists name of defendant, case number, and date of entry. Handwritten. Volumes average 400 pages. 10.5 x 7 x 2. Assignment room, Criminal Court Building.

689. CRIMINAL FILES
1899—. 775 file boxes (case number 1-460,000).
Contain indictments and whatever pleadings are filed with the case, such as motions, demurrers, briefs, etc. In order of case numbers. Handwritten and typed. Each file box 13.75 x 4.75 x 10.75. 1899-1934, 730 file boxes, Room 71, County courthouse; current files, 45 file boxes, clerk's office, first floor, Criminal Court Building.

690. COMMON PLEAS RECORD
1810—.
A complete record of all cases in the civil and criminal branches of the common pleas court. For complete description see number 556. Volumes from 1810-1882 combine civil and criminal cases. From 1883—, civil and criminal cases are entered in separate volumes.

691. CRIMINAL JOURNAL
1857—. 57 volumes, 1-57.
Lists name of defendant, case number, docket number, and entries of all proceedings pertaining to the case. Typed. Volumes average 600 pages. 16 x 14 x 4. 1857-1927, 43 volumes, 1-43, Room 34, County courthouse; 1927—, 14 volumes, 44-57, clerk's office, first floor, Criminal Court Building.

692. CRIMINAL APPEARANCE DOCKET
1899—. 91 volumes, 1-91.

Lists name of defendant, names of attorneys, date, case and docket numbers, and a statement of proceedings. In chronological order. For index see number 693. Handwritten on printed forms. Volumes average 600 pages. 18 x 12 x 3. Clerk's office, first floor, Criminal Court Building.

693. CRIMINAL INDEX
1899—. 10 volumes.

An alphabetical index of defendants, listing case number and date of entry. Handwritten. Volumes average 400 pages. 10.5 x 7 x 2. Clerk's office, first floor, Criminal Court Building.

694. CRIMINAL RECOGNIZANCE
1858—. 94 volumes, 1-94.

Gives name of defendant, crime for which indicted, case number, recognizance number, amount of bond, names and addresses of bondsmen, location of real estate listed for surety, and name of clerk or deputy who swore in bondsmen. Alphabetically index of defendants and each volume; for index, 1858-1885, see number 695. Handwritten and printed. Volumes average 600 pages. 15 x 11.5 x 4. 87 volumes, 1-83, 85-88, second floor, Hart Building; 4 volumes, 84, 89-91, Room 34, County courthouse; 3 volumes,92-94, Clerk's office, first floor, Criminal Court Building.

695. INDEX TO CRIMINAL RECOGNIZANCE
1858-1885. 1 volume.

An alphabetical index of defendants and bondsmen, listing nature of crime, name and address of bondsmen, and amount of bond. Handwritten. 600 pages. 15 x 14 x 3.5. Second floor, Hart Building.

696. RECORD OF CONVICTIONS
1901—. 5 volumes.

Lists case number, name of defendant, nature of crime, sentence imposed, general remarks, and name of presiding judge. Contains alphabetical indexes of defendants for each term of court. Handwritten. Volumes average 428 pages. 16 x 11 x 3. Clerk's office, first floor, Criminal Court Building.

697. INDICTMENTS
1927—. 2 volumes.
Contains the findings of the grand jury and information returned by the prosecutor, giving name of defendant, case number, and the charge. In chronological order. Handwritten. Volumes average 450 pages. 14 x 9 x 2. Clerk's office, first floor, Criminal Court Building.

698. COMMITMENT ORDERS
1900—. 15 volumes.
A record giving name of plaintiff and of defendant, case number, disposition of case, and date of commitment. In chronological order. Typed. Volumes average 600 pages. 18 x 12.5 x 3. 1900-1925, 6 volumes, second floor, Hart Building; 1926—, 9 volumes, Clerk's office, first floor, Criminal Court Building.

699. EXECUTIONS (Execution Docket).
October 1927—. 2 volumes.
A record listing date of entry, execution docket number, file number, and name of defendant. Contains an alphabetical index of defendants. Handwritten. 368 pages. 9.25 x 10.5 x 1.5. Clerk's office, first floor, Criminal Court Building.

700. NO BILLS
1927—. 1 volume.
A record of the findings of the grand jury when a "no bill" is returned. Handwritten. In chronological order. 300 pages. 11.5 x 9.5 x 1.5. Clerk's office, first floor, Criminal Court Building.

701. *PRECIPE* BOOK
1853—. 5 volumes, 1-5.
A record of *precipes* showing names of parties, case number, and dates of receipt, and the execution of the *precipe*. In chronological order. Handwritten. Volumes average 440 pages. 14 x 9 x 2. 1853-1931, 3 volumes, 1-3, second floor, Hart Building; 1931—, 2 volumes, 4-5, Clerk's office, first floor Criminal Court Building.

702. GRAND JURY SUBPOENAS
1899—. 2 file drawers; 1 bin.

List name and addresses of witnesses, case number, and the reason for issuing subpoenas. Handwritten on printed forms. 1899-1935, 1 bin, Hart Building; January 1935—, 2 drawers, 23.5 x 16 x 23, Clerk's office, first floor, Criminal Court Building.

703. MINUTE BOOK, CRIMINAL COURTS
1856-1882. 1 volume.

Lists name of defendant, crime indicted for, case and docket numbers. In chronological order. Handwritten. 350 pages. 14 x 12 x 2.5. Second floor, Hart Building.

704. CRIMINAL EXECUTION DOCKET
1856-1882. -5 volumes, 1-5. (Also, see number 699).

Lists name of defendant, crime for which indicted, case number, criminal appearance docket number, and disposition of case. In order of case numbers. Handwritten. Volumes average 400 pages. 18 x 14 x 3. Room 34, County courthouse.

705. CRIMINAL RECORD
1856-1882. 7 volumes, 1-7.

Gives name of defendant, crime for which indicted, previous criminal record, and disposition of case. For index see number 707. Handwritten on printed forms. Volumes average 400 pages. 17 x 13 x 3. Room 34, County courthouse.

706. CRIMINAL APPEARANCE DOCKET
1856-1882. 2 volumes, 1-2. (Also, see number 692).

Lists name of defendant, case number, docket number, crime charged, disposition of case, and date of entry. For index see number 707. Handwritten. Volumes average 675 pages. 17 x 14 x 2.25. Second floor, Hart Building.

707. CRIMINAL INDEX
1856-1882. 4 volumes.

An alphabetical index of defendants, listing crimes for which indicted, case number, and appearance docket number. Handwritten on printed forms. Volumes average 400 pages. 18 x 14 x 2.5. Room 34, County courthouse.

708. CRIMINAL RECEIPT AND DISBURSEMENT RECORD
September 1911-July 1913. 1 volume.

Lists date of action taken by the grand jury, names of witnesses, date voucher was issued, amount of mileage for witnesses, and old voucher issue date. This information is found under the following headings; Grand Jury, *Nolle* or Not Guilty, and Misdemeanors or Felonies. In chronological order. Handwritten. 400 pages. 17 x 15 x 2. Second floor, Hart Building.

709. CASE WITNESS BOOK
1900—. 9 volumes.

Lists names of witnesses, number of days served, and voucher number. In chronological order. Volumes average 350 pages. 17.5 x 13.5 x 1.75. 1900-1929, 6 volumes, second floor, Hart Building; 1930—, 3 volumes, Clerk's office, first floor, Criminal Court Building.

710. ERROR DOCKET
1923—. 1 volume.

A record of cases appealed from mayor, justice of peace, or other courts. Lists name of defendant, case number, error of lower court, and all court entries. This information is also listed in the appearance docket. In chronological order. Handwritten and typed. 240 pages. 9 x 14 x 1.25. Clerk's office, first floor, Criminal Court Building.

711. RELEASE BOOKS
1933—. 3 volumes.

Last name of defendant, case number, date, and disposition of case. All releases are signed by the sheriff. Handwritten on printed forms. In chronological order. Volumes average 150 pages. 9.5 x 14 x 1. Clerk's office, first floor, Criminal Court Building.

712. BOARD OF ELECTIONS LIST OF CONVICTIONS
1931—. 1 file box.

Clerk of courts' reports of convictions, listing name of defendant, his age, address, and date of conviction. A second copy is filed with the board of elections, and a third with the jury commission. Filed chronologically. Clerk's office, first floor, Criminal Court Building.

713. PENITENTIARY AND REFORMATORY COST BILLS
September 1926—. 8 file boxes.

Contain certificates for allowances of guards and certificates of issuing executions. List name of defendant, charge, case number, various costs, names of witnesses, witnesses fees, and recapitulation of costs. Filed chronologically. File box 10.5 x 12 x 4.5. Clerk's office, first floor, Criminal Court Building.

714. WORKHOUSE COST BILLS
September 1921—. 3 file boxes.

List case number, name of defendant, names of witnesses, amount paid to each witness, various fees, and miscellaneous costs. Filed chronologically. Each file box 10.5 x 12 x 4.5. Clerk's office, first floor, Criminal Court Building.

715. GRAND JURY REPORTS
June 1882—. 1 file box.

General report of grand jury of investigations, findings, and special activities. Filed with presiding judge for each term of court. Chronological. Handwritten and typed. File box 10.5 x 12 x 4.5. Clerk's office, first floor, Criminal Court Building.

716. COST CLERK'S SENTENCE BOOK
1932—. 1 volume.

Date, case number, name of defendant, crime, various costs, and sentence. Chronological. Handwritten on printed forms. 95 pages. 19 x 16 x 1. Clerk's office, first floor, Criminal Court Building.

717. RECEIPT BOOK
1932—. 1 volume.

Lists receipts for moneys received by criminal branch of clerk of courts for cash bonds, fines, costs, etc. Handwritten on printed forms. Chronological. 200 pages. 11 x 8 x .5. Clerk's office, first floor, Criminal Court Building.

718. GRAND JURY WITNESS BOOK
1895—. 24 volumes.

Lists name of witnesses, number of days served, mileage, voucher number and date voucher issued. Alphabetical indexes of witnesses for each term of court. Handwritten. Volumes average 90 pages. 17 x 13.5 x 2. 1895-1924, 16 volumes, second floor, Hart Building; 1925-1929, 5 volumes, Room 71; 1931—, 3 volumes,

Clerk's office, first floor, Criminal Court Building.

719. GRAND JURY WITNESS CERTIFICATES OF FEES
1930—. 29 volumes.

List name of defendant, case number, date, name of witness, mileage, and days served. In order of certificate numbers. Handwritten on printed forms. Volumes average 250 pages. 18 x 12 x 2. 24 volumes, Room 34, County courthouse; 5 volumes, Clerk's office, first floor, Criminal Court Building.

720. PETIT AND GRAND JURORS' CERTIFICATES OF FEES
1921—. 1 cardboard box; 1 burlap bag; 50 volumes.

Show certificate number, name of juror, term of court, amount of fee, and date of payment. Arranged chronologically. Handwritten on printed forms. These are issued by the civil branch except in cases of special venire or first degree murder cases. Volumes average 250 pages. 14 x 3.75 x 1; box 9.5 x 11 x 36. Box and bag, second floor, Hart Building; 50 volumes, Room 71, County courthouse.

The following departments are under the direct jurisdiction of the Court. Their records are not kept by the Clerk of Courts:

Jury Commission

Pursuant to an act of the general assembly of April 23, 1894, the judges of the court of common pleas, in counties having a population of not less than 33,000 nor more than 50,000, were empowered to appoint four residents of the county to serve as a jury commission for a term of one year. They were to receive compensation of $3.00 per day. It was the duty of this commission to determine the qualifications and fitness of persons to be selected as jurors. (91 O. L. 176). An amendment in 1913 provided for the appointment of jury commissioners who were also to act as assignment commissioners. (103 O. L. 513). The act as amended in 1915 provided that in every county a jury commission of two resident electors shall be appointed, neither of whom shall be an attorney at law, nor of the same political party. In 1921 the common pleas court of Cuyahoga County appointed assignment commissioners to act as jury commissioners, and on September 1, 1929 an amendment became effective providing for the appointment of full-time jury commissioners. (106 O. L. 106; 113 O. L. 264).

The jury code, which became effective August 2, 1931, was in large part based on the work of the jury commission in Cuyahoga County and provided for a permanent jury commission of the same number and qualifications as previously provided for, to hold office at the pleasure of the judges of the common pleas court, and whose duty it shall be to meet and select prospective jurors, both grand and petit, for the ensuing year, for my list of electors provided by the board of elections. (114 O. L. 213). The jury commission selects prospective jurors, for civil and criminal cases as well as for the grand jury. They select jurors for the probate court, juvenile court, other minor courts, and all cities and villages where there are no established municipal courts.

721. JURY EXAMINATION RECORD
September 1930—. 6 volumes.

Lists name and address; date of examination; whether accepted; ward, precinct, and township; and remarks. Each volume contains an alphabetical index of jurors by wards, precincts, and townships. Typed on printed forms. Volumes average 400 pages. 14 x 17 x 2. Room 141 ½, County courthouse.

722. JURORS EXEMPTED
September 1930—. 120,000 cards in 30 file boxes.

Cards list all jurors exempted from jury service, giving name, address, ward, precinct, township, date on which called, date of examination, and reason for exemption. Alphabetical as to jurors by wards, precincts, and townships for each year. Handwritten on printed forms. Each file box 5 x 6 x 24. Room 141 ½, County courthouse.

723. RECORD OF JURORS
September 1930—. Approximately 180,000 in 24 file boxes.

Lists name and address; precinct, ward, and township; juror's place of employment, occupation, length of service; size of family; age; whether native; and whether juror has served, has been given an extension, or has been excused. Filed chronologically. Indexed alphabetically for each year according to wards, precincts, and townships. Typed on printed forms. Each file box 13.5 x 5 x 30. Room 141 ½, County courthouse.

724. RECORDS OF JURORS CALLED FOR SERVICE
September 1930—. 1 volume; 2 bundles.
Lists name and address, precinct, ward, township, date when name was drawn from jury wheel, when assigned to court, when drawn and returned to secretary, when service started, extended date, when excused, name of person who excused juror, and remarks. Contains an alphabetical index for each period of service. Handwritten on printed of forms. 300 pages. 19 x 15 x 2. Room 141 ½, County courthouse.

725. INDEX TO JURORS
September 1930—. 1 revolving metal file.
An alphabetical index of jurors listing address, precinct, ward, township, and indicating in code whether juror has served, has been excused, or has been given an extension. Typed. Room 141 ½, County courthouse.

726. EXTENSION BOOK
September 1930—. 1 volume; 2 bundles.
A record of jurors who have been drawn to appear and of those who service has been excused to a later date. It lists name and address, ward, precinct, township, date on which each juror was to serve, and date of extension. Alphabetical index of jurors by wards, precincts, and townships for each year. Handwritten on printed forms. 500 pages. 17 x 12 x 2. Room 141 ½, County courthouse.

Domestic Relations Bureau

The problem of disposing of an increasing volume of business coming into the common pleas court was met by the establishment of a court of domestic relations, which immediately took over a large portion of the business arising from litigation pertaining to divorce and domestic relation cases.

The jurisdiction of this court in Cuyahoga County results, not from a specific act, but from a statute of 1923, authorizing the chief justice of the court of common pleas to classify and distribute the business of the court. (110 O. L. 52, sec. 1558). However, the bureau was actually organized in 1920, but it was not until January 1, 1929 that the court work pertaining to litigation growing out of domestic relations was segregated and put in the hands of one judge for a period of six months. The domestic relations bureau promotes reconciliations and conducts investigations, as the Court directs, in the matter of temporary alimony, custody of children, conditions in homes, character of persons, and makes recommendations in contempt proceedings.

727. DOMESTIC RELATIONS - OFFICIAL DOCKET
1921—. 2 volumes.

Lists date of entry, case number, name of plaintiff and of defendant, names of their attorneys, date on which notice was published, cause of action, and disposition of case. In chronological order. Typed on printed forms. Volumes average 500 pages. 17.5 x 15 x 2.5. Room 45, County courthouse.

728. DOMESTIC RELATIONS - UNOFFICIAL DOCKET
January 1921—. 2 volumes.

Lists date of entry, case number, name of husband and wife, number of children in family, cause of complaint, action taken in case, and result of action. In chronological order. Typed on printed forms. Volumes average 500 pages. 17.5 x 15 x 2.5. Room 45, County courthouse.

729. MOTION CASE FILES
January 1921—. Approximately 8000 in 6 file drawers.

Files of cases to which motions have been attached, and recommendations by the chief of the domestic relation bureau. In order of case numbers. For index see number 730. Typed. Each file drawer 27.5 x 12.75 x 11.5. Room 45, County courthouse.

730. MOTION CASE INDEX
January 1921—. Approximately 15,000 cards in 7 metal file boxes.

An alphabetical card index of plaintiffs and defendants, listing addresses, case numbers, and all records of motions in each case. Typed. Each file box 5 x 3 x 15. Room 45, County courthouse.

731. CASE FILE
January 1921—. Approximately 41,250 in 33 file drawers; 66 bins.

All common pleas court cases pertaining to litigations referred to the division of domestic relations. For index see number 732. Typed. Each file drawer 12.75 x 11.5 x 27, each bin 17 x 19 x 10.5. Room 45, County courthouse.

732. INDEX TO ACTIVE CASES

January 1921—. Approximately 4000 cards in 20 file boxes.

An alphabetical card index of plaintiffs and defendants, listing addresses and case numbers. Typed. Each file box 18 x 5.5 x 5.75. Room 45, County courthouse.

733. INDEX TO DIVORCE CASES

January 1921—. Approximately 48,000 cards in 9 file drawers.

An alphabetical card index of plaintiffs and defendants, listing addresses and case numbers. Typed. Each file drawer 12.5 x 5 x 25.5. Room 45, County courthouse.

Criminal Record Department

The need for a systematic compilation of individual criminal records led to the creation of the criminal record division of Cuyahoga County. A superintendent of criminal records was appointed by the judge of common pleas court in January 1925.

The main function of the department is to furnish the presiding judge of the criminal branch with a synopsis of the crime committed, including in it the elements of the specific crime with which he is charged, together with additional crimes committed about the same time with which the defendant is not charged, but in which he has either been identified or has admitted to his guilt. The records also show all previous arrests or dealings with the police, thus aiding the court in fixing bail, and pronouncing the sentence, or referring the individual to probation.

The department renders valuable service to police departments, peace officers, and magistrates of courts of the various subdivisions throughout the city, county, and state. It supplies detailed information about persons charged with crime who passed through common pleas courts to such organizations as the election board, the United States Army, and Navy recruiting offices, many branches of the Federal Government, hotels, banks, retail credit organizations, and all penal institutions.

The department is assisted in its work by the police of railroads as well as of private industries, the bureau of identification, the bureau of investigation, the department of ballistics, the auto bureau, and the detective bureau of the Cleveland police department.

The system, as now operated, has simplified and expedited the disposition of criminal cases brought to the attention of the court. All records compiled become permanent information, available only to persons directly affected or legally interested in the person charged. (G. C. sec. 1541).

734. ORIGINAL ARREST SLIPS
June 1927—. Approximately 28,000 in 3 file drawers.
List date of arrest, name of arresting officer, name of defendant, residence and occupation, crime charged, previous record, fingerprint classifications, nativity, marital status, sex, race, and age. Arranged alphabetically as to defendants. Typed on printed forms. Each file box 13.5 x 5 x 30. Criminal record room, first floor, Criminal Court Building.

735. THE BLOTTER
September 1925—. 2 loose-leaf volumes.
Lists case number and name of defendant; crime indicted for; nativity, marital status, sex, race, age, and previous record; grand jury action; prison sentenced to; and name of presiding judge. Arranged as to type of crime. Typed on printed forms. Volumes average 2000 pages. 16 x 19.5 x 12.5. Criminal record room, first floor, Criminal Court Building.

736. CASES BY NAME
June 1927—. Approximately 28,000 cards in 8 metal file drawers.
Lists case number; name of alias of defendant; crime indicted for; name of arresting officer; section of the General Code under which indicted; occupation; age, race, and marital status; amount of bail bond; date bound over to grand jury; date of the general jury hearing; date indictment was returned; disposition of case; name of presiding judge; fingerprint numbers of defendant; date defendant was sentenced; and the institutional number of the defendant. Arranged alphabetically as to defendants. Typed on printed forms. Each file drawer 13.5 x 5 x 30. Criminal record room, first floor, Criminal Court Building.

737. CRIMINAL INDEX BY NAME
September 1925—, 2 loose-leaf volumes.
An alphabetical index of defendants, listing case number, fingerprint number, crime indicted for, address, file number, previous record, age, disposition of case, name of presiding judge, and date defendant was sentenced. Typed on printed forms.

Volumes average 2000 pages. 15 x 12.5 x 8. Criminal record room, first floor, Criminal Court Building.

738. CASES BY NUMBERS
June 1927——. Approximately 28,000 cards in 6 file drawers.
List case number; name of defendant; residence, occupation, nativity, age, and race; aliases; crime indicted for; date of arrest; and amount of bail bond required. In order of case numbers. Typed on printed forms. Each file drawer 13.5 x 5 x 30. Criminal record room, first floor, Criminal Court Building.

739. CRIMINAL RECORD SHEETS
September 1925——. Approximately 28,000 in 24 file boxes.
List name of defendant, date of arrest, crime charged, date of grand jury hearing, Bertillon photograph number, aliases of defendant, and last crime arrested for, if any. In order of case numbers. Typed on printed forms. Each file box 10.25 x 4.5 x 20. Criminal record room, first floor, Criminal Court Building.

Grand Jury

The institution of the grand jury existed for centuries as part of the English law. (DeLome, *Constitution of England,* XIII, 170). In Ohio law the establishment of the procedure for organizing grand juries was always incumbent upon the legislative body. However, the Jury Code now definitely specifies the qualifications of a juryman and procedure in selecting a jury. (114 O. L. 193).

The law also provides that the grand jury of the county may at any time visit and inspect any of the benevolent or correctional institutions. They may also compel witnesses to attend and testify. (66 O. L. 272). It is the statutory duty of the grand jury to visit the county jail once during each term of court, to examine its state and condition, and to inquire into the discipline and treatment of the prisoners, their habits, diet and accommodation. They must report their findings in writing. (113 O. L. 161).

The grand jury from its origin has been a commission to acquire into the charges preferred against a subject and is meant to be protection against unjust and vindictive prosecutions. It is the duty of the grand jury to conduct investigations of matters which may be presented or which may come to its knowledge, and to determine the action to be taken. The prosecuting attorney is not permitted to be present during the expression of views or the taking of a vote. It may return indictments based wholly upon facts within its own knowledge, without the support of the testimony of a single witness, and it may indict originally without a charge having been made in an inferior court. When a case comes before the grand jury upon a charge preferred in a police court, it has the power to return an indictment according to the facts and evidence, even though it differs from the original charge. The proceedings before the grand jury inquest do not constitute a trial. No adverse party is present, and the person who is conduct is being investigated has no right to appear except by permission and then not as a party, but only as a voluntary witness. The jury is not controlled by any technical rules of evidence, and is not required to disclose proceedings unless called upon by a court of justice. The grand jury may appoint one of its members as clerk, to preserve the minutes of its proceedings. (113 O. L. 158-159).

The Jury Code of 1931 specifies that the grand jury shall consist of fifteen persons, who shall serve for one term of court and shall be selected from the persons who names are contained in the annual jury list. The judge presiding in the criminal branch of common pleas court in this county may appoint any qualified elector, whose name is not included in such a list, to preside as foreman. Twelve members of the jury must concur in returning an indictment. (114 O. L. 203).

The inquisitorial powers of the grand jury commence immediately after they are charged by the court and retire with the officer appointed to attend it. They may consider not only the cases of those persons bound over by the magistrates, but may take in charge matters presented by the court or the prosecuting attorney, and other matters disclosed and brought to the light during the investigations. It is comparatively without limit in the score of its investigation, the bills that it may return, and the general findings that it may make. (22 A. L. R. 356).

740. GRAND JURY CALENDARS
1892——. 37 loose-leaf volumes.
List case number, name of defendant, crime indicted for, date of grand jury hearing, date bound over to the grand jury, and names and addresses of witnesses. Alphabetical index of defendants in each volume. Typed on printed forms. Volumes average 300 pages. 15 x 17 x 2.5. 1892-1928, 29 volumes, second floor, Hart Building; January 1929, 8 volumes, criminal record room, first floor, Criminal Court Building.

Psychiatric Clinic

This clinic is under the directorship of a qualified physician trained in neuro-psychiatry. The clinic furnishes the trial judge with a report showing the mental condition of the prisoner, thus aiding the judge to determine whether hospitalization is preferable to punishment.

741. PSYCHIATRIC DIVISION
January 1, 1925—. 4472 folders.

Records of individual cases, containing social history, report of physician, psychiatric examination, physical examination, and report to the court. Alphabetical as to names of defendants. Typed. Each folder 18 x 12 x .5. Basement, Criminal Court Building.

Probation Department

The common pleas court used its inherent power in 1920 to establish a probation department, with court constables in charge. However, it was not until July 21, 1925 that the department was officially provided for by statute. The law provides that the judges of the court of common pleas of Cuyahoga County, if they deem it advisable, may with the concurrence of the board of county commissioners create a department of probation. It was provided that the department consists of a chief probation officer and such number of other probation officers and employees, clerks, and stenographers as may be fixed from time to time by the judges. The judges have the power to appoint persons to positions within the department, fix the salaries of the appointees within the amount appropriated therefore by the board of county commissioners, and supervise their work; but the persons so appointed must possess such training, experience, and other qualifications as may be prescribed by the department of public welfare of the state. All positions are now classified under the civil service rules of Cuyahoga County.

This department has custody and legal control and supervision of any person resident within the county who may have been placed upon probation by order of any other court exercising criminal jurisdiction in the state, whether within or without the county, upon the request of such court and subject to their continuing jurisdiction; they also received into legal custody or supervision any person paroled or conditionally paroled from a penal, reformatory, or correctional institution and residing or remaining in the county, if requested by the department of public welfare, or other authority having power to parole from any such institutions. (111 O. L. 423).

In all cases in which the probation department acquires custody of or supervision over a person paroled or conditionally paroled from a state penal, reformatory or correctional institution, the common pleas court and the department are governed by the rules and regulations of the state board of clemency applicable to such cases. In case of other persons placed in its control or under its supervision, the department administers the orders and conditions of the authority so placing such persons. The common pleas court may exercise discretionary rules and regulations not inconsistent with law or with the rules and regulations of the state board of clemency which shall be observed and enforced by the probation officers of the department. (111 O. L. 423-July 21, 1925; G. C. sec. 1554-3).

All persons on parole report periodically and are visited by members of the division. Detailed records of the work of the department are kept, and such reports are furnished to the State Department of Public Welfare as may be required. (G. C. sec. 1554-5).

For violation of any of the conditions of parole or rules and regulations of the department, upon written order or complaint of the chief probation office, the person charged is arrested and sentence is executed according to the terms of the original sentence. (111 O. L. 423; G. C. sec. 1554, 1925).

742. PROBATION CASE RECORD

1922—. 7 volumes.

Lists case number, name of defendant, date of sentence, name of presiding judge, or the defendant is in jail or on bail, name of attorney, name of probation officer assigned to the case, date on which case is to be heard before the court, disposition of case, and docket number. In order of case numbers. Handwritten on printed forms. Volumes average 600 pages. 14 x 11 x 1.5. Basement, Criminal Court Building.

743. OFFICE PROBATION RECORD CARDS

1922—. Approximately 6000 in 5 metal file boxes.

List name and description of defendant, address, name of presiding judge, docket number, beginning and final dates of probation, date defendant is to report, name of probation officer, name of case investigator, and all other information known in the case. Alphabetical as to defendants. Handwritten on printed forms. Each file box 8.5 x 5.5 x 24. Basement, Criminal Court Building.

744. PROBATION FILES

1922—. Approximately 12,000 in 45 metal file drawers.

Contain defendant's application for probation, historical record, clearinghouse shoot, synopsis of case, letters of character references, report of investigation, and record of visits made to homes and references. In order of case numbers. Handwritten and typed. Each file drawer 14.5 x 10 x 27. Basement, Criminal Court Building.

745. RECEIPT BOOKS

1922—. 55 volumes.

A record listing name of defendant who makes payment; purpose for payment, such as for restitution, reparation, support, court costs, or fines; and receipt number. In order of case numbers. Handwritten on printed forms. Volumes average 100 pages. 10.5 x 9.5 x .75. Basement, Criminal Court Building.

Court of Appeals

The court of appeals, which superseded the circuit court, was created by the constitution of the State of Ohio and acquires its jurisdiction directly from the constitution as amended September 3, 1912. The amendment provided that the court of appeals shall have original jurisdiction in *quo* warrants, *mandamus, habeas corpus,* prohibition, and precedents. It provided that unless a suit comes under one of these five original writs, the court of appeals has no original jurisdiction thereof. (Ohio Const., Art. 4, sec. 6; 110 O. Jur. 821).

Appellate jurisdiction of the court of appeals was originally divided into two classes; first, the trial *de novo* of chancery cases; and second, the jurisdiction to review, affirm, modify or reverse the judgments of the court of common pleas, superior courts, and other courts of record within the district as provided by law. By Amendment of September 17, 1935, effective January 1, 1936, the filing of a petition in error as a means of review was abolished, and the court of appeals retained only appellate jurisdiction. (116 O. L. 104-130).

The present court of appeals is comprised of three resident judges. Each district has three judges, one of whom is chosen every two years and holds his also for six years. At least one term of the court of appeals is held in each county each year. Additional terms are held at county seats in the district as the judges of the district may determine. (103 O. L. 411).

746. COURT OF APPEALS OPINIONS
January 13, 1913—. 44 volumes, 1-44.
Written opinions by the court giving a complete description of the case and the final decision rendered, lists name of plaintiff, defendant and case number. Alphabetical index of plaintiffs and defendants in each volume. For separate index see number 747. Typed. Volumes average 642 pages. 11 x 12 x 3. Room 215, County courthouse.

747. INDEX TO OPINIONS OF COURT OF APPEALS
January 13, 1913—. 24 file boxes.
An alphabetical card index of plaintiffs and defendants, listing case number, date of entry, record volume and page number. Typed. Each file box 3.5 x 5 x 16. Court of Appeals, second floor, County courthouse.

748. ORIGINAL PLEADINGS AND TRANSCRIPT OF JOURNAL ENTRIES FILED IN COURT OF APPEALS
1913—. 178 Bins; 20 drawers.
Bills of exception and exhibits in all actions filed in court of appeals listing name of plaintiff , defendant, and case number. In order of case numbers. Handwritten and typed. Each bin 30 x 16 x 14; each drawer 26 x 20 x 10. 1913-1927, 88 bins, second floor, Hart Building; 1927-1932, 90 bins, Room 71; 1932—, 20 drawers, Room 254, County courthouse.

749. COURT OF APPEALS FILES
1913—. (Cases 1-15, 500).
All pleadings, motions, *demurrers*, briefs, and other papers pertaining to the case. Handwritten and typed. Each bin 24 x 24 x 18. 320 bins, cases 1-7999, second floor, Hart Building; 84 bins, cases 8000-12, 999, Room 71; 48 bins, cases 13,000-15,500, Room 28; pending cases, 70 bins, 18 x 18 x 10, Room 254, County courthouse.

750. COURT OF APPEALS TRIAL DOCKET
1913—. 23 volumes.
Lists name of plaintiff and defendant, docket number, case number, and disposition of the case. Alphabetical index of plaintiffs and defendants in each volume. Handwritten. Volumes average 600 pages. 14 x 11 x 3. 1913, 1 volume, second floor, Hart Building; 1914-1926, 13 volumes, Room 34; 1927—, 10 volumes, Court of Appeals, second floor, County courthouse.

751. COURT OF APPEALS MOTIONS AND DEMURRER DOCKET
January 1913—. 13 volumes.
Lists name of plaintiff and defendant, case number, docket number, type of case, and final disposition of case. In chronological order. Alphabetical index of plaintiffs and defendants in each volume. Handwritten on printed forms. Volumes average 310 pages. 13.5 x 9 x 2. 5 volumes, Room 34; 8 volumes, Court of Appeals, second floor, County courthouse.

752. COURT OF APPEALS APPEARANCE AND EXECUTION DOCKET
1913—. 16 volumes, 1-16.
Lists name of plaintiff and of defendant, names of attorneys, cost to plaintiff or to defendant, statement of proceedings, docket number, and case number. Alphabetical index of plaintiffs and defendants in each volume. Handwritten on printed forms. Volumes average 600 pages. 18.5 x 12.75 x 3. Volumes, 1-8, Room 34; volumes, 9-16, Room 254, County courthouse.

753. INDEX TO CASES OF COURT OF APPEALS
1913-1922. 1 volume.
An alphabetical index of plaintiffs and defendants, listing the volume and page of the execution docket, date of trial, and case number. Handwritten on printed forms. 400 pages. 16 x 10 x 2. Room 34, County courthouse.

754. COURT OF APPEALS JOURNAL
January 1913—. 10 volumes, 1-9.
Lists name of plaintiff and defendant, case number, and journal entries of cases that have been reviewed by the court of appeals. Journal entries can be traced by case number from the civil appearance docket or from the docket index. Typed. Volumes average 800 pages. 13.5 x 16.5 x 2. Volumes 1-9, Room 34; 1 volume, Room 254, County courthouse.

Supreme Court

The supreme court of Ohio was created by the constitution of 1802, and consists of three judges, appointed by a joint ballot of both houses of the general assembly. (Ohio Const., Art. 3, sec. 1, 2, 8). By statute in 1803 the supreme court was granted original and appellate jurisdiction within the state. The same act provided the time of holding court in each county. (1 O. L. 35). An act of 1831 provided that supreme court should hold court in banc annually, for the final adjudication of all such questions as may be reserved in any county for decision. (29 O. L. 93). The supreme court has provided for in the Constitution of 1851 succeeded the supreme court in banc as a distinct and separate tribunal. (Ohio Const., Art. 4, sec. 1). The district court, created in 1852, succeeded in part to the jurisdiction of the supreme court on the circuit court. (51 O. L. 473).

755. SUPREME COURT RECORDS
1810-1851. 14 volumes, A-M.
A record giving name of plaintiff and defendant, date of entry, and history and disposition of the case. In chronological order. Alphabetical index of plaintiffs and defendants in each volume. Handwritten. Lions average 500 pages. 17 x 12 x 3. Room 34, County courthouse.

756. SUPREME COURT JOURNALS
1810-1852. 4 volumes, A-D.
List name of plaintiff and defendant, case number, and entries of all proceedings in the case. Handwritten. Volumes average 300 pages. Volumes A, B, 9.5 x 7.75 x 1.75; volume C, 14.5 x 9.5 x 1.5; volume D, 15.5 x 11 x 2.25. Room 34, County courthouse.

757. EXECUTION DOCKET
1810-1852. 2 volumes.
Lists name of plaintiff and defendant, case number, date of entry, court cost, disposition of case, and names of witnesses. Alphabetical index of plaintiffs and defendants in each volume. Handwritten. Volumes average 400 pages. 13.25 x 8.75 x 1.75. Room 34, County courthouse.

District Court

The district court, in 1852, succeeded to the jurisdiction and the powers of the supreme court on the circuit, although the court was acting as early as March 21, 1845 under limited jurisdiction. District courts were composed of the judge of common pleas court of the respective districts, and one judge of the supreme court, and three of whom constituted a *quorum*. The court had original jurisdiction with the supreme court, and such appellate jurisdiction as was conferred by law. (Ohio Const., 1851, Art. 4, sec. 5-6; 51 O. L. 473). The nine common pleas court districts were apportioned into five judicial districts for the purpose of the district courts. (50 O. L. 69). Although the court succeeded too many of the powers and much of the jurisdiction of the supreme court on the circuit, it did not succeed to the right of the supreme court to try criminal cases upon election by the accused. Trials of murder cases were assigned to the district court only because of the constitutional right to transfer pending business to other courts. (51 O. L. 474). The circuit court became the successor of the district court by a constitutional amendment of 1883. (80 O. L. 382).

758. DISTRICT COURT FILES
1852-1885. Approximately 3900 in 78 bundles.
Contain all documents filed in each case of the district court. In order of case numbers. Handwritten and typed on printed forms. Each bundle 10 x 13 x 4.5. Second floor, Hart Building.

759. FILES IN CASES REFERRED IN COMMON PLEAS AND DISTRICT COURTS
1858-1864. 1 volume.
Contains a record of all files taken into court and returned to the office of the clerk of courts, and lists case number, name of plaintiff and defendant, title of cause, name of party to whom case was referred to, name of party who referred the case, date on which file was taken to court, and date file was returned to the clerk of courts. Contains an alphabetical index of plaintiffs and defendants. Handwritten on printed forms. 300 pages. 14 x 9 x .75. Second floor, Hart Building.

760. DISTRICT COURT JOURNAL
1852-1885. 6 volumes, D-I.

Lists name of plaintiff and of defendant, date of entry, and case number and gives a complete history of the case. Journal entries can be traced by case number through the appearance docket; if the case number is not known, they can be traced by the name of plaintiff or defendant in the appearance docket index. Handwritten. Volumes average 378 pages. 16 x 11 x 2.5. Room 34, County courthouse.

761. DISTRICT COURT RECORD
1852-1885. 18 volumes, N-Z; 1-5.

Lists name of plaintiff and of defendant, amount of suit, petition filed, *precipe* filed, sheriff's return, transcript and proceedings of the case, date notices were published, date first venire was drawn, names of jurors, and disposition of the case. In chronological order. Handwritten. Volumes average 640 pages. 18.25 x 12 x 2.5. Room 34, County courthouse.

762. DISTRICT COURT DOCKET
1852-1885. 4 volumes.

Lists the case and docket numbers; plaintiff, defendant, and attorneys; cause of action; and disposition of the case. Arranged as to terms of court. For index see number 763. Handwritten on printed forms. Volumes average 350 pages. 14.5 x 9 x 1.75. 1852-1885, 2 volumes, second floor, Hart Building; 1877-1884, 2 volumes, Room 34, County courthouse.

763. DISTRICT COURT INDEX
1852-1885.1 volume.

Contains an alphabetical index of plaintiffs and defendants, listing the volume and page of the docket, and case number. Handwritten on printed forms. 300 pages. 10.75 x 7.25 x 2. Room 34, County courthouse.

764. DISTRICT COURT EXECUTION DOCKET
1852-1885. 3 volumes, D-F.

Lists plaintiff, defendant, and attorneys; a statement of the proceedings; case number; circuit court case number; and costs taxed to plaintiffs and defendants. In chronological order. Alphabetical index of plaintiffs and defendants in each volume. Handwritten on printed forms. Volumes average 600 pages. 18.5 x 12.75 x 3. Room 34, County courthouse.

765. NEW LIST - DISTRICT COURT
1852-1882. 2 volumes.
A record listing name of plaintiff and defendant, docket number, case number, cause of action, and disposition of the case. In chronological order. Handwritten. Volumes average 200 pages. 14 x 9 x 1.5. Second floor, Hart Building.

Circuit Court

The circuit court became the successor to the district court by an amendment of 1883 to the Constitution of Ohio. This amendment provided that the circuit court have original jurisdiction with the supreme court and such appellate jurisdiction as might be provided by law. It left to the legislature the problem of determining the number of judges and the number of circuits. (Ohio Const., Art. 4, sec. 6).

The legislature took cognizance of this when they met in 1884, and divided the state into seven circuits. They provided that three judges were to hold court in each circuit; that one was to be elected for two years, one for four years, and one for six years, beginning February 1885; but thereafter a judge should be elected every two years at the state and county election for a term of six years. All powers and duties of the former district court were conferred by this bill upon the supreme court. (81 O. L. 168-172). In 1885 they were given the right to review all criminal cases which had been decided in inferior courts. (82 O. L. 39). In 1888 they were given the power to grant injunctions. (85 O. L. 151-152). However, the circuit court was superseded by the court of appeals in 1912 by an amendment to the constitution. (Ohio Const., Art. 4, sec. 6).

766. CIRCUIT COURT FILES
1885-1912. Approximately 13,000 in 139 bundles.
Contains all documents filed in each case, including affidavits, depositions, positions, executions, and all legal papers pertaining to the case; and lists name of plaintiff and of defendant, and case number. In order of case number. Handwritten on printed forms. Each bundle 10 x 13 x 4.75. Second floor, Hart Building.

767. CIRCUIT COURT TRIAL DOCKET
1885-1912. 44 volumes.

Lists name of plaintiff and defendant, common pleas case number, docket number, cause of action, and disposition of the case. In chronological order. Handwritten on printed forms. Volumes average 260 pages. 14 x 9 x 1.75. Second floor, Hart Building.

768. CIRCUIT COURT JOURNAL
1885-1912. 13 volumes, 1-13.

Lists name of plaintiff and of defendant, case number, date, cause of action, and disposition of the case. 1885-1906, handwritten; 1906-1912, typed. Volumes average 484 pages. 16.5 x 11.5 x 2.5. Room 34, County courthouse.

769. CIRCUIT COURT APPEARANCE DOCKET
1885-1912. 6 volumes, 1-6.

Lists case number, parties involved, attorney's action, docket number, name of sheriff, return time, pleadings, file date of summons, when returnable, when returned, date of answer, and court entries. Alphabetical index of plaintiffs and defendants in each volume. Handwritten on printed forms. Volumes average 600 pages. 18 x 12.5 x 2. Room 34, County courthouse.

770. CIRCUIT COURT INDEX TO PENDING CASES
1885-1912. 2 volumes.

An alphabetical index of plaintiffs and defendants, listing docket volume and case number. Handwritten on printed forms. Volumes average 400 pages. 11.5 x 7.25 x 1.75. Room 34, County courthouse.

771. CIRCUIT COURT MOTION AND DEMURRER DOCKET
1885-1912. 5 volumes.

Lists name of plaintiff and of defendant, case number, docket number, cause of action, and disposition of case. Contains an alphabetical index of plaintiffs and defendants. Handwritten on printed forms. Volumes average 200 pages. 14 x 9.5 x 2. Second floor, Hart Building.

772. CIRCUIT COURT BILLS OF EXCEPTION
1891-1903. Approximately 13,000 in 4 bins.
Testimony, affidavits, and exhibits in each case that are filed in circuit court, listing name of plaintiff and of defendant, and case number. In order of case numbers. Handwritten and typed. Each bill of exception 14.75 x 9.25 x .75. Second floor, Hart Building.

773. CIRCUIT COURT OPINIONS
December 1898-December 23, 1912. 12 volumes, 1-12.
Opinions and rulings with citations, giving status of case and decision rendered. Alphabetical index of plaintiffs and defendants in each volume. Typed. Volumes average 642 pages. 11 x 12 x 3. Room 215, County courthouse.

Old Superior Court

Courts in Ohio are divided into two classes; those established by the Constitution, and such other courts as the legislation may, from time to time, establish.

The first court to be created by the legislature in Ohio was the Superior Court of Cincinnati. The second was the Superior Court of Cleveland which was established in December 1847. It was given concurrent jurisdiction with the court of common pleas, in all civil cases, law, and in equity, and consists of one judge who was required to reside in the county of Cuyahoga, and to be appointed in the same manner, take the same oath, and hold his office for the same time as a presiding judge of the court of common pleas. He was to receive $1,000 per annum. The statute also provided that all cases pending in common pleas court at the time of the inception of the superior court could be removed to the latter court. (46 O. L. 21).

The Superior Court of Cleveland was abolished by the Constitution of 1852. The abolition, however, was expressly effective February 3, 1853. (Ohio Const., Art. 14, sec. 6). All powers, files, pending cases, journals, and dockets, passed to the court of common pleas. (51 O. L. 317).

774. JOURNAL
1848-1853. 3 volumes, 1-3.
Lists all journal entries of each case, name of plaintiff and of defendant, and case number. Handwritten. 450 pages. 17.5 x 12 x 2.25. Room 34, County courthouse.

775. GENERAL INDEX
1848-1953. 1 volume.
An alphabetical index of plaintiffs and defendants, listing volume number of appearance docket and case number. Handwritten. 450 pages. 17.5 x 12 x 2.25. Room 34, County courthouse.

776. RECORD
1848-1853. 11 volumes, 1-11.
Gives complete history of each case tried, and lists name of plaintiff and defendant, case number, cause of action, and disposition. In chronological order. Handwritten. 600 pages. 18 x 12.5 x 2.75. Room 34, County courthouse.

Late Superior Court

The act establishing the Late Superior Court of Cleveland was passed on May 5, 1873. The court which was presided over by three judges who were to be elected for a term of five years had the briefest tenure of any court in the history of the State of Ohio. The extent of its existence covered a period from June 1873 until March 1875. The act denominated limited jurisdiction for this court, both territorial and as to subject matter. Its jurisdiction was concurrent with the court of common pleas excepting jurisdiction in criminal, bastardy, divorce, alimony, insolvency, police court, and justice of the peace cases, and probate court appeals and condemnation proceedings. The evidence proposed in creating this court was to relieve the court of common pleas, since section 28 of the act provided for the elimination of one judge of that court. (71 O. L. 297-303). The great increase in the volume of civil cases was due in most part to the panic of 1873 and the consequent business failures.

By amendment in January 1875 the act was changed to extend to and to include the jurisdiction of the common pleas court except as to territorial limitations. In that respect its jurisdiction was purely municipal. (72 O. L. 189-190). In March of the same year, during the same session of the legislature, the court was abolished, and all pending matters and papers were transferred to the court of common pleas. (72 O. L. 105).

777. EXECUTION DOCKET

1873-1875. 8 volumes, 1-8.

Lists name of plaintiff and defendant, journal volume and page, court costs and disposition. Alphabetical index of plaintiffs and defendants in each volume. Handwritten. 600 pages. 18 x 13 x 2.75. Room 34, County courthouse.

778. JOURNAL

1873-1875. 4 volumes, 1, A, B, C.

Lists all journal entries of each case, name of plaintiff and defendant, and case number. Handwritten. 450 pages. 17.5 x 12 x 2.25. Room 34, County courthouse.

779. LEVY RECORD

1873-1875. 1 volume.

Lists name of plaintiff and defendant, case number, appraised value, order of sale, confirmation of sale and the amount received. Contains an alphabetical index of plaintiffs and defendants. Handwritten. 600 pages. 18 x 12.5 x 3. Room 34, County courthouse.

779a. APPEARANCE DOCKET

1873-1875. 3 volumes, 1-3.

Lists name of plaintiff and defendant, case number, execution docket number, date on which the pleadings were filed, date summons was issued, date returned, and date on which the answer is due. In order of case numbers. Handwritten on printed forms. 300 pages. 14 x 10 x 2. Volumes 1 and 3, second floor, Hart Building; volume 2, Room 34, County courthouse.

780. MOTION DOCKET

1873-1875. 1 volume.

Lists case number, name of plaintiff and defendant, type of motion, and disposition of motion. Arranged chronologically. Handwritten. 250 pages. 14 x 8.75 x 1.25. Second floor, Hart Building.

780a. RECORD

1873-1875. 10 volumes, 1, 12-21. (volume 13 missing)

Gives complete history of each case tried, lists name of plaintiff and defendant, case number, cause of action, and disposition. In chronological order. Handwritten. 600 pages. 18 x 12.5 x 2.75. Room 34, County courthouse.

781. MINUTE BOOK
1873-1875. 1 volume.

Lists case number, name of plaintiff and defendant, names of attorneys, name of presiding judge, date of entry, and disposition of the case. Arranged chronologically. Handwritten, 484 pages. 10.25 x 8.25 x 2. Second floor, Hart Building.

782. CALENDAR OF JURY CASES
1873-1875. 1 volume.

Lists name of plaintiff and defendant, docket number, case number, date of hearing, cause of action and disposition. Arranged chronologically. Handwritten. 200 pages. 14 x 8.75 x 1.25. Second floor, Hart Building.

783. WITNESS BOOK
1873-1875. 1 volume.

Lists names of witnesses, number of days served, mileage, voucher number, and date of issuance. Alphabetically arranged. Handwritten. 300 pages. 14 x 9 x 2. Second floor, Hart Building.

Insolvency Court

On March 11, 1896, in the General Assembly, Senate Bill number 87 was passed creating the court of insolvency for Cuyahoga County. (92 O. L. 475).

The insolvency court was created in order to relieve the probate court in matters relating to the mode of administering assignments for the benefit of creditors, the appropriation of land for public purposes, and the assessment of damages occasioned by a public improvement. The judge of insolvency court was originally elected for a term of five years, and in every respect had the same powers, discharged the same duties, and incurred the same penalties, as a judge of probate court, with reference to matters under his jurisdiction. (92 O. L. 475). The term of office was changed to four years in 1906. (98 O. L. 389). The judge of insolvency court was also designated judge of the juvenile court in 1908, and exercised concurrent powers in both of these courts. (99 O. L. 192).

The insolvency court was abolished by an act of 1931 which provided that the court function until December 31, 1934 at which time all matters pending in insolvency court, by which the juvenile court had jurisdiction should be transferred to that court; that all matters of which the common pleas court had jurisdiction be transferred to the common pleas court; and that all matters in which the probate court had jurisdiction, of which neither the juvenile court nor the common pleas court had jurisdiction, be transferred to probate court. (114 O. L. 44).

784. INSOLVENCY COURT FILES
1897-1934. 202 metal file boxes.
All papers filed in the case, such as summons, affidavits, petitions, answers, and the decree granted in the court. In order of case numbers. Handwritten and typed. Each file box 10.5 x 5 x 14. Second floor, Hart Building.

785. JOURNAL
February 1897-December 1828. 34 volumes, 1-34.
Contains all court entries giving name of plaintiff and of defendant, docket number, and case number. Journal entries can be traced by case number from the civil appearance docket or from the docket indexes. February 1897-December 1911, handwritten; 1912-1928, typed. Average 500 pages. 13 x 16 x 2.5. Room 34, County courthouse.

786. EXECUTION DOCKET
May 1898-September 1904. 1 volume, 1.
Gives name of attorney, names of parties, and statement of proceedings. Contains an alphabetical index of plaintiffs and defendants. Handwritten on printed forms. 600 pages. 13 x 16 x 3.5. Room 34, County courthouse.

787. ASSIGNMENT RECORD
1897-1934. 58 volumes, 1-58.
Gives a complete transcript of proceedings of assignment in trust for creditors, showing the case, docket and page numbers, title of case, deed of assignment filed, schedule of debts filed, inventory of estate filed, property appraisal, final report of assignee etc. For index see number 790. Typed. Volumes average 400 pages. 14 x 18.75 x 3.5. Volumes 1-31, Room 34; volumes 32-58, Room 254, County courthouse.

788. APPROPRIATION RECORD OF LAND
March 1897-1930. 11 volumes, 1-11.

Transcripts of proceedings to appropriate certain lands to public use, giving the title of case, its number, docket and page number, application to assess compensation filed, description of land involved, verdict rendered, etc. Some of the older records contain the sketches and drawings submitted to the court as exhibits, showing the property involved. Volumes 1-4 contain an alphabetical index, and are handwritten; the others are indexed under number 790, and are typed. Volumes average 400 pages. 15 x 18 x 3.5. Room 34, County courthouse.

789. CIVIL APPEARANCE DOCKET
February 1897-1934. 31 volumes, 1-31.

Gives name of attorney, the parties, the date, statement of proceedings, and case number. Docket contains references to all court proceedings in insolvency court. In order of case numbers. For index see number 790. Handwritten on printed forms. Volumes average 1000 pages. 13 x 18.75 x 2.75. Room 34, County courthouse.

790. INDEX TO CIVIL DOCKETS
February 1897-1929. 3 volumes, 1-3.

An alphabetical index of plaintiffs and defendants, listing case number and general remarks. Also an index to record of assignments and appropriation record of land. Handwritten on printed forms. Volumes average 460 pages. 13 x 18 x 2.75. Room 34, County courthouse.

791. RECORD OF APPEALS
July 1897-February 1903. 2 volumes, 2-3. Volume 1 missing.

Gives the legal proceedings of the original case, docket number, name of plaintiff and of defendant, case number, and application for appeal. Contains an alphabetical index of plaintiffs and defendants. Handwritten. Volumes average 550 pages. 13 x 18.75 x 3. Room 34, County courthouse.

792. PROCEEDINGS IN APPROPRIATION OF PROPERTY BY MUNICIPAL CORPORATIONS
1926. 36 envelopes in 2 bundles.

Includes various papers filed in the matter of appropriation of property by municipal corporations, such as description of the property, application to assess compensation, cross-petitions, and attorneys' correspondence. In order of case numbers. Handwritten and typed on printed forms. Each bundle 9.75 x 14.75 x 2. Second floor, Hart Building.

793. RECORD OF LAND SALES
March 1897-February 1908. 3 volumes, 1-3.

Lists names of plaintiff and defendant and volume and page number; includes a copy of notices filed; and gives an account of the legal proceedings. Contains an alphabetical index of plaintiffs and defendants. Handwritten. Volumes average 600 pages. 13 x 18 x 3. Room 254, County courthouse.

794. DIVORCE RECORD
March 1910-August 1925. 24 volumes, 1-24.

Copies of petitions filed, of affidavits or publication, of proof of publication, of motion to advance, of granting of the motion, and the courts decision concerning the granting of the decree. Lists names of plaintiffs and defendants, and case number. Typed. Volumes average 1400 pages. 14 x 18 x 3. Room 34, County courthouse.

795. ALIMONY ACCOUNTS
July 1910-April 1925. 4 volumes, 1-4.

Lists date and amount of payment, of whom received, case number, and to whom paid. Alphabetical index of plaintiffs and defendants in each volume. Handwritten on printed forms. Volumes average 500 pages. 14 x 16 x 3.5. Room 34, County courthouse.

796. CASH BOOK
March 1914-December 1934. 7 volumes, 1-7.

Lists the docket number; case number; by whom paid; total fund; individual funds for sheriff, witnesses, interest, awards, deposits, and sundries; and date of disbursement. In chronological order. Handwritten on printed forms. Volumes average 500 pages. 17 x 19 x 2.5. Room 71, County courthouse.

The predecessor of the probate court was the ecclesiastical court of England. William the Conqueror separated the civil and the ecclesiastical jurisdictions, and forbade tribunals of either class from assuming cognizance of cases pertaining to the other. (Holdsworth, *op. cit.,* I, 580).

A court of probate was established by an ordinance of the Northwest Territory, published August 30, 1788, defining its powers and jurisdiction. (Pease, *op. cit.,* 9). However, under the Ohio Constitution of 1802 (Art. 3, sec. 5) the court of common pleas was given jurisdiction in all probate and testamentary matters. The probate court was restored as a separate court in 1851 under the new constitution, which defined the jurisdiction of the probate court as follows: "The probate court shall have jurisdiction in probate and testamentary matters, the appointment of administrators and guardians, and such jurisdiction in *habeas corpus,* the issuing of marriage licenses, and for the sale of land by executors, administrators, and guardians, and such other jurisdiction, in any county or counties as may be provided by law." The judge of probate court was elected for a term of three years. (Ohio Const., 1851, Art. 4, sec. 7-8).

The probate court, upon its establishment, succeeded to all probate jurisdiction previously invested in the court of common pleas. The code of civil procedure adopted in 1853 interrupted the constitutional provisions affecting the probate court, listing in detail the powers implicit in the constitution of 1851. It defined all cases in which the probate court shall have exclusive jurisdiction and all cases in which it shall have concurrent jurisdiction; it outlined the organization of the court; and describe the powers and duties of the probate judge in civil and criminal actions. The code specifies that the following records be kept by the probate court: criminal record, civil docket, journal, record of wills, final record of causes, record of inventory, record of accounts, and execution docket. It also required that all records contain complete alphabetical indexes. (51 O. L. 167-178).

The civil code provided that the probate court make inquests respecting insane persons, and deaf and dumb persons subject by law to guardianship. In 1856 the court acquired statutory jurisdiction for the commitment of idiots, imbeciles and lunatics to institutions maintained for that purpose and also empowered to appoint and remove guardians over the estates of such persons. (53 O. L. 81-96). Two years later the court was given power to appoint and remove guardians over minors. (55 O. L. 54). In 1870 they were authorized to render adoption decrees. (67 O. L. 14). In 1889 they were empowered to appoint and remove guardians over the estates of a habitual drunkard. (86 O. L. 196). In 1913 the court was authorized to appoint and remove guardians or persons confined in state, benevolent, or penal institutions under the order of any court. (103 O. L. 471).

The probate court originally had limited criminal jurisdiction in cases in which the sentence did not impose capital punishment. The civil code also provided that the court of common pleas have appellate jurisdiction in all matters arising in probate court. (51 O. L. 173).

The court was given full equity jurisdictions by the act of April 12, 1858, relative to the sale of property of deceased persons in proceedings to discharge debts. (55 O. L. 157). In 1888 a measure was adopted which provided that all banks and persons engaged in loaning money for profit file with the court an annual statement of all unclaimed deposits, and that a special record be kept for that purpose. (85 O. L. 65-67).

The Ohio direct inheritance tax law was enacted in 1894 (91 O. L. 166) and declared unconstitutional in 1895. (53 O. S. 325). A year before the act was passed, a collateral inheritance tax law was enacted. (90 O. L. 14). The letter was sustained by the supreme court in 1897 (55 O. S. 613), and contained to be the law until 1919 when the present law was enacted. (108 O. L. pt. 1, 561). A second direct tax law was passed in 1904 but repealed in 1906. (97 O. L. 398; 98 O. L. 229). An amendment was written into the constitution in 1912 which provided that the inheritance tax laws either direct or collateral may be enacted. (Ohio Const., 1912, Art. 12, sec. 7). In accordance with the present law enacted in 1919 applications for the determination of such taxes are filed with a probate court, which directs the county auditor to appraise the property belonging to the decedent's estate. On the return of appraisal, the probate court determines and assesses the tax, which is paid to the county treasurer. (108 O. L. pt. 1, 561).

In 1906 a measure was adopted which provided that the probate judge appoint six persons to serve as a board of county visitors for the inspection of all charitable and correctional institutions supported in whole or in part from county or municipal funds. (98 O. L. 29). Births and deaths were registered with the probate court until May 5, 1906, when an act of legislature provided for the proper registration as such vital statistics in cities, villages, and townships under the supervision of the secretary of state. (99 O. L. 206-307). This was amended in 1921 to the effect that a copy of all certificates of birth and deaths must be transmitted to the probate judge. (109 O. L. 403).

The registration of licensed physicians was required in 1896; and a similar act affecting registered nurses was passed in 1915. (92 O. L. 47; 106 O. L. 193).

In 1913 the court was given the power by statute to grant injunctions. (103 O. L. 427). Two years later the probate judge was made a member of a county board for the appointment of a county board of revision. This act was repealed in 1917. (106 O. L. 433-434; 107 O. L. 29). In the same session the court was given jurisdiction in road condemnation proceedings. (105 O. L. 583).

In 1917 a measure was enacted which provided for the creation of park districts for the purpose of preserving natural resources. The probate court was given the power to receive applications for the creation of such park districts, and was also empowered to appoint three persons to constitute a board known as the Metropolitan Park Board. (107 O. L. 65-66).

The probate judge was authorized in 1921 to determine the territory of a county library district, and to certify such action to deputy state supervisors of elections, who then submit the question of establishing a library to the electors residing in the territory and comprising the proposed library district. (109 O. L. 351). The Cuyahoga County Library was organized in 1924.

An act of 1929 provided that any owner of property to be assessed or taxed for improvements, may appeal to probate court from the action of the county commissioners in order to determine the necessity of improvement, the boundaries of the assessment district and the tentative apportionment of the assessment. (113 O. L. 289).

On January 1, 1932, a new Ohio probate code became effective codifying all the statutes affecting the probate court. In addition, such amendments were made as were deemed necessary. Among the significant changes affecting the probate court at the time was the repeal of statutes granting the court limited criminal jurisdiction, the granting of jurisdiction in the construction of wills and declaratory judgments, and changes in the dower statute and the statute pertaining to descent and distribution. An amendment adopted in 1931 provided that five days must elapse after application, before marriage licenses be issued. (114 O. L. 320-481).

An amendment of May 23, 1935 provided that a probate judge shall be elected quadrennially in each county, and that he shall be a practicing attorney or a probate judge at the time the act was passed (116 O. L. 481). Assignments for the benefit of creditors were originally under the jurisdiction of the probate court until 1897 (92 O. L. 475), when the insolvency court assumed jurisdiction. Upon the abolition of the insolvency court in 1935, such jurisdiction was returned to the probate court. (114 O. L. 44).

Each probate judge has the care and custody of the files, papers, and records belonging to the probate court. He is authorized to perform the duties of clerk of his own court, and appoint a deputy clerk or clerks, who may perform the duties appertaining to the office of clerk of court. (53 O. L. 137; 114 O. L. 321).

The probate court has been held to have limited and special jurisdiction as provided by the constitution and statutory law. However, the probate court has plenary power at law and inequity to dispose fully of any matter properly before the court, unless the power is expressly or otherwise limited or denied by statute.

General Records

797. COURT CALENDARS
February 1898—. 456 volumes.
List date of case, case number, names of persons involved, title of action, and general remarks. In the chronological order. Handwritten and typed on printed forms. Volumes average 200 pages. 12 x 14.25 x 2.5. February 1898-1932, 410 volumes, Room 27; 1933—, 46 volumes, Room 250, County courthouse.

798. COMMON PLEAS FILE DOCKET A
Mar. 1811-1852. Approximately 1050 files in 21 file boxes.
Wills, probations of wills, affidavits, final statements, and other papers pertinent to probate cases. Filed by case number. Handwritten. Each file box 4.75 x 10.75 x 14. Room 250, County courthouse.

799. PROBATE FILES
1852—. 7629 file boxes, A-K-278. (Cases 1-246,000).
Wills, probation of wills, affidavits, final statements, and other papers pertinent to the case. In order of case numbers. Handwritten and typed. Each file box 4.75 x 10.75 x 14. Room 250, County courthouse.

800. JOURNAL
March 1852—. 434 volumes. (March 1852-October 1886, 26 volumes, A-Z; October 1886—, 408 volumes, 27-434).
Contains accounts of all court proceedings, giving the term of court, docket number for which entry was made, case number, title of case, and name of plaintiff and defendant. March 1852-August 1904, handwritten; August 1914—, typed. Volumes average 576 pages. 13 x 18.75 x 3. Room 250, County courthouse.

801. CIVIL APPEARANCE DOCKET
1852—. 243 volumes, 1-276 (excluding insane dockets).

A record containing abridged entries of the proceedings of all cases appearing in probate court. It lists title of case, names of parties involved, case number, and a reference to the records in which the original accounts of all proceedings are recorded. Among the types of actions listed are land sales, adoptions, insolvents, change of name, determination of heirship, declaratory judgments, condemnation of property, etc. For indexes see numbers 802, 803, 804, and 805. 1852-1917, handwritten; 1917—, typed. Volumes average 1000 pages. 18 x 12 x 3. Room 250, County courthouse.

802. INDEX TO CIVIL APPEARANCE DOCKET
1852—. 14 volumes (March 1852-June 1901, 1 volume, A-P, 17-61; February 1901—, 13 volumes, 4-17, which cover original docket volumes 17—.

An alphabetical index of plaintiffs and defendants, decedents, wards, adopting parents, guardians, etc., listing docket number and the cause of action. Handwritten, printed, and typed on printed forms. Volumes average 500 pages. 16 x 18.75 x 3.5. Room 250, County courthouse.

803. INDEX TO ESTATES
March 1811-December 1896. 1 volume, A-Z.

An alphabetical index of guardians, listing case number, docket number, and record volume and page. Handwritten on printed forms. 190 pages. 9.25 x 12.25 x 1.25. Room 250, County courthouse.

804. INDEX TO ADMINISTRATION DOCKET
March 1888—. 16 volumes, 1-16.

An alphabetical index of decedents, listing docket number, name of administrator or executor, and general remarks. Handwritten and typed on printed forms. Volumes average 428 pages. 16 x 18.75 x 3.5. 15 volumes, Room 250; volume 12, Room 27, County courthouse.

805. INDEX TO GUARDIANS DOCKET
1862—. 13 volumes (1862-1888, 1 volume; February 1888—, 12 volumes, 1-12).

An alphabetical index of parents and guardians, listing docket number, case number and name of ward. 1862-1888, 1 volume, 150 pages, 12.5 x 18.75 x 2, Handwritten on printed forms, Room 27; 1888—, 12 volumes, 1-12, average 400 pages, 16 x 18.75 x 3.5, handwritten and typed on printed forms, Room 250, County courthouse.

806. COMMON PLEAS PROBATE DOCKET
1811-1851. 2 volumes, A-B.

Lists case number, title of case, names of parties involved, date of filing, and all proceedings of the case. Alphabetical index of plaintiffs and defendants in each volume. Handwritten. Volumes average 600 pages. 18 x 12 x 3. Room 250, County courthouse.

807. COMMON PLEAS PROBATE DOCKET
1811-1934. 1 volume.

Lists name of plaintiff and defendant, case number, cause of action, disposition of case, and volume and page of the journal indicating all journal entries. Alphabetical index of plaintiffs and defendants in each volume. Handwritten. 360 pages. 17 x 13 x 1. Second floor, Hart Building.

Estates and Guardianships

808. RECORD OF WILLS
March 1852—. 234 volumes (March 1852-September 1883, 26 volumes, A-Z; 1883—, 208 volumes, 27-234).

Exact copies of all wills filed in Cuyahoga County. Contains applications for probate of will, notices of applications to admit will to probate, presentation to the court for probate and record of will, and a record of the will and testament. It lists the civil docket numbers, case number, and the volume and page of the journal. An alphabetical index of names of testators in each volume. March 1852-January 1911 handwritten; January 1911—, typed. Volumes average 590 pages. 13 x 18.75 x 3.5. Room 250, County courthouse.

809. DETERMINATION OF HEIRS, DECLARATORY JUDGMENTS AND CONSTRUCTION OF WILLS

1932—. 6 file boxes (pending); 1932—, 14 file boxes (completed). Approximately 600 in 20 file boxes.

Petitions, together with various pertinent papers, with the name of the decedent and the case number on the face of the jacket. In order of case numbers. Handwritten and typed on printed forms. Each file box 4.75 10.75 14. Room 250, County courthouse.

810. RECORD OF EXECUTOR'S BONDS

1870—. 14 volumes.

List name of executor, amount of bond, date posted, name of decedent, oath of executor, and his signature. Alphabetical index of executors in each volume. Handwritten on printed forms. Volumes average 600 pages. 13 x 18 x 2.5. Room 250, County courthouse.

811. RECORD OF ADMINISTRATION BONDS

1862—. 77 volumes, 1-77.

Gives name of administrator, bond, amount, when posted, name of decedent, jurat, and signature of administrator. Alphabetical index of administrators and each volume. Handwritten on printed forms. Volumes average 600 pages. 13 x 18 x 2.5. Room 250, County courthouse.

812. RECORD OF GUARDIANSHIP BONDS

April 1862—. 43 volumes, 1-43. (Record of Guardians' Bonds and Letters, 1862-1925, 31 volumes, 1-31; Record of Guardians Bonds, Minors, 1925—, 9 volumes, 32, 34, 35, 38-43; Record of Guardians, Improvident, 1922—, 4 volumes, 33, 34, 36, and 37. For records prior to and following these dates, see Miscellaneous Records).

Lists name of guardian, amount of bond, date of posting the condition of the obligation, and signature of guardian. Contains an alphabetical index of minors. Handwritten on printed forms. Volumes average 1050 pages. 12 x 16 x 2.5. Room 27; current volumes, Room 250, County courthouse.

813. INHERITANCE TAX DOCKETS
June 1919—. 21 volumes, 1-21.

Lists name of administrator; docket number; case number; name of decedents and their residence; date and place of death; administrator's or executor's address; estimated value of real property; value of personal property per inventory; value of auditor's appraisal for real and personal property; total value of auditor's appraisal; value as fixed by probate judge for real and personal property; total value; total of indebtedness; total cost of administration; net value of estate; heirs at law; names, addresses, and relationship of heirs; names and addresses of legatees and devisees; list of properties inherited, real and personal; value, exemptions, and net value subject to tax; amount of inheritance tax; rate of taxation; where tax originated; city, village, or township; date of accrued tax; date of payments; and amount paid. Alphabetical index of decedents in each volume. Typed on printed forms. Volumes average 575 pages. 13 x 18.75 x 3.5. Room 250, County courthouse.

814. INHERITANCE TAX RECORDS
1919—. 110 volumes, 1-110.

A record of the entire proceedings, listing name of decedent; civil docket number; case number; application for determination of inheritance tax; designation of court if court action is taken; a sworn statement by executor of will being filed in probate court, with an itemized statement of assets and liabilities, and of beneficiaries under the will with their names and ages, and their relationships to the deceased person; a journal entry by the court determining the inheritance tax, if any, to be paid; and court costs accrued during these proceedings. Alphabetical index of decedents in each volume. Typed. Volumes average 600 pages. 13 x 18.75 x 3.5. 36 volumes, 1-36, Room 27; 74 volumes, 37-110, Room 250, County courthouse.

815. LAND SALES RECORD
1852—. 220 volumes (March 1852-October 1888, 26 volumes, A-Z; October 1887, 194 volumes, 27-220).

Gives name of plaintiff and defendant; civil docket number; case number; petitions; description of land involved; schedule of debts; *precipe*; summons; summons returns; answer and cross petitions of the defendants; finding of the court as recorded in the journal, giving the journal volume and page, order of appraisal, order of appraisal returned, order of sale, report of sale, confirmation of sale, amount realized, distribution of proceeds of sale, settlement by the court, and court costs. Alphabetical index of plaintiffs and defendants in each volume. March 1852-

January 1911, handwritten; 1911—, typed. Volumes average 600 pages. 12.25 x 18.75 x 3.5. Volumes A-Z, 27-180, Room 27; volumes 181-220, Room 250, County courthouse.

816. RECORD OF ASSIGNMENTS
September 30, 1859-November 1897, 37 volumes.

Complete record of the various proceedings involved in assignments for the benefit of creditors. Chronological. An alphabetical index in each volume. Handwritten. Volumes average 700 pages. 12 x 16 x 3.5. Room 27, County courthouse.

Psychiatric Division

817. INSANE APPEARANCE DOCKET
1852—. 36 volumes (23, 36, 51, 62, 69, 80, 87, 94, 105, 110-112, 115, 120, 125, 130, 135, 145, 160, 166, 175, 180, 185, 190, 195, 206, 215, 225, 230, 235, 240, 245, 250, 255, 260, 265, 275).

These volumes are contained in the complete insane and civil appearance docket. They list name of insane person, case number, and status of action. In order of case numbers. For separate index see number 818. Contains an alphabetical index of insane persons and guardians. 1852-1917, handwritten; 1917—, typed. Volumes average 1000 pages. 18 x 12 x 3. Room 250, County courthouse.

818. INDEX TO INSANE CASES
1852—. 4 volumes, 1-4.

An alphabetical index of insane persons, listing the insane docket number and the case number. 1852-1924—, typed. Volumes average 1000 pages. 18 x 12 x 3. Room 250, County courthouse.

819. INQUEST OF LUNACY
April 1904—. 98 volumes, 1-98.

A complete record of all lunacy inquest, listing filing date of complaint, names of friends or relatives, date of warrant for arrest, if issued, statement of its return, record of inquest, doctor's certificate, volume and page of the civil docket, and case number. Alphabetical index of insane persons in each volume. 1904-1916, handwritten; 1917—, typed. Volumes average 600 pages. 12.5 x 18.75 x 3.5. 1904-1926, 72 volumes, 1-72, Room 27; 1927—, 26 volumes, 73-98, Room 250, County courthouse.

820. INSANE RECORD
1912-1913. 1 volume.

Lists docket number, date of commitment, date of discharge. Alphabetical index of insane persons. Handwritten on printed forms. 400 pages. 14 x 18 x 2.5. Room 250, County courthouse.

821. CARD SYSTEM INDEX TO INSANITY CASES (Active and Inactive Cases).
1913—. 18 file boxes.

Each card list name of patient, place of commitment, case number, date of commitment, and name of examining physician. Arranged alphabetically by names of insane persons. Handwritten on printed forms. Each file box 19 x 4 x 6. 12 file boxes, inactive cases; 3 file boxes, active cases; 3 file boxes, feeble-minded and epileptic cases. Room 250, County courthouse.

822. APPLICATIONS FOR COMMITMENT TO THE INSTITUTION FOR FEEBLE-MINDED
1930—. 3 file boxes.

Applications for less urgent cases that have not been examined or certified. Each list the name and residence of parents, guardians, or others making the application; birthplace of applicant; date of birth; question of physical and mental fitness; general capabilities; family weaknesses, etc. General correspondence pertaining to the case is filed with the application. Handwritten on printed forms. Filed alphabetically. Each file box 17 x 11.5 x 4.5. Room 250, County courthouse.

Accounts and Inventories

823. INVENTORY AND SALES RECORD
1852—. 203 volumes (March 1852-August 1889, 16 volumes, A-P; June 1889—, 187 volumes, 1-187).

Lists filing date of inventory and appraisal, fiduciaries' or ward oaths, schedules of personal goods and chattels belonging to the estates, and liabilities of the estates. Alphabetical index of estates in each volume. 1852-1920, A-P, 1-86, handwritten; 1915—, 87-187, typed. Volumes average 600 pages. 13 x 18.75 x 3. 1852-1927, A-P, 1-143, Room 27; 1928—, 44 volumes, Room 250, County courthouse.

824. RECORD OF PARTIAL AND FINAL ACCOUNTS
March 1911—. 506 volumes; 153 file boxes. (Common Pleas Probate Record, March 1811-1878, 25 volumes, A-H, J-Z; Record of Accounts 1878-1933, 481 volumes, 1-481, 1933—, 153 file boxes of accounts not recorded).

Volumes A-H, 1811-1852, are records of the common pleas court pertaining to probate matters. Contains a description of the estate, record of wills, a listing of partial and final accounts, and docket volume and page. Alphabetical index of estates in each volume. 1811-1925, handwritten; March 1925—, typed. Volumes average 600 pages. 13 x 19 x 3.5; each file box 9 x 11.25 x 3. 1811-1927, 281 volumes, A-H, J-Z, 1-251, Room 27; 1928—, 225 volumes, 153 file boxes, Room 250, County courthouse.

825. RECEIPTS PERTAINING TO ESTATES
1852—. 1709 bundles.

All receipts marked "paid." They pertain to the expenditures and disbursements of an estate and are filed in the original jackets. The serial numbers of the case is recorded on each bundle. Handwritten on printed forms. Each bundle 10 x 6 x 4. Room 27, County courthouse.

826. CARD INDEX OF UNPAID ACCOUNTS
January 1895—. Approximately 3800 cards in 76 file boxes.

Statements of expenses and costs accrued during probate proceedings. They are not posted in the record of accounts until paid. In order of case numbers. Handwritten on printed forms. Each file box 4.75 x 10.25 x 14. Room 245, County courthouse.

827. ACCOUNT DOCKET
September 1915—. 65 volumes,

Lists accounts for estates, guardianships of minors, insane or incompetent persons, trustees, etc. The record contains a brief notation of partial and final payments, giving case number and amount of payment. In order of case numbers. Typed on Printed forms. Volumes average 200 pages. 9 x 15 x 2. Room 27; current volume, Room 250, County courthouse.

828. GENERAL CIVIL DOCKET
1897-1905. 3 volumes, 41-43.

This record was kept as an office memorandum for accounts advertised. These accounts came up for hearing the first Monday of each month. In chronological order. Handwritten on printed forms. Volumes average 200 pages. 12 x 18 x 1.5. Room 27, County courthouse.

Cashier's Records

829. PROBATE FEE BOOK
1881—. 6 volumes. (1881-1883 1 volume; January 1907-December 1922, 4 volumes, 1-4; 1926—, 1 volume.

A record of fees received by the court, listing case number; names of fiduciaries, plaintiffs, and defendants; costs paid by each; date of payment; and name of writ. Alphabetical index of payees in each volume. Handwritten on printed forms. Volumes average 500 pages. 12.5 x 18 x 2.75. 1881-1883, 1 volume, second floor, Hart Building; January 1907-December 1922, 4 volumes, Room 27; 1926—, 1 volume, Room 250, County courthouse.

830. CASH BOOK
1888—. 99 volumes (1888-1913, 20 volumes, 1-20; 1913-1924, 25 volumes, 1-25; 1924—, 54 volumes, 26-79).

A record of all cash receipts and disbursements, listing the case number; date; total payment; by whom paid; name of county; itemized accounts for fees, witnesses, recorder, sheriff, daily papers, foreign sheriff, sundries; date of disbursements and payments received; to whom paid; and total amount expended. Alphabetical index of payees or recipients in each volume. Handwritten on printed forms. Volumes average 200 pages. 17 x 17 x 2.5. 1888-1924, 45 volumes, 1-45, Room 27; 1924—, 54 volumes, Room 250, County courthouse.

831. JUROR AND WITNESS FEES
1888—. 79 volumes.

Contains stubs of certificates, showing certificate number, person to whom paid, amount, docket number, and date. In order of certificate numbers. Handwritten on printed forms. Volumes average 400 pages. 14 x 15.5 x 1.5. 1888-1928, 68 volumes, Room 27; 1928—, 11 volumes, Room 250, County courthouse.

832. FOREIGN SHERIFF AND WITNESS FEES
January 1920—. 8 volumes.

Contains receipt stubs, and indicate cashbook and page number, name of payee (either witness or foreign sheriff), and amount. In order of receipt numbers. Handwritten on printed forms. Volumes average 400 pages. 14 x 15 x 1.5. Room 250, County courthouse.

833. RECORD OF ACCRUED FEES
1907—. 60 volumes (8 volumes, 1-8; 22 volumes, 9-20, each number covering 2 volumes marked parts I and II; 12 volumes, 21-24, each number covering volumes marked parts I, II and III; 8 volumes, 25-26, marked parts I, II, III and IV; 6 volumes, 27-28, each number covering 3 volumes marked parts I, II, and III, 4 volumes, 29, each number covering 4 volumes marked parts I, II, III and IV).

Lists case number, title of case, charges, credit, nature of proceeding, amount due the probate court from the county, date of payment, and sundries. In chronological order. Handwritten on printed forms. Volumes average 500 pages. 15 x 17 x 4.25. Room 250, County courthouse.

834. UNCLAIMED DEPOSITS OF BANKS
July 1899—. 1 volume, 1.

A record listing name of bank and of depositor, amount due plus interest, and a sworn statement of bank officer confirming the list. Alphabetical index of depositors in each volume. Handwritten on printed forms. 500 pages. 12 x 18.75 x 3. Room 250, County courthouse.

835. PROBATE COURT RECEIPTS
1918—. 573 volumes.

List receipt number, case number, cashbook volume and page, date of receipt, person received from, number and name of estate, itemized statements, and the total amount for which receipt is given. In order a receipt numbers. Handwritten on printed forms. Volumes average 400 pages. 11 x 14 x 1.75. 1918-1924, 462 volumes, Room 27; 1924—, 111 volumes, Room 250, County courthouse.

836. INSANE INVOICES
December 1904-August 1907. 5 volumes, 14-28.
Includes cost bill; record of the individual fees for filing the affidavit, docketing the case, holding inquest, and sheriff's charges; and name of insane party and of judge. Alphabetical index of insane persons in each volume. Handwritten on printed forms. Volumes average 175 pages. 10 x 16 x 2. Room 27, County courthouse.

837. DAY BOOK
1897-1903. 4 volumes.
Lists case number, to whom charged, amount charged, amount of cash received, and remarks. This record was evidently supplementary to the daily cash record. In chronological order. Handwritten on printed forms. Volumes average 356 pages. 11.5 x 16 x 2. Room 27, County courthouse.

838. RECAPITULATION BOOK
November 1888-April 1889. 1 volume.
A record of monies received by the cashier from all departments of probate court. In chronological order. Handwritten on printed forms. 100 pages. 10 x 14 x 18. Room 27, County courthouse.

Criminal Records

839. CRIMINAL DOCKET FILES
1852-December 1931. 56 file cases.
A file of all papers pertaining to the case, such as motions, criminal bonds, cost bills, affidavits , subpoenas, etc. In order of case numbers. Handwritten and typed on printed forms. Each file box 4.5 x 10.25 x 13.5. Room 27, County courthouse.

840. CRIMINAL EXECUTION DOCKET
August 1852-December 4, 1931. 7 volumes, A-G.
Lists case number, names of defendant, prosecuting attorney, judge, sheriff, and justice of peace; date of filing transcript; names of witnesses; decision of the court; and general remarks. This is a docket of cases referred from justice of peace courts to probate court for final jurisdiction. Alphabetical index of defendants in each volume. Handwritten on printed forms. Volumes average 800 pages. 12.5 x 18.75 x 3. Volumes A-F, Room 27; volume G, Room 250, County courthouse.

841. CRIMINAL JOURNAL
1878-1886. 1 volume, 1.

Gives a complete history of the case from the time the official charges made by the prosecutor to the final decision of the court. It also includes testimony, cross-examinations, motions for new trials, etc. Alphabetical index of defendants. Handwritten. 500 pages. 12.25 x 18.75 x 2.25. Room 27, County courthouse.

842. DAILY JOURNAL
1913-1915, 3 volumes.

Lists number and names of parties involved in court proceedings. Alphabetical index of defendants in each volume. Handwritten on printed forms. Volumes average 200 pages. 10 x 18 x 1.5. Room 72, County courthouse.

Licenses and Certificates

843. MARRIAGE RECORD (and Banns)
1810—. 176 volumes, 1-176.

Shows application number and date license was issued; name, age, residence, place of birth, and occupation of each party; names of parents and minister; date as to previous marriage, if any; and date marriage was performed. Beginning in 1891 banns were recorded in separate volumes designated "Banns;" previously they were listed in the back of each volume. Prior to 1928 each volume contains an alphabetical index. For subsequent index and separate index for complete series see number 844. 1810-1918, handwritten; 1918—, type on printed forms. Volumes average 500 pages. 12 x 19 x 3.5. Room 250, County courthouse.

844. MARRIAGE INDEX
1810-1907, 4 volumes, 1-4. (Banns not included).

Alphabetically arranged by periods (1810-1875, 1875-1890, 1890-1902, 1901-1907) giving name, and record volume and page number. Typed on printed forms. Volumes average 500 pages. 15 x 19 x 3. Work of completing this index has been temporarily suspended. Room 250, County courthouse.

Index to marriage records, 1928—. 4 volumes, 1-4.
      For description see "Marriage Index" above. Room 250, County courthouse.

845. MARRIAGE LICENSE (Banns)
1889—. Approximately 8500 in 20 file boxes.
Gives date of marriage, names of parties and person performing marriage. Filed numerically. Handwritten on printed forms. Each file box 4.5 x 10.5 x 14. 1889-July 1918, 14 file boxes, Room 27; 1918—, 6 file boxes, Room 250, County courthouse.

846. APPLICATIONS FOR MARRIAGE LICENSES
February 1892—. Approximately 299,000 in 628 file boxes.
For description see number 843. Arranged numerically. Typed and handwritten on printed forms. Each file box 3.5 x 10.5 x 14. Room 250, County courthouse.

847. MARRIAGE LICENSE APPLICATIONS (not called for)
July 1931—. Approximately 800 in 3 file boxes. A1-28909.
Filed numerically. Handwritten and typed on printed forms. Each file box 4.5 x 10.5 x 14. Room 250, County courthouse.

848. RECORD OF APPLICATIONS FOR MARRIAGE LICENSES
February 1831-April 1875. 25 volumes.
Shows names of parties to proposed marriage; declaration by application of their legal ages, and that neither party has a wife or husband living; date of application; names of probate judge and deputy; and signature of the applicant. Arranged chronologically. Handwritten on printed forms. Volumes average 200 pages. 9.25 x 14 x 1.5. Room 250, County courthouse.

849. MARRIAGE CONSENTS
December 1888-December 1890. Approximately 1500 in 3 file boxes.
Name of applicants for marriage, names of parents or guardians giving consent, date of consent, signature of parents or guardians. From 1898 to date consents are filed with licenses and applications. Handwritten on printed forms. Each file box 4.75. X10.75 x 14. Room 27, County courthouse.

850. RECORD OF MINISTERS' LICENSES
June 1922—. 5 volumes, 1-5.
Lists name of minister, date and place ordained, and date recorded in Cuyahoga County. Ministers' licenses issued by probate court of Cuyahoga County are entered in the journal. These volumes record licenses not issued in Cuyahoga County. For

index (1852—), see number 851. Handwritten. Volumes average 300 pages. 7.25 x 8.5 x 1.5. Room 245, County courthouse.

851. INDEX TO MINISTERS' LICENSES
March 1852—. 2 volumes, 1-2.

An alphabetical index of ministers, listing docket volume and number of case, volume and page of the journal, and volume and page of the "Record of Ministers' Licenses." Typed on printed forms. Volumes average 795 pages. 13 x 18.75 x 3. Room 245, County courthouse.

852. INDIVIDUAL LETTERS FROM THE PUBLIC REQUESTING COPIES OF BIRTH AND MARRIAGE CERTIFICATES
1898—. Approximately 21,000 in 72 file boxes.

Arranged alphabetically. Handwritten and typed. Each file box 4.25 x 10.5 x 14. 1898-1932, 68 file boxes, Room 27; 4 file boxes, Room 250, County courthouse.

853. RECORD OF PHYSICIANS' CERTIFICATES
May 1896—. 2 volumes, 1-2.

Lists date received and recorded, certificate number, name of physician, name and location of school from which degree was received, date, certification by the Board of Medical Registration of the State of Ohio, and remarks. Alphabetical index of physicians in each volume. Handwritten on printed forms. Volumes average 400 pages. 12.5 x 18.75 x 2.5. 250, County courthouse.

854. RECORD OF NURSES' CERTIFICATES
May 1916—. 3 volumes, 1-3.

Lists date received and recorded; name, county, and state; date of graduation; name and location of training school; diploma; certification by the Ohio State Medical Board; the nurses' examining committee; name of the chief examiner and of the secretary; and remarks. Alphabetical index of nurses in each volume. Handwritten on printed forms. Volumes average 500 pages. 13 x 18.75 x 2.75. Room at 250, County courthouse.

855. RECORD OF LIMITED PRACTITIONERS CERTIFICATES
March 1916—. 1 volume, 1.

Lists date received for record, name and address of applicant to whom certificates was issued, name of county, name of the secretary and of the president of the Ohio State Medical Board, and remarks. Alphabetical index of nurses in each volume. Handwritten on printed forms. Volumes average 500 pages. 13 x 18.75 x 2.75. Room 250, County courthouse.

Record of Birth and Death

856. RECORD OF BIRTHS
July 1867-May 1918. 10 volumes, 1-10.

Lists number of births per month; name and full; date of birth; city, town, or township; county and state; names and addresses, sex, color, age, nationality, religion, and occupation of parents; and date of recording. 1867-1889, alphabetical index of children's name in each volume. For index (1890-1908) see number 857. Handwritten on printed forms. Volumes average 275 pages. 11 x 12 x 2.5. Room 250, County courthouse.

857. INDEX TO BIRTHS
July 1867-May 1908. 2 volumes, 1-2.

An alphabetical index to certain periods, listing name and certificate number. Handwritten on printed forms. Average 450 pages. 13 x 18.75 x 3. Room 250, County courthouse.

858. BIRTH CERTIFICATES
May 1899-May 1908. Approximately 300 in 1 file box.

Gives date and place of birth; sex; maiden name of mother; nativity, age, and color of mother; full name of father; nativity, age, and color of father; and signature and address of medical attendant. Handwritten on printed forms. In chronological order. File box 4.75 x 10.75 x 14. Room 27, County courthouse.

859. RECORD OF DEATH
January 1867-June 1908. 17 volumes, 1-17.

List record number; name of decedent; date of death; whether married, single, or widowed; age, sex, color, occupation, and religion; place of birth; name of parents; nationality of parents; direct cause of death; indirect cause of death; last place of residence; county and state; name of physician, clergyman, and undertaker; burial lot number; section number of cemetery; and date recorded. For index see number 860. Handwritten on printed forms. Volumes average 325 pages. 13 x 18.75 x 3. Room 250, County courthouse.

860. INDEX TO DEATHS
January 1867-June 1908. 4 volumes, 1-4.
An alphabetical index for certain periods, giving name of decedent and certificate number. Handwritten on printed forms. Volumes average 425 pages. 13 x 18.75 x 3. Room 250, County courthouse.

861. DEATH CERTIFICATES
March 1907-June 1908. Approximately 450 in 1 file box.
Give name of decedent; date and place of death; sex, age, color, occupation, and residence; county and state; whether married, single, or widowed; place of birth; name of father and of mother; last place of residence; name of attending physician; name of clergyman; and place of burial. In chronological order. Handwritten on printed forms. File box 4.75 x 10.75 x 14. Room 27, County courthouse.

862. VITAL AND SOCIAL STATISTICS
August 1882-August 1908. 17 pamphlets.
Annual reports of mortality statistics, listing the color, age, and sex of deceased person, as well as the cause and date of death. Causes for mortality are classified as zymotic, constitutional, local, and developmental diseases, and violent deaths. Handwritten on printed forms. Pamphlets average 28 pages. 11.75 x 18.75 x .125. Room 27, County courthouse.

Naturalization Records

863. RECORD OF NATURALIZATION
May 1859-July 1901. 26 volumes, 1-26.
Contains copies of petitions listing number of certificate, name of person, date of application, native country, arrival date, occupation, address at time of application, names and addresses of witnesses, and date of naturalization. Alphabetical index of aliens in each volume. Handwritten on printed forms. Volumes average 490 pages. 9.5 x 14.25 x 2.5. Room 250, County courthouse. Naturalization records from 1902 to date are registered in the common pleas court and in the Federal court.

864. DECLARATION OF MINORS
May 1859-August 1901. 16 volumes, 1-16.
Lists name of minor, native country, age, and date of arrival. Alphabetical index of minors in each volume. Handwritten on printed forms. Volumes average 490 pages. 9.5 x 14.25 x 2.25. Room 250, County courthouse.

865. DECLARATION OF ALIENS
June 1859-March 1887. 12 volumes, 1-12.
Lists name of applicant; native country; date of arrival; intention of becoming a citizen; abjuration of allegiance to his native sovereign; name of native king, queen, etc.; date of declaration; and applicant's signature. Alphabetical index of aliens in each volume. Handwritten on printed forms. Volumes average 580 pages. 9.5 x 14 x 2.75. Room 250, County courthouse.

Miscellaneous

866. MISCELLANEOUS AND ADOPTION RECORDS
1857—. 34 volumes; 5 file boxes. (Volumes 1-35; Number 32 is blank. File boxes contain papers not yet recorded. Beginning in 1921 adoption proceedings were segregated and are contained in separate volumes numbered 17, 18, 22, 23, 26-30, and 33-35 marked "Adoption Records").
Complete transcripts of road appeals, changes the name, adoptions and other proceedings that are not recorded in separate record series. Alphabetical index of petitioners in front of each volume. 1857-1911 handwritten; 1911—, typed. Volumes average 300 pages. 12.25 x 18.5 x 3.25. Room 250, County courthouse.

867. REGISTER OF BLIND
June 1904-October 1906. 1 volume, 1.
Lists name and residence of registered party, quarterly expenses, journal volume and page, date of registration, date of cessation of benefit, and cause for and date of discontinuance of benefit. Contains an alphabetical index of blind persons. Handwritten on printed forms. 110 pages. 9.25 x 14.25 x 1.5. Room 250, County courthouse.

868. PATENT RECORD

1861-1869. 1 volume, 1.

Lists name of article patented; patent number; name of judge and of applicant; residence and occupation of applicant; a record of the oath; date of application; signature of the judge, the deputy, and applicant; and date of Federal approval of the patent. In order of patent numbers. Handwritten on printed forms. 430 pages. 9.75 x 14 x 2.5. Room 249, County courthouse.

The juvenile court of Cuyahoga County was created by a legislative act of April 18, 1902 entitled "an act to establish a juvenile court in certain counties and to regulate the control of delinquent and neglected children." This act authorized counties having a population of more than 380,000 and an insolvency court to establish a juvenile court under an extension of the jurisdiction of the insolvency court. This provision made the law applicable only in Cuyahoga County. The act was to apply only to children under 16 years of age, and provided that a jury of six might be impaneled on demand of any person before the court or upon motion of the judge. The court was given jurisdiction over neglected children (such as are now defined as dependent) but had no authority to deal with adults who contributed to that condition.

Children under 12 years of age could not be committed to jail or detained at police stations. If unable to furnished bail, they could be committed to the sheriff, a police officer, a probation officer, or the agent of a child protective society "who shall keep such child in some suitable place, provided by the city or county, outside the enclosure of any jail or police station."

Probation officers, serving without pay, might be appointed by the judge who could parole delinquent children to them for supervision. The delinquent children could be placed in free homes or in boarding homes where support was voluntarily contributed, or they could be committed to the state institutions or accredited child caring agencies. (95 O. L. 785).

The act creating the Cuyahoga County Juvenile Court was in great part based on an act of the Illinois legislature of April 21, 1899 creating a juvenile court in Cook County, Illinois, the first two be created by legislature in the country. The Ohio Statute was passed following a movement in Cuyahoga County demanding a distinction in treatment between the delinquent juvenile and the criminal adult.

On May 5, 1904, a bill was passed providing for the employment of a paid probation officer, although Cuyahoga County had previously secured private funds for this purpose. The weakness of the original act regarding cases of neglected children was somewhat remedied by an amendment passed in 1906 permitting the court to impose fines and costs. This amendment increased the number of probation officers permitted and made the appointment of at least one woman mandatory. (97 O. L. 565-568).

An amendment passed in 1908 raised the jurisdictional age to 17 years both for dependents and delinquents. It provided that a delinquent boy 16 years or over who had committed a felony could be committed to the Ohio State Reformatory. Adults contributing to delinquency of minors could be punished by a fine ranging from ten to a thousand dollars, or imprisoned not less than 10 days or more than one year, or both. The same penalties were made to apply to adults contributing to dependency or neglect, county commissioners were directed to make an allowance out of the general funds for the support of the minor children of parents serving sentences for neglect. The same act authorized county commissioners to provide, by purchase or lease, for a detention home, if recommended by the judge. In the case of larger counties, the judge was given power to appoint the superintendent, matron, or other employees. (99 O. L. 192-203).

An act passed in 1911 further defined the powers and duties of probation officers and provided that the findings against a child in juvenile court could not be used as evidence against that child in any other court. The bill had been drawn primarily to establish juvenile courts in ten of the larger counties of the state. It simplified the procedure in filing complaints and provided that felonies committed by juveniles need not be taken before the grand jury or passed on by the county prosecutor. (102 O. L. 425).

In 1911 the legislature had authorized a commission "to revise, consolidate, and suggest amendments to the statute laws of the State of Ohio which pertain to children." A printed report was submitted by the commission which formed the basis of an entirely new code of laws pertaining to children and affecting juvenile courts. The act known as Senate Bill number 18 was passed April 28, and approved by Governor James M. Cox on May 9, 1913.

The act of 1913 raised the judicial age to 18 years, where it has since remained. In more clearly defined the powers and limitations of the court and also the terms "delinquent," "dependent," and "proper parental care." It provided for physical and mental examinations of all children committed to any institution. It raised the sum allowed for the support of children in neglected cases where the parent was committed to the workhouse from 40 cents to 50 cents per day. The first mothers' pension law was also included in the same act, and the responsibility of administering the fund placed upon juvenile courts. (103 O. L. 869).

In 1929 the court was given authority by statute to subject any person who came before it to a physical, psychometric (mental), and psychiatric examination, authorizing, at the same time the appointment of a full-time physician, psychologist, and psychiatrist. (113 O. L. 471).

The act abolishing the insolvency court and establishing a separate and independent juvenile court was passed April 7, 1931 and became effective midnight of December 31, 1934. (H. B. 175; 114 O. L. 45). The juvenile court of Cuyahoga County remains the only independent juvenile court in the state. There are seven other juvenile courts in Ohio, all attached to the courts of domestic relations. In their counties it is customary for a judge of the probate court to act as judge in juvenile cases.

Cashier' Records

869. LEDGER

1907—. (1907-1934, 11 volumes, 1-11; October 1, 1934—, ledger cards). A record of all accounts of juvenile court, listing name and address of person or corporation, case number, and amount of money debited or credited. Arranged alphabetically as to payees. Handwritten. Volumes average 500 pages. 10.25 x 15.5 x 2.5. 1907-1917, 3 volumes, Room 11; 1917-1934, 8 volumes, 1934—, ledger cards, Cashier's office, first floor, Juvenile Court Building.

870. CASH BOOK AND JOURNAL

1907—. (1907-1934, 23 volumes; October 1, 1934—, loose-leaf sheets). A record of money received and disbursed by the juvenile court, listing date of receipt or disbursement, amount, and voucher number. Arranged chronologically. Handwritten on printed forms. Volumes average 375 pages. 15 x 12 x 2. 1907-1932, 21 volumes, 1-21, Room 11; 1932-1934, 2 volumes, 22-23, and loose-leaf sheets, Cashier's office, first floor, Juvenile Court Building.

871. UNCLAIMED MONEY

1916—. 1 volume. A record of unclaimed money paid into the cashier's office, listing name and address of person making payment, date of payment, and amount. Contains an alphabetical index of payees. Handwritten. 300 pages. 10.25 x 15.5 x 1.75. Cashier's office, first floor, Juvenile Court Building.

872. CANCELLED CHECKS

1928—. Checks which have been issued by the juvenile court and paid by the bank. Each check lists name of payee, date, check never, and purpose for which issued. In chronological order. 1928-1934, Room 11; June 1934——, Cashier's office, first floor, Juvenile Court Building.

873. STATEMENT OF ACCOUNTS
1926——. 1 drawer.
Statements made monthly by cashier, showing money received and disbursed by cashier's office, and purpose of receipt and disbursement. Arranged by months. Typed. Drawer 9.5 x 4 x 18. Cashier's office, first floor, Juvenile Court Building.

874. WORK HOUSE RECORD
1927——. 2 volumes.
A record of fathers and mothers who defaulted in payment for the support of their children, listing name and address, amount in default, and date of commitment to workhouse. An alphabetical index in each volume. Handwritten. Volumes average 200 pages. 8.5 x 12 x 1.25. Cashier's office, first floor, Juvenile Court Building.

875. APPEARANCE AND GUARANTEE BONDS
1928——. 4 volumes; 1 bundle.
List amount of bond posted, name and address of defendant, date, and signature of bondsman. In order of case numbers. Handwritten on printed forms. Volumes average 300 pages. 10.25 x 14.25 x 1.75; bundle 5 x 9 x 12. Appearance bonds, 2 volumes, cashier's office; guarantee bonds, 1 bundle, Room 11; 2 volumes, Cashier's office, first floor, Juvenile Court Building.

876. UNOFFICIAL RECEIPTS
1927-October 1, 1934. 1 drawer.
Cards listing name of case, record number, name of payer and payee, dates of payment, and dates of disbursements. Filed alphabetically. Cashier's office, first floor, Juvenile Court Building.

877. RECEIPT BOOKS
1926——. (1926-1933, 3 bundles; 1936——, 50 books).
A record of money received, listing date and amount of payment, name of payer, and purpose of payment. In order of receipt numbers. Handwritten on printed forms. 3 bundles, 9 x 12 x 1, Room 11; 40 books, 12 x 24 x 36, Cashier's office, first floor, Juvenile Court Building.

878. INDEX TO ACCOUNTS
April 1936—. 1 cardex index.

List official and unofficial accounts, showing case number, record number, and names of payer and payee. In alphabetical order. Typed. Cashier's office, first floor, Juvenile Court Building.

879. MISCELLANEOUS CORRESPONDENCE
1934—. 2 letter boxes.

Letters of varied nature pertaining to business of cashier's office. Alphabetical as to correspondence. Handwritten and typed. Each letter box 10 x 12 x 18. Cashier's office, first floor, Juvenile Court Building.

880. PAYMENT CARDS, NEGLECT DIVISION
1931—. 1 cabinet, A-Z.

A record of both active and inactive cases of fathers, mothers, or organizations caring for children who have neglected payment for their support. It lists name and address, place of employment, amount paid towards support of children, and date of payment. Filed alphabetically. Typed on printed forms. Cabinet 5 x 10 x 24. Neglect division, first floor, Juvenile Court Building.

Clerk's Records

881. JUVENILE INDEX
1902—. 9 volumes.

An alphabetical index of cases, listing name and case number. Handwritten on printed forms. Volumes average 800 pages. 9.5 x 14 x 3. Room 107, Juvenile Court Building.

882. MINUTE BOOK
1910—. 8 volumes.

A record of the nature of the petition and name and address of petitioner, name and address of the individual against whom complaint is made, case number, age, sex, date of petition, date of hearing, and disposition of case. Handwritten. Volumes average 600 pages. 10.5 x 18.25 x 2. 1910-1933, 7 volumes, Room 11; 1933—, 1 volume, Room 107, Juvenile Court Building.

883. APPEARANCE DOCKET
1902—. 100 volumes. (1902-1903. 1 volume, Juvenile Trial Docket; 1903-1909, 12 volumes, Juvenile Record; 1909-1927, 37 volumes, Juvenile Appearance Docket; 1927—, 50 volumes.

Lists case number, name and address, filing date, and brief remarks pertaining to the case. In order case numbers. Handwritten on printed forms. Volumes average 500 pages. 10.25 x 16.5 x 3. 1902-1927, 50 volumes, Room 11; 1927—, 50 volumes, 50-99, Room 107, Juvenile Court Building.

884. JOURNAL
1908—.-42 volumes.

A record of the proceedings of the court, listing case number and title of case. In chronological order. Typed. Volumes average 700 pages. 14 x 18.5 x 2.5. 1908-1931, 34 volumes, Room 11; 1932—, 8 volumes, Room 107, Juvenile Court Building.

885. DETENTION HOME RELEASE BOOK STUBS
1930-1934. 7 volumes.

List date of entry, case number, name of juvenile, and release or commitment. In chronological order. Handwritten on printed forms. Volumes average 250 pages. 8.5 x 12 x .75. Room 11, Juvenile Court Building.

886. OFFICIAL CASE FILES
1902—. 596 file boxes.

Contains all writs used in each case, such as petitions, statements, warrants, medical certificates, subpoenas, etc. In order of case numbers. Typed and printed. Each file box 11 x 5 x 16. 1902-1926, 396 file boxes, Room 11; 1926—, 200 file boxes, Room 107, Juvenile Court Building.

887. COMMITMENT BOOK
1924—. 1 volume.

A record of commitments of minors to institutions, listing date of commitment, number of case, name, officer's name, and transportation charges. Listed under various institutions. Handwritten on printed forms. 200 pages. 14 x 8 x 2. Room 107, Juvenile Court Building.

888. WORK HOUSE COMMITMENT BOOK
1918—. 3 volumes.
List name and address of adult, date of admittance, date of release, and charge. Alphabetical index of cases in each volume. Handwritten. Volumes average 300 pages. 8.5 x 11 x 1. Room 11, Juvenile Court Building.

889. PENDING CASE FILE, CURRENT MONTH
Current month, 1-31, and "no date." 32 bins.
Unheard cases filed under assigned date of hearing. If date has not been assigned case is placed in "no date" bin. Each bin 12 x 4.5 x 7. Room 107, Juvenile Court Building.

890. GENERAL CORRESPONDENCE
1928—. 4 letter boxes.
Correspondence pertaining to crippled children, to various child-caring agencies, regarding payrolls, etc. One letter box contains letters pertaining to legal status of department as well as general correspondence. Letterbox 10 x 12 x 18. Cashier's office, first floor, Juvenile Court Building.

891. DAILY CALENDAR
1935—. Loose leaf-sheets; 1 bundle.
Record of all cases heard each day by chief probation officer and judge, listing case number, date of hearing, title of case, and various remarks. In order of case numbers. Typed and handwritten. Bundle 12.25 x 16.5 x 9. 1935, 1 bundle, Room 11; current sheets, record room drawer, Juvenile Court Building.

Case Records

892. OFFICIAL ACTIVE CASES
1920—. Approximately 22,000 in 15 drawers.
Record giving complete history of each case, with general correspondence, case record, reports of investigations, various other reports, etc. Each card lists family case number and name, address, age, occupation, birthplace, etc., of parents. Reports are different types, such as those on physical, educational, and mental condition of child. These investigations continue until child comes of age. In order of case numbers. For index see number 894. Handwritten and typed on printed forms. Each card 9.5 x 12; drawers 7 x 6 x 20. Room 108, Juvenile Court Building.

893. UNOFFICIAL ACTIVE CASES
1928—. Approximately 2650 in 11 drawers.
Cases handled by the chief probation officer, listing name of minor, case number, child's previous record, nature of offense, and disposition of the case. In order of case numbers. For index see number 894. Handwritten. Each drawer 12 x 10 x 18. Room 108, Juvenile Court Building.

894. INDEX TO ACTIVE CASES
1920—. Approximately 22,000 cards in 15 drawers.
An alphabetical card index to official and unofficial active cases, arranged as to names of minors, listing address, date of entry, and case number. Handwritten and typed. Each drawer 13.5 x 4.75 x 30; each card 5 x 8. Room 108, Juvenile Court Building.

895. OFFICIAL CLOSED CASES (Family Record)
1920—. Approximately 14,800 in 62 steel drawers.
A record of juvenile court investigations of children who have become of age, and whose cases consequently are automatically closed. In order of case numbers. Handwritten and typed. Each drawer 12 x 10 x 18. Room 11, Juvenile Court Building.

896. CLOSED UNOFFICIAL CASES
1928—. Approximately 500 in 2 drawers.
Cases which have been disposed of by the chief probation officer, and of which there is a complete history. In order of case numbers. Typed. Each drawer 12 x 10 x 18. Room 11, Juvenile Court Building.

897. MISCELLANEOUS CORRESPONDENCE
1934—. 1 drawer.
Letters of a varied nature referring to the active cases. Arranged alphabetically as to correspondence. Handwritten and typed. Drawer 10 x 12 x 18. Room 108, Juvenile Court Building.

898. CARBON COPY CASE FILE
1932—. 4 file drawers.
Carbon copies of all cases. Retained for four years. Filed alphabetically. Each drawer 20 x 13 x 11.5. Room 108, Juvenile Court Building.

899. UNOFFICIAL RECORDS
1929—. 4 steel file drawers, A-Z.
Gives accounts of the interviews relative to minor offenses, name and address of child, and date of entry. Alphabetical as to names of children. Typed and handwritten on printed forms. Each file drawer 9.5 x 12 x 18. Room 120, Juvenile Court Building.

Statistical Records

900. ANNUAL REPORT
1909—. (1909-1929, 20 reports in 2 bundles; 1932—, 4 volumes; 1930—, 3 printed reports).
Reports from 1909-1929 were made by the chief probation officer and listed statistical information pertaining to delinquency, dependency, neglect, and consent to the marriages of minors. The reports for 1928 and 1929 were prepared by the Federal Children's Bureau and were much less detailed. Reports for 1930, 1931-1932 and 1933-1934 were prepared by the juvenile court statistician and are compiled from the statistical ledgers which is based on the statistical cards kept for delinquent, dependent, and neglected children. Official and unofficial cases are separated. These reports also contain a description of the activities of the various departments. 1909-1929, typed; 1930—, printed. Volumes are handwritten on printed forms. Volumes average 100 pages. 9 x 11.25 x .75. Room 15, Juvenile Court Building.

901. STATISTICAL CARDS (Official Cases)
1930—. Approximately 20,000 in 13 drawers.
Distinct cards are kept for delinquent boys, delinquent girls, neglected minors, dependents, and transfers from the jurisdiction of the common pleas court. Delinquency cards list date, name, address, race, date of birth, complaint , sources of complaint, I. Q., where child is held, information pertaining to the members of the family, previous appearances, economic status, charges against parents or other children, adult contributors, and disposition of child. Neglect cards list similar

information and offense and disposition of adult. Dependent cards stress type of neglect and disposition of contributors. The transfer cards from common pleas court started January 1, 1936, and include all cases active at that time. Cards are filed in order of case numbers. Typed on printed forms. 6 drawers 9 x 6 x 16; 7 drawers 28 x 6.5 x 17.5. Room 15, Juvenile Court Building.

902. SPOT MAPS
1929—. 14 maps.

Spot maps of juvenile court cases, showing delinquency, dependency, neglect, etc., based on the census tracts of Greater Cleveland. Printed. Each map 20 x 30. Room 15, Juvenile Court Building.

903. DISPLAY CHARTS AND GRAPHS
1930—. 16 in 1 file drawer.

Charts and graphs showing various types of delinquency, and the relation of delinquency to employment, age, sex, etc. File drawer 40 x 24 x 5. Room 15, Juvenile Court Building.

904. MISCELLANEOUS FILE
9 file drawers.

General correspondence, pamphlets, newspaper clippings, reports, textbooks, commercial publications, and publications from local, state, and national organizations pertaining to child welfare. 3 drawers 8.5 x 13 x 6; 3 drawers 8.5 x 10.5 x 6. Room 15, Juvenile Court Building.

Mothers' Pension

The original act authorizing mothers' pensions was passed March 1, 1913. It provided that women whose husbands were either dead, imprisoned, permanently disabled, or have deserted them for three years or more, and who had a child or children less than 16 years old, were eligible to the mothers' pension. They must have resided in any county in the state for two years prior to making application and could not receive more than $35.00 per month for the first child and $10.00 for each additional child. (103 O. L. 878).

This act was amended in 1921 and again on April 6, 1936. The latter bill termed "Aid to Dependent Children" enlarges eligibility to meet requirements of the Federal Social Security Act. It provides for all qualifications enumerated in the old bill and includes children living with certain relatives. It reduces residence and desertion law to one year, and removes the maximum pension which can be given. It provides that the pension shall adequately meet the needs of the family on the basis of health and decency after deducting any income that may be in the family. (116 O. L. first session H. 610).

905. APPEARANCE DOCKET
1914—. 6 volumes, 1-6.
A record of all applications for mothers' pensions, listing name and address of applicant, case number, date of application, and various remarks. In order of case numbers. For index see number 906. Handwritten. Volumes average 500 pages. 15.5 x 18 x 3.25. Room 309, Juvenile Court Building.

906. INDEX TO APPEARANCE DOCKET
1914—. 2 volumes, 1-2.
An alphabetical index of applicants, listing case numbers. Handwritten. Volumes average 300 pages. 15 x 18.5 x 3.25. Room 309, Juvenile Court Building.

907. JOURNAL
1914—. 3 volumes, 1-3.
Gives case number, name of mother, date of journal entry, and remarks on hearing. In chronological order. Typed. Volumes average 500 pages. 15 x 18.5 x 3.5. Room 309, Juvenile Court Building.

908. FAMILY RECORDS (Active)
1920—. Approximately 1085 cases in 19 drawers.
Cards list case number, name and address of each applicant, date application was filed, investigator's reports, and amount of pension, if granted. In order of case numbers. For index see number 909. Typed. Each drawer 9 x 12 x 18. Room 309, Juvenile Court Building.

909. FAMILY RECORD PAYROLL INDEX (Active)
1925—. 1 drawer.

Cards list name of applicant, dates pension was granted, case number, present address, amount of pension, and monthly change in amounts. Filed alphabetically. Drawer 26 x 14 x 3. Room 309, Juvenile Court Building.

910. FAMILY RECORDS (Inactive)
1914—. Approximately 8400 cards in 56 drawers.

Records of closed cases, giving a complete history of each case, date on which payment was discontinued, and reason for such action. In order of case numbers. For index see number 911. Typed. Each drawer 9 x 12 x 18. Room 309, Juvenile Court Building.

911. FAMILY RECORD INDEX (Inactive)
1914—. 2 drawers.

An alphabetical card index of applicants, listing address, date of application, and case number. Typed and handwritten. Drawer 26 x 14 x 3. Room 309, Juvenile Court Building.

912. CANCELLED CHECKS
1925—. Approximately 42,000 in 12 cardboard file boxes.

Cancelled checks, listing name of person to whom check was issued, date and amount of check, and name of county treasurer. Filed with county commissioners. Typed. Each file box 24 x 9.5 x 3.25. Attic storeroom, fourth floor, County courthouse.

913. PAYROLL BOOK
1922—. 1 bundle; 1 loose-leaf binder. (1922-1924, 1 bundle; 1930—, 1 binder) 1925-1929 missing.

A record of payments received by mothers, listing name and address of each mother, case number, and amount of payment. In order of case numbers. Typed. Bundle 11.5 x 15 x 3.5; binder 12 x 16 x 2. Bundle, Basement storeroom; binder, Room 309, Juvenile Court Building.

Detention Home for Dependent and Delinquent Children

An act passed April 23, 1908 provided for the purchase or lease of a place to be known as a detention home. This act authorized the county commissioners upon the advice and recommendation of the judge exercising proper jurisdiction in such matters to provide a detention home for delinquent, dependent, or neglected minors under the age of 18 years, where they may be detained until their final disposition. (99 O. L. 192). This act followed the failure of an appeal to the public for funds for a detention home.

Temporary quarters were used until February 1917 when a residence which had been purchased for this purpose in 1914 was occupied as a permanent detention home for boys and girls. Residences on either side of the first one were purchased in 1919 and 1924. However, both were condemned in 1930, increasing the congestion in the original building. The building of the present home was started in 1931 and completed in 1932. The new building completely separates delinquent from dependent children.

The Cuyahoga County detention home receives children brought in by the police and other law enforcement officers, those held by the court, and those brought in by parents and social agencies, and held with the consent of the court. Delinquent children remain in the home until the court hearing is completed or until they are removed to an institution. Dependent children remain until satisfactory foster or boarding homes can be found.

914. DAILY ENTRANCE BOOK
1917—. 10 bundles; 1 loose-leaf volume.
Lists date of entrance, name and address of child, and name of arresting officer in charge. In chronological order. Handwritten on printed forms. Volumes, 150 pages. 7 x 12 x 1. 1917-1934, 10 bundles, Basement storeroom; 1935—, 1 volume, Room 102, Detention Home.

915. DAILY ATTENDANCE BOOK
1917—. 1 volume; 6 bundles.
Lists date received, child's name, total number of days spent in the detention home, date of leaving, and the disposition or comment. Handwritten on printed forms. Volumes, 600 pages. 9.75 x 12.5 x 3; each bundle 3 x 5 x .5. 1917-1934, 6 bundles, Basement storeroom; 1 volume, Room 102, Detention Home.

916. FILE CARDS
1917—. 10 file drawers, A-Z.

List file number, name and address of child, name of father and mother, case number, age, nationality, religion, school, name of officer, date, and charge. Filed alphabetically. Handwritten and typed on printed forms. Each drawer 28 x 13 x 5.5. Room 102, Detention Home.

917. RECORD FILES
1923—. 40 file drawers.

Contain physical, conduct, psychological, and in some cases psychiatric reports for each child. Originals are in the juvenile court files. Filed alphabetically. Each drawer 13 x 11.5 x 28. 1923-1929, 12 drawers, Basement storeroom; 1930—, 28 drawers, Room 102, Detention Home.

918. EXPENSE BOOK
1917—. 3 volumes.

List date of purchase, name of firm where purchased was made, and total amount for various items for the month. In chronological order. Handwritten. Contains quarterly and semi-annual reports. Volumes average 200 pages. 15.5 x 13 x 1.5. 1 volume, 1917-1923, Basement storeroom; 2 volumes, 1924—, Room 102, Detention Home.

The prosecutor was originally known in England as the "king's attorney," "narrator for the king," and the "king's sergeant." Later he called an "attorney-general" and "director of criminal prosecutions." However, criminal prosecutions in England were often instituted by private persons. (Holdsworth, *op. cit.,* VI, 458).

Under the laws of the Northwest Territory, the attorney-general was the prosecutor-in-chief, and he appointed and commissioned various persons to prosecute cases in their respective counties. He did the actual work in his own county and traveled on circuit. (Pease, *op. cit.,* 506).

In 1803 the legislature passed an act authorizing the supreme court to appoint in each county an attorney to prosecute cases in behalf of the state. (1 O. L. 50). In 1805 this right was transferred to the court of common pleas with the provision that the prosecutor hold office during the pleasure of the court. (3 O. L. 47).

A bill was passed in 1831 which provided that it shall be the duty of the prosecutor to prosecute for and in behalf of the state, all complaints, suits and controversies in which the state shall be a party, within the county for which he shall have been appointed, both in the supreme court and court of common pleas. It also stipulated that his compensation was to be determined annually by the court. (29 O. L. 413). An amendment to this act passed in 1939 provided that he give a bond conditioned upon faithful performance. (37 O. L. 37).

In 1833 the office became elective for a term of two years and it was provided that no person shall be eligible as a candidate for the office who is not a duly licensed attorney. In 1881 the term of office was made three years, and again reduced to two years in 1906. (78 O. L. 260; 98 O. L. 271-272). It was increased to four years and 1936. (116 O. L. pt. 2, 1st ses, H. 603).

In 1935 the prosecutor was authorized to superintend the collection of cost of all felony cases, and if necessary to sue for the cost in the name of the state of Ohio. (33 O. L. 44). Three years later it was made the duty of the prosecutor, when directed by the governor, supreme court, or the general assembly, to file information, in the nature of a quo warranto, in cases of the illegal holdings of public office, and the usurpation or misuse of corporate rights. (37 O. L. 70). The same session of the legislature provided that the superintendent of common schools (the county auditor) take an account of all funds and property given in any way for the support of education, and report any instance of waste to the prosecutor, who in turn shall petition for an injunction against the trustees or persons guilty and cause proper investigation to be made by the court. (36 O. L. 21). This act was appealed in 1841. (47 O. L. 24).

In 1842 a bill was passed which provided that the prosecutor must keep a case book of cost, which he must deliver to his successor on the expiration of his term. (40 O. L. 25). In 1847 provision was made that when a report of an investigating committee appointed by the court shows a breach of the auditor's bond by the illegal drawing of money in the county treasury, an action in the name of the state, for the benefit of the county, must be brought by the prosecuting attorney against the auditor and sureties of his bond. (45 O. L. 42). A measure enacted in 1852 provided that the prosecutor, if requested, must report annually to the attorney general. (50 O. L. 262). Another act, approved two years later, provided that prosecuting attorneys, upon request, are entitled to advise from the attorney general respecting their duties in all complaints, suits and controversies in which the state is, or maybe, a party. (50 O. L. 267). A measure was adopted in 1861 providing that the prosecutor must make an annual report to the county commissioners. (58 O. L. 58).

In 1865 the prosecutor was required to prepare official bonds for all county officers, and certify as to their sufficiency. (62 O. L. 173). Three years later an act was carried which provided that he furnished certain statistical information regarding crime to the secretary of state upon request. (65 O. L. 32). In 1869 a measure was adopted which provided that the prosecuting attorney endorse his certificate upon all contracts for public works involving an amount above a stipulated sum, made by the county commissioners. (66 O. L. 52). In the same session a statute was enacted which provided for the sale of stolen, embezzled, or falsely obtained property left in the custody of an officer, and directed that the prosecutor supervised such sale. (66 O. L. 287).

During the next decade numerous duties were added to the office. The prosecutor was required to investigate and report to the governor, upon his request, regarding applications for the surrender of persons held in custody, or under recognizance. (66 O. L. 171). The prosecutor was required to act as legal counsel for all school boards within his county. If, however, an action should arise between two school boards therein, he is not required to act for either of them. (70 O. L. 195). A bill was passed which required the prosecutor to institute a civil action for recovery of penalty from members of a school board in certain instances. (72 O. L. 59). He was required to prosecute the county commissioners for failure to make their annual report to the court of common pleas. (73 O. L. 141). It was made his duty to attend to all suits instituted on behalf of hospitals for the insane. (75 O. L. 64). In the same session it was provided that he receive information from the coroner in all cases of investigation of deaths (75 O. L. 570).

In 1881 the statutes relating to the office of county prosecutor were revised, make it him the legal advisor of the county commissioners, and all other county officers, and also of all township officers. (78 O. L. 260).

The duties of the prosecutor were further expanded during the next two decades. He was authorized, upon the request of the attorney general, to act in certain matters relating to the department of agriculture. (84 O. L. 90). He was required to prosecute for penalties under the Unknown Depositor's Law. (85 O. L. 65). Statutes were enacted providing that whenever an examination is made of a public office the report thereof must be filed with the prosecuting attorney (95 O. L. 514) and that certain county officers must file reports of their fees with the prosecuting attorney. (98 O. L. 90). The same session of legislature authorized the prosecutor to act for the public utilities commission upon its request. (98 O. L. 357).

In 1908 three bills were passed in relation to the office: The first authorized the prosecutor, upon the request of the secretary of state medical board, to act regarding violation of laws relating to the practice of medicine; the second authorized a similar procedure upon request of the secretary of state dental board; the third authorized him to prevent public meetings in buildings declared unsafe, whenever requested by the mayor or chief executive of a municipality. (99 O. L. 503; 99 O. L. 70; 99 O. L. 233). Two years later increased duties were imposed upon him regarding the collection of taxes. (101 O.L. 399).

In 1911 the prosecutor was empowered to appoint a secret service officer to aid in the collection and discovery of evidence to be used in grand jury investigations and in the trial of criminal cases. He was authorized to act for the state tax commission in certain instances, and upon their request. Another act specified that he be notified of all violations of the laws relating to taxation for which a penalty, either civil or criminal, is provided. (102 O. L. 77-78; 102 O. L. 224; 102 O. L. 225). Minor changes were made in the latter act in 1915. (103 O. L. 798; 106 O. L. 264).

Numerous duties and powers were added in 1913. The prosecutor was authorized upon request, to act for the state industrial commission, the board of awards thereof, and the state civil service commission. It was made his duty to prosecute and keep the attorney general advised in cases of illegal expenditures of public funds, and he was empowered to examine the accounts and records of companies executing charitable trusts. The state inspector of building and loan associations was required to furnish the prosecutor with information relating to such associations. (103 O. L. 95; 103 O. L. 72; 103 O. L. 698; 103 O. L. 509; 103 O. L. 535; 103 O. L. 181).

The prosecutor's duties were further expanded two years later. He was required to prosecute and defend all suits which the board of deputy state supervisors and inspectors of elections of his county may direct, or to which it is a party, and was made its legal advisor. He was required to prosecute a county auditor for delay in making a report. An additional act provided that he may be directed by the attorney general to collect or institute a civil action, in the name of the state, to recover the amount due upon any delinquent charge for state taxes or revenues. Another act stipulated that in no event shall his salary exceed $5,500.00 (106 O.L. 452; 106 O. L. 488; 106 O. L. 500; 106 O. L. 327).

An act was passed in 1917 which authorized him in behalf of the highway commissioners to bring civil action for the recovery of damages or injuries to inter-county highways, culverts, and bridges. In the same session he was given the duty of taking charge of appeals from revocation or suspension of certificates of registration of motor vehicles. (107 O. L. 59; 107 O. L. 644).

Additions were made to the duties and powers of the county prosecutor in 1919. He was designated president of the county board of trustees of the sinking fund, and he was made legal advisor of the district board of health, with the responsibility of representing it in all legal proceedings. He was authorized, upon request, to act for the fire marshal in relation to violations of statutory provisions regarding hotels, and for the superintendent of the county infirmary im regard to the return of escaped inmates. (108 O. L., pt. 1, 561-577; 108 O. L. pt. 1, 236-243; 108 O. L. pt. 1, 291; 108 O. L. pt. 2, 1127).

In 1927 he was made a member of the county budget commission. (112 O. L. 399). Two years later the prosecutor was given the authority to contract for broadcasting of information concerning violent crime in his county. (113 O. L. 139). In the same session an act was carried which provided that a record of the evidence relating to false statements regarding campaign expenditures be transmitted to the prosecuting attorney, among other officers, by the board of elections. (113 O. L. 307).

Since 1932 the prosecutor has been required to file with the court of common pleas transcripts of judgment in all cases involving concealment or embezzlement of assets by an executor, administrator, or guardian. (114 O. L. 280).

Although the prosecutor was originally intended to protect the county in violations of state law, his civil duties have greatly increased. He is constantly called on in an advisory capacity, and has done a great deal to prevent unnecessary foreclosures of property. With the growth of crime and litigation the prosecutor has become increasingly important in the administration of county government.

Criminal Branch

919. CRIMINAL CASE FILES

1897—. Approximately 133,000 files in 655 file drawers and 5 bundles. Each envelope (15 x 9.5) contains the indictment, memorandum of the grand jury, and statements taken by the police department. On the outside of the envelope is listed name of defendant; charge; date indicted; day arranged; plea on arrangement; bond fixed; day of crime; date of arrest; attorney or defendant; date of trial; verdict; sentence; judge before whom tried; name of prosecutor; list of witnesses for state, if any; and proceedings in court of appeals or supreme court. In order of case numbers. Handwritten and typed. 619 file drawers 10.25 x 4.75 x 20; 33 file drawers 15.5 x 11 x 24.5. 643 drawers, 5 bundles, Basement vault; 12 drawers, Room 102, Criminal Court Building.

920. PROSECUTOR'S CRIMINAL DOCKET

1879—. 34 volumes.

Lists name of defendant, title of case, crime indicted for, whether defendant is on bond, date indictment was returned, date of arrangement, plea of defendant, date of trial, verdict, name of state's attorney and of trial judge, and the sentence. In chronological order. Handwritten on printed forms. Volumes average 560 pages. 18 x 13 x 2.75. 1879-1928, 27 volumes, Prosecutor's vault; 1929—, 17 volumes, Room 102, Criminal Court Building.

921. RECORD OF PROSECUTING ATTORNEY

1929—. 2 volumes.

Lists case number, name of defendant, crime charged, sentence, name of judge, name of prosecutor, date of sentence, and remarks. Alphabetical index of defendants in each volume. Listed as to type of crime for each year. Handwritten on printed forms. Volumes average 550 pages. 18 x 13 x 2.75. Room 102, Criminal Court Building.

922. PROSECUTOR'S POLICE RECORD

1929—. 3 volumes.

A daily record listing name of defendant, crime charged with, and disposition of case in police court. In chronological order. For index see number 923. Handwritten on printed forms. Volumes average 300 pages. 14 x 11.25 x 2.25. 2 volumes, Basement vault; 1 volume, Room 102, Criminal Court Building.

923. INDEX TO PROSECUTOR'S POLICE RECORD
1929—. 2 volumes.
Lists name of defendant and page of police record. Handwritten. Volumes average 100 pages. 10.5 x 8 x .5. Room 102, Criminal Court Building.

924. CASES PENDING IN COURT OF APPEALS
Current cases. 1 file drawer.
Complete case files for cases pending in the court of appeals. In order of case numbers. Drawer 15.5 x 11 x 24.5. Room 102, Criminal Court Building.

925. COUNTY PROSECUTOR'S RECORD
1900-1908. 1 volume.
Lists name of defendant, names of attorneys and witnesses, case number, date of entry, date petition was filed, and sentence. Contains an alphabetical index of defendants. Handwritten on printed forms. 600 pages. 14 x 9.5 x 1.75. Prosecutor's vault, Criminal Court Building.

926. DAILY COURT CALENDAR
1909-1912. 4 volumes.
Lists name of defendant, crime charged or cause of action, date defendant was arrested, date arranged, date indictment was returned, name of attorney for defendant, date of trial, name of presiding judge and prosecutor, and disposition of the case. Alphabetical index of defendants in each volume. Handwritten on printed forms. Volumes average 650 pages. 16 x 12.5 x 3.75. Prosecutor's vault, Criminal Court Building.

927. PROSECUTOR'S TRIAL DOCKET
1885-1919. 7 volumes.
Lists name of defendant; case number; crime or cause of action; date of arraignment; date of trial; name of attorney; plea of defendant; verdict; and names of presiding judge, prosecutor, bondsman, and witnesses. Alphabetical index of defendants in each volume. Handwritten on printed forms. Volumes average 800 pages. 14 x 11.5 x 2. Prosecutor's vault, Criminal Court Building.

928. CASES FOR TRIAL
1899-1914. 3 volumes.

Lists name of defendant, case number, crime defendant is charged with or cause of action, date arranged, date of trial, name of attorney for defendant, defendant's plea, verdict in the case, and name of presiding judge, prosecutor, bondsman, and witnesses. Alphabetical as to names of defendants in each volume. Handwritten on printed forms. Volumes average 476 pages. 14.25 x 9.25 x 1.25. Prosecutor's vault, Criminal Court Building.

Civil Branch

929. CIVIL CASE FILES
1929—. 22 file drawers.

Contain all proceedings in civil cases in which the prosecutor acts for the plaintiff or defendant. In order of case numbers. Each drawer 15.5 x 11 x 24.5. 10 file drawers, prosecutor's vault; 12 file drawers, Room 102, Criminal Court Building.

930. CIVIL DOCKET
1929—. 2 loose-leaf volumes.

Lists name of plaintiff and of defendant, case number, file number, cause of action, names of attorneys, date petition is filed, date answer is due, and disposition of the case. Alphabetical index of plaintiffs and defendants in each volume. In chronological order. Typed on printed forms. Volumes average 600 pages. 15 x 9 x 5. Room 102, Criminal Court Building.

931. OPINIONS OF COUNTY PROSECUTORS
1895—. Approximately 10,500 in 15 volumes and 94 letter boxes.

Written opinions and correspondence pertaining to requests of county, village, and township officials, the board of elections, etc., for legal opinions on various matters. Filed chronologically. Typed. Each letter box 12 x 11.25 x 4. Volumes average 500 pages. 13 x 18 x 4. 1895-1916, 15 volumes, 1917-1934, 67 letter boxes, Prosecutor's vault; 1935—, 27 letter boxes, Room 102, Criminal Court Building.

932. OPINION BOOK
1931—. 3 volumes.

Lists date request is received, official or board making the request, name of assistant prosecutor to whom the matter is assigned, and date request is answered. Contains an annual summary of opinions rendered. In chronological order. Handwritten. Volumes average 150 pages. 12 x 8 x 1.5. Room 104, Criminal Court Building.

933. DAILY CALENDAR OF PLEADINGS
1931—. 5 volumes.

Lists full title of case, case number, title of pleading, and name of assistant prosecutor or clerk to whom assigned. Handwritten. Volumes average 100 pages. 12 x 3 x 1.5. Room 104, Criminal Court Building.

934. BAIL BONDS
1919—. 5 drawers.

Mainly appearance bonds and bonds for payment and neglect cases. List principal, surety, defendant, condition of the obligation, and charge. In chronological order. Each drawer 11.5 x 16 x 25. 1 drawer, Prosecutor's vault; 4 drawers, Room 102, Criminal Court Building.

935. FORFEITED BAIL BOND DOCKET
1919—. 4 volumes.

Lists amount claimed, charge, date of petition and answer, name of trial judge, judgment, date of judgment, amount of court cost, when judgment is paid, description of property pledged, and memoranda on case. Handwritten on printed forms. Volumes average 750 pages. 14.5 x 10.25 x 2.5. Room 102, Criminal Court Building.

936. LIQUOR TAX FILES
1929—. 2 file drawers.

Contain the pleadings and evidence in cases of liquor violation where taxes were certified against the county. Filed in order of case numbers. File drawer 11.5 x 16 x 25. Room 102, Criminal Court Building.

937. LIQUOR TRAFFIC DOCKET
1929-1931. 1 volume.

Docket of liquor violations in suits against officials to restrain the collection of liquor taxes. Lists name of plaintiff and of defendant, case number, tax, and finding of the court. In chronological order. Handwritten on printed forms. 200 pages. Prosecutor's vault, Criminal Court Building.

938. FORECLOSURES FILE
1935—. 1 file drawer.

Answers and cross-petitions filed, setting up lien of real estate taxes, personal property taxes, and inheritance taxes; and judgment on bail bonds. Filed in order of case numbers. Drawer 11.5 x 16 x 25. Room 102, Criminal Court Building.

939. REAL ESTATE TAX FILE
1934—. 6 drawers.

Contains answers, cross-petitions, etc., in cases where the treasurer was defendant in setting up a lien for real estate taxes. Filed in order of case numbers. Each drawer 11.5 x 16 x 25. Room 102, Criminal Court Building.

Tax Division

940. DELINQUENT TAX FORECLOSURE FILE
1932—. 2 file drawers.

All correspondence pertaining to delinquent taxes and a complete history of each case. The case history lists name of owner of property; address; location of property; general description of property giving land value, building value, etc.; amount of delinquent taxes due; name of mortgagee, if any; amount of mortgage; and reports of responses to correspondence pertaining to payment of taxes. Mortgages must be delinquent three years before the prosecutor receives an order to foreclose. Filed alphabetically. For index (1936—) see number 941. Each drawer 12 x 16.5 x 25. Room 121, Criminal Court Building.

941. GENERAL INDEX
April 1936—. 1 file drawer.

An alphabetical card index of persons involved in foreclosure cases, listing case number. File drawer 6 x 16.5 x 27. Room 121, Criminal Court Building.

942. GENERAL TAX TICKLER
1936—. 1 file drawer.

A chronological card file of foreclosure cases. The card which lists name and file number is filed under the date assigned for the next action in the case. File drawer 6 x 16.5 x 27. Room 121, Criminal Court Building.

943. TAX DOCKET
1933—. 6 volumes.

Lists common pleas case number, certificate number, abstract number, amount of delinquent taxes, name of plaintiff and of defendant, date, and progress of case. Each assistant prosecutor keeps a separate docket. In order of case numbers. Handwritten on printed forms. Volumes average 250 pages. 19 x 13 x 2.5. Room 121, Criminal Court Building.

944. ACTIVE CASES, SETTLED
1932—. 1 file drawer.

Files of civil cases relating particularly to tax matters and mortgages given to the county by banks which have defaulted. Filed by case numbers. Drawer 12 x 16.5 x 25. Room 121, Criminal Court Building.

945. JOURNAL ENTRIES
1932—. 2 file drawers, A-Z.

Court decrees regarding foreclosure suits. Filed alphabetically. Each file drawer 12 x 16.5 x 25. Room 121, Criminal Court Building.

946. FORFEITED TO THE STATE
1932—. 2 file drawers.

Reports of land forfeited to the state because of failure to pay taxes. Filed alphabetically. File drawer 12 x 16.5 x 25. Room 121, Criminal Court Building.

In early English law the coroner had wide judicial powers, and looked out for the pecuniary interests of the king at all times. If a man committed suicide or was convicted of a felony, the coroner, in the name of the king, took his chattels which were forfeited by law. (Holdsworth, *op. cit.,* I, 82-85).

An ordinance of the Northwest Territory, published in 1788, provided for the appointment of a coroner, by the governor, in each county within the territory. It also defined the duties and authority of the coroner. He was empowered to do any act which could be done by the sheriff. He also had the duty of holding inquests over the bodies of all persons found within the county who were believed to have died by violence or casualty. (Pease, *op. cit.,* 272).

The Ohio Constitution of 1802 definitely provided for the office of coroner, making it elective for a term of two years. (Ohio Const., Art. 3, Sec. 1). A statute enacted in 1805 set up the duties and authority of the coroner. He had, in substance, the same powers and obligations which the coroner possessed under the laws of the Northwest Territory, except that concurrent jurisdiction with the sheriff was not re-invested in him. It also provided that the remuneration was to be by fees and that whenever the office of sheriff became vacant due to death, resignation, or otherwise, the coroner was temporarily to execute the sheriff's duties. (3 O. L. 158-161). The latter stipulation was repealed in 1887. (84 O. L. 108-210). In 1831 a statute was enacted which provided that the coroner return a report of his findings in inquests to the clerk of the court of common pleas. He was also empowered to cause the arrest of the person or persons, who, through force or violence, caused the death of the deceased. (29 O. L. 112).

The Constitution of 1851 left the office unchanged. A bill was carried in 1853 which provided that the coroner when required by the probate court, must attend court, and that he may serve or execute subpoenas or attachments for witnesses, issued from any court. (51 O. L. 167, para. 61). Three years later a measure was adopted which provided that the coroner must notify the relatives of the deceased after the inquest of the latter's death, and of his findings, and give a statement of property found on the body. (53 O. L. 48, para. 2).

The Constitution of 1912 also had no provision which affected the office of coroner, and not until recent years have any laws been passed which changed its status. In 1921 the law of 1831 was amended in that he was empowered to make autopsies, if authorized by the county prosecutor, the results of which he must also report to the clerk of the common pleas court. The same act somewhat changed the rule as to the circumstances under which inquests were to be held. The law now read "when informed that the body of a person whose death is supposed to have been caused by unlawful or suspicious means has been found within the county" the coroner shall hold an inquest. The law therefore invested in him a certain discretion as to whether the circumstances warranted an inquest. (109 O. L. 543). In the same year a bill was carried which provided that in all counties having a population of 100,000 or more only licensed physicians be eligible for the office of coroner. The same bill made the coroner the official custodian of the morgue. (109 O. L. 544).

In 1927 a bill was passed which set the salary of the coroner at $6000.00 per year in all counties having a population of 400,000 or more. It also authorized him to appoint one stenographer, a secretary, and three assistant custodians of the morgue. (112 O. L. 204-205). In 1929 a bill was voted, which empowered the coroner to appoint a pathologist who was to serve as a deputy coroner, to make chemical examinations and autopsies. (113 O. L. 497). The last act which affected the office was passed in 1936, changing the term of office from two to four years. (116 O. L. pt. 2, 1st s. sec. H. 603).

947. CORONER'S FILES
October 1833—. Approximately 45,000 files in 363 file boxes.
Contain a complete history of the case, date of death, coroner's verdict, name of witnesses, results of the autopsy, police reports, coroner's testimony, and a record of coroner's view slip. In order of case numbers. Handwritten, typed, and printed. Each file box 4.25 x 10.75 x 13.5. October 1833-1923, 216 file boxes, 1-27999, Basement storeroom; June 1923—, 147 file boxes, 28000-44738, Inquest room, Morgue.

948. INDEX TO CORONER'S INQUESTS
October 1833—. 6 volumes.
An alphabetical index of deceased persons, listing case number, date of death, locality where deceased was found, and cause of death according to the judgment of the coroner. It also records property found on the body and disposition of the property. The first two volumes contain a record of unknown and unclaimed dead for the years 1833-1903. Handwritten on printed forms. Volumes average 460 pages. 15.5 x 18.75 x 2.5. Inquest room, Morgue.

949. RECORD OF UNKNOWN AND UNCLAIMED DEAD
September 1904—. 2 volumes.

Lists place, date, and probable cause of death, and includes a photograph of the decedent, and complete description of body. In chronological order. Handwritten on printed forms. Volumes average 250 pages. 12.75 x 18.75 x 2.75. Inquest room, Morgue. Records from October 1933-September 1904 will be found in the first two volumes of the Index to Coroner's Inquest.

950. CORONER'S RECORD
January 1898—. 3 volumes.

Lists case number; date of death; name, age, and nativity of decedent; whether married or single; occupation; residence; number of witnesses to the corpse; fees for informants and constable; and general remarks. In order a case numbers. Handwritten and typed on printed forms. Volumes average 300 pages. 12.5 x 16.25 x 2.5. Inquest room, Morgue.

951. CORONER'S RECORD BOOK
February 1928—. 1 volume.

Lists cause of death, if known; occupation, age, sex, color, and other facts about decedent; and totals of deaths from each of various causes. In chronological order. Handwritten on printed forms. 130 pages. 15 x 17.5 x 1.2. Inquest room, Morgue.

952. DEATH REPORT RECEIVED (Outside Book)
July 1926—. 3 volumes, 2-4.

Reports of deaths in which the body is not brought to the morgue, giving name and address of decedent; time, place, and cause of death; and address of the undertaker. Alphabetical index of deceased persons in each volume. Handwritten on printed forms. Volumes average 1,000 pages. 10 x 11.5 x 3. Inquest room, Morgue.

953. RECORD OF BODIES RECEIVED
October 1927—. 22 volumes, 6-27.

Lists name and address of the decedent, date and hour at which death occurred, a complete description of the body, a statement as to the probable cause of death, the name of person to whom body is released. Alphabetical index of deceased person in each volume. Handwritten on printed forms. Volumes average 500 pages. 10.75 x 12 x 2.25. Inquest room, Morgue.

954. CORONER'S REPORTS
April 1914-January 1922. 1 volume.
List case number, name of deceased, and date of death. In chronological order. Handwritten on printed forms. 300 pages. 9.75 x 14.5 x 1.75. Inquest room, Morgue.

955. CORONER'S PROPERTY BOOK
September 1926—. 17 volumes, 10-26.
Lists personal property found on the body and in the clothing of the decedent, date the body was received, name of decedent, where body is received from. It also gives the names of the first witnesses who discovered the body. Personal property is listed under the headings of clothing, money, jewelry, and miscellaneous. Handwritten and typed on printed forms. Volumes average 250 pages. 6.5 x 12 x 2. Inquest room, Morgue.

956. PROPERTY BOOK (Releases)
September 1926—. 3 volumes, 6-8.
Records listing property of deceased person, name of person by whom it is claimed, and signature of the claimant. Order for disposition of property obtained from probate court is also listed. Alphabetical index of deceased persons in each volume. Handwritten on printed forms. Volumes average 500 pages. 11.25 x 15.75 x 4. Inquest room, Morgue.

957. CORONER'S CASH BOOK
February 1928—. 1 volume.
A record of money received and disbursed by the coroner's office, listing case number; name and address of deceased; to whom fees are due, such as morgue, sheriff, and miscellaneous fees; and date of which money is received or disbursed. In chronological order. Handwritten on printed forms. 250 pages. 10.5 x 16 x 1.75. Inquest room, Morgue.

958. CORONER'S FEES
September 1910-July 1921. 1 volume.
Charges of the coroner for services rendered, listing case number; name and address of deceased person; corpse number; and amount paid to witnesses, informants, and constables. In chronological order. Handwritten on printed forms. 300 pages. 12 x 16.5 x 2.5. Inquest room, Morgue.

The office of county sheriff had its inception in England during the Anglo-Saxon period. The word sheriff originated with the two words shire-reve (or reev). The sheriff in England was a ministerial officer who executed process, kept the king's peace, took bail, witnessed contracts, put laws into execution, and presided at the hundred court. During the Anglo-Norman period the power of the sheriff increased until he became the leading officer of the county. He was responsible for the county's revenue, its military force, its police, its jails, its courts, and for the execution of the writs of all courts. Beginning with the 17th century, the sheriff's duties became more nominal and he acted as little more than an executive agent of the courts. (George Crabb, *A History of English Law,* 1831, 24-25; W. S. Holdsworth, *op. cit.,* 1, 65-66).

The office of sheriff was incorporated in the governmental organization of American colonists, and by provision of the laws of the Northwest Territory the governor was authorized to appoint and commission a sheriff who took an oath of office, gave bond, and whose duty it was to keep peace, suppress all affrays, routs, riots, and insurrections. He was to pursue, apprehend and commit to jail, all felons and traitors; he executed all warrants, writs, and other process appertaining to his office, or directed to him by legal authority. He attended upon all courts of record of his county. (Pease, *op. cit.,* 8).

The constitution of 1802 provided for the election of a sheriff in each county for a term of two years, and stipulated that no person shall be eligible for a longer term than four years in any term of six years. (Ohio Const. Art. 6, sec. 1). In the same year the general assembly authorized the sheriff to procure ballot boxes, at the county's expense, and place one in each township where elections were to be held, and give notice by proclamation, of the time of holding election and the names of the officers to be chosen. (1 O. L. 77).

The duties of the sheriff prescribed by the general assembly in 1905, were similar to the duties imposed upon him by the laws of the Northwest Territory. By provision of the same act he was empowered to summon to his aid such persons as he deemed necessary to assist him in the exercise of his awful duties. He was designated custodian of the county jail. His compensation was received from fees collected by him. (3 O. L. 156). In the same year the sheriff was made county executioner, and he carried out death sentences as imposed by the court. (3 O. L. 13). Public executions by the sheriff were prohibited in 1844. (42 O. L. 71). Later his duties as executioner were transferred from the sheriff to the warden of the Ohio State Penitentiary. (83 O. L. 145).

In 1804 the sheriff was designated county tax collector. (2 O. L. 171). A later this statute was repealed. (3 O. L. 108).

The sheriff was authorized in 1818 to appoint deputies subject to their approval of the court of common pleas (16 O. L. 128), and to summon persons selected for jury service. (22 O. L. 101).

The keeping of an execution docket by the sheriff, in which every execution, order, decree and other process issuing from any court in the state was recorded, was authorized in 1838. (36 O. L. 18). He is also required to keep a jail register, of which he made a report in writing, to the clerk of courts, to the county auditor for the use of the county commissioners, and to the secretary of state. (41 O. L. 7.). A cash book is kept by the sheriff in which a record of all money received by him in his official capacity is entered (65 O. L. 114), and he accounts annually to the county commissioners for all fines and costs collected by him during the year, and the amount paid by him to the clerk of courts. (41 O. L. 71).

The sheriff is required to serve subpoenas and execute warrants emanating from different state departments and boards, among which were any standing or select committee of the general assembly or any house thereof (69 O. L. 61), the bureau of inspection and supervision of public offices (97 O. L. 271), the state board of pharmacy (107 O. L. 541), the state fire marshal (108 O. L. pt. 1, 288), and the state medical board. (109 O. L. 585).

In 1910 the governor was empowered to remove the sheriff from office if he were proved guilty of negligence in affording a prisoner adequate protection from mob violence. (101 O. L. 109). The sheriff is authorized to arrest any person for parole violation. (103 O. L. 405). He is also required to forward to the state bureau of criminal investigation all finger prints of persons arrested for a felony. (109 O. L. 585).

The fee system for compensation of county officers was abolished in 1906, and the sheriff's salary at that time was limited to $6,000 a year. (98 O. L. 117). The constitutional provision limiting the term of office for the sheriff to four years in any term of six years was repealed by a constitutional amendment adopted November 7, 1933. (Ohio Const., Art. 10, sec. 3). Three years later an act was passed providing that a sheriff be elected quadrennially in each county. (115 O. L., pt. 2, H. 603).

The changes in the sheriff's duties as executive agent of the courts have been insignificant. He is still the active custodian of the county jail and submits all bills to the county commissioners for the feeding and care of the prisoners. He is still authorized to transport prisoners to other counties for safe-keeping. He is required to attend the court of appeals and the court of common pleas during session, and when required, upon probate court, and to execute all writs, warrants and subpoenas directed to him by lawful authority.

Although still recognized as the chief peace officer of the county, the sheriff has relinquished most of his powers in law enforcement to the police department of the municipalities in his county and to the state highway patrol; only when they refuse or neglect to act according to law, or when requested by them, does he exercise the power vested in him.

Civil Branch

Service

959. RECORD OF ACCRUED FEES
January 1911—. 21 volumes.
A record of accrued fees for service rendered by the sheriff, listing case number, date received, kind of writ, date returned, and sheriff's cost. Arranged chronologically. Handwritten on printed forms. Volumes average 650 pages. 13 x 18.5 x 3.5. 1911-1934, 20 volumes, Basement storeroom; 1934—, 1 volume. Room 257, County courthouse.

960. PENDING CASES
1935—. Approximately 6000 in 12 file boxes.
Writs which have not been served because of inability of the deputies to locate person to whom they were directed. In order of case numbers. Handwritten on printed forms. Each file box 12 x 11.75 x 3. Room 257, County courthouse.

961. DEPUTIES' RETURNS
1901—. 236 volumes.
Individual deputy sheriffs' records of service obtained on writs, giving case number; kind of writ; name and address of party served; kind of service–whether personal, residential, etc.; date; and any remarks necessary as to conditions at time service was obtained, or whether the service could not to be made. In chronological order.

Handwritten. Volumes average 320 pages. 14.5 x 17 x 1.25. 1901-1933, 209 volumes, Basement storeroom; 1933—, 27 volumes, Room 257 annex, County courthouse.

962. DIVORCE SUMMONS
1935—. 3 file boxes, A-Z.

Defendants' copies of the petition and summons on which return has been made. Filed alphabetically. Handwritten and typed on printed forms. Each file box 12 x 11.75 x 3. Room 257, County courthouse.

963. OUT-OF-STATE SUMMONS DOCKET
July 1927—. 1 volume.

A record of summonses originating outside the State of Ohio to be served on Cuyahoga County defendants. It lists title of case, names of parties involved, nature of writ, date writ was received, when returned, and amount of fee for serving the writ. Contains an alphabetical index of plaintiffs and defendants. Handwritten on printed forms. 500 pages. 14.5 x 17 x 3.25. Room 257 annex, County courthouse.

964. FOREIGN SUMMONS DOCKET
1881—. 21 volumes (September 1881-September 1898, 2 volumes; January 1907-1928, 12 volumes; 1929—, 7 volumes). 1898-1906 missing.

A record of summonses issued on Cuyahoga County defendants which originated outside of Cuyahoga County. It lists case number, name plaintiff and defendant, nature of summons, date summons was received, date returned, amount of fee, and date of payment. Alphabetical index of plaintiffs and defendants in each volume. Handwritten on printed forms. Volumes average 800 pages. 15 x 16.75 x 4. January 1881-1928, 14 volumes, Basement storeroom; 1929—, 7 volumes, 13-19, Room 257, County courthouse.

965. SHERIFF'S DAY BOOK
January 1907-December 1911. 2 volumes, 1-2.

A record of writs received by the sheriff's office from the courts, listing case number, name of plaintiff and of defendant, date on which writ was received by the sheriff, date returned, court from which writ was issued, type of writ, names of attorneys, and fees for serving writ. Chronological. Handwritten. Volumes average 480 pages. 15.25 x 16 x 2.25. Basement storeroom, County courthouse.

966. EXECUTION DOCKET
September 1848-March 1919. 3 volumes (September 1848-December 1874,
1 volume; January 1907-March 1919, 2 volumes). January 1875-December
1906 missing.
A record of all writs served by the sheriff's office, listing name of plaintiff and of
defendant, date execution was issued, date received by sheriff's office, when
returned, net fees for service, and remarks. Alphabetical index of plaintiffs and
defendants in each volume. For separate index see number 967. Handwritten on
printed forms. Volumes average 460 pages. 14 x 17.5 x 3. Basement storeroom,
County courthouse.

967. INDEX TO EXECUTION DOCKET
1848-1919. 3 volumes.
Alphabetical index of plaintiffs and defendants, listing volume and page of the
docket. Handwritten. Volumes average 100 pages. 11 x 16 x .75. Basement
storeroom, County courthouse.

968. COURT ORDERS
1922-1927. Approximately 2000 in 4 bundles; approximately 390 in 1 file
box.
Various executed court orders, such as notices to garnishees, copies of journal
entries, injunctions, restraining orders, citations, bench warrants, etc. Handwritten
and typed on printed forms. Each bundle 9 x 5 x 3; file box 11.75 x 12 x 3.
Basement storeroom, County courthouse.

Executions

969. DOMESTIC EXECUTION DOCKET
1923—. 44 volumes, 1-44.
A record of executions originating in Cuyahoga County courts, listing name of
plaintiff and of defendant, date when writ originated, date received by the sheriff's
office, and pertinent remarks. Alphabetical index of plaintiffs and defendants in
each volume. Handwritten on printed forms. Volumes average 650 pages. 12.5 x
17.75 x 6.5. 1923-1935, 42 volumes, 1-42, Basement storeroom; 1935—, 2
volumes, 43-44, Room 257, County courthouse.

970. FOREIGN EXECUTION DOCKET
1881—. 9 volumes, 1-9.

A record of executions originating outside of Cuyahoga County, listing name of plaintiff and of defendant, date of writ, date when received, name of person who received it, the county and court where originated, date served, date returned, amount of writ, and various remarks. Alphabetical index of plaintiffs and defendants in each volume. Handwritten on printed forms. Volumes average 180 pages. 13 x 17.25 x 2.25. January 1881-1923, 6 volumes, 1-6, Basement storeroom; 1923—, 3 volumes, 7-9, Room 257, County courthouse.

971. EXECUTIONS
1928—. 5 bundles; approximately 2400 in 12 file boxes.

Executed writs, including various types of summonses, attachments, evictions, replevins, and foreclosure of chattels, in jackets. Jacket list date levy was made, when advertised, paper advertised in, date of sale, purchaser, amount sold for, and names of attorneys. In order of case numbers. Handwritten and typed on printed forms. Each bundle 12 x 11 x 5; each file box 12 x 11 x 3. 1828-1930, 5 bundles, Basement storeroom; 1931—, 12 file boxes, Room 257, County courthouse.

972. LAND LEVIES
1926-1930. Approximately 900 in 9 bundles.

Land levy forms, listing name and address of defendant, description of the land, date and hour at which writ was served, name of deputy who served the writ, and amount of sheriff's fees. (Copies are now posted in the execution docket; originals are returned to the clerk). Arranged chronologically. Handwritten and typed on printed forms. Each bundle 6 x 9 x 6. Basement storeroom, County courthouse.

973. PLAINTIFF'S REPLEVIN BOND FORMS
1921. Approximately 200 in 1 bundle.

Each form lists amount of bond in a replevin action, date on which bond was posted, and name of plaintiff and of sheriff. (Bonds are now recorded and execution docket). In chronological order. Typed on printed forms. Bundle 10.5 x 4.25 x 4.5. Basement storeroom, County courthouse.

974. ATTACHMENTS AND REPLEVINS
1922-1926. Approximately 85 in 1 bundle.
Attachments and replevins listing name of plaintiff and defendant, date served, and various remarks. Arranged chronologically. Handwritten and typed on printed forms. Bundle 12 x 9 x 5. Basement storeroom, County courthouse.

Evictions

975. EVICTION WRITS
September 1934—. Approximately 900 in 3 file boxes.
Eviction writs, listing date of eviction, name of plaintiff and defendant, case number, title of case, and fees. In order of case numbers. Typed on printed forms. Each file box 5 x 12.5 x 13. Room 257, County courthouse.

Foreclosures

976. SHERIFF'S SALES RECORD
1921—. 23 volumes, 1-23.
Record of all real property sold by sheriff, listing case number, sales number, name of attorney, title of case, day writ received, day appraised, amount appraised for, date advertised, paper advertised in, day sold, to whom sold, amount sold for, sheriff's fees, and appraiser's and others' fees. Alphabetical index of plaintiff in each volume. Volumes average 500 pages. 13 x 18 x 2.5. 1921-1932, 13 volumes, Basement storeroom; 1932—, 9 volumes, Room 257, County courthouse.

977. CONFIRMATIONS AND DISTRIBUTIONS (Foreclosures)
1927—. 189 file boxes.
Orders of sale, reports on distribution of proceeds, tax bills, clerk's cost bills, and special entries which may be filed in the case. Filed by case numbers. Each file box 11.75 x 12 x 3. 1927-1931, 71 file boxes, Basement storeroom; 1931—, 118 file boxes, Room 257, County courthouse.

978. CONFIRMATIONS OF SALE (Foreclosures)
1923-1924, 1 bundle; 1924-1927, 6 volumes.
Records of decrees of confirmation by court certifying sales of foreclosed property by sheriff were legally executed. Alphabetical index of plaintiffs in each volume.

Printed and typed. Volumes average 150 pages. 9 x 17.75 x 3.5. Basement storeroom, County courthouse.

979. LAND APPRAISALS
1934—. Approximately 880 in 22 file boxes.
Land appraisal forms listing case number; title of case; location, address, and description of property; date of appraisal; amount appraised for; date copy filed; date of advertising; date of sale; purchaser; amount sold for; name of attorney; and a sketch of property. In order by case numbers. Handwritten and typed on printed forms. Each file box 12 x 11.75 x 3. Room 257, County courthouse.

980. FINAL FORECLOSURE REPORTS
June 1932—. Approximately 7200 in 12 file boxes.
Uncalled-for sheriff's deeds, and reports on foreclosures of property. In order of case numbers. Handwritten and typed on printed forms. Each file box 12 x 11.75 x 3. Room 257, County courthouse.

981. TAXES PAID
1922-1927. Approximately 6240 tax bills in 16 letter boxes.
Paid tax bills on foreclosed property. Arranged alphabetically by names of property owners. Handwritten and typed on printed forms. Each letter box 11.25 x 12 x 3. Basement storeroom, County courthouse.

982. ORDER OF SALES
April 1879-November 1912. 2 volumes.
A record of writs received by sheriff ordering him to sell property described in writ. Lists docket volume, case number, name of plaintiff and defendant, date writ received, appraised value of property, date and hour of sale, name of purchaser, amount of purchase price, date of final settlement, and various remarks. In chronological order. Handwritten on printed forms. Volumes average 330 pages. 12.75 x 13.25 x 1.25. Basement storeroom, County courthouse.

983. TAX CERTIFICATES REDEEMED AND TAX CERTIFICATES FOR WHICH DEEDS ARE MADE
1877-1880. 1 volume.

A sheriff's record of land sold for delinquent taxes. A certificate by the auditor was given to the county surveyor, listing the delinquent taxes on the land, township in which land was located, original lot and sublot numbers, allotment block, amount of tax together with the penalty, name of purchaser, amount, and date of sale. Arranged chronologically. Handwritten on printed forms. 400 pages. 8.75 x 12 x 2.5. Basement storeroom, County courthouse.

984. POUND KEEPER'S RECORD
September 1923-October 24, 1923. 1 volume, 16.

Gives description of dog; owner's name and address; date dog was impounded; manner and date of disposition; cost bill for pick-up, housing, and feeding of dog; whether dog is sold; purchaser's name and address; amount paid for the animal; and date of sale. In chronological order. Handwritten on printed forms. 600 pages. 12 x 16.5 x 2.75. Basement storeroom, County courthouse.

Cashier's Records

985. CASH DISBURSEMENTS
1924—. 18 volumes, 1-18.

A record of all monies paid by the sheriff's office, listing case number, check number, amount, payee, amounts paid to the sheriff's fee fund, court costs, judgments, sales, deposits, and sundries. Arranged chronologically. Handwritten on printed forms. Volumes average 460 pages. 17.75 x 19.5 x 2. February 1924-1935, 17 volumes, Basement storeroom; current volume, Room 257, County courthouse.

986. CASH RECEIPTS
1924—. 12 volumes.

A record of all cash received by the civil branch of the sheriff's office, listing case number, receipt number, name of party from whom received and of party to whom due, amount due, amount received, date, fee fund, sheriff's fees, sheriff's sales, court cost, judgments, and date on which payments were received. Arranged chronologically. Handwritten on printed forms. Volumes average 350 pages. 17.5 x 20.5 x 1.75. 1924-1930, 7 volumes, Basement storeroom; 1931—, 5 Volumes, Room 257, County courthouse.

987. CASH RECEIPTS AND DISBURSEMENTS
January 1907-January 1924. 9 volumes, 1-5, 5-8.

A record of cash received and disbursed by the sheriff's office, listing case number, date on which money was received or paid, and name of payee and payer. Beginning February 1924, this record was broken down, separating the recording of the receipts from the disbursements. Volumes 5-8 have an alphabetical index of plaintiffs and defendants in each volume. Handwritten on printed forms. Volume average 320 pages. 13 x 18.5 x 3.75. Basement storeroom, County courthouse.

988. RECEIPT BOOKS
1919—. 158 books.

Receipts for payments made in the sheriff's office, showing name of payee and of payer, dates of payments, and receipt numbers. Handwritten on printed forms. Books average 100 pages. 8.75 x 14.25 x 1.25. 1919-1932, 410 books, Basement storeroom; 1932—, 8 books, Room 257, County courthouse.

989. CHATTEL RECEIPTS
1927- October 1933. 1 volume.

Chattel receipts posted in volume and show case number, title of case, amount, and signature of person receiving funds. Now in general receipt books. Chronological. 200 pages. 11 x 15.5 x 2.5. Room 257, County courthouse.

990. CASH BOOK
1907-January 1919. 6 volumes.

Record of money received on foreclosures sales, listing sale number, date of sale, name of person from whom money was received, and amount received. Chronological. Handwritten on printed forms. Volumes average 300 pages. 10 x 11.75 x 1.5. Basement storeroom, County courthouse.

991. CASH AND EXECUTION DOCKET
January 1877-May 1919. 8 volumes (February 1877-December 1880, 1 volume; January 1881-May 1919, 7 volumes, 1-7).

Record of monies received and disbursed by sheriff's office, listing name of person receiving money, person from whom it was received, dates, amounts, and purpose for which money was paid or received. Volumes 3-7 have alphabetical index of plaintiffs and defendants in each volume. Handwritten on printed forms. Volumes average 300 pages. 14 x 17.5 x 3.25. Basement storeroom, County courthouse.

992. MISCELLANEOUS DISBURSEMENTS, CORRESPONDENCE, AND RECEIPTS

1925—. 27 letter boxes.

Small bills paid by the sheriff, miscellaneous receipts, and general correspondence. Arranged chronologically and as to subject matter. Handwritten and typed on printed forms. Each file box 11.25 x 12.25 x 3.25. 5 letter boxes, Basement storeroom; 22 letter boxes, Room 257, County courthouse.

993. MONTHLY STATEMENTS TO STATE EXAMINERS

1927—. 10 volumes.

A recapitulation of the month's business, listing bank balance, outstanding checks, balance shown on check stubs, cash receipts entered, money used in transportation of prisoners to state institutions, sheriff's fees collected, court costs, and total amount of checks drawn by the sheriff. In chronological order. Volumes average 175 pages. 9 x 15 x 1.5. 9 volumes, Basement storeroom; 1 volume, Room 257, County courthouse.

994. LIST OF UNCLAIMED MONIES PAID TO TREASURER

June 1920—. 1 volume.

Record of unclaimed monies paid to the treasurer, listing case number, name of party to whom money is due, number of order certificate, date of issue, volume and page of the fee book, amount due, and various remarks. Contains an alphabetical index of plaintiffs and defendants. Handwritten on printed forms. 300 pages. 12.5 x 15.75 x 2.25. Room 257, County courthouse.

995. CANCELLED CHECKS

1914—. 43 file boxes.

Checks which have been paid by the bank on which they have been drawn and returned to the sheriff. In order of check numbers. Handwritten and typed on printed forms. Each file box 10.5 x 4.5 x 27. 1914-1930, 33 boxes, Basement storeroom; 1931—, 10 boxes, Room 257, County courthouse.

996. CHECK STUBS
1921—. 11 bundles.
These check stubs show amount of the check drawn, check number, name of payee, and date on which check was drawn. In order of check numbers. Handwritten and typed on printed forms. Each bundle 9 x 14 x 5. 1921-1936, 10 bundles, Basement storeroom; 1936—, 1 bundle, in safe, Room 257, County courthouse.

997. UNPAID COST
1927-1929. 4 volumes.
Lists case number, name of plaintiff and of defendant, and amount due by plaintiff or defendant. In order of case numbers. Typed on printed forms. Volumes average 125 pages. 10 x 16 x 1. Basement storeroom, County courthouse.

998. COST BILLS
1924-1927. Approximately 2860 in 11 file boxes.
Statements of court costs, listing case number, name of plaintiff and defendant, itemized statement of cost, and total. Arranged alphabetically as to plaintiffs. Handwritten and typed on printed forms. Now filed with foreclosure proceedings file. Each file box 11.75 x 12 x 3. Basement storeroom, County courthouse.

999. TRAVELING EXPENSE AND TRANSPORTATION SHEETS OF DEPUTIES
1928. Approximately 3000 in 3 bins.
List fees and traveling expenses of deputy sheriffs for serving writs, summonses, etc. Handwritten on printed forms. Each bin 3 x 1.5 x 1.25. Attic storeroom, fourth floor, County courthouse.

1000. PROBATE COURT FEE BOOK
1881-1883, 1 volume; 1907-1922, 4 volumes.
A record of fees obtained by the sheriff for service rendered the probate court, listing case number, name of plaintiff and defendant, date service rendered, court costs, amount paid by plaintiff or defendant, and title of the case. Alphabetical index of plaintiffs and defendants in each volume. Handwritten on printed forms. Volumes average 450 pages. 12.5 x 18 x 2.75. 1881-1883, 1 volume, second floor, Hart Building; January 1907-December 1922, 4 volumes, 1-4, Basement storeroom, County courthouse.

1001. SHERIFF'S INSANE FEE BOOK
January 1907-June 1910. 4 volumes, 1-4.
A record of money received by the sheriff for service rendered in insane cases, listing case number, name and address of insane party, name of writ, date on which writ was received by sheriff, date writ was served, name of deputy, total cost, name of person who paid the cost, and date of payment. Alphabetical index of plaintiffs and defendants in each volume. Handwritten on printed forms. Volumes average 450 pages. 13.25 x 18.5 x 3.75. Basement storeroom, County courthouse.

1002. STATE OF OHIO FEE BOOK
January 1907-March 1919. 7 volumes, 1-6; 1 volume not numbered.
A record of fees obtained through service rendered for the State of Ohio, listing case number, date of writ, cost to plaintiff and to defendant, amount of cost paid by each, and title of writ. Alphabetical index of plaintiffs and defendants in each volume. Handwritten on printed forms. Volumes average 510 pages. 13.25 x 18.25 x 3.5. Basement storeroom, County courthouse.

1003. SHERIFF'S COMMON PLEAS FEE BOOK
January 1907-January 1922. 23 volumes, 1-23.
Record of fees obtained by the sheriff for service rendered the common pleas court, listing case number, names of plaintiff and defendant, date service rendered, court costs, amount paid by plaintiff or defendant, and title of writ. Alphabetical index of plaintiffs and defendants in each volume. Handwritten on printed forms. Volumes average 500 pages. 13.75 x 18.5 x 3. Basement store room, County courthouse.

1004. INSOLVENCY COURT FEE BOOK
January 1907-May 1924. 3 volumes, 1-3.
A record of fees obtained through the service of writs for the insolvency court, listing date of fees accrued, name of plaintiff or defendant, dates of payments, and name of writ. Alphabetical index of plaintiffs and defendants in each volume. Handwritten on printed forms. Volumes average 450 pages. 13 x 17.5 x 2.25. Basement storeroom, County courthouse.

1005. JUVENILE FEE BOOK
November 1907-July 1926. 2 volumes, 2-3.
A record of fees for service of writs for juvenile court, listing case number, names of plaintiff and defendant, name of writ, and total cost for service rendered. Alphabetical index of plaintiffs and defendants in each volume. Handwritten on printed forms. Volumes average 500 pages. 13 x 17.5 x 2.5. Basement storeroom, County courthouse.

1006. FEES FROM COUNTY CLERK
February 1907-December 1912. 3 volumes, 1-3.
A record of fees obtained for service rendered the county clerk, listing the docket number, case number, name of plaintiff and of defendant, amount of fee, and various remarks. Arranged chronologically. Handwritten on printed forms. Volumes average 300 pages. 11.25 x 16.5 x1.75. Basement storeroom, County courthouse.

1007. DIVORCE FEE BOOK
1881-1919. 10 volumes. 1883-1906 missing.
A record of fees obtained for service rendered in divorce proceedings, listing case number, names of plaintiff and defendant, title of writ, date served, court costs, and amount paid by plaintiff or defendant. Alphabetical index of plaintiffs and defendants in each volume. Handwritten on printed forms. Volumes average 450 pages. 13 x 17.25 x 3. 1881-1882, 2 volumes, second floor, Hart Building; January 1907-September 1920, 8 volumes, 1-8, Basement store room, County courthouse.

Criminal Branch

1008. RECORD OF PRISONERS CONVICTED AND SENTENCED
1920—. 5 volumes.
Lists name and address of defendant, crime convicted of, race and social status, date of admission, date discharge, and sentence ordered. Alphabetical index of defendants in each volume. Handwritten. Volumes average 336 pages. 16 x 11.5 x 1.5. Fourth floor, Criminal Courts Building.

1009. VOUCHERS FOR THE RELEASE OF PRISONERS
1927—. 1 bundle; 10 boxes.
List case number and name of prisoner, of judge, and of court. In order of case numbers. Handwritten on printed forms. Bundle 10 x 8 x 3; each box 30 x 24 x 14.

1927-1930, 1 bundle, Basement storeroom; 1930—, 10 boxes, 13th floor, Criminal Courts Building.

1010. REQUISITION ORDER BOOK
1930—. 1 loose-leaf volume.

A record of competitive bidding requisitions on all supplies, including food for prisoners requested for the sheriff's office and county jail. In chronological order. Typed. 1500 pages. 13 x 10 x 3.5. Fourth floor, Criminal Courts Building.

1011. GENERAL CORRESPONDENCE FILES
1930—. 11 file drawers.

General correspondence, monthly reports, board bills for county commissioners, federal reports, files of special deputies, and copies of competitive bids. In order of subject matter. Handwritten and typed. Each file drawer 11 x 13 x 24. Fourth floor, Criminal Courts Building.

1012. COUNTY JAIL REGISTER
1918—. 10 volumes.

Lists name and address of defendant, charge, race and social status, date committed to jail, date discharged, and disposition of case. Arranged alphabetically as to names of defendants. Handwritten. Volumes average 200 pages. 14.75 x 17 x 1.25. Fourth floor, Criminal Courts Building.

1013. FEDERAL BOOKING OF PRISONERS
1931—. 1 loose-leaf volume.

Lists name and address of defendant, date of admission to county jail, the charge, race and age, place of birth, length of sentence, and institution to which sentence. In chronological order. Handwritten. 300 pages. 24 x 16.5 x 1.5. Fourth floor, Criminal Courts Building.

1014. CITY JAIL REGISTER
1920—. 3 loose-leaf volumes.

Lists name and address of defendant, charge, date of admission to jail, race and social status, date of discharge, disposition of case. Alphabetical index of defendants in each volume. Handwritten. Volumes average 100 pages. 16.5 x 16 x 1. Fourth floor, Criminal Courts Building.

1015. JUVENILE DELINQUENT REGISTER
1919—. 5 volumes.

Lists name and address of delinquent, the charge, race and social status, date of admission, date of discharge, and disposition of case. Alphabetical index of defendants in each volume. Handwritten. Volumes average 200 pages. 14.75 x 17 x 1.75. Fourth floor, Criminal Courts Building.

1016. INDICTMENT BOOK
1921—. 4 volumes.

Lists name of defendant, date on which indictment was returned, and the charge. Alphabetical index of defendants in each volume. Handwritten. Volumes average 150 pages. 10 x 8.25 x 1. Fourth floor, Criminal Courts Building.

1017. LEDGER - OBSERVATION CASES
1925—. 1 volume.

Gives name and address of person held for observation; race, age, and social status; history; complete report of the observation; date admitted; and date discharged. Contains an alphabetical index of persons in each volume. Handwritten. 440 pages. 14 x 9 x 2. Fourth floor, Criminal Courts Building.

1018. FEDERAL JAIL REGISTER
1919-1933. 8 volumes.

Lists name and address of defendant, the charge, race and social status, date of admission, date of discharge, and disposition of the case. In chronological order. Handwritten. Volumes average 200 pages. 14.25 x 17 x 1.25. Fourth floor, Criminal Courts Building.

1019. GENERAL JAIL REGISTER
1887-1891. 1 volume.

Lists name and address of defendant, date of admission, and date discharged or transferred to another institution. Contains an alphabetical index of defendants. Handwritten. 200 pages. 17 x 15 x 1.75. Fourth floor, Criminal Courts Building.

The auditor's office is probably the most complex of all the county offices and has acquired, as had the office of county commissioners, a miscellany of duties not elsewhere delegated by statute. Strictly speaking, the auditor is the financial officer of the county and although the treasurer is the actual dispenser of county funds, no payment can be made except upon warrant of the county auditor. The auditor issues most of the licenses required by statute except for a few issued by the county recorder as clerk of courts. He is secretary of the budget commission, a member of the board of revision, and a member of the board of trustees of the sinking fund. The auditor appraises and assesses all real and personal property in the county and makes up the tax duplicate for real, personal, and inheritance taxes.

The auditor's office can be traced in England to 1118 A. D. It was then known as the upper division of the board of Exchequer - later known as the Chancellory of the Exchequer. Twice a year, at Easter and Michaelmas, the sheriff and other persons who had received money on behalf of the crown appeared before the board, composed of the more important state officials. At such times legal disputes as to payments were decided, and accounts were settled between the crown and its debtors or accountants, chief of whom was the sheriff who served as official tax collector. (Holdsworth, *op. cit.,* I, 42).

A law of the Northwest Territory adopted in 1799 provided for an auditor of public accounts appointed by the governor. It was his duty to receive and liquidate all accounts against the territory and to certify to the treasurer the balance due the territory. He was obliged to keep all accounts, vouchers, an account of treasurer's receipts and certificates, and a copy of warrants issued by him on the treasurer. Such file and records were open to examination by the legislature. Tax collection was made by the sheriff or an appointed collector. The auditor was compensated by a specified percentage of the fees. Township assessors, by an act of 1792, were appointed by the judges of the court of common pleas. (Pease, *op. cit.,* 71).

The Ohio Constitution of 1802 provided for a state auditor to be chosen triennially by a joint ballot of both houses of the legislature. (Ohio Const., Art., 6, sec. 2). In 1803 a statute was enacted requiring the state auditor of public accounts to perform all duties required of the auditor of public accounts of the Northwest Territory and to act as auditor of each county. (1 O. L. 71).

An act passed in 1804 provided that the county commissioners assess all county taxes and that the clerk of the common pleas court make out duplicates of the land tax, one for the county collector and one for the state auditor.

The commissioners were also required to file an annual report with a judge of the common pleas court. (2 O. L. 154, 169).

In 1819 provision was made for an auditor for each county, appointed annually by joint resolution of the general assembly. He was required to take an oath as to faithful performance of office and gave a bond to the state, and it was his duty to make out from lists and books delivered by him by the county commissioners, a complete list of all land within his county; and to take from each proprietor a list of land in his possession within the county. The act further stipulated that the auditor of the state make a list of all lands in each of the several counties within the state, with the amount of taxes, interest and penalties thereon and transmit the list to the county auditor. The county auditor was required to make out annually a complete duplicate of all lands subject to taxation within his county, in three copies, one of which he retained, one of which he gave to the county treasurer, and the last of which he delivered to the county collector who was appointed each year by the county commissioners. Each collector settled annually with the county auditor of his county and the county auditor then compiled from the collector's duplicate, a list of all lands on which taxes were delinquent.

The auditor was required to give to the collector a certificate of the amount to be paid to the state treasurer. The collector was required to turn over to the treasurer of state, all money collected by him on his duplicate. He paid to the county treasurer such proportion as the auditor directed, not exceeding the county's net proportion. The county treasurer's receipt for the county's share of taxes collected and accepted by the state treasurer was charged to the county. The county auditor submitted to the state auditor, by the collector, a list of all lands within his county on which taxes were delinquent.

On receiving the list of land the second time delinquent from the state auditor, the county auditor was required to proceed to the courthouse of the county where the lands were, to sell as much of each tract so delinquent as would be sufficient to pay the tax, interest and penalties charged thereon. All deeds of land sold for taxes conveyed to the purchaser, all rights, title and interest of the former proprietor. (Chase, *The Statutes of Ohio, II, 1102*).

A bill approved February 2, 1821 provided that the county auditor by virtue of his office shall be clerk of the board of county commissioners. (2 Chase, 1195). On February 23, 1824, the office of county auditor was made elective for a term of two years, and the same acts required the auditor to keep an accurate record of all corporate proceedings of the county commissioners; to examine and allow all account debts, and the demands chargeable to the county; and to make out alphabetical duplicates of the county tax, assessed by the commissioners of the county. It also provided that upon receiving from the collector of land tax the receipt of the county treasurer for moneys paid by the collector into the county treasury, he charge the treasurer with the amount thereof. (Ibid., 1376).

An act was passed on February 8, 1825 which amended the procedure as to collection of tax, delinquent tax and sale of property for tax. (Ibid., 1493).

In 1829 the county auditor was empowered to draw his order on the county treasury for maintenance of a poor house. (Ibid., III, 1619).

In the thirties a few additional duties were added. By a measure adopted in 1830 the incomes of lawyers and physicians in the county were subject to a tax not exceeding $5. (29 O. L. 304). This law was repealed in 1852. (50 O. L. 126). In 1831 the county auditor and the county prosecutor were made public informers with respect to the sale of liquor and the operating of a ferry without license. (29 O. L. 310; 28 O. L. 447).

An act of July 18, 1833 permitted taxes erroneously charged or collected to be deducted or refunded. In the same year the county auditor was given the power to discharge from imprisonment any person confined to jail for non-payment of any fine due the county. (30 O. L. 18). A statute was enacted in 1835 stipulating that all costs collected by the county prosecutor and received by the county treasurer shall be charged to the treasurer by the county auditor. (33 O. L. 45). An act passed in 1838 made the county auditor county superintendent of common schools. (36 O. L. 21).

More significant changes were made during the next decade. In 1840 a bill was passed providing for a county board of equalization to consist of the county auditor, county assessor, and county commissioners. They were to meet annually for the purpose of hearing complaints, equalizing assessments and revaluing all real and personal property within the county. (40 O. L. 54; 43 O. L. 67).

A bill passed in 1842 permitted justice of the peace to retain moneys collected as cost in criminal cases. The county treasurer was liable to the justice for unpaid to cost. An amendment allowed the justice to retain and collect cost in the event the case was not dismissed by him. (40 O. L. 54; 43 O. L. 67).

In 1845 a comprehensive tax measure was enacted. It was clarified by amendment in 1852, and as amended provided for the assessment and taxation of both real and personal property, specifically mentioning all moneys, credits, investments in bonds, stocks, joint stock companies and corporations, and included all banks, manufacturers and brokers. (50 O. L. 136).

In the same year it was made incumbent on the town directors to account to the auditor each year for money received by them through the sale of town lots. (43 O. L. 20). Another act provided that taxes be levied on real and personal property, specifying that a portion of the taxes appropriated by the act be used for the construction, and a portion for the maintenance of free turnpike roads; the amounts to be apportioned by the auditor upon certificate of the board of free turnpike commissioners. (43 O. L. 107).

An act of 1846 made the county auditor, in place of the county commissioners, the county sealer of weights and measures. (44 O. L. 56). The following year the auditor was authorized to open accounts with new townships. (46 O. L. 53).

A comprehensive act affecting public schools was passed in 1849 providing for district boards of education and divesting the county auditor of his office as superintendent of common schools. However, all expenditures for school sites or construction had to be certified to the county auditor and assessed and collected in each school district. (47 O. L. 24). In the same year an act required the obtaining of a permit from the auditor for any public exhibition in the county. (47 O. L. 51).

In 1850 an act was passed empowering the auditor to issue orders on the county treasurer for the payment of all reasonable expenses (not over certain stipulated amounts) arising out of the adjudication, care, and support of lunatics. (48 O. L. 86). Two years later the general assembly abolished the office of tax collector and empowered the county treasurer to receive and collect taxes for the county. (52 O. L. 124).

A statute was enacted in 1853 making it lawful for the trustees of any township to purchase or improve a cemetery for the use of the township upon the approval of a majority of the township voters. The auditor, upon proper notification, was given the duty of entering the necessary assessments upon the tax duplicate. (51 O. L. 97).

Another measure adopted in 1853 provided that the county commissioners empower the county auditor to contract for repairs or improvements of public buildings or grounds, providing that the cost and no instance exceeded $50. (51 O. L. 422-424).

The auditor and the commissioners were also required to determine annually the amount to be raised for various county purposes, and stipulated that the auditor ascertain the net value collected for each purpose, none of which was to be diverted to other uses. (51 O. L. 478).

The following year, the auditor was authorized to sell drained and reclaimed swamp lands within his county, at the appraised value; appraisal to be made by the county commissioners. (52 O. L. 51).

In 1856 a measure was adopted which provided that no money shall be disbursed except by the county treasurer upon the warrant of the county auditor. The auditor was also required to make a quarterly report to the commissioners of all moneys collected by him in fees and percentages. (53 O. L. 156).

Four acts were passed in 1858 affecting the auditor's office. One act gave the auditor power to appoint a deputy; another specified that no money be paid into the county except on his draft, with the exception of taxes charged on the tax duplicate; a third provided for the semi-annual payment and accounting of taxes; and the last measure required that the auditor and the treasurer jointly, make a quarterly financial report to a newspaper of general circulation. (55 O. L. 21; 55 O. L. 63; 55 O. L. 62; 55 O. L. 99).

During the following year additional changes were made. The auditor's bond was raised to $20,000. It was provided that no claims against the county be paid otherwise then upon the allowance of the county commissioners and upon the warrant of the county auditor, except in cases where the amount is fixed by law. A county board for the equalization of real and personal property was provided for, to be composed of the commissioners and the auditor. Another county board for equalization of real property to consist of the county auditor, surveyor, and commissioners were provided for. This was a board of assessment in contrast to the board of revision and was to meet once every six years. One assessor was elected in each township, town and ward, and in the event that the elected assessor failed to qualify, the auditor was to fill the position by appointment. (56 O. L. 129; 56 O. L. 130; 56 O. L. 146; 56 O. L. 193; 56 O. L. 156).

In 1859 it was stipulated that when a person deposits with the auditor, any receipt given by the treasurer, the auditor shall file it in his office and charge the treasurer with the amount which it represents. (56 O. L. 130).

A number of statutes affecting the auditor were passed in 1861. The auditor was required to make a semi-annual settlement with the treasurer, first ascertaining the amount collected by the treasurer, and then making in duplicate an abstract of moneys collected and uncollected, one copy to be given to the treasurer and one to be forwarded to the state auditor. It was also made the duty of the county treasurer, recorder, sheriff, prosecutor, and clerk of courts to file annually with the county auditor statements showing the fees collected by each during the preceding year, and to forward a copy of the statement to the state auditor, together with a similar statement by the auditor; a third made it the auditor's duty to annually submit to the state auditor a list of all deaf, dumb, blind, insane, and idiotic persons in the county. (57 O. L. 6; 58 O. L. 40).

The following year saw the passage of two bills which affected the office: one made it the auditor's duty to grant state license to peddlers; a second specified that the auditors of the several counties in which a railroad may have its roadway in whole or part shall constitute a board of assessors thereof. (50 O. L. 40; 59 O. L. 89).

In 1866 a measure was enacted which provided that a writ of peremptory *mandamus* may be awarded by any court having jurisdiction against any board of county commissioners, city council or board of education, commanding them to levy and assess such taxes as may be required by law for the purpose of paying the debt upon which the *mandamus* has been awarded, or for the purpose of creating a sinking fund for the gradual extinguishment of it. When such *mandamus* is addressed to the auditor, he shall be responsible for its execution as if he were an officer of the court. In 1869 an amendment provided that in case he neglects to do this, he shall forfeit to the state the sum of $50. (63 O. L. 15-16; 66 O. L. 26). In 1868 the sexennial board of equalization became a decennial board. (65 O. L. 168-169). In 1869 a bill was passed which levied a tax upon all federal treasury bonds, notes, and fractional currency. This act required all banks to make statements of such investments to the ward and township assessors who turned them over to the county auditor, who placed them on the tax duplicate. (66 O. L. 342-343).

Three enactments were passed in 1870 which related to the office: one provided that did directors of each county infirmary organize a school for the benefit of all inmates who were of school age, and that the auditor transfer to the poor fund a proportionate amount of school funds; a second stipulated that he keep an account current with the treasurer and receive a daily statement from him; a third required him to make a monthly financial statement in duplicate, one copy to be posted in his office, one to be filed with the commissioners. (67 O. L. 58-59; 67 O. L. 123; 67 O. L. 103).

In 1872 a measure was adopted which provided that whenever two thirds of the resident taxpayers living on the line of any state, county, or free turnpike road, desire any extra tax for the improving or repairing of that road, they may petition the auditor to levy a tax for that purpose. In the same session it was provided by enactment that the county commissioners shall require their surveyor to make maps and plots of original surveys in a form suitable for the preservation and that they shall be filed in the office of the county auditor. (69 O. L. 179;

69 O. L. 111). Another act passed in 1872 required the auditor to give to the auditor of state a complete and detailed abstract of the funded and unfunded indebtedness, and of the livestock statistics of each political division or subdivision. (70 O. L. 251; 70 O. L. 60-61).

The following year a bill was carried which gave any municipal board of health the power to abate or remove any nuisance within its jurisdiction and assess the necessary cost upon the property where the nuisance was situated. This assessment went certified by the president of the board to the auditor became a lien to be collected by him in favor of the municipality. (72 O. L. 159).

In 1875 an enactment was passed which provided that every railroad which has a right of way in any county must file with the county auditor thereof a statement showing the quantity of land embraced by it so that the proper reductions may be made from the parcel of the tax duplicate. (72 O. L. 75).

An enactment, adopted in 1876, required the auditors of the several counties composing a children's home district to meet at the home semi-annually, to adjust accounts. (73 O. L. 69).

Two measures were adopted in 1877 regarding the auditor's office: one extending the term of office to three years; the second requiring the county auditor to annually file with the state auditor a report of the sheep killed by dogs. (74 O. L. 381; 74 O. L. 179).

In 1881 a statute was enacted which established city boards for the equalization and revision of the value of personal property, moneys and credits. The auditor was made a member of the board. (78 O. L. 179-180).

In 1882 the first measure to provide for the taxation of persons engaged in the sale of intoxicating liquors was adopted. The assessors of personal property made the list of such persons to be turned into the county auditor, for assessment. (79 O. L. 66-69).

A statute enacted on February 17, 1887, specified that on warrant of the auditor, the treasurer shall, on order of the county commissioners pay the cost of burial of a pauper or unidentified person. (84 O. L. 29).

An act of March 6, 1888 provided for an annual salary of $5,000 per year to the county auditor. (85 O. L. 69). A statute enacted April 10, 1888 stipulated that the county commissioners, county auditor and county treasurer, were empowered to employ any person to make inquiry and furnish the county auditor the facts as to any omission of property subject to tax. (85 O. L. 170).

An act passed on April 11, 1888 contained the requirement that the treasurer shall settle annually on September 1, with the county auditor, for the preceding school year. (85 O. L. 194).

A bill passed in 1891 provided for the meeting of the decennial board of equalization of Cuyahoga County as a board of revision. (88 O. L. 339). In the same session the legislature a bill empowered the auditor of Cuyahoga County to appoint 40 assessors for the city of Cleveland, not more than half of whom are to be of the same political party, and whose duties are to be the same as formally provided for in respect to township assessors. (88 O. L. 341).

An act of 1891 created a state school-book board, and made the county auditor custodian of all school books of his county, specifying that the clerks of the district, special, and city schools, annually file with the auditor a list of all books required in their schools for the succeeding year. (88 O. L. 568).

By enactment of 1892 the county auditor was made Secretary of the newly created board of equalization of the city of Cleveland and was authorized to appoint a ditch commissioner, whose duty it would be to keep ditches clear. (89 O. L. 283, 305).

The first act for taxation of cigarettes was passed in 1893, the county auditor being authorized to assess the amount of tax. (90 O. L. 235). The initial collateral inheritance tax was passed in 1893, (90 O. L. 14-17), and amended in 1894, changing the exemption and rate of tax. (91 O. L. 166). In the same year a direct inheritance tax was approved imposing a graduated tax depending on the amount of inheritance. (90 O. L. 14-18). The cigarette tax was amended and 1894, lowering the tax rate, and prohibiting the enclosing of a picture or coupon, as premium, within the package. (91 O. L. 311-314).

A measure adopted in 1896 required depositories of county funds to notify the county auditor, in writing, on the first business day of each month, of the amount of deposits made by the county treasurer for the preceding month, and the balance due the county. (92 O. L. 356). Two years later the county auditor was made an ex officio member of the board of road commissioners but was given a vote only in case of a tie vote on any question before the board. (93 O. L. 423).

In 1902 all city boards of equalization and revision were abolished, and one city board of review was established which was to meet annually, with the county auditor as secretary. (95 O. L. 481). Another act gave the auditor, or any person he authorized in writing, permission to examine and make memoranda from the recorder's anywhere in the county. (95 O. L. 573).

Certain changes were made regarding taxation of inheritance. The Supreme Court of Ohio, in 1895, declared unconstitutional the act of 1894 imposing a direct-inheritance tax. The county auditor was authorized two years later to issue warrants on the county treasurer in favor of all persons who had paid the tax, for twenty-five percent of the tax so paid. (93 O. L. 374). An act to oppose a tax upon the right to succeed to, or inherit property was passed on April 24, 1904 and repealed the same year except as to states in which inventories had been filed. (97 O. L. 398; 98 O. L. 229).

When the fee system for all county officers was established in 1906, the legislature provided that all fees be paid quarterly into the county and that the county auditor was to receive, annually, an amount proportionate to his department's income in fees, but which in no event was to exceed $6,000. (98 O. L. 93).

The duties of the auditor regarding taxation were increased during the next decade. An act pass May 31, 1911 provided that the county auditor transmit quadrennially to the state tax commission an abstract of the real property of each taxing district of his county. (102 O. L. 256). Two years later the state tax commission was required to direct and supervise the assessment for taxation of all real and personal property in the state, with the aid of district assessors to be appointed by the governor. In each assessment district the state tax commission annually appointed a district board a complaint composed of three members, by which the county auditor was secretary. (103 O. L. 786). The offices of district assessors, and district boards of complaint were abolished in 1915 and the county auditor was made the chief assessing officer of the county, both as to real and personal property. (106 O. L. 246-272). The elective officers of township and ward assessors remained.

In the same session a bill was carried which provided that the treasurer, prosecutor, probate judge, and president of the board of commissioners of each county constitute a county board for the appointment of three members of a county board of revision. All appointments were to be made before April 1917, and were to be subject to the approval of the state tax commission. (106 O. L. 433-434). This act was repealed in 1917, and the county auditor became assessor of all real estate in the county. In addition, the auditor, the treasurer and president of the board of county commissioners were constituted the new board of revision which was to meet annually. (107 O. L. 534).

Certain duties were imposed by statute upon the county auditor March 21, 1917 in respect to the registration and licensing of dogs and dog kennels, the issuance of certificates of registration and transfer of ownership, and the keeping of a permanent record in a dog kennel register. (107 O. L. 534).

In 1919, by amendment, the county auditor was made the inheritance tax appraiser for his county. (108 O. L. 561-577). Another enactment that year provided that in each county having a bonded indebtedness, there shall be a board designated as trustees of the sinking fund, to be composed of the auditor, treasurer and prosecutor, to provide for the payment of interest on all bonds issued by the county. (108 O. L., Part I, 700-702).

By amendment and 1920, the term of office of the county auditor was changed to four years. (108 O. L., Part ii, 1994). In 1921 is salary was made proportionate to the population of his respective county and could not exceed $6,000 per year. (109 O. L. 614).

In 1923 the office of township assessor was established and a county board of assessors created, such board to be composed of the county auditor, prosecutor, and president of the board of county commissioners, making the county a unit for taxation purposes. (110 O. L. 386). In 1925 this act was repealed and the auditor designated as chief assessor of all real property in the county, excepting property of any public utility. (111 O. L. 419).

A bill passed in 1925 provided that the county auditor shall be assessor for, and list and value for taxation all personal property and his county. (111 O. L. 486).

On August 10, 1927, a statute was enacted which created in each county a budget commission consisting of the county auditor, treasurer, and prosecutor of which the auditor is secretary. They were to meet annually for the purpose of adjusting the rate of taxation and fixing the amount of taxes to be levied each year. Their decisions were to be determined by the amount of taxable property as shown on the auditor's duplicate, or by the auditor's estimate. (112 O. L. 399).

The intangible tax law passed on June 11, 1931 extended the personal property tax to cover such intangibles as certificates of deposits, savings and other deposits in financial institutions outside of the state yielding in excess of 4% per annum; and royalties and other contractual obligations for the payment of money. It provided that when a corporation allots shares to employees, it shall be deemed a trust and levied and assessed accordingly. It also emitted tax on household equipment.

In 1931 a measure was adopted which provided for the payment of delinquent taxes in five semi-annual installments. A similar act was approved in 1933 as an emergency measure for three years, and is known as the Whittmore law. It also provides for a remission of interest and penalties. A proposed amendment to this is now being considered by the general assembly. The first act has never been repealed. (115 O. L. 162).

In 1933 a bill popularly known as the Annat Bill, was passed to provide direct housing relief to indigent persons. Although the clerk of the board of county commissioners was designated by this law as the officer to whom the commissioners were to delegate the administration of such relief, the county auditor was given the duty of issuing tax warrants to the landlords, and deducting the amount represented by them from that due each taxing subdivision. (115 O. L. 194-195).

General Accounting and License Division

Certification and Appropriation Ledgers

1020. GENERAL LEDGER
September 1860—. 30 volumes (1860-1888, 2 volumes; 1888-1904, 6 volumes; 1901-1920, 13 volumes; 1921-1933, 7 volumes, 1934—, 2 volumes.
Lists date, reason for expenditure, folio number, debits, credits, and credit and debit balance. Alphabetical index of funds in each. Volumes 1860-1934, handwritten; 1934—, typed. Volumes average 500 pages. 13 x 12.5 x 6. 1860-1888, 2 volumes, Hart Building; 1888-1914, 6 volumes, marked "Record of County Funds," Hart Building, 1904-1920, 13 volumes; Room 70; 1921-1933, 7 volumes, Room 43; January 1, 1934—, 2 volumes, Room 149, County courthouse.

1021. APPROPRIATION LEDGER
April 1, 1912-December 1933, 38 loose-leaf volumes.
A record of receipts and disbursements, listing date of entry, from whom money was received, purpose of entry, receiving order number; a recapitulation of total receipts (debit), of the county treasurer's (balance), and of total disbursements (credit); the total amount received, and name of account charged. These accounts are listed under the various funds. Disbursements list date of entry, name to whom warrant was issued, warrant number, account, and distribution of the money

expended for various accounts. The amounts appropriated to these various accounts are also shown. Arranged chronologically. Each volume contains a marginal index as to the name of the fund. Handwritten and typed. Volumes average 1000 pages. 26 x 14.5 x 1.5. 1912-1920, 16 volumes, Hart Building; 1920-1827, 15 volumes, Room 70; 1928—, 7 volumes, Room 149, County courthouse.

1022. AUDITOR'S CERTIFICATE RECORD
January 1923-1933. (1923-1928 1 bundle; 1929-1933, 3 loose-leaf volumes.)

A recapitulation of the certificates issued, listing date, warrant number, amount certified, amount paid, number of certificate, bills payable, balance, and the difference funds. Alphabetical index of funds and appropriations in each volume. Handwritten. 1923-1929, 1 bundle, 17.5 x 18.5 x 3.75, Room 70. Volumes average 800 pages. 17.5 x 18.25 x 3.75. January 1929-1931, 2 volumes, Room 70; 1932-1933, 1 volume, Room 149, County courthouse.

1023. CERTIFICATION RECORD
March 1923-December 1933. 7 volumes.

Contains the certification of the county auditor that sufficient money is in the treasury to make proper payments, and list date, warrant number, amount paid, and number of certificate. Alphabetical index of names of funds in each volume. Handwritten on printed forms. Volumes average 2000 pages. 15.5 x 18 x 3.75. March 1923-November 1927, 6 volumes, Room 70; 1927-1933, 1 volume. Room 149, County courthouse.

1024. APPROPRIATION AND CERTIFICATION LEDGER
January 1, 1934. 2 volumes and loose-leaf.

A record of total appropriations, amount certified against appropriations, certified amount paid, total expenditure, and fee balance remaining in appropriation. Total amounts certified and unpaid certifications. Arranged alphabetically as to funds in accounts. Typed on printed forms. Volumes average 1500 pages. 14 x 14 x 6. Room 149, County courthouse.

1025. CONTRACT CERTIFICATION LEDGER
April 28, 1902—. 4 volumes.
A record of moneys expended for contracts let for improvements, showing contract number, date, amount of debt side of ledger and amounts of various estimates paid until the project is completed. Listed numerically as to contract numbers. Each volume contains an index (front) arranged alphabetically as to name of improvement. Handwritten. Volumes average 372 pages. 10.5 x 16 x 2. 1902-1910, 3 volumes, Hart Building, 1 volume, Room 149, County courthouse.

1026. APPROPRIATION AND CERTIFICATION JOURNAL
January 1, 1934—. 2 volumes.
Appropriation journal sheets, showing amount of certification for payment; amounts of expenditures, appropriations, and unpaid bills; warrant number; and name of person to whom warrant was issued. In chronological order. Typed on printed forms. Volumes average 500 pages. 18.75 x 17.5 x 5. June 1934-December 1934, 1 volume; Room 70; January 1935—, 1 volume, Room 149, County courthouse.

Journals

1027. RECORD OF ORDERS (General Disbursements of County)
September 1870-November 1879. 3 volumes.
A record of warrants drawn on the treasury, listing warrant number, name of payee, purpose for which paid–whether for witness fees, jurors, or judges, etc.; and totals charged to general fund, bridge fund, and building fund. Arranged chronologically. Handwritten on printed forms. Volumes average 700 pages. 21 x 15 x 3. Room 70, County courthouse.

1028. AUDITOR'S JOURNAL
March 1876-September 1888. 1 volume.
A journal record of moneys expended for various county funds. In chronological order. Handwritten. 640 pages. 18.5 x 13 x 3. Room 70, County courthouse.

1029. RECORD OF WARRANTS DRAWN BY THE COUNTY AUDITOR ON THE COUNTY TREASURER
1883-1888. 2 volumes.

A record of indebtedness accrued by various county departments and paid by the county treasurer, showing number of warrant and voucher, or whom drawn, purpose and description, and amount of order; distribution county general and poor fund according to (a) county officers and employees; (b) Cleveland police court, (c) justices of peace and constables, (d) miscellaneous, (e) stationary and advertising, (f) assessor's and board of equalization, (g) miscellaneous fees, coroner's and insane, (h) transient poor and (i) tax refund; county road and bridge fund; liquor tax- fund; county sheep fund; soldiers' relief fund; county ditch fund; miscellaneous fund; township and village funds; the total; and unpaid orders. Arranged chronologically for each fund. Handwritten on printed forms. Volumes average 500 pages. 19 x 16 x 2.5. Room 70, County courthouse.

1030. RECORD OF MONEYS DISBURSED
September 1889-June 1896. 2 volumes. (September 1889-May 1890, 1 volume; September 1894-June 1896, 1 volume). May 1890-September 1894 missing.

Lists date and number of warrant; name of person to whom payable; and amount distributed to the miscellaneous fund, undivided fund, sheep fund, bridge fund, soldiers' relief fund soldiers' monument fund, liquor tax fund, general fund, county treasurer, and county depository. Arranged chronologically. Handwritten on printed forms. Volumes average 450 pages. 12.5 x 18 x 2. Room 70, County courthouse.

1031. DIVISION OF FUNDS
February 1902-1911. 2 volumes. (February 1902-August 1903, 1 volume, 2; September 1909-1911, 1 volume, 6). 1904-908 missing.

Shows date on which warrant was issued, warrant number, and for whom drawn; lists amounts expended for general fund expense, court expenses, fees and salaries, officers and employees, charitable institutions, expense of criminals, expense of county buildings, appraising of property, etc. Contains a marginal alphabetical index as to names of various funds. Handwritten on printed forms. Volumes average 200 pages. 19.5 x 22 x 2.25. Room 70, County courthouse.

1032. AUDITOR'S JOURNAL OF WARRANTS ISSUED AND OF PAYMENTS
1908—. 27 volumes.

An itemized record of receipts and disbursements listing date of warrant; name of person to whom issued; purpose and number of warrant; amount of warrant credited to county treasurer; and amount of warrant to be debited to the general fund, or to the State and county road fund, or to various other funds. Arranged as to warrant numbers. Handwritten. Volumes average 340 pages. 15.25 x 20.5 x 2. September 1, 1908-August 31, 1920, 10 volumes, Hart Building; September 1920-1927, 8 volumes, Room 43; 1928-1933, 6 volumes, Room 46; 1934—, 3 volumes, Room 149, County courthouse.

1033. EMERGENCY AND C.C.R.A. RELIEF JOURNAL
November 1933-November 1935. 3 volumes.

Schedules giving recapitulation of vouchers issued monthly, showing schedule number; name and address of person to whom warrant was issued; amount; number and date of warrant; commodity purchased; and whether charge to C.C.R.A. State funds, cash relief, or county funds. In chronological order. Typed and handwritten. Volumes average 1000 pages. 17.5 x 11.75 x 4.5. Room 149, County courthouse.

Vouchers, Receipts, Warrants, Check Stubs, and Contracts

1034. VOUCHERS ON EXPENDITURES DRAWN ON COUNTY AUDITOR AND PAID BY COUNTY TREASURER
1921—. 1233 file boxes.

Payroll statements, and bills contracted by the county for stationary, equipment, etc., purchased for county purposes. Vouchers are numbered, and show name of person from whom drawn, the purpose, name of fund, data filing, amount and distribution of expense. In order of voucher numbers. Handwritten on printed forms. Each file box 9 x 4 x 12. 1921-1928, 426 file boxes, Attic storeroom; 1928- October 1934, 473 file boxes, Room 70; October 1934—, 344 file boxes, Room 149, County courthouse.

1035. PAYROLLS, VOUCHERS, AND RECEIPTS
1920-1926. 1 cardboard box.

A list of names of employees, showing salaries and the receipts. Handwritten on printed forms. Cardboard box 22 x 16 x 12. Fourth floor, County courthouse.

1036. VOUCHERS MAY COMPANY
1919-1923. Approximately 40 in 2 file boxes.

Vouchers issued for payments on clothing furnished to insane persons. In order of voucher numbers. Typed on printed forms. Each file box 13.25 x 10.75 x 4.75. Room 149, County courthouse.

1037. VOUCHERS, MEMORIAL BUILDING FUND
1920-1921. 1 file box.

Vouchers issued to cover the expense paid for the memorial building fund. Arranged as to voucher numbers. Handwritten and typed. File box 13.5 x 10.75 x 4.75. Room 149, County courthouse.

1038. VOUCHERS, PUBLIC COUNTY BUILDING
1902-1914. 7 file boxes.

Vouchers to cover expenses incurred for the account of public county buildings. Arranged as to voucher numbers. Handwritten and typed. Each file box 13.25 x 10.75 x 4.75. Room 149, County courthouse.

1039. AUDITOR'S VOUCHERS FOR THE SHERIFF'S BOARD BILL FOR PRISONERS
November 1919-1929. 5 bundles.

Food bill marked "paid," and the vouchers which have been approved for payment by the county commissioners. Arranged as to dates of payment and voucher numbers. Handwritten on printed forms. Each bundle 10 x 8 x 4. Attic storeroom, fourth floor, County courthouse.

1040. TREASURER'S RECEIPTS, MONEY PAID INTO TREASURY BY COUNTY AUDITOR, AND OUTSTANDING CHECKS
August 1913—. 1 file box.

In chronological order. Handwritten and typed. File box 13 x 10.75 x 4.75. Room 149, County courthouse.

1041. WARRANTS
1928—. 162 books.

Stubs of warrants listing date on which warrant was drawn, name of person in whose favor drawn, purpose for which drawn, amount and fund to which warrant was charged, and warrant number. In order of warrants numbers. Handwritten on printed forms. From January 1934 used for Sinking Fund only. For general warrants, January 1934—, see number 1042. Books average 125 pages. 24 x 18 x 1; 52 books, 15.25 x 5.25 x 1. 1928-1932, 104 books, Attic storeroom, fourth floor; 1929-1935, 6 books, Room 149; 1930-1935, 52 books, Room 70, County courthouse.

1042. DUPLICATE WARRANTS
January 1934—. 41 volumes.

Duplicates of all general warrants issued by county auditor to the treasurer, showing date issued, warrant number, to whom payable, name of fund, amount and tax note or in cash, total amount and the purpose for which warrant is issued. Arranged in order of warrant numbers. Typed on printed forms. Volumes average 24 x 18 x 4. January 1934-December 1935, 25 volumes, Room 72; January 1936—, 16 volumes, Room 149, County courthouse.

1043. WARRANTS, METROPOLITAN PARK BOARD
September 1930-November 1933. 6 volumes.

Stubs of the warrants issued by the county auditor for the metropolitan park board. In order of warrant numbers. Handwritten on printed forms. Volumes average 250 pages. 5.75 x 15 x 1. Room 70, County courthouse.

1044. TREASURER'S RECORD OF COURT WARRANTS ISSUED BUT STILL OUTSTANDING
December 1922—. 1 volume.

Lists date on which warrant is drawn, name and amount and number of warrant. Arranged chronologically. Handwritten. 400 pages. 12 x 18 x 2. Room 149, County courthouse.

1045. AUDITOR'S RECORD OF COURT WARRANTS ISSUED
1917—. 20 volumes.

A record listing warrant number, date and name of party to whom issued. Under heading of common pleas court is indicated the amount charged for petit jurors, grand jurors, grand jury witnesses, and for witnesses in criminal cases; under police court is shown separately the amounts charge for jurors and witnesses; and amounts charged for witnesses in probate court, insolvency court, minor court, and coroner's court. Arranged as to warrant numbers. Handwritten on printed forms. Volumes average 500 pages. 18 x 12.5 x 2. 1917-193, 14 volumes, 10-23, Attic storeroom, fourth floor; 1931-1932, 3 volumes, 24-26, Room 43; 1933-1935, 2 volumes, 27-28, Room 70; 1935— 1 volume, 29, Room 149, County courthouse.

1046. VOUCHERS-WITNESS, INTERPRETER'S FEES ETC.
1918-1933. Approximately 600 in 2 file boxes.
Vouchers issued for witness fees, interpreter's fees, etc., principally from probate court. In order of voucher numbers. Handwritten and typed. Each file box 13.25 x 10.75 x 4.75. Room 149, County courthouse.

1047. CANCELLED CHECKS
1927—. 41 bundles; 105 file boxes.
Checks drawn from various funds. In order of check numbers. Handwritten. Each bundle 13 x 9 x 4; each file box 13.25 x 10.75 x 4.75. 1927-1931, 41 bundles, 80 file boxes, Room 70; 1931—, 25 file boxes, Room 72, County courthouse.

1048. CHECKS
1933. 1 metal filing cabinet.
Checks which were offered in payment of taxes but which were not honored during the time the banks were closed in March 1933. Handwritten on printed forms. Cabinet 24.25 x 18 x 11.25. Room 149, County courthouse.

1049. CHECKS (Stubs)
July 1920-August 1921. 1 book.
Stubs of seven checks that were issued for a memorial building fund. In order of check numbers. Handwritten on printed forms. 125 pages. 13.25 x 10.75 x 4.75. Room 149, County courthouse.

1050. CHECKS (Stubs)
January 1924-April 1929. 1 book.
Stubs of seven checks issued for public county building Number 2 Fund, or for jail and courthouse improvements. In order of check numbers. Handwritten on printed forms. 125 pages. 5.75 x 15 x 1. Room 149, County courthouse.

1051. GENERAL CONTRACTS
January 1929—. Approximately 1480 in 37 metal file boxes, 6849-8256. Copies of contracts entered into with various firms and individual persons by the county commissioners for supplies, services, etc. Filed as to contract numbers. Typed and printed. Each file box 13.25 x 10.75 x 4.75. Room 149, County courthouse.

1052. COUNTY BUILDING COMMISSION CONTRACTS
1907-1910. 1 file box.
Copies of contracts entered into by the county for material to be furnished or services to be rendered for the county building commission. In order of contract numbers. Handwritten and typed. File box 13.5 x 10.75 x 4.75. Room 149, County courthouse.

1053. CONTRACTS, CLEVELAND METROPOLITAN PARK DISTRICT
1924—. 3 metal file boxes.
Contracts entered into by the commissioners of the Cleveland Metropolitan Park Board for work and services. Arranged as to contract numbers. Typed. Each file box 13.5 x 10.75 x 4.75. Room 149, County courthouse.

1054. CLEVELAND METROPOLITAN PARK DISTRICTS
August 15, 1917-January 10, 1928. 1 volume.
A record of payments made for services and supplies for the Cleveland Metropolitan Park district, listing date, name of claimant, amount of claim, and voucher number. Arranged numerically as to contract numbers. Handwritten. 500 pages. 9 x 14 x 1. Room 70, County courthouse.

1055. OLD BILLS
1917-1923. 1 metal file box.
Vouchers that have been checked and ordered paid. Filed as to voucher numbers. Handwritten and typed. File box 13.25 x 10.75 x 4.75. Room 149, County courthouse.

1056. STATE EXAMINER'S BILLS
March 1933—. 6 metal file boxes.

Vouchers for the daily expenses of state examiners. Arranged in order of voucher numbers. Handwritten and typed on printed forms. Each file box 13.25 x 4.75 x 10.75. Room 149, County courthouse.

1057. BOARD OF ELECTION PAYROLL
September 1911-February 1913. 3 file boxes.

Vouchers for services rendered by election officials. Arranged by voucher numbers. Typed and handwritten. File box 13.25 x 9.75 x 4.5. Room 149, County courthouse.

1058. ELECTION OFFICERS' PAYROLL SHEETS
November 1933—. 23 books.

Duplicates checks issued for payment of services of election officials. In order of check numbers. Typed. Books averaged 750 pages. 11.5 x 13 x 1.5. November 1933-March 1935, 8 books, Room 70; 1933-1935, 15 books, Room 149, County courthouse.

1059. AUDITOR'S DOCKET OF BILLS FILED
July 15, 1904—. 12 loose-leaf volumes. (1922-1930 missing).

Record of all bills of county, giving date of bill, name of claimant, purpose of payment, amount of bill, date of filing, date and amount of approval, date paid, and warrant number. Alphabetical order by claimants. Handwritten. Volumes average 500 pages. 21.5 x 16 x 3.25. July 15, 1904-October 30, 1913, 5 volumes, A to E, Room 70; November 1913-December 1929, 4 volumes; January 1930- December 1934, 2 volumes; January 1935—, 1 volume, Room 149, County courthouse.

Securities and Bonds

1060. BONDS AND COUPONS
1908—. 2 volumes.

Record of bonds and coupons paid and returned to county auditor, giving date of payment, amount paid to county treasurer, amount of bonds and coupons returned to county auditor, amount and number of bonds and coupons outstanding, and voucher number. Alphabetical index of funds in each volume. Handwritten on printed forms. Volumes average 600 pages. 21.5 x 16 x 4. 1908-1924, 1 volume, Room 70; 1925—, 1 volume, Room 149, County courthouse.

1061. BOND RECORD (Refunding Bonds)
October 1929—. 2 volumes. (1913—, Bridges and Buildings, 1 volume; 1929—, 1 volume, Bonds).
Bonds issued to cover bridges, buildings, and county roads. In order of bond numbers. Handwritten. Volumes average 1000 pages. 21.5 x 16.5 x 4. Room 149, County courthouse.

1062. CERTIFICATE AND BOND RECORD
May 1921—. 5 volumes. (Sanitary Department, 1921—,2 volumes; County Roads, may 1925—, 3 volumes.
A register of bonds issued for county roads and the sanitary engineering department, listing date issued, date delivered and redeemed, date of maturity, number of bond, and amount. Arranged as to improvement funds numbers. Handwritten. Volumes average 1600 pages. 17.5 x 11.75 x 4. Room 149, County courthouse.

1063. FUNDING BONDS RECORD
1909. 1 volume.
Redeemed, funding bonds and interest coupons, arranged according to bond numbers. Printed. 560 pages. 20 x 16 x 5. Attic storeroom, fourth floor, County courthouse.

1064. SPECIAL ASSESSMENT BONDS
1923-1932. 2 wooden boxes.
Redeemed bonds of various kinds for which vouchers were issued between January and March 30, 1936. Filed chronologically and as to bond numbers. Photostat and handwritten. Boxes 15 x 42 x 12.5 and 13 x 17 x 7.5. Room 70, County courthouse.

1065. CERTIFICATES FOR ISSUANCE OF REFUNDING BONDS
1934—. Approximately 300 in 1 file box.
Certificates authorizing the issuance of refunding bonds. Filed alphabetically as to taxing districts. Typed. File box 13.5 x 10.75 x 4.75. Room 149, County courthouse.

1066. OUTSTANDING BONDS AND CERTIFICATES OF INDEBTEDNESS
1928—. 1 volume.
List date of issue, amount of original issue, rate, maturity, bonds outstanding not registered, bonds outstanding registered, bonds due not registered in April, bonds

due in April registered, and number of bonds due not registered in April. Alphabetical by names of funds. Handwritten. 1000 pages. 17.5 x 11.75 x 4. Room 149, County courthouse.

1067. BONDS (original)
1935—. 24 cardboard file boxes.
All county bonds such as building, road, sewer, and special assessment bonds. Arranged in order of bond numbers. Printed. Each file box 12 x 10.75 x 5.5. Room 149, County courthouse.

1068. CANCELLED BONDS AND NOTES
1929-1935. 4 bundles.
Bonds exchanged for notes and cancelled registered bonds. In chronological order. Each bundle 13.5 x 12 x 16. Room 70, County courthouse.

1069. BONDS AND INTEREST COUPONS
December 1933-December 1935. 57 file boxes.
Improvement bonds and other redeemed bonds, such as special assessments, sinking funds, etc., for which vouchers have been issued for amount of the bonds and interest coupons. Filed as to voucher numbers. Handwritten and photostat. Each file box 12 x 10.75 x 5.5. Room 70 County courthouse.

1070. VOUCHERS FOR INTEREST COUPONS
December 1933—. Approximately 126 in 7 file boxes.
Vouchers that have been issued for interest on various bonds. In order of voucher numbers. Handwritten on printed forms. Each file box 13.5 x 4.75 x 10.75. Room 149, County courthouse.

1071. AUDITOR'S RECORD OF REGISTERED BONDS
1909-1923. 1 volume.
A record of registered bonds. Arranged by bond numbers. Handwritten on printed forms and printed. 500 pages. 15 x 9 x 2.75. Attic storeroom, fourth floor, County courthouse.

1072. REGISTERED BOND RECORD
October 1909—. 1 volume.
Lists amount of bond, name and address of owner, date of issue and of maturity,

rate of interest, and interest paid. Chronological as to dates of registration. Handwritten on printed forms. 200 pages. 16 x 18.5 x 1.75. Room 149, County courthouse.

1073. RECORD OF MISCELLANEOUS BONDS
September 1905-April 1935. 8 volumes. (September 1905-October 1934, 4 volumes, 1-4; October 1921-April 1935, 4 volumes).

Retired bonds and coupons pasted in the volumes. Arranged as to dates of issue. Printed. Volumes average 520 pages. 21.5 x 15 x 4. Now filed with vouchers that pay the bonds and interest. Room 70, County courthouse.

1074. RECORD OF PUBLIC BUILDING BONDS–NUMBER 2 JAIL
1918-1919. 4 volumes.

Volumes contain interest coupons which are pasted in when paid. Volumes are paged consecutively with the numbers for bonds. Printed. Volumes average 360 pages. 16 x 21.5 x 4.75. Room 70, County courthouse.

1075. RECORD OF PUBLIC BUILDING BONDS
July 1902-October 1924. 22 volumes. (1902-1921, 4 volumes, 1-1000; 1906-1924, 18 volumes, 1001-5500.

Redeemed public building bonds and interest coupons. Some volumes contain only interest coupons. In order of bond numbers. Volumes average 500 pages. 22.5 x 18.5 x 2. Room 70, County courthouse.

1076. RECORD OF BRIGHTON-BROOKLYN BRIDGE BONDS
December 1913-May 1914. 4 volumes.

Contains interest coupons of bonds issued on the Brighton-Brooklyn Bridge. Filed as to bond numbers. Printed. Volumes average 500 pages. 16 x 21.5 x 4. Room 70, next to upper county courthouse.

1077. RECORD OF CHAGRIN RIVER BONDS
May 1895-April 1906. 1 volume.

Redeemed bonds and interest coupons on the construction of a new bridge across Chagrin River at Bentleyville. In order of bond numbers. Printed and typed. 70 pages. 18.5 x 16.5 x 1.75. Room 70, County courthouse.

1078. RECORD OF DETROIT-SUPERIOR BRIDGE BONDS
July 1911-October 1920. 23 volumes.

Redeemed bonds and interest coupons issued to cover the construction of the Detroit-Superior Bridge. In order of bond numbers. Printed. Volumes average 500 pages. 16 x 21.5 x 4. Room 70, County courthouse.

1079. RECORD OF HARVARD- DENISON BRIDGE BONDS
1909-October 1928. 3 volumes.

Redeemed bonds and interest coupons issued to cover the construction of the Harvard-Denison Bridge. In order of bond numbers. Printed. Volumes average 520 pages. 21.5 x 15 x 4. Room 70, County courthouse.

1080. RECORD OF ROCKY RIVER BRIDGE BONDS
September 1, 1908-September 1, 1928. 1 volume.

Redeemed bonds and interest coupons pasted in the volume. Arranged as to bond numbers. Printed. 520 pages. 15 x 21.5 x 4. Room 70, County courthouse.

1081. SOUTH ROCKY RIVER BRIDGE BONDS
May 10, 1894-August 9, 1906. 1 volume.

Redeemed bonds and interest coupons issued to cover the construction of the South Rocky River Bridge, under authority of House Bill 925. In order of bond numbers. Printed. 300 pages. 18 x 16.5 x 3.5. Room 70, County courthouse.

Financial Reports

1082. ANNUAL FINANCIAL REPORT
August 1905-August 1923. 1 loose-leaf volume.

A general, financial report of all county receipts and expenditures. Arranged alphabetically as to the various departments. For detail see published report number 1083. Handwritten and printed on forms. 600 pages. 30 x 18 x 2. Room 149, County courthouse.

1083. ANNUAL REPORTS
1906—. 2 file boxes.

Annual financial reports of county receipts and expenditures made up on four forms; also a summary of the receipts and expenditures of districts whose funds are administered by the county auditor and treasurer. "Schedule A" is a listing of total receipts, payments, and balances by fund, showing the January 1st balance; receipts (revenue and non-revenue); total receipts and balance; payments (total; operation, maintenance, and interest; outlay; non-governmental cost payments); and balance on December 31, other following funds; general; county road and bridge; state road and bridge; motor vehicle and gasoline tax; dog and kennel; sewer and water districts; bond retirement; sinking; emergency relief; total of funds belonging to county government; undistributed tax and trust funds belonging to other governmental units; county board of education; county health district; metropolitan park district; county library district, and orders afloat. It also shows total of funds not belonging to county government and total of all funds. "Schedule B-1" is a summary of receipts by sources as follows; taxes (classified as to kind); special assessments (classified); licenses and permits (classified); fines, cost and forfeitures; gifts and donations; rents; interest, and fees, sales, charges for service, etc., (classified as to offices or source). "Schedule B-2" is a summary of payments by function as follows: general government (classified as to offices); protection to person and property; agriculture; health; sanitation and drainage; charities and correction (classified); highways (classified); education; recreation; public service enterprises - water supply; miscellaneous and interest and grand total of payments. These items are segregated as to operation, maintenance, interest, and outlay. "Schedule C" is a detailed exhibit of receipts and payments by fund, conforming to the classification of accounts prescribed by the Bureau of Inspection Supervision of Public Offices. It is prepared directly from the appropriation and receipts ledgers. The accounts are similar to those enumerated under "Schedules B-1 and B-2". Under the district funds are listed the county board of education, county health district fund and any other fund which is administered by the county auditor and treasurer. This report also includes general county statistics as to population, last census; tax valuation for year of report; tax levy for county purposes; and total salaries, fees and wages for the year. A copy of each report is filed with the state auditor. Filed chronologically. Handwritten on printed forms. Each file box 9.75 x 4.5 x 13.25. Room 149, County courthouse.

1084. COMBINED WITH 1086.

1085. CLERK'S FINANCIAL REPORTS
January 1934-September 1935. Approximately 2000 in one metal file box. Reports prepared by the clerk of courts at the end of each term of court, showing name of jurors summoned, dates of service, number of days served, amount of

mileage, and fees received; and listing number of jurors under the headings of petit jury, grand jury, and criminal court jury. Report also gives a summary of the number of days served, the amount of mileage, and the total expenditures by weeks. In chronological order. Typed on printed forms. File box 13.25 x 10.75 x 4.75. Room 149, County courthouse.

1086. ANNUAL REPORT OF COUNTY COMMISSIONERS AND AUDITOR TO THE JUDGES OF THE COURT OF COMMON PLEAS September 1880—. 34 volumes. (Missing, June, 1888-August 1902; September 1910-September 1911).

Detailed summary of receipts and disbursements of county funds, showing county commissioners' budget and tax levy; funds necessary for year, purposes for which funds are to be used, and a copy of the commissioners resolution certifying these amounts to auditor. Also contains a report of receipts and disbursements of all moneys passing through treasury during year; balance the various funds remaining with t county treasurer and county depositories, specifying whether in bonds or funds. A summary of receipts by sources, and disbursements by funds, or source of expense during year; shows depositary interest settlement and transfers from other funds. Chronological order. Typed and handwritten. Volumes average 100 pages. 11.75 x 18 x 1. Room 149, County courthouse.

Budgets

1087. BUDGETS 1911—. 25 file boxes.

Budgets of school districts listing year for which budget is required, date filed, purpose, amount estimated, estimated balance at the end of year, estimated applicable receipts during coming year from other sources then taxation, net amount of levy required, and amount of expenditures for each month of the previous year. Arranged alphabetically as to taxing districts. Handwritten and typed. Each file box 13.25 x 10.75 x 4.75. Room 149, County courthouse.

1088. APPROPRIATION CERTIFICATES AND BALANCES 1926—. 10 file boxes.

Copies of ordinances passed to provide funds for current and other expenses of the city, township, village, etc., showing sums to be set aside and appropriated for the purpose enumerated in the ordinance, to each of which is attached a certificate of the official estimate of balance and revenue in the city, township, or village concerned. Alphabetical as to names of taxing districts. Handwritten and typed. Each file box 13.25 x 10.75 x 4.75. Room 149, County courthouse.

1089. BOND RESOLUTIONS, AVERAGE RATE
1923—. 2 file boxes.
Resolutions, passed by the various taxing districts, pertaining to the issuance of bonds. Arranged alphabetically as to taxing districts. Typed and handwritten. Each file box 13.25 x 10.75 x 4.75. Room 149, County courthouse.

1090. PERMISSION TO ISSUE BONDS, BUREAU OF I. S. of P. O.
1932—. 1 file box.
Copies of resolutions adopted by the various taxing districts and letters from the state auditor approving the issuance of bonds. Arranged alphabetically as to taxing districts. Handwritten and typed. File box 13.25 x 10.75 x 4.75. Room 149, County courthouse.

1091. APPROPRIATION ORDINANCES AND RESOLUTIONS
1926—. 1 file box.
Enactments passed by the various city, township and village officials. Filed alphabetically as to districts. Typed and handwritten. File box 13.25 x 10.75 x 4.75. Room 149, County courthouse.

1092. BOND ORDINANCES AND SPECIAL ASSESSMENTS
January 1922—. 18 metal file boxes.
Certified copies of ordinances pertaining to bonds and special assessments passed by various school districts, townships, villages, and cities. Alphabetically arranged as to taxing districts. Typed and handwritten. Each file box 13.25 x 10.5 x 4.5. Room 149, County courthouse.

1093. RECORD OF BONDS AND ORDINANCES
December 1922—. 1 volume.
Shows amount of bonds issue, due date of bonds, name of township, whether bonds are for poor relief or for other fund, how bonds are payable, rate of interest, date of issue, and expiration date. In chronological order. Handwritten. 1000 pages. 16.25 x 21.5 x 4. Room 149, County courthouse.

1094. SETTLEMENT SHEETS
March 1919——. 30 volumes.

Settlement sheets for all taxes levied for State of Ohio funds, township funds, corporate tax, county funds, schools funds, county library funds, etc., listing name of township, village, or city; the amount of the levy for the tax year; amount of delinquency; interest on delinquent taxes; and the total. One or more sheets are prepared for each class of funds, headings vary according to the different funds. Arranged chronologically. Handwritten. Volumes average 200 pages. 32.5 x 21.5 x 1.5. Room 149, County courthouse.

1095. SETTLEMENT RECEIPT BOOK
1874——. 8 volumes. (Missing, 1878-1895).

A record of moneys received by various cities, townships, and villages, listing the amount for township, village, or school purposes; or roads, poor relief, and other funds. Alphabetical as to school districts or villages. Handwritten on printed forms. Volumes average 800 pages. 11.5 x 14.5 x 3. 1874-September 22, 1921, 5 volumes, Room 70; April 1922——, 3 volumes, Room 149, County courthouse.

1096. SETTLEMENT BOOK
1896——. 5 volumes.

Abstracts of the yearly tax duplicate, showing real and public utility values, together with total values. The abstracts list special school, township, county, and municipal taxes, as well as their totals; it also lists the delinquent taxes for that particular year and for the prior years separately, and the total of delinquency. Arranged chronologically and alphabetically as to taxing districts. Handwritten on printed forms. Average 100 pages. 19.5 x 16 x 2.25. Room 149, County courthouse.

1097. SETTLEMENT OF SCHOOL DISTRICT FUNDS
1905-1923. 4 volumes.

A record of the auditor's account with each school district for each year, showing statements of distribution by tax settlements; receipts for building, tuition, schoolhouse, and contingent expenses; bonds and interest; and total expenditures, which lists any amount received prior to settlement, etc., and balance if any, of funds. Alphabetical as to school districts. Handwritten. Volumes average 300 pages. 13 x 18.25 x 2.5. Room 70, County courthouse.

1098. DISTRIBUTION OF SCHOOL FUNDS FROM THE TAX COLLECTIONS
1828-1842. 1 volume.

Lists total tax collection and amount allocated to school funds. Arranged by date of distribution. Handwritten on printed forms. Volumes average 300 pages. 19 x 17 x 3. Room 70, County courthouse.

1099. RECEIPTS FOR TOWNSHIP MONEY
1874-1878. 1 volume.

Receipts signed by township treasurers for orders on county treasurer received from auditor for full payment for moneys collected for townships and for amount of State and Western Reserve school fund. This fund is apportioned for roads; township purposes; the poor; corporation purposes; and school purposes, such as tuition, for the State and Western Reserve common school fund, taxes levied by township board of education, purposes other than tuition, and proceeds of special taxes on taxable property. Chronological. Handwritten on printed forms. 700 pages. 14.5 x 9.5 x 3. Room 70, County courthouse.

1100. STATEMENT OF CONDITION OF FUNDS, SCHOOL DISTRICTS
August 1923—. 1 loose-leaf volume.

Statement of condition of funds of each school district, listing receipts for tuition, contingent, and building fund, bonds, interest and sinking fund, and retirement fund; total receipts; disbursements; and treasury balance. Alphabetical by school districts, chronological by dates of statements. Handwritten on printed forms. 4000 pages. 16 x 10.25 x 7. Room 149, County courthouse.

1101. RECORD OF FEES
October 1907—. 1 volume.

Lists date of entry; by whom paid; total payment; general settlement; other settlements; transfers; additions; and payments for ditches, pikes, and sundries. Chronological. Handwritten on printed forms. 200 pages. 10.75 x 16.25 x 1. Room 149, County courthouse.

1102. SCHOOL REPORTS
1908—. 11 file boxes.

School clerk's bonds, state auditor's reports, resolutions, etc., regarding school matters. Alphabetical by school districts. Handwritten, photostat, and typed. Each file box 13.25 x 10.75 x 4.75. Room 149, County courthouse.

1103. TAX RATES
1918—. 10 loose-leaf volumes.

Tax rate sheets listing taxing district; valuation total for municipality; name of fund; ten mill limit and particular funds belonging in this class such as general, library, university, firemen and police pension funds, etc.; municipal rates, no limit rates, school rates; and complete citations from the General Code as to tax rates. Arranged by taxing districts in each volume. Volumes for 1925—, have an index in each volume for cities, villages and townships. Volumes for 1923—, contain proceedings of budget commission. Typed and handwritten. Volumes average 300 pages. 10.25 x 16 x 3. Room 149, County courthouse.

1104. RATES OF TAXATION IN THE VARIOUS TOWNSHIPS, VILLAGES, CITIES IN CUYAHOGA COUNTY
1892—. 2 volumes.

List of rates levied by General Assembly, county commissioners and by township, village and city authorities, showing name of taxing district, and purpose for which levied. Chronological and alphabetical as to taxing districts. Handwritten. Volumes average 30 pages. 20 x 16 x 1. Room 149, County courthouse.

1105. INDEBTEDNESS
January 1910—. 19 file boxes.

Reports made to county auditor by various township, village, and city officials each January, giving an abstract of debts of county, city, village school district, city school and township. Abstract gives purpose for which indebtedness was created, total debt outstanding, rate of interest, etc., headings vary according to indebtedness reported. Chronological. Typed and handwritten on printed forms. File box 9.75 x 13.25 x 4.5. Room 149, County courthouse.

1106. DELINQUENCIES (abstract of delinquencies in various townships and villages)
August 1888-August 1907. 2 volumes. (1890-1905 missing).

Abstract records of delinquencies, giving name of townships, general tax, school tax, tax for specials and for liquor, and total tax; and showing any prior delinquency and total delinquencies. Handwritten. Volumes average 100 pages. 10.5 x 15.25 x .5. Room 70, County courthouse.

1107. WORKMEN'S COMPENSATION
1915—. 1 file box.
Various memoranda regarding workmen's compensation matters. In chronological order. Typed. File box 9.75 x 13.75 x 1.5. Room 149, County courthouse.

Copies of Court Journal Entries

1108. JOURNAL ENTRY, LIQUOR TAX
1909—. Approximately 260 in 2 file boxes.
Journal entries from court of common pleas pertaining to law violations in liquor cases. Filed by case numbers. Typed. Each file box 13.25 x 10.75 x 4.75. Room 149, County courthouse.

1109. APPRAISERS' FEES, INHERITANCE TAX COLLATERAL
1919-1926. Approximately 300 in 1 file box.
Certified copies of journal entries from probate court, in which the amount of the appraisers' fees in connection with the inheritance tax collateral is determined. In order of probate court case numbers. Typed on printed forms. File box 13.25 x 10.75 x 4.75. Room 149, County courthouse.

1110. BOARD OF STATE CHARITIES
1921-1926. Approximately 600 in 2 file boxes.
A record of the journal entries of the juvenile court recorded whenever a child is turned over to the public welfare department, listing date, name of child, birthplace, and name of parents if known. Chronological as to dates of journal entries. Typed on printed forms. Each file box 13.25 x 10.75 x 4.75. Room 149, County courthouse.

1111. JOURNAL ENTRIES, ASSIGNMENTS, ATTACHMENTS, ETC.
September 1909—. Approximately 380 in 4 file boxes.
Copies of journal entries, assignments, etc., filed with the auditor. Filed as to dates of receipt. Typed. Each file box 13.25 x 10.75 x 4.75. Room 149, County courthouse.

Housing Relief Records

1112. RECORD OF DISTRICT HOUSING RELIEF WARRANTS ISSUED AND RETURNED
December 1933——. 2 loose-leaf volumes.

Each warrant lists name and address of person for whom drawn; amount and number of warrant; date issued, date retired, and date posted; and page and line number of auditor's tax duplicate. Arranged as to warrant numbers. Typed. Volumes average 750 pages. 18.75 x 17.75 x 4. Room 149, County courthouse.

1113. HOUSING RELIEF WARRANTS CANCELLED
1934-1925. 13 file boxes.

Redeemed duplicate warrants listing case number, name of payee, amount drawn for, and purpose. Chronological by dates of various tax settlements. Handwritten and typed. Each file box 12 x 10.75 x 5.5. Room 149, County courthouse.

1114. ANNAT RECORDS
1933——. 7 bundles; 336 file boxes.

Give name of indigent tenant, amount allowed for premises that tenant occupies, name of landlord, and a description of his property. In chronological order. Typed. Each file box 14 x 9 x 6. Room 204, Marion building.

Inheritance Taxes

1115. INHERITANCE TAX BILLS (copies)
August 1924-August 1935. 4 loose-leaf volumes; 9 loose-leaf bundles.
(March 1928; September 1929; March 1930; August 1930, missing).

Amount of inheritance tax charge collected, inheritance tax charge number, probate court case number, date of charge entry, amount of tax, name and address of estate, date of accrued tax, amount fixed by court, discount allowed or interest, total amount paid, and date of payment. In order of inheritance tax charge numbers. Handwritten on printed forms. Volumes and bundles average 1000 pages. 12 x 13 x 4.5. Room 70, County courthouse.

1116. AUDITOR'S ADDITION BOOK OF INHERITANCE TAX
September 1894——. 1 volume.

Record showing list of taxes on additions made by auditor, and listing name of decedent and his inventory, names of heirs, names of collateral heirs, net amount taxable, date of entry, an amount of tax due at the expiration of one year. Contains an alphabetical index of decedents. Handwritten. 500 pages. 16 x 12 x 1.5. Room 149, County courthouse.

1117. INHERITANCE TAX RECAPITULATION SHEETS
March 1929-March 1932. 1 loose-leaf bundle.

A record of direct inheritance tax collected, listing auditor's file number, name of estate, name of person by whom tax was paid, date of payment, amount of tax, discount, interest, tax collected and due local taxing district, amounts of auditor's and sheriff's expenses, and balance of tax. This record also contains typed statements made up semi-annually by the probate court under the heading "District Inheritance Tax for _____ Period." Statements show item number, court case number, name of estate, and amount of tax. In chronological order. Handwritten and typed on printed forms. Bundle 17 x 11 x 2. Room 70, County courthouse.

1118. DETERMINATION OF INHERITANCE TAX
January 1931—. Approximately 4800 in 16 metal file boxes.

Probate court journal entries showing the amount of inheritance tax to be levied without the auditor's appraisal, listing name, age, and relationship of successor; value of succession as found by the court; amount of exception; balance subject to tax; accrued date of tax; name of person by whom tax should be paid; and name of township or municipal corporation. In order of auditor's record numbers. Typed on printed forms. Each file box 13.25 x 10.75 x 4.75. Room 149, County courthouse.

1119. INHERITANCE TAX PAID
September 1935—. 1 file box.

Transcripts of journal entries that have been removed from the files titled "Determination of Inheritance Tax" following payment. Filed numerically. Typed. File box 13.25 x 10.75 x 4.75. Room 149, County courthouse.

1120. INHERITANCE TAX CERTIFICATIONS FOR PAYMENTS
1920—. 3 file boxes.

Journal entries from probate court determining the amount of inheritance tax to be levied against individual persons. Filed alphabetically. Typed on printed forms. Each file box 13.25 x 10.75 x 4.75. Room 149, County courthouse.

1121. INHERITANCE TAX FUND RECEIPTS
October 1919—. 3 volumes, 5 bundles. (October 1919-November 1931, 2 volumes, 5 bundles; 1934—, 1 volume.

Lists number of receipt, name of administrator from whom tax is received, name of decedent, amount of tax to be placed to the credit of the inheritance fund, amount of tax as fixed by the court, interest added or discount allowed, amount collected, and signature of county treasurer. In order of receipt numbers. Typed on printed forms. Volumes and bundles average 1500 pages. Each volume and bundle 5 x 10.25 x 4. 1919- November 1931, 2 volumes, 5 bundles, Room 70; 1934—, 1 volume, Room 149, County courthouse.

1122. INHERITANCE TAX PAID
October 1919—. 3 volumes.

A record of direct inheritance tax collected in the county, listing auditor's file number, name of estate, name of taxpayer, date of payment, amount of tax, discount, amount collected, amount due local tax district, auditor's expenses, court costs, and balance. Arranged chronologically. Handwritten. Volumes average 500 pages. 11.5 x 17.5 x 2.5. Room 149, County courthouse.

1123. INHERITANCE TAX, COLLATERAL
February 9, 1897-March 1919. 2 volumes.

Semi-annual statements of inheritance taxes prepared by the probate court for the auditor, giving case number, name of decedent, amount of property (real, personal or total) taxed, amount that will accrue, and amount due but unpaid. Alphabetical index. Handwritten and typed. Volumes average 200 pages. 10 x 18 x 2.75. February 9, 1897-December 10, 1913, 1 volume, Room 70; December 1913-March 1919, 1 volume, Room 149, County courthouse.

Claims

1124. CLAIMS AGAINST THE COUNTY
February 1891-July 1902. 2 volumes.

Lists date of case, name of claimant, title of case, nature and amount of allowance, date of payment, voucher number, and general remarks. Contains an alphabetical index of claimants. Handwritten on printed forms. Volumes average 350 pages. 15 x 18.75 x 1.75. Room 70, County courthouse.

1125. SHEEP CLAIM (Animal Claims)
September 1892—. 1 volume.
The auditor's record of claims against the county for sheep and other animals or livestock destroyed by dogs. Lists name and address of claimant, nature of claim, amount, date paid, and number of voucher. In order of claims numbers. Handwritten on printed forms. 200 pages. 14.5 x 18.5 x 1. Room 149, County courthouse.

1126. ANIMAL CLAIMS
1910—. Approximately 450 in 3 file boxes.
Pertaining to sheep and other animal claims. In November, 1929 wording on claimed form was changed from "Sheep Claim." Filed numerically. Handwritten and typed. Each file box 13.25 x 10.75 x 4.75. Room 149, County courthouse.

Surety Bonds

1127. BONDS FORFEITED TO STATE OF OHIO
May 1884—. 3 volumes. (May 1884-January 1925, 2 volumes; April 1924—, 1 volume).
A record showing who forfeited bond and who gave bond, the date, amount, name of court, when bond was forfeited, when it was delivered to prosecuting attorney, and collections if any. In chronological order. Handwritten. Volumes average 350 pages. 12.5 x 9 x 1.25. Room 149, County courthouse.

1128. AUCTIONEERS' BONDS
July 1913-April 1924. Approximately 50 in 1 file box.
Bonds filed with the county auditor by auctioneers. Arranged chronologically. Typed and photostat. File box 13.75 x 10.75 x 4.75. Room 149, County courthouse.

1129. RECORD OF BONDS
1810-1933. 1 volume.
Lists the surety bonds filed with the county by all county officials upon taking office. In chronological order. Handwritten. 2000 pages. 9.25 c 13.5 c 2.75. Room 149, County courthouse.

Requisitions

1130. REQUISITION BOOK
March 1921—. 2 loose-leaf volumes.
Requisitions and purchase orders for supplies, work to be done, etc., by county departments. Numerical by requisition numbers. Typed on printed forms. Volumes average 1000 pages. 12.75 x 9.5 x 5. Room 149, County courthouse.

1131. PURCHASE ORDERS, AUDITOR'S COPY
1933-December 1934. 6 bundles.
Date of order, number, name of firm where purchase , quantity, description, and total cost of materials or services purchased, name of person receiving delivery, name of department for which materials or services were obtained. Arranged by departments. Typed on printed forms. Each bundle 9 x 11.5 x 7. Room 70, County courthouse.

1132. REQUISITION FOR STOREROOM SUPPLIES
1931—. 5 bundles.
Reports of storekeeper, listing amounts of stationary and office supplies issued to various departments; receipts for supplies received. Chronological. Handwritten and typed on printed forms. Each bundle 7.5 x 6 x 5. Room 70. Current records, Room 149, County courthouse.

Soldiers' Relief Commission Records

1133. SOLDIERS' RELIEF WARRANT BOOK
1925- December 1933. 2 volumes. (1928- 1931 missing).
Stubs issued to indigent soldiers, name of soldier, amount of warrant, warrant number. Arranged by warrant numbers. Handwritten on printed forms. Volumes average 250 pages. 14 x 13.75 x .75. May 1931-December 1933, 1 volume, Room 149; 1925-1928, 1 volume, Room 70, County courthouse.

1134. SOLDIERS' RELIEF COMMISSION: INVESTIGATORS EXPENSE ACCOUNT
April-May 1932. Approximately 40 books in 1 bundle.
Expense accounts, in book form, showing name of investigator, date of expense,

distance from one point to another, and amount of fare. Chronological. Handwritten. Bundle 5.75 x 2.5 x 2.75. Room 70, County courthouse.

1135. SOLDIERS' RELIEF RECORD
February 1897-1935. 24 volumes; 1 bundle. (February-December 1897, 1 volume; 1906-1928, 21 volumes; 1930-1931, 1 volume; 1931-1932, 1 bundle; 1934, 1 volume).
Record of allowances paid by soldiers' relief commission, listing name, age, address, and ward number of soldier; amount paid; date of payment. Alphabetical index of villages in 1934 volumes. Handwritten on printed forms. Volumes average 350 pages. 19.75 x 13.75 x 1.5. Room 70, County courthouse.

1136. RECORD OF COMMITTEE ON BURIAL OF EX-UNION SOLDIERS
1891—. 25 volumes.
Reports listing name of decedent, date of death, ward number, amount paid for funeral, and name of cemetery. Alphabetical index of deceased persons in each volume. Handwritten. Volumes average 420 pages. 9.75 x 14 x 1. 1891-1930, 19 volumes, Room 70; 1930—, 6 volumes, Room 149, County courthouse.

1137. VOUCHERS, SOLDIERS' RELIEF
1930—. Approximately 600 in 2 file boxes.
Vouchers for soldiers' relief expenses. Arranged by voucher numbers. Handwritten and typed. Each file box 13.75 x 10.75 x 4.75. Room 149, County courthouse.

Brewers' Wort and Malt Dealers' Licenses

1138. APPLICATION FOR BREWER'S WORT AND MALT DEALER'S LICENSE (with receipt stubs).
May 1934-January 1935. 500 in 1 bundle; 1 file box
License number, name and address of applicant. Alphabetical. Handwritten on printed forms. Bundle 3.75 x 8.75 x 7; file box 24.75 x 18 x 11.75. 1934, 1 bundle, Room 70; 1935, 1 file box, Room 149, County courthouse.

1139. BREWERS' WORT AND MALT LICENSES
1932—. 8 bundles.
Duplicate licenses listing license number, name and address of dealer, and place of

business. Alphabetical. Handwritten on printed forms. Each bundle 8.5 x 14 x 4. Room 70, County courthouse.

1140. AUDITOR'S WORT AND MALT DEALERS' LICENSE RECORD
1933—, 1 volume; 1 bundle.

Lists number of receipt, name of proprietor, location of business, date license was issued, and amount of tax due. Alphabetical by political subdivision. Handwritten on printed forms. 500 pages. 14.75 x 11 x 3. Room 149, County courthouse.

1141. BREWERS' WORT AND MALT LICENSES
1932—. 3 volumes.

Record listing license number, name and address of dealer, place of business. In order of license number. Handwritten on printed forms. Volumes average 400 pages. 8.5 x 14 x 4. 1932, 1 volume, Room 70; 1935—, 2 volumes, Room 149, County courthouse.

Vendors' Licenses

1142. REPORT OF CANCELLATION OF VENDORS' LICENSES
January 1, 1935—. 1 metal file drawer.

List vendor's name, license number, trade name, business address, residence address, status of business (whether terminated, sold, etc.), and whether license was incorrectly issued or not needed. Filed alphabetically. Typed on printed forms. Drawer 11.75 x 27 x 17. Room 149, County courthouse.

1143. DISCONTINUED APPLICATIONS FOR VENDORS' LICENSES
January 1935—. 10 bundles.

A record of vendors who returned their licenses to auditor for cancellation and whose applications were removed from active files and discontinued. Alphabetical by names of vendors. Handwritten on printed forms. Each bundle 8.5 x 11 x 5. Room 149, County courthouse.

1144. APPLICATION FOR VENDOR'S LICENSE TO SELL TANGIBLE PERSONAL PROPERTY AT RETAIL
January 1, 1935—. 50 bundles.

Lists name and address of each vendor, date and number of application, and gives a description of the business in which the vendor is to be engaged. Alphabetical by names of vendors. Handwritten on printed forms. Each bundle 8.25 c 11 c 3. Room 149, County courthouse.

1145. VENDORS' LICENSE TO SELL TANGIBLE PERSONAL PROPERTY AT RETAIL
January 1, 1935—. 54 bins; 3 file boxes; 6 bundles.

Duplicates of each vendor's license issued, showing name and address of vendor, date of issue, code number, and classification of vendor's business. Filed in order of license numbers. Each license 6.5 x 8; each file box 16.75 x 11.75 x 24.75; each bin 13.25 x 10.75 x 4.75. Room 149, County courthouse.

1146. DUPLICATE SALES TAX, LICENSE REPORTS
January 1, 1935—. 1 bundle.

Statement relating to duplicate license listing name of applicant, license number, code number, kind of business, to whom issued, business address, date of issue, and signature of clerk issuing duplicate license. Arranged as to license numbers. Handwritten and typed. 500 pages. 8.5 x 11 x 1. Room 149, County courthouse.

1147. LIST OF APPLICATIONS FOR LICENSE TO SELL TANGIBLE PERSONAL PROPERTY AT RETAIL
January 1935—. 3 file boxes.

A copy of a list prepared weekly and forwarded to the state treasurer, listing names and addresses of applicants, code number and license number. In order of license number. Typed on printed forms. Each file box 13.25 x 10.75 x 4.72. Room 149, County courthouse.

1148. STUBS OF VENDORS' LICENSE FEES
January 1935—. 3 cardboard boxes.

Stubs of vendors' license fees permitting the sale of tangible personal property at retail. In order of license numbers. Handwritten on printed forms. Each box 9.5 x 11 x 4. Room 149, County courthouse.

Dog Licenses

1149. DOG LICENSES
1923—. Approximately 442,000 in 240 file boxes. (1930-1932, missing).

Applications made yearly for the registration of dogs, giving name and address of owner, complete description of dog, amount of license fee paid, penalty if any, and date of application. In order of license numbers. Handwritten on printed forms. Each file box 13.5 x 10.75 x 4.75. 1923-1929, 135 boxes, Attic storeroom, fourth floor; 1933, 25 file boxes, Room 72; 1934, 27 file boxes; 1935—, 58 file boxes, Room 149, County courthouse.

1150. DOG AND KENNEL RECORD, REGISTRATION OF DOGS
1917—. 17 volumes.

Registered listing number and date of application; name of owner; sex of dogs; registration fee; letters O, K, or H, which indicates whether applicant is owner, keeper, or harborer; address of place where dog is kept or harbored; duplicate tags issues if any, their dates, and any fee that may have been paid. Alphabetical by names of owners. Typed. Volumes average 1000 pages. 17 x 14.5 x 4. 1917-1932, 15 volumes, Room 70; 1933—, current loose-leaf sheets, Room 149, County courthouse.

1151. KENNEL RECORD, DOGS IMPOUNDED
January 1925—. 8 loose-leaf volumes.

Contains information concerning dogs were impounded, giving A. P. L. number, date animal was picked up; name of county agent; name and address of owner; description of dog; date and manner of disposal; date of release; number of days in kennel; number of days charged for; amount charge for housing and feeding, and selling or destroying dog; and total of all charges. Arranged chronologically. Handwritten and types of printed forms. Volumes average 450 pages. 11.5 x 16 x 5. January 1925-April 1933, 7 volumes, Room 70; May 1933-August 1935, 1 volume, Room 149, County courthouse.

1152. KENNEL RECORD, DOGS DISPOSED OF
January 1929-1935. 2 loose-leaf volumes.

Lists receipt number; A. P. L. Stray dog number; date of impoundment; name of county agent; name and address of owner; description and sex of dog; possession and disposition; date released; number of days in kennel; number of days charged for; and amount charged for license, affidavit, seizure, notice, housing and feeding, or for selling the dog. Arranged chronologically. Handwritten and typed. Volumes average 500 pages. 18.75 x 11 x 2.75. May 1933-September 1935, 1 volume, Room 149; January 1929-April 1933, 1 volume, Room 70, County courthouse.

Cigarette Taxes and License

1153. APPLICATION FOR CIGARETTE DEALERS' LICENSE
May 1933—. 5000 in 4 file boxes.

Applications for wholesale and retail cigarette dealers' licenses, and receipt stubs, showing dealer's name and address, business address, taxing district, and date each application was filed. Receipt stubs show amount paid into tax treasury. Filed alphabetically. Handwritten on printed forms. Each file box 12 x 10.75 x 5.5. May 1933-1935, 3 file boxes, Room 70; May 1935—, 1 file box, Room 149, County courthouse.

1154. RECEIPTS FOR CIGARETTE DEALERS' LICENSE TAX
1933. 1 bundle.

Receipt stubs for taxes paid, listing amount paid for the license, name of party procuring license, business address and date license was issued. In order of license numbers. Handwritten. Bundle 7.5 x 5 x 4. Room 149, County courthouse.

1155. CIGARETTE DEALERS' LICENSE–WHOLESALE
May 1935—. 1 volume.

Duplicates of wholesale dealers' licenses, showing license number, name and address of dealer to whom it was issued and effective date. In order of license numbers. Handwritten on printed forms. 200 pages. 14.75 x 9.25 x 1.25. Room 149, County courthouse.

1156. CIGARETTE DEALERS' LICENSES–RETAIL
May 1932—. 12 loose-leaf volumes; 12 bundles.

Duplicates of retail cigarette dealer's licenses issued by the county, showing dealers name and address, taxing district, date license was issued, and date of expiration. In order of license numbers. Handwritten on printed forms. Volumes average 500 pages. 14.75 x 9.25 x 1; each bundle 13.75 x 8.5 x 4. Room 149, County courthouse.

1157. CIGARETTE RECEIPTS
1927-1928. 1 file box.

Lists name and address of vendor, license number, amount of tax, and receipt number. Filed alphabetically as to names of vendors. Handwritten on printed forms. File box 12 x 9.5 x 5. Attic storeroom, fourth floor, County courthouse.

1158. DISCONTINUANCE OF CIGARETTE TRAFFIC (Applications for Refunds)
1928-1931, 4 file boxes.
Affidavits for discontinuance of cigarette traffic, with request that tax be abated, to which is attached cigarette assessment receipt (license). On back of affidavit is listed voucher number, name and address of vendor, amount of claim, and receipt for amount received. In order of voucher numbers. Handwritten on printed forms. Each file box 12 x 10.75 x 5.5. June 1928-July 1929, 1 file box, Room 149; July 1925, 1929-August 10, 1931, 3 file boxes Room 70, County courthouse.

1159. AUDITOR'S CIGARETTE DUPLICATE
1922-1927. 5 volumes. (1923 missing).
Cigarette traffic tax duplicate, giving treasurer's receipt number, name of dealer, name property owner, description of property, date of tax assessment and amount, date of payment, amount unpaid at July settlement, amount assessed thereafter, amount allowed or discontinuance since the July tax settlement. Alphabetical index of names of dealers in each volume. Volumes average 560 pages. 17 x 19.5 x 2.25. Room 70, County courthouse.

1160. AUDITOR'S CIGARETTE DEALERS' LICENSE RECORD
July 1931—. 2 volumes; 2 bundles.
Lists license fee, receipt number, name of dealer and location of business, date license issued, and amount of tax. Alphabetical by dealers name for Cleveland; in numerical order for suburbs listed alphabetically. Handwritten on printed forms. Volumes average 300 pages. 14.75 x 12 x 2.5. Room 149, County courthouse.

1161. CIGARETTE TRAFFIC TAX NOTICE
May 1924-May 1934. 21 bundles.
A form certified that certain persons or firms will begin trafficking in cigarettes on certain dates. Chronological. Handwritten and typed on printed forms. Each bundle 5.5 x 14 x 6. Room 70, County courthouse.

1162. REFUND OF ASSESSMENTS
1904-1923. 1 volume.
Refunds of assessments for cigarette tax, giving date of refund, voucher number, name and address of person to whom refund is made, date of assessment, date of

discontinuance, and amount refunded. Arranged chronologically. Handwritten. 150 pages. 11 x 16 x 1.75. Room 70, County courthouse.

Miscellaneous Licenses

1163. COSMETIC LICENSE RECORDS
1933-1935. 2 bundles.
 Record listing cash receipt number, name and location of dealer, date license was issued, and amount of cosmetic tax. Arranged alphabetically for each year. Handwritten on printed forms. Each bundle 14.75 x 11.5. x3. Room 149, County courthouse.

1164. BEVERAGE LICENSE RECORD
1933-1935. 2 bundles.
Lists number of receipt for tax paid, name and address of dealer, date license was issued, and amount of tax. Alphabetical by names of dealers. Handwritten on printed forms. Bundles 14.75 x 11.5 x 3. Room 149, County courthouse.

1165. SOLDIERS' AND SAILORS' PERMITS
1921-1934. 34 volumes.
A record of permits to peddle and sell goods, listing name and address of soldier or sailor, and company and regiment in which he served. Filed chronologically. Handwritten on printed forms. Volumes average 200 pages. 13.5 x 4.5 x 1. Room 70, County courthouse.

1166. REPORT OF SALE OF MOTOR VEHICLE LICENSES
1926-1931. 3 bundles.
Reports by the county auditor, showing number of licenses issued and amount of money collected for them. In chronological order. Handwritten and typed. Each bundle 15 x 18 x 5. Room 70, County courthouse.

Liquor Tax Records

1167. LIQUOR TRAFFIC TAX
November 22, 1902-September 28, 1917. 1 volume.
Letters and printed forms from the auditor of State directing the county auditor to enter certain liquor law violators upon the tax assessment duplicate together with

a penalty of 20 percent, giving date, name of dealer, and location and character of business. In chronological order. Typed and handwritten. 200 pages. 10.25 x 16 x 3. Room 70, County courthouse.

1168. LIQUOR AND CIGARETTE TAX COLLECTIONS, DISBURSEMENTS, AND STATEMENTS
July 1, 1896-August 31, 1900. 1 volume.

Shows voucher number, name and address of trafficker, amount of voucher, amount of unpaid tax, date of discontinuance of traffic, balance of treasurer's fees, and number of new applications. Arranged according to voucher numbers and dates of periods for which statements were prepared. Handwritten. 100 pages. 10.5 x 15.75 x .5. Room 70, County courthouse.

1169. CERTIFICATION OF PERSONS OR CORPORATIONS AS BEING LIABLE FOR LIQUOR TRAFFIC ASSESSMENT
September 1921-April 1932. 2 volumes.

A record of certification to the county auditor, showing name and address of trafficker and whether or not he is an owner of real estate, and giving a description of any real estate owned. Contains an alphabetical index of traffickers. Printed and typed. Volumes average 600 pages. 9.75 x 11.75 x 2. Room 149, County courthouse.

1170. ORDER OF REMITTER LIQUOR TAX ASSESSMENT
January 1924-December 1933. 1 volume.

Orders received from the auditor of state releasing claims against owners of real estate and asking the county treasurer to collect the liquor assessment made against liquor-law violators. Filed chronologically. Typed and printed. 1200 pages. 9 x 14 x 5. Room 149, County courthouse.

1171. LIQUOR DISCONTINUANCES
May 25, 1903-August 1, 1904. 1 volume.

Lists voucher number, date of issue, name and address of trafficker, date of liquor tax assessment, amount, date of discontinuance, amount refunded, and name of successor if any. Chronological as to dates of entry. Handwritten. 100 pages. 10.5 x 15.75 x .5. Room 70, County courthouse.

1172. AUDITOR'S LIQUOR DUPLICATE
1909—. 2 volumes.
A record of assessments for liquor traffic, listing name of violator, location of property, name of owner, date of assessment, amount assessed, the penalty, and amount paid on liquor duplicate. Alphabetical index of violators in each volume. Handwritten on printed forms. Volumes average 400 pages. 19 x 15.25 x 2. Room 149, County courthouse.

Miscellaneous Records

1173. MONTHLY STATEMENT OF CONDITION OF APPROPRIATIONS
April 1934—. 2 bundles.
A report of the condition of the appropriations for all departments in the county listing code number for each account, total appropriation, total amount certified, unpaid certifications, total amount paid, and the free balance remaining. Bundles 11 x 9 x 6. Room 149, County courthouse.

1174. COUNTY AUDITOR'S DAILY STATEMENT SHOWING AMOUNT OF MOTOR VEHICLE TAXES COLLECTED
1925-1932. 4 volumes. (1930 missing).
A statement of motor vehicle taxes collected by the county auditor by sale of auto tags, showing district and registration; whether passenger cars, trucks, or motorcycles; dealer's fee from State commissioner; and total fees. Arranged chronologically. Handwritten and typed. Volumes average 100 pages. 14 x 20 x 3.5. Room 70, County courthouse.

1175. STATEMENT OF AUTO REGISTRATION FEES
January 1932—. 1 volume.
A statement made out by the State commissioner of motor vehicles concerning auto fees due this county, listing taxing district, total fees, and distribution of fees as follows: 23 percent to the State, 5 percent for equalization, 47 percent to the county, and 25 percent to the district of registration; and amounts in each case. In chronological order. Typed. 100 pages. 12 x 9.5 x .75. Room 149, County courthouse.

1176. TRANSFER FEE BOOK
1903—. 27 volumes. (1908-1912 missing).

A record of fees received in the transfer of property, listing name and address of grantee, location of property, number of parcels, and amount of fee. In chronological order. Handwritten on printed forms. Volumes average 800 pages. 18 x 14 x 3. 1903-1907, 2 volumes, 6-7, Room 70; 1913-1931, 21 volumes, 12-32, Attic storeroom, fourth floor; 1932—, 4 volumes, 33-36, Room 149, County courthouse.

1177. RECORD OF MONEYS RECEIVED BY COUNTY TREASURER
September 1898-August 1902, 1 volume.

Lists date of entry; from whom money is received; account to which credited; amount received; amount received in addition to taxes and receipts from liquor tax, cigarette tax, and undivided tax; total cash receipts; name of county treasurer; and amount deposited in county treasury. In chronological order. Handwritten on printed forms. 186 pages. 13 x 18.25 x 2. Room 70, County courthouse.

1178. DAILY STATEMENT OF COUNTY TREASURER
July 1918—. 7 volumes. (July 22, 1918- November 7, 1919, 2 volumes; June 28, 1920-December 31, 1920, 1 volume; January 3, 1921-August 27, 1921, 1 volume; January 1, 1930-December 31, 1931, 1 volume; July 1933, 2 volumes). (November 1919-1920; August 1921-December 1930; January 1932-June 1933, missing).

Lists various funds, amount deposited, amount distributed by check or cash, and total amount. In chronological order. Handwritten on printed forms. Volumes average 800 pages. 10.25 x 16 x 3. July 1918-December 1931, 5 volumes, Room 70; July 1933—, 2 volumes, Room 149, County courthouse.

1179. PUBLIC COUNTY BUILDING FUNDS
1911-1924. 1 volume.

A record of construction of county buildings, showing receipts and disbursements, warrant number, name of person to whom warrant was issued, for what purpose issued, balance in treasury, amount disbursed, amount received, accrued interest, and all loans and premiums. Arranged by names of funds. Handwritten. 1000 pages. 17 x 14.5 x 4. Room 149, County courthouse.

1180. UNCLAIMED MONEYS, FEES, COST, ETC., PAID TO THE COUNTY TREASURER
1891—. 7 volumes. (1891-1935, 1 volume, Probate Court; 1901—, 5 volumes, 1-5, Court of Common Pleas; 1914-1932. 1 volume, Insolvency Court).

Record of unclaimed moneys, such as court fees and costs, paid into county treasury by the various courts. It lists number and page of the fee book, court case number, name of person to boom unclaimed money was payable, and amount, certificate order on the treasurer for recovery of this money, date of issue, and general remarks. Contains an alphabetical index of courts in each volume. Handwritten. Volumes average 440 pages. 11.25 x 14.75 x 2.25. Room 149, County courthouse.

1181. TREASURER'S RECORD OF OVERPAYMENTS
1917—. 14 volumes.

Lists original lot and sublot numbers, overpayment number, name and address of party making payment, date of payment, amounts of double payment and of overpayment, page and line number of tax assessment book, treasurer's certificate number, auditor's warrant number, and amount and date refunded. Arranged by treasurer's tax-duplicate book number and year dates. Numerical by tax duplicates. Handwritten. Volumes average 600 pages. 15 x 14.75 x 5. Room 149, County courthouse.

1182. REPORT OF EXAMINATION BY STATE AUDITOR
April 1918. 1 loose-leaf volume.

A copy of the report made to the state auditor by the state examiner covering his examination of offices at Atlanta, Ohio. Typed, table form. 200 pages. 6 x 8 x 1. Attic storeroom, 4 floor, County courthouse.

1183. REPORT OF EXAMINATION BY STATE AUDITOR
September 1911-October 1917. 7 volumes. (September 1911-January 1916, 3 volumes, Cuyahoga County; April 1913-June 1914, 1 volume, Marion County; April 1914-July 1915, 1 volume, Lorain County; July 1915-April 1917, 1 volume, Fayette County; January 1916- October 1917, 1 volume, Perry County).

Copies of reports made by the state examiner to the state auditor covering the examinations of various county offices. Typed, table form. Volumes average 200 pages. 13 x 8 x .5. Attic storeroom, fourth floor, County courthouse.

1184. REPORT OF EXAMINATION BY STATE AUDITOR OF VILLAGE SCHOOL DISTRICTS

Cuyahoga County, 1920-1924. 1 loose-leaf volume.

A copy of a report addressed to the state auditor, covering the examination of village school districts made by the state examiner from 1920 to 1924. In chronological order. Typed, table form. 200 pages. 6 x 8 x 1. Attic storeroom, fourth floor, County courthouse.

1185. OPINIONS

October 15, 1909-May 21, 1919. 1 volume.

Letters from the attorney general, the prosecuting attorney, and the state examiner, containing opinions on various matters. Inside alphabetical index of subjects. Typed and printed. 240 pages. 11.5 x 16 x 3. Room 70, County courthouse.

1186. RECORD OF TAX DEEDS MADE BY COUNTY AUDITOR

1884—. 1 volume.

Gives name of owner and township; description of property, including frontage, street, amount of tax, date of sale, to whom sold, and to whom deeded. Arranged chronologically. Handwritten on printed forms. Volumes average 150 pages. 13.5 x 17.5 x 1. Room 149, County courthouse.

1187. LAND REDEMPTION

February 1906-February 1914. 1 volume.

A record of redeemed lands, showing date of redemption, name of party to whom land was sold, description of property, certificate number, deposit made to redeem land, amount of advertising fees, voucher number, and pay-in order number. Arranged by date of redemption. Handwritten. 800 pages. 14.75 x 11 x 4. Room 149, County courthouse.

1188. BOUNTY RECORD –CIVIL WAR (receipts).

July 1862-1864. 1 volume.

A record of bounties paid by Civil War veterans in Cuyahoga County, giving name of veteran, ward number, amount, certificate filed, date of enlistment, battery, family and residence; contains telegrams (in longhand), letters and petitions requesting payment. Handwritten. 500 pages. 14 x 10 x 1. Room 149, County courthouse.

1189. RECORD OF BLIND RELIEF
January 6, 1905-October 10, 1931. 4 volumes.
Lists amounts allotted for blind and relief, giving name and address of person receiving relief, yearly amount allowed, amount allowed quarterly, date of payment, and voucher number. Alphabetical by names of clients. Handwritten. Volumes average 200 pages. 14 x 17 x .75. Room 70, County courthouse.

1190. FEES, COSTS, ETC., DUE CUYAHOGA COUNTY
January 1924-January 1925. 1 volume.
A record of fees, court costs, etc., due Cuyahoga County and common pleas court, incurred up to January 1, 1924, and remaining unpaid January 1, 1925, listing case numbers, amount due, etc. In order of court case numbers. Typed. 500 pages. 8.5 x 14 x 3. Room 149, County courthouse.

1191. MEMORANDUM OF ALLOWANCES BY COUNTY COMMISSIONERS IN STATE CASES TO JUSTICES AND CONSTABLES
September 1, 1912. 1 volume.
An alphabetical index of justices and constables and list amounts of allowances, and dates. Handwritten. 400 pages. 15 x 13.25 x 2. Room 149, County courthouse.

1192. SCRIP REGISTER
September 1932—. 12 volumes.
A register of Cuyahoga County scrip, listing each piece of scrip by number, classified by series of issue and denomination. Handwritten on printed forms. Volumes average 400 pages. 15 x 18 x 3. 1932-1933, 11 volumes, Room 43; 1933—, 1 volume, Room 149, County courthouse.

1193. FEES AND PAYROLL
October 16, 1899-May 15, 1926. 3 volumes.
A record of payroll funds of the various county offices, listing date of fiscal year, date and number of voucher, salaries of individual employees and officials, and total payroll. Alphabetical index of names of various county offices. Typed and handwritten. Volumes average 450 pages. 11.5 x 16.25 x 2.25. Room 70, County courthouse.

1194. CLAIMS AGAINST THE COUNTY APPROVED AND ORDERED
PAID BY BOARD OF COMMISSIONERS
November 1883-February 1916. 4 volumes. (November 1883-June 1889,
1 volume; June 1893-July 1898, 2volumes, October 1902-February 1916,
1 volume).
List volume and page of journal, date of approval and date on which ordered paid,
name of claimant, reason for claim, amount of payment, number of voucher, and
date of payment. Alphabetically indexed by claimants. Handwritten on printed
forms. Volumes average 350 pages. 15.5 x 18.5 x 2. Room 70, County courthouse.

1195. SCRAP BOOK
December 1907-April 1913. 1 volume.
Contains clippings regarding county affairs and especially concerning the
construction of the new courthouse. In chronological order. 240 pages. 20.5 x 24 x
2. Room 70, County courthouse.

Miscellaneous Files

1196. PAYROLLS
1926-1930. 14 bundles in 4 bins.
Payroll sheets made by various county offices and sent to auditor for record.
Chronological by dates of payrolls. Typed and handwritten. Each bundle 11 x 10
x 5. Room at 70, County courthouse.

1197. PAYROLL CHANGES
March 1918—. 4 volumes; 2 bundles; 1 folder.
Certifications of changes in payrolls by various department heads of county offices.
Arranged alphabetically by county office. Typed. Each bundle 8.5 x 11 x 1.
Volumes average 1000 pages. 12.5 x 16 x 4. 1918-1932, Room 70; 1932—, Room
149, County courthouse.

1198. JUSTICE OF PEACE TRANSCRIPTS
May 1909-1924. Approximately 500 in 1 metal file box.
Criminal cost bills for justice of peace courts which have been approved and
ordered paid by the county commissioners. Filed chronologically. Handwritten and
typed on printed forms. File box 13.5 x 10.75 x 4.75. Room 149, County
courthouse.

1199. PROBATE COURT CRIMINAL TRANSCRIPTS
1911-1925. Approximately 250 in 1 metal file box.

Transcripts covering cases in probate court, showing date of transcript, name of offender, and amount of court costs. Filed numerically. Handwritten and typed. File box 13.25 x 10.75 x 4.75. Room 149, County courthouse.

1200. CIVIL SERVICE COMMISSION AND TAX COMMISSION
1913-1926. 1 file box.

Various letters and reports passed between the civil service commission and tax commission. Arranged alphabetically by subject matter. Typed. File box 12 x 11 x 4. Room 149, County courthouse.

1201. RESOLUTIONS PASSED BY COUNTY COMMISSIONERS
October 1928-September 1932. Approximately 250 in 1 bundle.

Various resolutions regarding appointments, resignations, changes in payroll, etc., passed by county commissioners. In chronological order. Typed. Bundle 3.5 x 8.5 x 4. Room 70, County courthouse.

1202. DITCH PROCEEDINGS
February 1913-January 1923. 2 metal file boxes.

A record of legal proceedings, notices, ordinances, etc., regarding ditches in the county. Alphabetical by names of taxing districts. Typed. Each file box 13.5 x 10.75 x 4.75. Room 149, County courthouse.

1203. MISCELLANEOUS LETTERS
June 24, 1892-September 7, 1909. 1 volume.

Contains letters on various subjects pertaining to the office of the county auditor. Alphabetical index of the subject matter. Handwritten and typed. 470 pages. 10 x 15.5 x 4. Room 70, County courthouse.

1204. BOX FILES
1925—. Approximately 6600 in 22 file boxes.

Miscellaneous papers, reports, insurance renewals, assessments, bills of sales, etc., pertaining to auditor's office. Arranged chronologically. Typed, photostat, and handwritten. Each file box 13.25 x 10.75 x 4.75. Room 149, County courthouse.

1205. EUROPEAN CORN BORER CONTROL NOTICES
May-June 1927. Approximately 500 in 1 metal file box.
Copies of notices sent to farmers by State Department of Agriculture, instructing
them to destroy their corn. Chronological. Typed and handwritten. File box 13.25
x 10.75 x 4.75. Room 149, County courthouse.

1206. WILLS (uncalled-for)
June 1907-June 1918. 1 file box.
Alphabetical by names of testators. Typed. File box 13.25 x 10.75 x 4.75. Room
149, County courthouse.

1207. WORKHOUSE REPORTS
December 1907-May 1932. Approximately 500 statements in 1 file box.
Statement of cost, fines, upkeep expense of prisoners at workhouse. Chronological.
Typed on printed forms. File box 13.25 x 10.75 x 4.75. Room 149, County
courthouse.

1208. ELECTION FUND
1925-1929. Approximately 30 sheets in 1 file box.
Expense sheets for printing election ballots, etc. Chronological by dates of sheets.
Typed. File box 13.25 x 10.75 x 4.75. Room 149, County courthouse.

1209. ELECTION NOTICES
November 29, 1909—. 3 volumes. (November 29, 1909-November 22,
1919, 1 volume; November 6, 1919-June 9, 1928, 1 volume; November
1929—, 1 volume).
Notices by village clerks listing names of officers elected in village or township.
Alphabetical by names of officers. Typed and handwritten. Volumes average 200
pages. 10.5 x 16 x 3. November 29, 1909-June 9, 1928, 2 volumes, Room 70;
November 1929,—, 1 volume, Room 149, County courthouse.

1210. MONTHLY REPORT OF RECEIPTS AND DISBURSEMENTS
December 1925-1926. 1 bundle.
Trial balances showing name of funds in which money was credited or debited;
monthly balances of accounts, total receipts, disbursements, balances. Arranged by
months. Handwritten on printed forms. 1000 loose-leaf pages. 13.25 x 29 x 6. Room
70, County courthouse.

1211. STATEMENT OF FINES
1908—. Approximately 600 in 3 metal file boxes.
Shows fines assessed in various justice of peace courts listing name of person fined, amount of fine, amount of court cost, and date on which costs and fines were assessed. Chronological by dates of statements. Typed and handwritten on printed forms. Each file box 13.25 c 10.75 c 4.75. Room 149, County courthouse.

1212. TRANSFER OF FUNDS
October 1905—. Approximately 1600 in 4 file boxes.
Various resolutions passed by county commissioners regarding transfer of funds. Chronological by dates of resolutions. Typed. Each file box 13.25 x 10.75 x 4.75. Room 149, County courthouse.

1213. EXPENSE REPORTS (deputy sheriffs')
February 1925-1928. 2 bins. (1926-1927, missing).
Lists date of entry, case number, name of court, kind of writ served, number of miles traveled, and destination; and shows amount of expense incurred by deputy sheriffs in serving various writs throughout the county so deputies may be fully reimbursed. Handwritten. Each bin 9 x 11 x 15. Room 70, County courthouse.

1214. STATEMENT OF EXPENSES FOR DEPENDENT CHILDREN
1928-1931. 47 bundles.
Itemized accounts–statements submitted by superintendent of Division of Charities, Department of Public Welfare, Columbus, to auditor, who has issued vouchers in payment of expense, listing name of child and amounts expended for hospital care, board, clothing, and miscellaneous items. Typed on printed forms. Each bundle 8.5 x 11 x .75. Room 70, County courthouse.

1215. BLUEPRINTS OF PLANS AND SPECIFICATIONS OF THE CUYAHOGA COUNTY DETENTION HOME, AND THE JUVENILE COURT BUILDING
June 1931. 1 circular copper container.
A typewritten estimate of the total cost of buildings, land, and furnishings is attached to blueprints, which are kept in the container. Each blueprint 17.25 x 38.75. Room 70, County courthouse.

Real Estate Appraisal Divisions

Tax Accounting

Property Maps

1216. PROPERTY MAPS
1860—. 171 volumes.

Maps designate dimensions of each individual parcel of land in the county listing names of all successive owners and date of each purchase. The volumes for 1860 also contain an assessment of land record listing description of property; owner's name; acres; value per acre; value of land and buildings; total valuation; number of acres of land in plow, meadow, and wood. Volumes arranged by villages, townships, wards, and taxing districts. Volumes 1870-1880 contain index of property owners for each village or township. For separate index see number 1217. Volumes average 60 pages. Sizes vary from 12.5 x 15 x 1.75 to 24.5 x 30.5 x 2. Room 59, Current maps, Room 30, County courthouse.

1217. INDEX MAPS, no dates
3 maps.

These maps serve as index to property maps. On wall in Room 30, County courthouse.

(a)   A detailed street map of Cuyahoga County showing the boundaries of all taxing districts in the county and indicating the reference numbers used in the property maps. Scale, one half-inch to the mile. 7' x 6'. Publisher, Foreman-Bassett Company.

(b)   A map of Cleveland and vicinity showing boundaries of all taxing districts in the city and vicinity and indicating reference numbers used in the property maps. Scale, one inch to the quarter mile. 7' x 7'. Publisher, Foreman-Bassett Company.

(c)   Map showing all school districts in Cuyahoga County and indicating reference numbers used in the property maps. Scale, two inches to the mile. 7' x 6'. Drawn by John McWilliams.

Tax Duplicate and Transfer Record

1218. MASTER CARDS OF REAL ESTATE LIST
1934——. 240 metal file drawers (384,000 cards).

A card file of all real property, listing owner's name, address, description of property, sublot, foot frontage, where located, land valuation, building valuation, total valuation, tax rate, mills, fractions, total general tax, auditor's code number, project, year dates, and purpose of assessment. Arranged alphabetically under each taxing district, and cards arranged alphabetically by name of property owner. Typed and handwritten. Each file drawer 25 x 5.5 x 6.5. Room 150, County courthouse.

1219. ASSESSMENT CHARGE CARDS
1934——. 615 metal file drawers (700,000 cards).

Individual card for each assessment charged against real property owners. For description see number 1218. Arranged alphabetically under each taxing district; cards arranged alphabetically by name of property owner. Typed and handwritten. Each file drawer 16 x 8.5 x 5.75. Room 150, County courthouse.

1220. AUDITOR'S DUPLICATE OF REAL AND PERSONAL PROPERTY
1820——. 4066 volumes. (Missing; 1905, 1 volume, 48; 1906, 4 volumes, 45-48; 1908, 1 volume, 50; 1909, 1 volume, 50; 1910, 1 volume, 54; 1912, 2 volumes, 66-67; 1924, 2 volumes 90-91).

The auditor's duplicate, made each year for taxation, contains a list of owners of all property in the county. From 1820 to 1850 includes: owner's name, range, tract, section, original lot, sublot, what part of lot owned, acreage, frontage, depth, assessed value, state tax, county tax, school tax, road tax, township tax, bridge tax, total tax, and amounts of payments paid on each parcel. Personal property tax entered in duplicate after each city, township, or village, listing name of owner, number of cattle, number of horses, merchant capital, cash on interest, assessed value, state and county tax, road tax, and total tax. From 1851 to 1857 the following items were added to the duplicate: district school tax, delinquent tax, penalty, and interest. From 1820 to 1857 taxes paid annually. From 1858 to date taxes collected semi-annually. From 1880 to date following items were added: sewer districts, special assessments, and a description of assessments. Arranged alphabetically by names of owners in each section of the city and in each city, township, and village. 1820-1850 handwritten; 1851-1905, handwritten on printed forms; 1906——, handwritten and typed on printed forms. (And delinquent taxes from 1820-1860 was 30 percent; 1861-1879, 20 percent; 1880-1923, 15 percent; 1923—, 10 percent; prior to 1923 the penalty charged on general and school tax only. Since 1923 penalty has been charged on general and all special assessments). Volumes average 440 pages. 20 x 22.5 x 2. 1820-1921, second floor, Hart Building; 1922-1932, Room 42; 1934—, Room 150, County courthouse.

1221. AUDITOR'S TRANSFER RECORD OF REAL PROPERTY
1820—. 2057 volumes. (Missing; 1829-1835, 1 volume, 2; 1921-1923, 2 volumes, 69-70).

Lists date of recording, name of present owner, map district number and map page number of the parcel, name of subdivision, original lot number, sublot number, frontage and depth of lot or number of acres, the land value, building value if any, total value, name of grantor, and date of conveyance. The consideration is shown also if it appears on deed. Alphabetical and chronological according to date a recording. 1820-1856, handwritten; 1856—, handwritten on printed forms. 1820-1899, volumes average 550 pages; 1891—, volumes average 300 pages. 1820-1856, 13 x 9 x 1.5; 1856-1889, 15 x 12 x 2; 1876-1891, 18 x 14 x 3; 1883—, 16 x 14 x 2. 1820-1923 Room 70; 1923-1927, Room 59; 1927—, Room 30, County courthouse.

Additions and Abatements

1222. AUDITOR'S ADDITIONS ON REAL AND PERSONAL PROPERTY
1879—. 48 volumes.

A list of taxes on additions made by auditor in cities, townships, and villages on real and personal property, giving name of owner, number of ward or map, date, name of subdivision, original lot number, sublot number, what part of sublot owned, frontage, street, tax value, gain to duplicate, general tax, special tax, prior delinquencies, total tax, amount collected in December, amount collected in June, amount uncollected for the year, date of mailing list, petition number, and reason why additions were made. Contains alphabetical index of owners in each volume. Handwritten on printed forms. Volumes average 240 pages. 18.5 x 17 x 2.5. 1879-1912, second floor, Hart Building; 1913-1921, Attic storeroom, fourth floor; 1922—, Room 158, County courthouse.

1223. ABATEMENTS ALLOWED ON REAL AND PERSONAL PROPERTY

1879—. 45 volumes. (1891, 1904, missing).

A list of abatements allowed on real and personal property in cities, townships, and villages for clerical errors, building razed, etc., listing stub number, number of abatement, date of entry, to whom given, name of owner, number of ward or map, name of subdivision, original lot number, sublot number, what part of sublot owned, frontage, street, tax value, loss to duplicate, general tax, special tax, prior delinquencies, total tax, amount allowed in December collection, amount to be allowed in June collection, amount actually allowed in June collection, amount unallowed for the year, petition number, and reason why abatement was allowed. Alphabetical index by names of owners in each city, township, and village. Handwritten on printed forms. Volumes average 325 pages. 18.5 x 17 x 3.5. In 1879-1920, 29 volumes, second floor, Hart Building; 1921-1925, 5 volumes, Room 72; 1926-1934, 10 volumes, Room 158, County courthouse.

1224. ABATEMENT AND ADDITION PETITIONS

1917—. 146 file boxes.

Abatement petitions, or applications, filed by the property owner for reduction in land or building values or abatements of penalty that have been acted on favorably by the county auditor, listing name of owner, subdivision, sublot number, frontage, name of street, and amount of abatement or addition. Chronological by dates of petitions. Handwritten on printed forms. Each file box 8.5 x 3.5 x 11.5. 1917-1929, 124 file boxes, Room 72, County courthouse; 1930—, 22 file boxes, second floor, Hart Building.

1225. AUDITOR'S DUPLICATE OF AUTOMOBILES

1924. 16 volumes. (East and West of River, 13 volumes, 90-102; Townships and Villages, 3 volumes, 103-105).

Auditor's list of taxes on automobiles showing name of owner, house number, street, name of car, style of car, year's model, license number, tax value, total tax, amount paid in December collection, amount unpaid and due in June, and amount unpaid in June collection and carried to the record of the delinquent personal property. Arranged alphabetically by names of owners. Typed on printed forms. Volumes average 370 pages. 20 x 19 x 2. Attic storeroom, fourth floor, County courthouse.

1226. AUDITOR'S ADDITIONS, OMITTED AUTOMOBILES
1925-1930. 9 volumes.

List of taxes on additions made by the auditor on automobiles, showing name of owner who failed to make a tax return, house number, street, make of car, type, year's model, list price, tax value, total tax due, and amount of tax collected if any. Alphabetical by names of owners. Typed on printed forms. Volumes average 340 pages. 18.5 x 16 x 3. 1925, 1 volume, 1926, 1 volume, 1928, 1 volume, 1929, 1 volume, Attic storeroom, fourth floor; 1928, 1 volume, Room 158, County courthouse; 1925-1927, 2 volumes, 1930, 1 volume, second floor, Hart Building.

1227. AUDITOR'S RECORD OF CORRECTIONS ON 1934 DUPLICATE
1934. 31 volumes.

Record of corrections made on auditor's tax duplicate, showing how record reads before and after corrections, and giving taxing district, book and bill number, name of owner, and description of property. Chronological by dates of correction. Handwritten on printed forms. Volumes average 200 pages. 13 x 8 x 1. Room 72, County courthouse.

Special Assessments

1228. DELINQUENT SPECIAL ASSESSMENT RECORD
1875—. 26 volumes.

Record of delinquent special assessments in cities, townships, and villages, giving name of owner, description of property, name of subdivision, original lot or block number, sublot number, frontage, street or avenue, depth of improvement, amount of tax, amount paid in March settlement, and amount paid in August settlement; and containing list of delinquent special assessment in the county. Arranged alphabetically by names of funds. Each city, township, and village listed separately. Alphabetical by names of project and property owners. Handwritten on printed forms. Volumes average 300 pages. 19 x 15 x 3. Room 158, County courthouse. East of River, 4 volumes, 1-4. West of River, 3 volumes, 1-3. Township and Villages, 19 volumes.

1229. SPECIAL ASSESSMENT REVISIONS
1927-1928. 1 volume.

Revised assessments listing original assessments and amount of increase. For further description see number 1230. Front index lists volume and page number, name of street, improvement, exact location of work, years to run, total to be collected and amounts paid each year. Arranged alphabetically by street name or numerically if numbered street, then alphabetically by owners' names. Handwritten and typed on printed forms. 315 pages. 19.5 x 19 x 2.5. Room 72, County courthouse.

1230. SPECIAL ASSESSMENTS
1886—. 972 volumes. Each number covers from 1 to 22 volumes. (Missing; 1914, 1 volume, 2; 1915, 1 volume, 2; 1916 1 volume, 2; 1917 1 volume, 2; 1918, 1 volume, 3; 1919, 1 volume, 3; 1920, 5 volumes, 2, 3, 6, 7, 8; 1921, 2 volumes, 7, 8; 1922, 2 volumes, 7, 8; 1923, 2 volumes, 9, 10; 1924, 1 volume, 10).There are 19 volumes of Lakewood special assessments, 1902-1920, at Lakewood City Hall. It is possible that additional missing volumes may be found in other political subdivisions).

Lists street name, exact location of work, kind of improvement, owner's name, line number, subdivision, rate, penalty, original lot are blocked number, sublot number, what part, frontage, total amount of tax, December collection, amount due in June, June collection, amounts delinquent, page number, whether county or municipal fund, acres, yearly installment, amount percent interest on unpaid balance, total to be collected for the year, reduction, credits, and amount of abatement. First volume of each series has front index, showing volume and page number, name of street, improvement, exact location of work, years to run, total to be collected and amount paid each year. Arranged alphabetically by street name or numerically if numbered street, then alphabetically by owners' names. Handwritten and typed on printed forms. Volumes average 800 pages. 20 x 17 x 4. Originally stored in attic storeroom, fourth floor, County courthouse. Removed in part to second floor, Hart Building.

1231. DELINQUENT SPECIAL ASSESSMENTS
1874-1928. 26 volumes.

Record of delinquent special assessments in cities, townships, and villages, giving name of owner, description of property, name of subdivision, original lot or block number, sublot number, frontage, street or avenue, depth, name of improvement, amount of tax, amount paid in March settlement, and amount paid in August settlement. Each city, township, and village is listed separately. Alphabetical by project and property owners charged with assessment. Handwritten on printed forms. Volumes average 300 pages. 19 x 15 x 3. 1874-1926, 24 volumes, second floor, Hart Building; 1927, 2 volumes, Room 148, County courthouse.

1232. SPECIAL ASSESSMENT INDEX
1922—. 5 volumes.

An index of special improvements in cities, townships, and villages, listing name of street, name of improvements, years to run, book number, and number of page. 1922-1934, alphabetical by taxing district and project; 1934—, arranged numerically by code number and streets. Typed on present forms. Volumes average 300 pages. 19 x 19 x 1.5. Room 150, County courthouse.

1233. ORIGINAL ASSESSMENTS (county roads, ditches, sewers, and water mains).
1901—. 38 volumes.

Record of assignments charged to property owners in various townships and villages, listing name of improvement, years to run, amount of interest on bonds issued, name of owner, original lot number, name of subdivision, sublot number, street, what part of lot owned, and amount of district assessment. Each volume contains alphabetical index of owners for each township and village. Typed on printed forms. Volumes average 520 pages. 20 x 17 x 3. Room 150, County courthouse.

Delinquencies

1234. DELINQUENCIES
1920-1932. 80 volumes.

Record of delinquent taxes of August semi-annual settlement, listing name of owner; section; name of tract or subdivision; original lot number; sublot number; frontage; street or avenue; number of acres; value; improvements; general tax; penalty on general, special, and county funds; delinquencies of former years unpaid; total tax due; and remarks. Alphabetical by owners in each city, township, or village. Handwritten on printed forms. Volumes average 772 pages. 17.5 x 15 x 3.5. Second floor, Hart Building.

1235. AUDITOR'S DUPLICATE OF TAX CERTIFIED DELINQUENT
1918-1934.

Record of delinquent lands certified to auditor of state; also record of interest, advertising, and certification fees paid on lands redeemed. Record lists name of owner, map district, name of subdivision, original lot or block number, sublot number, what part of lot owned, frontage, street, depth, total tax value, total tax certified delinquent, amount of interest collected, advertising costs and certification fee. Alphabetical index by names of owners in each city, township, and village. Typed on printed forms. Volumes average 600 pages. 20 x 20 x 2. Second floor, Hart Building. From 1934 to date record of delinquencies kept in tax duplicate.

1236. RECORD OF DELINQUENCIES ADVERTISED
1874-1915. 10 volumes. (1877, 1881-1882, 1893, missing).

Record of all real estate returned delinquent by treasurer and prepared for publication in daily papers as required by law. Alphabetical by names of owners in each taxing district in each volume. Handwritten on printed forms. Volumes average 250 pages. 18.5 x 16 x 4. Second floor, Hart Building.

1237. DELINQUENT ANALYSIS TAX CARD
1936—. 66 drawers.

List all delinquencies to date. Each card gives name of owner, name of subdivision, original lot number, sublot number, frontage, name of street, and description of property; it also contains an analysis of each year's delinquent tax and amount paid if any after each collection. Alphabetical by names of owners in each city, township, and village. Handwritten on printed forms. Each drawer 11 x 11 x 28. 57 drawers, Room 159; 9 drawers, Room 59, County courthouse.

1238. DELINQUENT PROPERTIES CERTIFIED FOR FORECLOSURE
1918-1927. 8 volumes.

Record of real estate on which taxes have not been paid for five years. Statement sent to the State auditor for foreclosure, listing name of owner, taxing district, name of subdivision, original lot, sublot number, what part of lot owned, frontage, street, depth, and total amount of delinquent tax. No action has been taken by the State or foreclosure on certified delinquent taxes since the 1927 certifications. Alphabetical by names of owners. Handwritten on printed forms. Volumes average 800 pages. 17.5 x 14 x 5. Second floor, Hart Building.

1239. RECORD OF TAX SALES
1822-1914. 11 volumes. (1830-1937 missing).

A record of sales of land in the county because of delinquent taxes, listing name of owner, name of allotment, original lot number, sublot number, what part of sublot owned, name of street, frontage, acreage, tax value, total amount of tax, date of sale, to whom sold, redemptions if any, and to whom assigned. Alphabetical index of owners in each volume. Handwritten on printed forms. Volumes average 300 pages. 17 x 14 x 2.5. Second floor, Hart Building.

1240. CERTIFICATES OF REDEMPTION
1918-1931. 164,000 in 41 bundles.

Certificates issued by auditor to property owner when prior delinquencies paid plus 8 percent interest thereon. Arranged chronologically. Handwritten on printed forms. Each bundle 15 x 10 x 5. Second floor, Hart Building.

1241. RECORD OF FORTIFIED LANDS TO THE STATE OF OHIO
1880—. 1 volume.

List of all property in the county reverting to the state of Ohio for failure of owner to pay taxes, giving name of owner, name of subdivision, original lot number, sublot number, what part of sublot owned, frontage, name of street, depth, acreage, value of property, and tax and penalty at time of forfeiture. Alphabetical by names of owners. Handwritten on printed forms. 300 pages. 18.5 x 12 x 2.5. Room 30, County courthouse.

1242. RECORD OF PAYMENTS
1933—. 426 volumes.

Record of taxes paid and accounted for by tax settlement dates, listing book and page number, item number, total paid, restored checks, overpayments, transfers out, general tax, school tax, special assessments, delinquencies of former years, name and description, municipal assessments, and county assessments. Arranged by tax book numbers and in order of dates of payments. Handwritten. Volumes average 50 pages. 18 x 18 x 1. 1933, 120 volumes, 1-120; 1934, 120 volumes, 1-120, Room 59; 1935, 186 volumes, 1-186, Room 150, County courthouse.

1243. WHITTMORE INSTALLMENT UNDERTAKINGS
1933—. 35 volumes, 1-35.

Separate sheets for each delinquent taxpayer who agrees to pay delinquent taxes and assessments less penalties, interest, and other charges in 6 annual installments. In order of dates of payments. Handwritten on printed forms. Volumes average 500 pages. 15 x 8 x 4. Room 158, County courthouse.

1244. COUNTY TREASURER'S CERTIFICATE OF FULL PAYMENT OF DELINQUENT TAXES AND ASSESSMENTS
April 1933—. 18 bundles; 58 file boxes.

Lists name of owner, amount of money received, and the year which the taxes cover. It also shows the district where the land is located, date received, and book and bill number. In order of dates of payments. Handwritten on printed forms. Each file 8 x 4 x 12. 58 file boxes, Room 150; 18 bundles, Room 159, County courthouse.

Building Assessing

1245. BUILDING VALUE MAPS
1895—. 113 volumes.

Building maps showing location of buildings on each parcel of land in county. Photostat. Volumes arranged by villages, townships, wards and taxing districts. Volumes average 52 pages. 20 x 15 x 1. Scale, 50 feet to the inch. Room 16 and 59, County courthouse.

1246. BUILDING BOOK
1911-1915. 10 volumes.

A record of improvements added, removed, or destroyed on real property in Cleveland district east and west of river. Lists name of owner to whom permit was issued, subdivision, original lot number, what part of lot is owned, number of building card, name of street or avenue, house number, material used, finished, or unfinished, occupancy, value fixed for taxation. Alphabetical by owners. Handwritten on printed forms. Volumes average 140 pages. 19 x 17 x 1.5. Second floor, Hart Building.

1247. APPRAISEMENTS OF NEW BUILDINGS
1908-1916. 13 volumes. (1909-1910 missing). (1908, 1 volume, City Townships and Villages 1911-1916, 12 volumes, Cities Townships and Villages).

Record of buildings erected, improved, destroyed, or removed, lists name of owner on each duplicate, name of person permit is issued to, name of subdivision, original lot number, sublot number, street, house number, material, height, value finished, value unfinished, board value, occupancy, and board record numbers. Alphabetical by names of streets in city, township, and villages. Handwritten on printed forms. Volumes average 400 pages. 14.5 x 9 x 2. Room 72, County courthouse.

1248. BUILDING CARDS
1910—. 697 file boxes.

Individual cards for each building or addition thereto in county, giving name of owner and description of property where building located, taxing district, to whom permit issued, date and number of permit, kind of building, and estimated cost. Gives exact description of building, showing area and material used in construction, and appraised value for taxation. Filed according to street addresses. Handwritten on printed forms. Each file box 9.5 x 4.5 x 14. Room 16, County courthouse.

1249. BUILDING PERMITS RECORD
1911—. 33 volumes. (1911-1914, 4 volumes, Cities, Townships, and Villages; 1916-1925, 10 volumes, Cities Townships and Villages, 1-10; 1926—, 19 volumes, Cities, Townships, and Villages). (1915, missing).

Each permit lists permit number, date of issue, sublot number, to whom issued, name of street and house number, kind of building, reported value, and value assessed for taxation. Arranged by permit numbers for each city, township, or village. Handwritten on printed forms. Volumes average 200 pages. 17 x 16 x 1.5. 1911-1914, 4 volumes, Room 72; 1916—, 29 volumes, Room 16, County courthouse.

1250. DISTRICT ASSESSOR'S RETURNS
1870, 1880, 1890, 1900. 38 volumes.

District assessor's returns of land and buildings in Cuyahoga County, listing transfer remarks; name of owners; subdivision; section; tract; original lot; sublot; what part of lot; frontage; street or avenue; acres of arable or plow, of meadow and pasture, of wood and uncultivated; total acreage; value per foot a footage; average value of per acre; value of lands as fixed by district assessors; value of dwellings, barns, and out houses; stores, mills, shops, factories, and miscellaneous; total value of lands, buildings, and improvements as fixed by district assessor; additions and deductions made by county decennial board of equalization; value as amended by county board of equalization; additions and deductions made by state decennial board of equalization; net taxable value, exempt property, railroad property, and remarks on the nature of all miscellaneous buildings. Alphabetical by names of owners and cities, townships, and villages. Handwritten on printed forms. Volumes average 220 pages. 19.5 x 18 x 2. Second floor, Hart Building.

1251. QUADRENNIAL ASSESSORS' RETURNS
1910, 59 volumes. (West of River, 22 volumes, 1-12; East of River, 37 volumes, District 21-39).

Reports of 1910 general reappraisal of all buildings in city of Cleveland. Each record list name of owner; map district; subdivision; original lot; sublot; what part of lot; frontage; name of street; depth; acreage; value of land per foot front; value of land, dwellings, barns, stores, mills and shops, engines, boilers and fixed machinery; total value of lands, buildings, etc., fixed by district assessor; additions and deductions made by board of review; value as amended by board of review; additions and deductions made by State board of equalization; and net value for taxation, exempt property, and railroad property. Alphabetical index of owners. Handwritten on printed forms. Volumes average 192 pages. 18 x 22 x 1.5. Room 72, County courthouse.

1252. ASSESSOR'S LIST OF REAL ESTATE RECORD
1914-1935. 2109 volumes.

Lists transfer remarks (with page number of transfer book and name of person to whom transferred), name of owner, map district, map page, name of subdivision, original lot or block number, sublot number, part of sublot owned, frontage, name of street, depth, total tax value, value of lots or lands exclusive of buildings, value of buildings; reappraisement if any by assessor or board of revision showing addition or deduction and new value which is set for taxation and designating any changes made by state tax commission. Arranged alphabetically by names of owners and cities, townships, and villages. Typed and handwritten on printed forms.

Volumes average 100 pages. 20 x 19 x 2. 1914-1930, 1275 volumes; 1932-1934, 240 volumes, Attic storeroom, fourth floor; 1931, 120 volumes, Room 154; 1935, 186 volumes, Room 72; 1936, 186 volumes, Room 16, County courthouse; 1934, 120 volumes, second floor, Hart Building.

1253. AUDITOR'S LIST OF EXEMPT REAL PROPERTY
1930—. 3 volumes. (1 volume, East of River; 1 volume, West of River; 1 volume, Township and Villages).

Name of owner, subdivision, original lot number, sublot number, frontage or acreage, land value, building value, total value, and reason for which exemption is allowed. Alphabetical by owners. Typed on printed forms. Volumes average 150 pages. 17.5 x 14 x 1.5. Room 16, County courthouse.

1254. REAL ESTATE COMPLAINT INDEX–CITY, TOWNSHIP, VILLAGE
1910—. 19 volumes.

Complaint number, name of owner, address, taxing district, amount added to tax value, amount deducted from tax value, addition or abatement number, date of filing complaint, and remarks. Alphabetical by names of owners. Handwritten on printed forms. Volumes average 130 pages. 17 x 15 x 1.5. Room 16, County courthouse.

1255. AUDITOR'S REAL ESTATE EXEMPTION
1896. 1 volume.

Lists name of owner; section, tract, or subdivision; original lot or block number; sublot number; what part is owned; and frontage, name of street or avenue, depth, acreage, value, and remarks. Arranged alphabetically for each city, township, and village. Handwritten on printed forms. 230 pages. 20 x 17 x 2. Room 70, County courthouse.

Real Estate Appraisal Divisions

Land Assessing

1256. FIELD MAPS
1929-1935. 2 file boxes.

Field index maps of all taxing districts in county which have been used by assessor in preparation for sexennial re-appraisals of land. Blue on white. Each file box 15 x 21 x 12. Room 154, County courthouse.

1257. LAND VALUE MAPS
1890-1931. 232 volumes.

Maps indicating the rate per foot front on each street in county and rate per acre. Photostat. Volumes arranged by taxing districts. Volumes average 40 pages. 29 x 17 x 1.5. Scale, 50 and 100 feet to 1 inch. Rooms 59, 72, and 154, County courthouse.

1258. LAND VALUE CARDS
1931. Approximately 103,950 in 693 file boxes.

Cards for each parcel, and valuation thereof. Alphabetically arranged by owners for each city, township, and village. Handwritten on printed forms. Each file box 9.5 x 4.56 x 14. Room 154, County courthouse.

1259. INFORMATION INDEX FILE
1924——. 75 file boxes, 1-14, 200.

Data pertaining to real estate in Cuyahoga County assembled from such sources as newspapers, realtors, etc. Filed numerically. File box, 10 x 12 x 2.5. Room 154, County courthouse.

1260. RESUME RECORDS
Approximately 1900——. File started in 1933. 24 loose leaf-books in 12 file boxes.

Detailed records of all 99 year leases in county listing all data on the property secured from lease and other sources. In order of streets and street numbers. Typed. Volumes average 200 pages. Includes sketch of property. 10 x 12 x 2.5. Room 154, County courthouse.

1261. PUBLIC UTILITIES, SCHEDULES AND CORRESPONDENCE
1920-1932. 1 file box.

Schedules of properties owned by public utilities showing values of such properties, and relevant correspondence. Indicates location of property, general description listing number of lot and acre, and present assessed value and reassessed value, showing value of each lot, tract or parcel, total value in each taxing district, and total value in the county. File box 15 x 21 x 12. Room 154, County courthouse.

1262. REEVALUATION OF REAL PROPERTY
1840. 1 volume, City.

Lists name of owner, sublot number, part of lot owned, frontage, name of street, depth of lot, and value of property. Arranged alphabetically by owners. Handwritten on printed forms. 200 pages. 13 x 8 x 1. Second floor, Hart Building.

Personal Property Assessing and Inheritance Tax Division

Tax Lists

1263. DUPLICATE CLASSIFIED TAX CERTIFICATES
1932-1935—. 87 volumes.

Lists name and address of taxpayer, certificate number, total amount of tax, and taxing district in which property is located. Alphabetical by names of taxpayers. Typed on printed forms. Volumes average 1000 pages. 4.75 x 10.5 x 4.5.Room 141, County courthouse.

1264. TAX AND ASSESSMENT CERTIFICATES
1932-1935. 1932-1934. 9 file boxes, A-Z; 1935, 3 volumes, A-Z.

Lists name and address of taxpayer, total amount of assessment, payment number, amount still due, assessment number, and tax return number. Alphabetical by taxpayers. Handwritten and typed on printed forms. Volumes average 1000 pages. 8.5 x 14 x 3; each file box 5.5 x 10.5 x 27. 1932-1934, 9 file boxes, A-Z, Room 42; 1935, 3 volumes, A-Z, Room 141, County courthouse.

1265. AUDITOR'S DUPLICATE PERSONAL PROPERTY
1932. 10 volumes, (121-130; volumes are also marked A-Z and titled Classified Individuals, Classified Judiciaries, Classified Unincorporated, Classified Unincorporated Supplemental, General Individual, General Fiduciaries, General Unincorporated, Classified Corporations, Inter-County Corporation, Financial institutions, (Banks) Dealers and intangibles, insurance companies, public utilities, Corporations Supplemental and General Corporations).

List the assessment certificate number, name of taxpayer, address, productive investments, 5 percent tax rate, unproductive investments 2 mills, deposits 2 mills, credited 3 mills, final assessment, and amount of tax, money and other taxable intangibles, total tax for the year, amount of tax due, advance payment, date paid, and unpaid taxes for the year. Arranged alphabetically by taxpayers names. Typed on printed forms. Volumes average 300 pages. 19 x 17 x 2. Room 141, County courthouse.

1266. BUSINESS RETURNS OF TAXABLE PERSONAL PROPERTY OF PARTNERSHIPS, FIRMS AND INDIVIDUALS
1913. 2 volumes, A-Z.

Lists kind of business, name and address of partnership or firm, date of entry, date returned to county auditor, and date added by the county auditor. Alphabetical by names of partnerships or firms. Handwritten and typed. Volumes average 500 pages. 18 x 19 x 3.25. Room 72, County courthouse.

1267. INCORPORATED RETURNS OF TAXABLE PERSONAL PROPERTY
1924-1930. 25 volumes.

Lists kind of business; name and address; date return received by county auditor; date of certification by county auditor; all moneys in possession or on deposit; amount of excess credits; total amount of material; total amount of merchandise; total amount of all tools, machinery, and equipment; total amount of all moneys invested in stocks and bonds, or otherwise; average value of property converted into non-taxable securities. Alphabetical by names of corporations. Handwritten and typed. Volumes average 500 pages. 18 x 19 x 3.25. Room 72, County courthouse.

1268. ASSESSOR'S RETURNS OF PERSONAL PROPERTY OF BANKS
1930. 1 volume.

Lists name and address of owner, ward number, and tax value of property. Alphabetical by owners. Typed. 200 pages. 18 x 19 x 1. Room 72, County courthouse.

1269. ASSESSOR'S DUPLICATE OF PERSONAL PROPERTY
1928. 2 volumes.

Lists name and address of owner, listing number, and tax value of personal property. Alphabetical by names of owners in villages and townships. Typed. Volumes average 350 pages. 19.75 x 19 x 2. Room 72, County courthouse.

1270. UNINCORPORATED COMPANIES, RETURNS OF TAXABLE PERSONAL PROPERTY
1924-1929. 12 volumes.

Lists type of business; name and address; date return filed with county auditor; date return certified by county auditor; total amount of all moneys in possession or on deposit; total amount of excess credits; total amount of material; total amount of merchandise; total value of all tools, machinery, and equipment; total amount of all money invested in stocks or bonds, or otherwise; average value of property converted into non-taxable securities; total amount of office furniture and fixtures; total value of all automobiles, motor trucks, and other vehicles owned; total value of all livestock owned; and total value of all other personal property not listed. Alphabetical by names of unincorporated companies. Handwritten and typed. Volumes average 500 pages. 19 x 19 x 3.25. Room 72, County courthouse.

1271. TAX RETURNS OF NATIONAL AND STATE BANKS
1921-1930. 9 volumes. (1927, missing).

Lists name and address of owner, number of ward in which property is located, listing number, and tax value of property. Alphabetical by owners. Handwritten and typed. Volumes average 250 pages. 18 x 19 x 2.25. Room 72, County courthouse.

1272. AUTOS, CITY, TOWNSHIPS, AND VILLAGES
1924. 11 volumes, 94-104.

A list of taxes on automobiles for which returns were not made, listing name of owner, his address, make of car, type, year's model, list price, tax value, total tax due, and amount of tax collected if any. Alphabetical by owners. Typed on printed forms. Volumes average 200 pages. 18.5 x 16 x 3. Second floor, Hart Building.

1273. INCORPORATED COMPANIES' TAX RETURN
1898-1908. 7 volumes.

Shows amount listed for taxation by incorporated companies, name and address of company, amount of returns to auditor, amount added by board of revision, and total amount to be taxed. Alphabetical by names of property owners. Handwritten on printed forms. Volumes average 190 pages. 18.5 x 13 x 2. Room 70, County courthouse.

1274. JOURNAL OF ASSESSMENTS ON PERSONAL PROPERTY
1884-1891. 1 volume.

Lists name and address of owner, amount of assessments, and kind of personal property taxed. Arranged in order of board numbers. Handwritten. 200 pages. 14.5 x 20.5 x 2.75. Room 72, County courthouse.

1275. RECORD OF INDIVIDUAL AND PARTNERSHIP TRADERS
1884-1886. 1 volume.

A record of names and addresses of partners and kind of business. Arranged alphabetically. Handwritten on printed forms. 640 pages. 20 x 15 x 3. Room 70 County courthouse.

Returns

1276. CORPORATION TAX RETURNS
1932—. 12 file boxes; 196 volumes.

Gives names and addresses of corporations, kind of business, all tangible personal property, amount of stocks and bonds owned, total value of livestock owned, total value of machinery and tools owned, the depreciated book value of merchandise and material inventory, and sworn statement or affidavit of officials of corporations to truth of all statements made in returns. Alphabetical by names of corporations. Handwritten and typed on printed forms. Each file box 25 x 16 x 11; each cabinet 15 x 10.5 x 27. 1932, 10 file boxes, Attic storeroom, fourth floor; 1933, 54 volumes, Room 72; 1934, 68 volumes, Room 139; 1935, 74 volumes, Room 139; 1936, 2 file boxes, Room 139, County courthouse.

1277. ORIGINAL RETURNS, INCORPORATED COMPANIES
1923-1930. 205 volumes.

Personal property tax returns, listing name and address of owner, type of business, taxing district, what state laws organized under, authorized capital stock, stock subscribed but not paid for, issued and outstanding, principal office as specified in charts, principal accounting office, and properties owned. Alphabetical by owners. Handwritten and typed on printed forms. Volumes average 720 pages. 14 x 8.75 x 3. 1923, 24 volumes, second floor, Hart Building; 1927-1930, 181 volumes, Room 74, County courthouse.

1278. ORIGINAL PERSONAL PROPERTY RETURNS
1927-1930. 406 volumes. (1927, 96 volumes; 1928, 102 volumes; 1929, 101 volumes; 1930, 107 volumes).

Give name and address of owner, post office, and itemized list of properties. Alphabetical by property owners. Handwritten and typed on printed forms. Volumes average 800 pages. 14 x 8.75 x 3. Attic storeroom, fourth floor, County courthouse.

1279. ORIGINAL PROPERTY TAX RETURNS, INCORPORATED COMPANIES
1931. 50 volumes.

Gives name and addresses of incorporated companies, type of business, taxing district where business located, name and state under whose laws business is organized, amount of authorized capital stock, amount of stock subscribed for, amount of stock subscribed but not paid for, amount of stock outstanding, principal office of the corporation as specified in its charter, principal accounting office of corporation, and an itemized list of all property owned. Alphabetical by names of companies. Handwritten and typed on printed forms. Volumes average 700 pages. 14 x 8.75 x 3. Attic storeroom, fourth floor, County courthouse.

1280. INDIVIDUAL TAX RETURNS
1933. 222 volumes.

List name and address of owner, number, ward number, tax value of property, and amount of taxes. Alphabetical by owners. Handwritten and typed on printed forms. Volumes average 500 pages. 8.5 13.75 x 1.5. Room 72, County courthouse.

1281. BALANCE SHEETS OF INDIVIDUALS AND CORPORATIONS OF TOWNSHIPS
1929-1930. 4 volumes, A-Z.

List assets and liabilities, capital stock, and the complete financial status of individual corporations or personal property tax listing. Alphabetical by names of corporations. Handwritten and typed on printed forms. Volumes average 200 pages. 9 x 14 x 2. Room 42, County courthouse.

1282. NO PROPERTY REPORTS
1933-1935. 5 bundles, A-Z.
Give names and addresses of persons and corporations who have no personal property listing, and their reasons for not having personal property in Cuyahoga County. Alphabetical by names of persons and corporations. Handwritten and typed. Each bundle 15.5 x 10.5 x 27. 1933, 1 bundle, Room 72; 1934, 2 bundles, Room 42; 1935, 2 bundles, Room 42, County courthouse.

1283. INDIVIDUAL AND UNINCORPORATED PROPERTY TAX RETURN DUPLICATES
1932—. 41 file boxes; 349 volumes; 2 file cabinets.
Give names and addresses of owners, a list of all property owned, and tax evaluation of all property. Alphabetical by property owners. Handwritten and typed on printed forms. Each file box 8.5 x 14 x 3; each cabinet 15 x 10.5 x 27. Volumes average 8.5 x 14 x 2. 1932, 41 file boxes, Room 42; 1933, 139 volumes; 1934, 102 volumes; 1935, 108 volumes, Room 72; 1936, 2 large file cabinets, Room 141, County courthouse.

1284. ORIGINAL UNINCORPORATED BUSINESS RETURNS
1923-1930. 398 volumes. (1923, 72 volumes; 1927, 77 volumes, 1-78; 1928, 82 volumes, 1-84; 1929, 85 volumes, 1-85; 1930, 82 volumes, 1-83). (Missing: 1923, 3 volumes; parts of 1927, 1 volume, 16; 1928, 2 volumes, 11, 17; 1930, 3 volumes, 16).
Personal property tax returns, listing name; business and resident address of owner; taxing district; kind of business; telephone number; and properties owned. Alphabetical by owners. Handwritten and typed on printed forms. Volumes average 700 pages. 14 x 8.75 x 3. 1923, 72 volumes, second floor, Hart Building; 1927-1930, 326 volumes, Room 74, County courthouse.

1285. UNINCORPORATED BALANCE SHEET RETURNS SUBMITTED TO COUNTY AUDITOR
1930-1931. 110 volumes, (1930, 50 volumes, 1-50; 1931, 51 volumes, 1-51).
List type of business owner is operating, name and address of owner, date return received by county auditor, and date return certified by county auditor. Alphabetical by owners. Handwritten and typed. Volumes average 100 pages. 18 x 19 x 12. Room 72, County courthouse.

1286. ORIGINAL UNINCORPORATED BUSINESS RETURNS
1931. 81 volumes.

Gives name and address of unincorporated business, residence address of owner, taxing district, kind of business, telephone number, and itemized list of property. Alphabetical by owners. Handwritten and typed on printed forms. Volumes average 600 pages. 14 x 8.75 x 3. Attic storeroom, fourth floor, County courthouse.

1287. OMITTED AUTOS RETURNS
1925. 65 volumes. (1 volume, Cleveland, HA-HE, missing).

Gives name and address of owner, taxing district, make and model of car, list price and tax value. Alphabetical by owners. Handwritten and typed on printed forms. Volumes average 250 pages. 9 x 6.25 x 2.25. Second floor, Hart Building.

1288. OMITTED AUTO RETURNS
1927-1930. 59 volumes. (1929, missing).

Show name and address of owner; taxing district in which property is located; and make, model, list price, and tax value of the automobile. Alphabetical by owners. Handwritten and typed on printed forms. Volumes average 800 pages. 8.75 x 6.25 x 3. Attic storeroom, fourth floor, County courthouse.

1289. TREASURER'S MISCELLANEOUS RETURNS
1912. 1 volume, Cities, Townships, and Villages.

Lists affidavits by the real value of personal property, moneys on hand and on deposit, credits subject to taxation, ward number, date of affidavit, and name and address of person making return. Alphabetical by owners. Handwritten on printed forms. 300 pages. 11 x 9 x 3. Second floor, Hart Building.

Delinquent Tax List

1290. AUDITOR'S DUPLICATE-UNPAID TAXES ON PERSONAL PROPERTY
1883-1930. 43 volumes. 1906-1909, missing.

A record of unpaid taxes on personal property in city, township, and villages, listing name and address of owner; tax value; amount of unpaid tax; the penalty; and total tax. Alphabetical by owners in each city, township, and village. Handwritten on printed forms. Volumes average 190 pages. 20 x 17 x 1. Second floor, Hart Building.

1291. DUPLICATE UNPAID TAXES PERSONAL PROPERTY (Auditor's List of Unpaid Taxes on Personal Property Listed on Duplicate), 1920—. 43 volumes.
Lists name and address of owners and accumulated unpaid taxes. Alphabetical by names of owners. Handwritten and typed. Volumes average 1000 pages. 8.25 x 12 x 5. Room 141, County courthouse.

1292. DELINQUENCIES OF PERSONAL PROPERTY AND INCORPORATED COMPANIES
1922-1931. 8 volumes. (1926, 1929, missing).
A record of delinquent taxes made up semi-annually, listing semi-annual settlement, name of owner of property, house number, name of street, tax value, amount of general tax due, penalty for non-payment of taxes, in total amount of delinquent taxes on the property. Alphabetical by property owners. Handwritten and typed on printed forms. Volumes average 460 pages. 17.5 x 15 x 2. Room 70, County courthouse.

1293. INDEX OF DELINQUENT PERSONAL PROPERTY TAXES
1920-1929. 1 volume.
Index of owners, listing address, listing number, amount of delinquent tax and penalty. Handwritten and typed. 250 pages. 18 x 19 x 1.5. Room 42, County courthouse.

1294. COUNTY AUDITOR'S CUMULATIVE DELINQUENT PERSONAL AND PUBLIC UTILITY TAXES
1932. 5 volumes, 1-5. (1-4, A-Z; 5 Townships, Villages, and Cities).
List name of taxpayer; address; year entered; book, page and line number; certificate number; amount of delinquent tax, 10 percent penalty; total amount due; and taxing district. All taxes not general are entered as classified. Arranged alphabetically by name of taxpayer. Typed. 540 pages. 27 x 24 x 4. Room 141, County courthouse.

1295. UNPAID TAXES, PERSONAL PROPERTY
1885-1930. 37 volumes. (Missing: 1886-1888, 1906-1909, 1920-1923).
Lists name and address of owner, tax value, amount of unpaid tax, penalty, total amount due, date of payment, and date of settlement. Alphabetical by names of owners. Handwritten on printed forms. Volumes average 350 pages. 19.5 x 16.5 x 2.75. Second floor, Hart Building.

1296. DELINQUENT CHATTELS OF INDIVIDUALS
1920-1929. 2 volumes.
Lists listing number, name and address of owner, value of property, amount of unpaid tax, amount of penalty, total amount to be paid, and date of payment. Alphabetical by names of delinquent taxpayers. Typed. Volumes average 200 pages. 18 x 19 x 1. Room 72, County courthouse.

1297. DELINQUENT CHATTELS OF INCORPORATED AND UNINCORPORATED COMPANIES
1920-1930. 3 volumes.
Gives listing number, name and address of owner, total tax-dollar value, total amount of unpaid taxes, total amount of penalty, total amount due, dates on which payments made, and amount of payments. Alphabetical by names of owners. Typed. Volumes average 200 pages. 18 x 19 x 1. Room 72, County courthouse.

1298. UNPAID AUTO TAXES
1924-1930. 11 volumes. (1924, 3 volumes; 1925, 3 volumes, 103-105; 1926, 1 volume, 106; 1927, 1 volume, 113; 1928, 1 volume, 115; 1929, 1 volume, 118; 1930, 1 volume, 119).
Record of taxes on automobiles, showing name of owner who has failed to make a tax return on his car, and giving house number, name of street, make of car, type, year's model, list price, tax value, total tax due, amount of tax collected if any, and amount of tax unpaid. Alphabetical by owners. Typed on printed forms. Volumes average 200 pages.18.5 x 16 x 3. Second floor, Hart Building.

Abatements and Additions

1299. PERSONAL PROPERTY CERTIFICATES OF CORRECTIONS
1924—. 23 volumes.

Give name and address of property owner, taxing district in which property is located, and brief statement of reason for correction. Alphabetical by property owners. Handwritten on printed forms. Volumes average 250 pages. 7 x 8.25 x 1.5. 1924-1930, 18 volumes, second floor, Hart Building; 1932—, 5 volumes, Room 141, County courthouse.

1300. TAX ABATEMENT CERTIFICATES
1921-1925. 18 volumes.

Show certificate and abatement numbers, amount of abatement and date, name and address of owner to whom abatement was issued, reason for abatement, whether for first or last half of tax year, and total abatements. Arranged chronologically. Handwritten on printed forms. Volumes average 500 pages. 16.25 x 5.5 x 1.5. Attic storeroom, fourth floor, County courthouse.

1301. ADDITIONS AND ABATEMENTS
1927-1930. 6 file boxes.

Personal property complaints, listing petition number, abatement number, date complaint filed, name and address of owner, and reason for complaint. Arranged in order of statement numbers. For index see number 1302. Handwritten and typed on printed forms. Each file box 12 x 10.75 x 5. Room 42, County courthouse.

1302. INDEX OF PERSONAL PROPERTY ADDITIONS AND ABATEMENTS FOR UNINCORPORATED BUSINESS HOUSES, INDIVIDUALS AND ESTATES
1920-1930. 1 volume.

An index of owners, listing address, amount of delinquent tax, amount of penalty, and total amount of delinquent tax and penalty. Handwritten and typed. 250 pages. 18 x 19 x 1.5. Room 42, County courthouse.

1303. ASSESSOR'S ADDITIONS–OMITTED AUTOS
1926-1930. 6 volumes. (1926, 1 volume; 1928, 1 volume; 1929-1930, 4 volumes).

Lists number of entry, name and address of owner, make of car, type, year's model, license number, list price, tax value, amount paid if any, and date of payment. Alphabetical by owners. Typed on printed forms. Volumes average 350 pages. 19.5 x 19.5 x 1.75. Second floor, Hart Building.

Inheritance Taxes

1304. INHERITANCE TAX RETURNS
1933—. 219 file boxes.

Gives auditor's file number, name of estate, date order was received from court, date notice of appraisal was filed, date appraisal was made, date report of appraisal was filed, and an itemized statement of appraisal value of estate. Arranged in order of file numbers. For index see number 1305. Handwritten and typed. Each file box 5 x 10.5 x 13. Room 141, County courthouse.

1305. INDEX TO INHERITANCE TAX RETURNS
1919—. 3 volumes.

An alphabetical index of names of decedents, listing auditor's file number, name of executor or administrator, date application for release was filed, date release was granted, date appraisal was ordered, date notice of appraisal was published, date appraisal was made, and total amount of appraisal. Handwritten. Volumes average 300 pages. 20.5 x 14.5 x 5. Room 141, County courthouse.

Miscellaneous

1306. INDEX TO PERSONAL PROPERTY TAX RETURNS
1932—. 195 file drawers, containing cards; 395 drawers, containing addressograph plates with cards attached.

Alphabetical index of taxpayers, giving address of taxpayers, taxing district, and assessed value of property taxed. Typed. Card file drawers, 4.75 x 3.5 x 22; addressograph file drawers (card system), Room 139. Unincorporated business returns, 194 file drawers, and individual personal property returns, 196 file drawers (addressograph system), Room 141, County courthouse.

1307. CITATIONS FOR PERSONAL PROPERTY TAX
1933—. 6 volumes.

Notices to appear at the personal property tax department of the county auditor's office to clarify the personal property tax returns filed by the recipients. Lists name and address of the taxpayer and the citation number. Alphabetical by names of taxpayers. Typed on printed forms. Volumes average 2000 pages. 11 x 6.25 x 6.5. Periodically destroyed. Room at 141, County courthouse.

1308. CERTIFICATES OF CLASSIFIED PERSONAL PROPERTY TAX
1934. 5 file boxes.

Pay-in-orders listing bill number, name and address of property owner, taxpayers listed valuation of property owned, total amount of tax due, date bill was issued, and date return was filed. In order of taxing districts. Typed on printed forms. Each file box 5.5 x 10.5 x 27. Periodically destroyed. Room 42, County courthouse.

1309. CERTIFICATES OF TANGIBLE PERSONAL PROPERTY TAX
1934. 5 file drawers.

Pay-in- orders listing bill number, name and address of property owner, taxpayers listed valuation of property owned, total amount of tax due, date bill was issued, and date return was filed. In order of taxing districts. Typed on printed forms. Each file box 5.5 x 10.5 x 27. Periodically destroyed. Room 42, County courthouse.

1310. CERTIFICATES OF ADVANCE TAX PAYMENTS
1933. 13 file boxes.

Advance payment certificates, listing name and address of taxpayer, bill number, date bill was issued, tax return number, total listed tax valuation, total estimated amount of tax, amount of advanced payment, and date on which advanced payment was made. In chronological order. Typed on printed forms. Each file box 25 x 10.5 x 5. Periodically destroyed. Attic storeroom, fourth floor, County courthouse.

1311. CORRESPONDENCE FILES
1925—. 12 letter boxes.

General correspondence of the personal property and inheritance tax departments. Alphabetical by correspondence. Handwritten and typed. Each letter box 12 x 12 x 3. Room 42, County courthouse.

1312. STOCKHOLDERS' LISTS
1927—. 7 file boxes; 4 bundles. (1927-1931, 3 file boxes, 4 bundles; 1931—, 4 file boxes).

Bank lists, giving name and address of stockholder, the listing number, and number of shares owned. Alphabetical by names of stockholders. Handwritten and typed on printed forms. Each file box 5.5 x 10.5 x 27. 1927-1931, 3 file boxes, 4 bundles, Room 42; 1932—, 4 file boxes, Room 141, County courthouse.

1313. RESTORED CHECKS RECORD
1933. 1 file box.

Lists name and address of person issuing check to auditor's office, amount of check issued, date check was restored, and manner in which check was restored. Alphabetical by persons who issued the checks. Handwritten and typed on printed forms. File box 5.5 x 10.5 x 27. Room 42, County courthouse.

1314. PERSONAL PROPERTY COMPLAINTS
1925-1927. 2 file boxes.

Give name and address of taxpayer making complaints, petition number, abatement number, date complaint was filed, and complete record of actions taken. In order of petition numbers. Handwritten and typed on printed forms. Each file box 12 x 10.75 x 5. Room 42, County courthouse.

1315. BANKRUPT LETTERS OF FIRMS AND INDIVIDUALS
1925-1930. 1 letter box.

Letters received by the auditor's office on bankruptcy proceedings filed against individual persons and corporations. Alphabetical by names of persons and corporations. Handwritten and typed. Letter box 12 x 12 x 3. Room 42, County courthouse.

1316. SCRAP BOOKS ON TAX MATTERS; NEWSPAPER CLIPPINGS
1930-1934. 2 volumes.

Scrap books containing newspaper clippings on all tax matters that have received publicity. In chronological order. Printed clippings. Volumes average 100 pages. 14.5 x 11 x 1.75. Room 42, County courthouse.

Division of Weights and Measures

1317. RECORD OF COUNTY SEALER
1925—. 3 volumes.

Permanent record of county sealers inspection reports. For items listed see number 1319. Handwritten on printed forms. Volumes average 300 pages. 16 x 15 x 1. Room 32, County courthouse.

1318. DAILY REPORT OF COUNTY SEALER
1935—. 25 volumes.

Individual daily reports listing reports number, kind of business, name and address of dealer; names of the various scales, weights and measures, whether correct, adjusted, condemned, or condemned for repairs, and the total inspected. Arranged chronologically. Handwritten on printed forms. Volumes average 100 pages. 9 x 4 x .5. Periodically destroyed every two years. Room 32, County courthouse.

1319. WEEKLY SUMMARY OF OPERATIONS OF COUNTY SEALER
1932—. 1 letter box.

Weekly reports listing the various kinds of scales, measures, weights, etc., and the result of sealer's findings, such as found correct, correct sealed, adjusted and sealed, incorrect and condemned, condemned for repairs, recalls after repairs, total inspected, and general remarks. Arranged chronologically. Handwritten on printed forms. Loose-leaf 11 x 8.5. Periodically destroyed about every four years. Room 32, County courthouse.

1320. ANNUAL REPORTS OF COUNTY SEALER
1912—. 2 letter file boxes.

Contains weekly, monthly and annual summaries of the county sealer's inspection reports. For items listed see number 1319. Handwritten on printed forms. File box 12 x 10 x 4. Room 32, County courthouse.

In English law the treasurer's office was known as the lower house of the Exchequer or the Exchequer of Receipt, and later known as the office of the Treasurer of the Exchequer. Here the money was received, weighed or otherwise tested. (Holdsworth, *op. cit.,* I, 42; IX, 34).

As early as 1792 the Northwest Territory provided for the appointment by the territorial governor, of a county treasurer. However, the treasurer was not responsible for the collection of taxes. In 1795 the county commissioners and assessors were authorized to appoint a person in every township whose duty it was to collect the taxes. The act of 1792 was repealed four years later. In 1799 the office was re-created, and the county treasurer was charged with the duty of receiving and keeping all moneys due, or accrued to the use of the county. (Pease, *op. cit.,* 68, 206, 257, 496).

In 1803, at the first session of the general assembly, a bill was carried which provided that it shall be the duty of the associate judges of the court of common pleas to appoint a county treasurer, his duties to be practically the same as under the laws of the Northwest Territory, and his compensation to be 30 percent of all moneys collected. The judges also were delegated the power, formally vested in the county commissioners and assessor, to appoint townships collectors of taxes. (1 O. L. 98).

An act was carried in 1804, which authorized the county commissioners to appoint annually a county treasurer, who was given bond and whose duty it was to keep an accurate account of all receipts and disbursements. It was also the treasurer's duty to settle his accounts annually with the commissioners at their June meeting. The treasurer, as his compensation, received 4 percent of all moneys collected by him. (2 O. L. 154). Another statute enacted that year made the sheriff of each county the collector thereof. (2 O. L. 171).

In 1805 it was provided that the lister of property in each township (appointed by the county commissioners) should also be the collector of taxes therein, and that he should turn into the county treasury annually the full amount of tax listed on the tax duplicate. (3 O. L. 108). The office of township collector was abolished in 1810 and the county commissioners were authorized to appoint a county collector whose business it was to demand and collect from each person in the county all taxes charged on the tax duplicate. (8 O. L. 319). By enactment of 1827 the office of county collector was abolished and the duties of the office were added to those of the county treasurer. (25 O. L. 31).

In the same year an act was passed considerably enlarging the duties of the county treasurer. It provided for the election biennially of the county treasurer for each county in the state. Each county treasurer was required to take an oath of office, and to give bond which was to be approved by the county auditor, and to be in such amount as the commissioners directed. He was elected for a two year term, and received his compensation and fees allowed him for all moneys collected by him as county treasurer. The county commissioners filled any vacancy which might occur in the office of treasurer. Each county treasurer was authorized to appoint one or more deputies, and was liable for their conduct in office. Each business day, the treasurer made a statement to the county auditor for the preceding day, showing the totals of money received and paid out, the balance in the depository, and the balance in the treasury. He was required to make an annual settlement with the county auditor, on the first Monday in January, and to make a return of delinquency on tax duplicate. For money paid to the county treasurer (excepting such as was paid on account of taxes charged on the duplicate) the treasurer issued duplicate receipts, one of which was deposited with the county auditor. He was required to post notices in three places in each township in the county, and to insert such notices in a newspaper of general circulation in his county for six successive weeks, stating the amount of tax to be charged for state, township, county roads, or other purposes, on each $100 of valuation; also, on what day the treasurer or his deputy would be present at the place for holding election in each township, for the purpose of collecting taxes. Each county treasurer, on or before January 15 of each year was required to pay over to the treasurer of state all moneys received by him for state purposes, agreeable to the certificate of settlement with the auditor of his county, and to take duplicate receipts therefor, one of which was deposited with the auditor of the state. The treasurer was also required to make a full annual settlement with the county commissioners of his county. (25 O. L. 25-31).

A statute enacted in 1836 stipulated that all costs collected by the county prosecutor and received by the county treasurer were to be charged to the treasurer by the county auditor. (33 O. L. 45).

The act of 1825 prescribing the duties of the county treasurer was amended in 1842 requiring him to receive taxes and prohibiting him to distrain goods and chattel with non-payments by taxes until December 20, of each year. All sales of lands for delinquent taxes were to be made on the second Monday of January, and settlement with the county auditor and with the state treasurer was to take place on the first Monday of February. (41 O. L. 4-5).

The county treasurer was declared liable to the justices of the peace for unpaid cost in criminal cases, providing the case was not dismissed by him. (40 O. L. 54; 43 O. L. 67). In 1850 an act was passed empowering the auditor to issue orders on the county treasurer for the payment of all reasonable expenses arising out of the adjudication, care, and support of lunatics. (48 O. L. 86). An act of the general assembly abolishing the office of tax collector and empowering the county treasurer to receive and collect taxes for the county was passed April 13, 1852. (52 O. L. 124). In 1856 a measure was adopted which provided that no money shall be disbursed except by the county treasurer upon warrant of the county auditor. (53 O. L. 157).

The general assembly passed a number of acts in 1858 to meet the increasing business of the treasurer's office. One measure provided again for an annual settlement with the auditor and further provided that except for payments of taxes charged on the tax duplicate, and except for advanced payments, all payments of money into the county treasury shall be on the draft of the county auditor in favor of the county treasurer. (55 O. L. 44-114). The auditor of state was authorized to appoint a competent accountant for the purpose of examining any county treasury and counting the funds therein. (55 O. L. 44-114; 114 O. L. 728). The act of 1831 also amended in 1858 provided that the county treasurer shall keep his office in a room or rooms provided by the county commissioners, which shall constitute the county treasury, in which all public moneys and property in his possession shall be kept at all times. (55 O. L. 44). Another act provided for the payment of taxes to the county treasurer semi-annually, on or before the 20th day of December and of June of each year (55 O. L. 62), and that each county treasurer settle with the county auditor semi-annually. (55 O. L. 63). Further legislation provided that the county treasurer, within ten days after settlement with the county auditor, present to the state comptroller of the treasury, the certificates of the county auditor, setting forth the amount the county treasurer is compelled to pay into the state treasury. (55 O. L. 64). An additional measure required that the treasurer and the auditor, jointly, make a quarterly financial report in a newspaper of general circulation. (55 O. L. 99).

In April 1859 a law was enacted which provided that no claims against the county shall be paid by the county treasurer, otherwise than upon the allowance of the county commissioners and upon warrant of the county auditor, except in cases where the amount is fixed by law. (56 O. L. 130). An act of 1861 required the county treasurer to submit semi-annually to the auditor a list of delinquent taxes with a description of the property and reason for non-collection. The auditor was required to ascertain the true amount collected by the treasurer and the amount remaining in the hands of the treasurer belonging to each fund, and to deliver to the treasurer and the state auditor duplicate certificates for separate sums collected by the treasurer. (58 O. L. 128).

An act passed in 1875 provided that the treasurer shall bring suit to enforce tax liens in his own name as treasurer. (72 O. L. 37). A statute enacted February 17, 1887 specified that the treasurer shall, on order of the county commissioners, and on warrant of the county auditor pay the cost of burial of any pauper or unidentified person. (84 O. L. 29). The following year it was stipulated that the treasurer settle annually on September 1 with the county auditor for the preceding school year. (85 O. L. 194).

A measure adopted April 2, 1896 provided that in each county the commissioners thereof shall designate the banks or trust companies situated in the county as depositories of the money of the county, and that the treasurer shall, upon the written notice of the commissioners stating the name of the depositories selected, deposits in them to the credit of the county, all money in his possession except such amounts as may be necessary for current demands. (92 O. L. 353).

In 1888 the treasurer's salary was set at $5,000 a year and was augmented by a percentage of all sums collected by him. (85 O. L. 69). The fee system was abolished in 1906, and it was provided that all fees must be paid quarterly into the county treasury and that the county treasurer's salary was in no event to exceed $6,000 a year. (98 O. L. 89-97; 98 O. L. 6).

A measure enacted in 1917, provided that the county treasurer, the county auditor, and the president of the board of commissioners constitute a county board of revision, which was to meet annually. (107 O. L. 29-46). Later that year provision was made that no foreclosure proceedings or delinquent lands were to be instituted by the treasurer, unless the taxes, assessments, penalties and interest had not been paid for four years. (107 O. L. 735). An act passed in 1919, provided that in each county having a bonded indebtedness, there shall be a board designated as trustees of the sinking fund, to be composed of the auditor, treasurer, and prosecutor to provide for the payment of interest on all bonds issued by the county. (108 O. L. pt. 1, 700-702). On August 10, 1927 a budget commission was provided for to consist of the county auditor, treasurer, and prosecutor, of which the auditor is secretary. (112 O. L. 399).

An act of 1931 provided for a semi-annual settlement by the treasurer with the auditor for all taxes collected on the general duplicate a real and public utility property, and for all advance payments of taxes on personal and classified property. (114 O. L. 731). It was also provided that when taxes, other than those upon real estate, are past due and unpaid, the county treasurer may distrain sufficient goods and chattel if found within the county and belonging to the person charged with such taxes, for payment taxes remaining due and for accrued cost. An amendment in 1931 to the act of 1917 provided that foreclosure may be instituted on delinquent lands in three years instead of four. (114 O. L. 1833). Another measure was adopted that year providing for the payment of delinquent taxes in five semi-annual installments. A similar act was approved in 1933 as an emergency measure for three years, and is known as the Whittmore Law. It also provided for a remission of interest and penalties. (114 O. L. 827; 115 O. L. 161-164).

In 1933 and amendment to the Ohio Constitution authorizing the creation of a charter commission, removed the disability by tenure of office of county officers. (Ohio Const., Art. 10, sec. 3). Buy enactment in 1933, the treasurer was authorized to invest county funds in his possession in short term federal bonds. (115 O. L. pt. 2, 64). Another measure was passed that year provided for the payment of assessments, by bonds issued for the payment of the improvement for which such assessment was made. (115 O. L. pt. 2, 326).

An act of 1936 provided that the county treasurer shall be elected quadrennially in each county. (116 O. L. pt. 2, 1079).

Tax Duplicate, Abatements and Additions

1321. TREASURER'S DUPLICATE OF REAL AND PERSONAL PROPERTY
1820—. 4187 volumes. (Missing: 1821-1833, 15 volumes; 1835-1843, 46 volumes; 1847, 1 volume; 1885, 1 volume; 1886, 8 volumes).
The treasurer's duplicate is an exact copy of the auditor's, and for the years 1880 to date contains a list of all property owners in the county, showing map district and page number, name of subdivision, original lot number, sublot number, what part of lot is owned, acreage, frontage, depth, land value, building value, total value, general tax, school tax, special assessments, delinquent tax, total tax, amounts due and collected in December, amounts due and collected in June, and total tax unpaid and carried to duplicate for the following year. For variations of forms used previously to 1880 see report of auditor's duplicate of taxes collected. Alphabetical

by owners in each city, township, and village. 1820-1850 handwritten; 1851-1905, handwritten on printed forms; 1906—, handwritten and typed on printed forms. Volumes 1820-1834, average 300 pages. 12.5 x 8.5 x 2. 1835-1877, 900 pages. 17 x 13 x 3. 1878-1933, 400 pages. 19 x 17 x 2.5. 1934, 140 pages. 20 x 22.5 x 2. 1820-1912, 1923-1924, second floor, Hart Building; 1913-1922, 1924-1933, Room 74; 1934, Race Track; 1935-1936, Race Track, County courthouse.

1322. TREASURER'S ADDITIONS
1879—. 43 volumes. (Missing: 1891, 1893, 1894, 1903).

A list of additions on real and personal property made by the auditor in each city, township, and village, showing name of owner, map and page number, date of addition, name of subdivision, original lot number, sublot number, what part of lot owned, frontage, name of street, tax value, gain to duplicate, general tax, special tax, prior delinquencies, total tax, amount collected in December, amount collected in June, amount uncollected for the year, date of mailing, petition number, and reason why addition was made. In order of abatement numbers. Handwritten on printed forms. Additions for personal property are listed separately for 1930 to date. Volumes average 500 pages. 18.5 x 17 x 2.5. 1879-1919, second floor, Hart Building; 1920-1933, Room 74; 1934—, Race Track, County courthouse.

1323. TREASURER'S ABATEMENT
1878-1896. 5 volumes. (1878-1889, 1 volume; 1886-1889, 1 volume; 1891-1893, 1 volume; 1894-1895, 1 volume; 1895-1896, 1 volume). (1890, missing).

Gives name of abatement, location of property, description of property, name of street, value of property, amount of tax, for which collection (December or June) abatement was allowed, and amount allowed. In order of abatement numbers. Typed on printed forms. Volumes average 400 pages. 15 x 18.5 x 2. Now listed in regular duplicate. Second floor, Hart Building.

Personal Property Tax Payments and Delinquencies

1324. TREASURER'S GENERAL PERSONAL PROPERTY DUPLICATE
1933—. 88 volumes.

Lists bill number, name of taxpayer, tax return number, type of return, class of property, total assessed value, penalty assessed, total assessments, rate, total tax, advance payment number, and amount; amount due, if any, and date paid.

Numerical by bill numbers and alphabetical by taxpayers in each taxing district. Typed and handwritten on printed forms. Volumes average 780 pages. 10.25 x 4.75 x 3.5. 1933-1934, 44 volumes, Room 74; 1935—, 44 volumes, Room A, County courthouse.

1325. TREASURER'S GENERAL PERSONAL PROPERTY TAX DUPLICATE ADDITION BOOK

1933—. 4 volumes.

Lists bill number, name of taxpayer, tax return number, type of return, class of property, total assessed value, penalty assessment, total assessment, rate, total tax; amount due, and date paid. Numerical by bill numbers and alphabetical by taxpayers. Typed and handwritten on printed forms. Volumes average 200 pages. 10.25 x 4.75 x 3.5. 1933-1934, 2 volumes, Room 74; 1935—, 2 volumes, Room A, County courthouse.

1326. TREASURER'S CLASSIFIED TAX DUPLICATE

1933—. 158 volumes.

Lists duplicate number, return number, type of return, taxpayer's name, class of property and rate, total value assessed, penalty assessment, total assessment, tax on each class of property, total tax, advance payment number, its amount, total due and date paid. In order of duplicate numbers and alphabetically by taxpayers by districts. Typed and handwritten on printed forms. Volumes average 1000 pages. 10.25 x 4.75 x 4.5. 1933-1934, 86 volumes, Room 74; 1935—, 72 volumes, Room A, County courthouse.

1327. TREASURER'S CLASSIFIED TAX DUPLICATE ADDITION BOOK

1932—. 10 volumes.

Lists duplicate number, return number, type of return, taxpayer's name, class of property and rate, total value assessed, penalty assessment, total assessment, tax on each class of property, total tax, advanced payment number, its amount, total tax due, and date paid. In order of duplicate numbers and alphabetically by taxpayers by districts. Typed and handwritten on printed forms. Volumes average 250 pages. 10.25 x 4.75 x 4.5. 1932-1934, 8 volumes, Room 74; 1935—, 2 volumes, County courthouse.

1328. ADVANCED PAYMENT PERSONAL TAX BILLS AND RECEIPTS, TANGIBLE AND INTANGIBLE

1931—. 15 cardboard storage cases; 6 file boxes.

Record of payments made at the time of tax returns. Arranged numerically. Typed on printed forms. Each case 25.5 x 10.5 x 8.5. Each file box 4.75 x 10.75 x 13.5. 1931-1935, 15 storage cases, Room 74; 1936—, 6 file boxes, Room A, County courthouse.

1329. CUMULATIVE DELINQUENT TAX DUPLICATE

1932—. 46 volumes.

Copy of delinquent list showing year entered, account or book number, page number, line number, principal amount of tax, amount of delinquent penalty, total amount of delinquent, semi-annual collection reports for each year, amount paid and date paid for each collection. Arranged alphabetically by taxing district and numbered by accounts. Volumes average 1000 pages. 11.75 x 9 x 5.5. Room A, County courthouse.

1330. DELINQUENT PERSONAL TAX BILLS

First half 1935. 69 bundles.

Tax bills returned by post office because of wrong address or non-delivery. Arranged in order of tax book numbers and bill numbers. Handwritten on printed forms. Each bundle 10 x 4.5 x 1.5. Second floor, Hart Building.

1331. PERSONAL DELINQUENT CORRESPONDENCE

1919-1934. 14 letter boxes; 1 cardboard storage case, 8 bundles.

Correspondence between the delinquent taxpayers and the county treasurer concerning failure to pay personal tax. Alphabetically by correspondents. Typed and handwritten. Each letter box 11.75 x 12 x 3; storage case 25.5 x 10.5 x 8.5; each bundle 10 x 12 x 4. Second floor, Hart Building.

1332. CORPORATION DISSOLUTION CORRESPONDENCE

1927-1930. 3 letter boxes.

Correspondence concerning the dissolving of corporations. Arranged alphabetically by names of corporations. Typed. Each letter box 11.75 x 12 x 3. Second floor, Hart Building.

1333. BANKRUPTCY CASES PENDING
1934——. 5 metal file drawers.
A card system showing case number, disposition, date, amount of tax, and name and address of taxpayer. Filed alphabetically. Typed and handwritten on printed forms. Each file drawer 8 x 12 x 6. Room A, County courthouse.

1334. BANKRUPTCIES
1934——. 3 metal file drawers.
Active bankruptcy case reports, and relevant correspondence. Filed alphabetically. Typed and handwritten on printed forms. Each file drawer 16 x 24.5 x 12. Room A, County courthouse.

1335. DISSOLVED CORPORATIONS
1934——. 1 metal file drawer.
General correspondence and reports of dissolved corporations. Indexed alphabetically. Handwritten and typed on printed forms. File drawer 16 x 24.5 x 12. Room A, County courthouse.

1336. DISTRESS ACTIONS
1934——. 1 metal file drawer.
Contains distress and pre-distress cases. Indexed alphabetically. Handwritten on printed forms. File drawer 16 x 24.5 x 12. Room A, County courthouse.

1337. CORRESPONDENCE
1934——. 3 metal file drawers.
Contains personal correspondence, letters and opinions of the Attorney General, Board of Revision notes, bills (Senate and House), legal opinions, etc. Filed alphabetically. Handwritten and typed. Each file drawer 16 x 24.5 x 12. Room A, County courthouse.

1338. MISCELLANEOUS
1934——. 2 metal file drawers.
Contains partial and full release of liens, affidavits, protest letters, and miscellaneous correspondence. Indexed alphabetically. Typed and handwritten. Each file drawer 16 x 24.5 x 12. Room A, County courthouse.

1339. GENERAL FILES

1934—. 11 letter file boxes.

Contain general correspondence, cases held for investigation, form letters, partial payments, extensions, notices of appeal and probate court certificates. Filed alphabetically. Typed and handwritten or printed forms. Each file box 12 x 11.5 x 3. Room A, County courthouse.

Delinquencies and Foreclosures

1340. TREASURER'S DUPLICATE OF TAXES CERTIFIED DELINQUENT

1918-1934. 52 volumes.

A record of delinquent lands certified to the auditor of state from Cuyahoga County; also a record of interest, advertising, and certification fees paid on lands redeemed, listing name of owner, map district number, name of subdivision, original lot or block number, sublot number, what part of lot owned, frontage, street, depth, total tax value, total tax certified delinquent, amount of interest collected, advertising costs, and certification fee. Alphabetical by names of owners in each city, township, and villages. Typed on printed forms. Volumes average 600 pages. 19.5 x 19.5 x 3.5. 1918-1919, 1921-1925, second floor, Hart Building; 1920, Attic storeroom, fourth floor; 1928-1931, Room 74; 1932, 1934, Room 53, County courthouse. 1935—, listed in Tax Duplicate.

1341. LIST OF DELINQUENT TAXES

1886. 1 volume, City, Townships, and Villages.

Gives certification number, name of owner, name of subdivision, original lot or block number, sublot number, description of property, total tax value, and total tax certified delinquent. Arranged alphabetically by names of owners. Handwritten on printed forms. 350 pages. 19 x 12 x 1.5. Second floor, Hart Building.

1342. TAX SALE

1900-1914. 12 volumes.

A record of property sold by the county for taxes, listing name of owner, book, page, line, bill number; and amount of tax. Alphabetical by owners. Handwritten. Volumes average 350 pages. 14 x 9.25 x 1.5. Second floor, Hart Building.

1343. CERTIFIED IN 1923 FOR FORECLOSURE
1923. 1 volume.

A record of delinquent property in the county, which was certified to the county treasurer by the state auditor for foreclosure. It lists name of owner, map district and page number of parcel, name of subdivision, original lot number, sublot number, name of street, and amount of delinquent tax. Alphabetical by owners in cities, townships, and villages. Typed on printed forms. 300 pages. 14.5 x 17 x 1.5. Second floor, Hart Building.

1344. COUNTY AUDITOR'S CERTIFICATE OF COSTS OF REDEMPTION OF LANDS CERTIFIED DELINQUENT
1918-1934. 53 volumes; 31 bundles. (1919, 1931, 1933, missing).

Gives location of property, certification number, name of owner, description of property, taxes and penalties, and total amount of interest. Alphabetical by owners. Typed on printed forms. Volumes average 1500 pages. 15.25 x 9.75 x 3; bundles average 3000 pages. 15.25 x 9.75 x 5.5. Second floor, Hart Building.

Cashier's General Records

1345. DAILY STATEMENT OF COUNTY TREASURER
1829—. 50 volumes; 1 bundle. (1829-1849, 2 volumes; 1888-1889, 1 volume; 1889-1890, 1 volume; 1890-1893, 1 volume; 1893-1894, 1 volume; 1894-1898, 1 volume; 1901-1902, 1 volume; 1904-1924, 27 volumes; 1907-1922, 5 volumes; 1906-1930, 5 volumes; 1926-1928, 1 volume; 1927, 1 volume; 1932, 1 bundle; 1932-1933, 1 volume; 1933, 1 volume; 1935—, 1 volume).

Daily statements of the treasurer to the auditor of moneys belonging to Cuyahoga County, showing amount recorded, amount disbursed, amount deposited in bank, balance in depository and in treasury at close of business, and date of each statement. In chronological order. Handwritten on printed forms. Volumes average 600 pages. 15 x 9 x 3. 1829-1930, second floor, Hart Building; 1926-1928, Room 43; 1932-1933, Room 74; 1935—, Room 162, County courthouse.

1346. TRANSFER JOURNAL OF DISBURSEMENTS
1860—. 43 volumes. (1860-1879, 2 volumes; 1878-1880, 1 volume; 1882, 1 volume; 1888-1894, 5 volumes; 1891-1896, 1 volume; 1896-1900, 2 volumes; 1897-1900, 2 volumes; 1900-1902, 1 volume; 1904-1909, 1

volume; 1910-1921, 3 volumes; 1924-1931, 3 volumes; 1908-1933, 13 volumes; 1933—, 8 volumes).

Copies of statements of the condition of county treasury, showing name of person to whom disbursed, number of warrant, name of depository, amount of warrant, and name of fund on which warrant was drawn. In chronological order. Handwritten on printed forms. Volumes average 600 pages. 17 x 11 x 2. 1860-1921, 19 volumes; 1908-1933, 13 volumes; second floor, Hart Building; 1924-1931, 3 volumes, Room 43; 1933—, 8 volumes, Room 162, County courthouse.

1347. TREASURER'S LEDGER

1886—. 17 loose-leaf volumes. (1886-1926, 14 volumes; 1923—, 3 volumes). (1927-1932, missing).

A record of receipts and disbursements of the county, showing under the names of various funds, the purpose for which entry was made, receiving order number, total receipts, balance in treasury, and amount disbursed. Arranged alphabetically by names of funds. Handwritten on printed forms. Volumes average 400 pages. 18 x 15 x 3. 1886-1926, 14 volumes, second floor, Hart Building; 1933—, 3 volumes, Room, 161, County courthouse.

1348. CASHIER'S COLLECTION SHEET

1913—. 39 loose-leaf volumes. (January 1, 1913- September 4, 1926, 25 volumes; January 18, 1932-first half 1934, 12 volumes; second half of 1934, 1 volume; first half of 1935, 1 volume). (1927-1931, missing).

Daily reports of collection of each cashier, listing name of cashier, number of sheets, date of collection, and amount of collection. Chronological. Handwritten and typed on printed forms. Volumes average 1000 pages. 12 x 17 x 6. 1913-1926, second floor, Hart Building; 1932-1934, Room 74; 1934-1935, Room 161, County courthouse.

1349. DEPOSITORY ACCOUNTS

November 1905—. 18 loose-leaf volumes, 1 bundle; 4 cardboard storage cases. (1905-1906, 2 volumes; 1909-1920, 4 volumes; 1925-1935, 11 volumes; 1928, 1 bundle; 1933-1935, 4 cardboard storage cases; 1936—, 1 volume). (1907-1908; 1921-1924 missing).

A record listing date and amount of deposit, amount withdrawn, balance, depository report, amount outstanding, and name of bonds. In order of depository numbers. Typed on printed forms. Volumes average 300 pages. 24 x 13 x 1; each bundle 24 x 12 x 4; each case 18 x 32 x 13. 1905-1924, second floor, Hart Building; 1925-1935, Room 43; 1936—, Room 161, County courthouse.

1350. TREASURER'S RECORD OF FEES
January 1, 1907-August 21, 1917. 1 volume.

Fees collected from the various county officials, listing date of each entry; by whom paid; total payment; general settlement; other settlements; transfers and additions; payments for ditches, pikes, and sundries. Chronological. Handwritten. 400 pages. 16.25 x 11.75 x 2. Second floor, Hart Building.

1351. INHERITANCE TAX CHARGE
1919—. 12 volumes. (October 4, 1919-October 5, 1923, 2 volumes; January 2, 1925-1934, 9 volumes; September 1935—, 1 volume). October 5, 1923-January 2, 1925, missing).

Lists name and address of decedent, date of accruement of tax, amount of tax fixed by court, discount allowed or interest charged, and total amount of tax paid. Chronological by dates of payments. Handwritten and typed on printed forms. Volumes average 1700 pages. 14.5 x 12.5 x 4.75. 1919-1923, 2 volumes, second floor, Hart Building; 1925-1934, 9 volumes, Room 74; September 1935—, 1 volume, Room 161, County courthouse.

1352. CANCELLED CHECKS
1915—. (1915-1918, 1 file box; 1921-1926, 29 bundles; 1933-1936, 67 cardboard file boxes; current checks, 1 bundle). (1927-1932, missing).

Checks covering various funds. Typed and handwritten on printed forms. File box 2.5 x 18 x 11; each bundle 8.5 x 10 x 3.5. 1915-1926 second floor, Hart Building; 1933-1936, Room 74; current checks, Room 159, County courthouse.

1353. CHECK STUBS
1933—. 3 cardboard storage cases, 12 books. (1933-1934, 3 cardboard storage cases; 1934—, 12 books).

Stubs of checks drawn on Central United Bank and the Cleveland Trust Company. In order of check numbers. Typed on printed forms. Books average 100 pages. 25.5 x 10.5 x 8.5. 1933-1935 Room 74; 1935—, Room 159, County courthouse.

Overpayments

1354. RECORD OF OVERPAYMENTS
1915—. 18 volumes. (1915-1916, 1 volume; 1917-1918. 1 volume; 1819-
1922, 2 volumes; 1923-1924, 1 volume; 1925-1926, 1 volume; 1931-1933,
4 volumes; 1933, 3 volumes; 1927—, 5 volumes).

Record of double and overpayments listing date of payment; name of remitter;
book, page and line number; name in which property is listed; name and address of
person to whom refunded; amount paid; amount due; amount overpaid; how
refunded, whether by check, cash, or stamps; name of bank; and number of check.
Chronological by dates of payments. Handwritten on printed forms. Volumes
average 600 pages. 16 x 14.5 x 3.5. 1915-1918, 1923-1933, Second floor, Hart
Building; 1919-1922, Room 74; 1933, 1927—, Room 162, County courthouse.

1355. SMALL OVERPAYMENT RECEIPTS
1919-1932. 24 letter boxes.

Regular tax bill receipts of overpayment of taxes. Arranged alphabetically by
owners. Handwritten. Each letter box 11.75 x 12 x 3. Second floor, Hart Building.

1356. REQUEST FOR REFUND OF OVERPAYMENT OF TAXES
1920—. 17 volumes.

Lists date and number of request; book, page, and line number of parcel on which
overpayment has been made; original lot number; sublot number; and location of
property. Chronological by dates of request. Handwritten on printed forms.
Volumes average 120 pages. 13.75 x 9.75 x .5. 1920-1933, 15 volumes, Room 74;
1934—, 2 volumes, Room 161, County courthouse.

Tax Collections, Real and Personal Property

1357. TAXES COLLECTED
1886—. 591 volumes. (1911 missing).

An itemized list of taxes collected by the treasurer, showing book, page and line
number of tax duplicate where payment is credited to owner; date and amount of
payment. Each volume numbered with inclusive numbers of volumes of duplicate
to which it refers; the entries within are in chronological order. Typed on printed
forms. Volumes average 350 pages. 19 x 17 x 1.5. 1886-1928, second floor, Hart
Building; 1929-1935, Room 74, County courthouse.

1358. TAXES COLLECTED BY VARIOUS SUBSTATIONS

Last half 1932, 1 loose-leaf volume; first half 1933, 1 loose-leaf volume.
A record of receipts issued to the collector of taxes in each subdivision, listing tax
book number, tax bill number, and amount of tax collected. Arranged
chronologically by dates of payments. Handwritten on printed forms. Volumes
average 100 pages. 11.5 x 11.5 x 1. This record discontinued September, 1933.
Room 74, County courthouse.

1359. TREASURER'S TOWNSHIP RECEIPTS

April 1861-August 1873. 2 volumes.
Receipts for moneys collected on duplicates turned over to township, with a listing
of items for which money was to be used. Arranged chronologically by dates of
receipts. Handwritten on printed forms. Volumes average 60 pages. 8.75 x 14 x 2.
Second floor, Hart Building.

1360. RECAPITULATIONS OF COLLECTIONS

1888—. 101 loose leaf volumes. (1888-1890, 1 volume; 1894, 3 volumes;
1896, 3 volumes; 1897, 3 volumes; 1898, 2 volumes; 1898-1902, 1 volume;
1899, 4 volumes; 1900, 3 volumes; 1901, 3 volumes; 1902, 3 volumes;
1905, 1 volume; 1906, 3 volumes; 1907, 1 volume; 1908, 2 volumes; 1909,
6 volumes; 1910, 8 volumes; 1911, 3 volumes; 1912, 1 volume; 1913, 2
volumes; 1914, 2 volumes; 1915, 1 volume; 1916, 2 volumes; 1917, 2
volumes; 1918, 2 volumes; 1919, 2 volumes; 1920-1930, 20 volumes; 1931-
1934, 6 volumes; 1933-1934, 2 volumes; 1934, 1 volume; 1935, 1 volume;
1935—, 4 volumes). (1891-1893, 1903, 1904, missing).

Lists date of each collection, number of tax duplicate in which posted, amount of
collection at each instance, and total amount collected daily. Entries are in
chronological order. The volume is identified by year, first half or last half.
Handwritten on printed forms. Volumes average 200 pages. 24 x 12 x 1.5. 1889-
1920, second floor, Hart Building; 1920-1930, Room 43; 1931-1935, Room 74;
1935, Room 159; 1936, Room 161, County courthouse.

1361. CHECKS RESTORED TO DUPLICATE
1921—. 10 letter boxes, 3 file boxes. (1921-1924, 10 letter boxes; 1933—, 3 file boxes). (1925-1932, missing)
So-called "rubber" checks, given as payments to apply on real or personal property taxes, posted on the duplicate to credit on property designated, sent to bank, return to treasurer because of insufficient funds, and filed away. Filed chronologically. Handwritten on printed forms. Each letter box 11.75 x 12 x 3. Each metal file box 4 x 8 x 12. 1921-1924, 10 letter boxes, second floor, Hart Building; 1933—, 3 metal file boxes, Room 161, County courthouse.

1362. CASHIER'S STUBS (retained by cashier or payment of taxes)
1926—. 158 cardboard storage cases. (1926 to first half 1932, 98 cardboard storage cases; last half 1932, 3 cardboard storage cases; first half 1933, 21 cardboard storage cases; last half 1933, 23 cardboard storage cases; first half 1934, 21 cardboard storage cases).
Show name of owner; book, page, and line number; sublot number; amount of tax paid; and date of payment. Alphabetical by names of owners in cities, townships, and villages. Handwritten on printed forms. Each case 25.5 x 10.5 x 8.5. 1926 to first half 1932, Room 43; last half 1932 to first have 1934, Room 74, County courthouse.

1363. DUPLICATE TAX RECEIPTS
First half 1934. 186 volumes, Cities Townships, Villages.
A duplicate of the regular receipt mailed to taxpayers, giving lot number; sublot number; description of property; and book, page, and line number of the tax duplicate. Alphabetical by names of owners. Handwritten on printed forms. Volumes average 100 pages. 16 x 5.5 x .75. Room 74, County courthouse.

License Tax Collections

1364. ITEMIZED LIST OF TAX PAID FOR LICENSES
1849-1917. 2 volumes. (1849-1961, 1 volume; 1907-1917, 1 volume).
Date of payment, name of taxpayer, and amount of taxes; contains names of peddlers, auctioneers, circuses, insurance companies, taverns, ferries, and sundries; and lists notes receivable belonging to the county, forfeited land sales, and total amount of cash received. Chronological by dates of payments. Handwritten. Volumes average 200 pages. 8 x 12.5 x 1. Second floor, Hart Building.

1365. CIGARETTE AND LIQUOR DUPLICATE
1894-1931. 29 volumes. (1894, 1 volume; 1906-1931, 28 volumes). (1895-1905, 1908, missing).

Shows date of assessment, amount of assessment, date of payment, and allowance for discontinuance. Alphabetical by vendors. Handwritten. Volumes average 200 pages. 19.5 x 16.5 x 2.5. Second floor, Hart Building.

1366. LIQUOR AND CIGARETTE TAX COLLECTED
1895—. 11 volumes. (no date, 1 volume; 1895-1897, 3 volumes; 1909-1923, 4 volumes; 1930-1932, 2 volumes; 1934—, 1 volume). (1898-1908, 1911, 1924-1929, missing).

Record of moneys collected by treasurer for liquor and cigarette taxes, listing date of payment; page, line and bill number; and amount of tax collected. Alphabetical by vendors. Handwritten. Volumes average 350 pages. 13.75 x 9.25 x 1.25. 1895-1923, second floor, Hart Building; 1930-1932, Room 74; 1934—, Room 161, County courthouse.

1367. RECEIPT STUB CERTIFICATE DEALERS' LICENSE TAX
1925—. (1925-1933, 6 bundles; 1934—, 22 books). (1928-1930 missing).

Stub lists ward number, number of license, page and line number of entry, name of person to whom issued, and name of property owner. In order of stub numbers. Handwritten on printed forms. Each bundle 15 x 10.75 x 4. Books average 150 pages. 4 x 4 x .5. 1925-1933, second floor, Hart Building; 1934-1935, Room 74; current stubs, Room 161, County courthouse.

1368. LIST OF TRAFFICKERS IN CIGARETTES
1894-1908. 10 volumes. (1897, 1904, 1905, 1906, 1907, missing).

Name and address of vendor, name of property owner, amount of assessment, penalty, total assessment and penalty due, date of payment. Alphabetical. Handwritten. Volumes average 150 pages. 19.5 x 17.75 x 1. Second floor, Hart Building.

1369. LIST OF DEALERS IN CIGARETTES WHO HAVE NOT OBTAINED 1931-1932 LICENSE
1930-1931. 1 letter box.

List of dealers examined and approved by the commanding officer in each precinct; and general correspondence relating to cigarette taxes. Arranged alphabetically.

Handwritten and typed. Letter box 11.75 x 12 x 3. Room 74, County courthouse.

1370. LIQUOR DUPLICATE
1884-1917. 33 volumes. (1884-1903, 20 volumes; 1905-1909, 5 volumes,; 1910-1917, 8 volumes). (1904, 1 volume missing).

Name of dealer, location of business, name of owner of property, description of property, amount of delinquency, amount assessed, date of payment, and amount collected. Alphabetical by dealers in taxing districts. Handwritten. Volumes average 500 pages. 21.75 x 18.75 x 2.5. Second floor, Hart Building.

1371. LIQUOR VIOLATIONS
1920. 1 volume. A-Z.

Name of violator, location of business, name of owner of property, description of property, date of assessment, amount of assessment, assessment including penalty, amount paid on liquor duplicate, amount paid on real estate duplicate, date of abatement or remittance, amount abated on real estate duplicate, amount remitted on liquor duplicate, date carried to real estate duplicate, and name of person against whom certified. Alphabetical by names of violators. Handwritten. 150 pages. 10.25 x 15.5 x 1. Second floor, Hart Building.

1372. SALOON KEEPERS
1900. 2 volumes.

Gives name and address of each saloon keeper, ward number, date of license issue, and pertinent remarks. Alphabetically arranged. Handwritten. Volumes average 125 pages. 13.25 x 17.25 x 1.25. Second floor, Hart Building.

1373. SALES REPORTS OF TAX STAMPS SOLD
1932-1935. 8 bundles.

Gives name and address of vendor to whom stamps were sold, quantity of stamps sold, and amount of sale. Arranged chronologically by dates of sales. Handwritten on printed forms. Each bundle 10.5 x 9.5 x 8. Room 74, County courthouse.

1374. INVENTORY AND SALES OF EXCISE STAMPS
October 1935—. 1 volume.

Lists date of each sale; denominations of tax stamps; number of stamps sold and on hand; and denominations for beer, wine, malt, cigarettes, and mixed beverages.

There is a separate form for individual persons. The old system was discarded in October 1935. Chronological by dates of sales. Handwritten on printed forms. 150 pages. 18 x 14 x 1.5. Room 159, County courthouse.

1375. BEVERAGE AND MALT DAILY STAMP SALES
July 1935—. 1 volume.

A record listing the number of stamps received from the state, date of receipt, number on hand, number sold, balance on hand, and amount of money received for stamps sold. Chronologically by dates of sales. Handwritten. 300 pages. 10.75 x 8.5 x 1. Room 161, County courthouse.

Bonds

1376. BOND RECORD
1924—. 1 volume. 1 metal file box.

Lists bonds of treasurers of various municipalities and townships in the county. Arranged chronologically by dates of issue. Typed and written. Volumes average 640 pages. 18.25 x 11.5 x 2.25. File box 4 x 8 x 12. Beginning 1933 bond record discontinued, and original bonds are now kept. 1 volume, second floor, Hart Building; 1 file box, Room 161, County courthouse.

1377. COUPONS REDEEMED
April 1935—. One loose-leaf volume.

Lists date of redemption, kind of coupon, name of bond, number and amount of coupon, and total amount redeemed to date. Arranged chronologically by dates of redemption. Typed on printed forms. 100 pages. 14 x 8.5 x .5. Room 74, County courthouse.

1378. RECORD OF CENTRAL ARMORY BONDS
1893-1918. 1 volume.

Redeemed bonds, with the amount of interest paid on them, pasted to the pages of the volume. Arranged chronologically by dates of payments. Typed on printed forms. 460 pages. 20 x 19 x 5. Second floor, Hart Building.

1379. TREASURER'S RECORD OF REGISTERED BONDS
1901-1902. 1 volume.

Record of registered bonds and interest payments. Chronological by dates of entries. Handwritten on printed forms. 300 pages. 9 x 14 x 2. Second floor, Hart Building.

Sales Tax

1380. VENDORS, PREPAID TAX RECEIPTS
April 1935—. 20 cardboard storage cases.

Sales tax stamp purchase slips or stubs. Arranged alphabetically by vendors. Handwritten on printed forms. Each case 25.5 x 10.5 x 8. 1935-1936, Room 74; 1936—, Room 159, County courthouse.

1381. DAILY INVENTORY AND SALES RECORD
1935—. 2 loose-leaf volumes.

A record of sales of tax stamps, listing amount received from state treasurer; other increases, or amount received from vendors for possible refunds; total amount on hand; deductions other than sales, or possible shortages of cashier; balance on hand; amount of sales; and date of entry. Chronological by dates of entry. Handwritten on printed forms and photostat. Volumes average 200 pages. 17 x 14 x 1.5. Room 159, County courthouse.

1382. DETAILED DAILY SALES RECORD OF SALES TAX RECEIPTS
1935—. 1 volume.

Lists name of vendor, license number, total value of sales, vendors discount, and amount collected. Chronologically by dates of tax stamp sales. Handwritten on printed forms. 200 pages. 17 x 14 x 1.5. Room 159, County courthouse.

Miscellaneous

1383. LETTER BOOK
1881-1910. 22 volumes. (1881, 1 volume; 1882, 1 volume; 1883-1887, 2 volumes; 1891, 2 volumes; 1892, 2 volumes; 1894, 1 volume; 1898, 2 volumes; 1899, 2 volumes; 1900, 2 volumes; 1901, 2 volumes; 1902, 2 volumes; 1906, 2 volumes; 1910, 1 volume). (Missing 1888-1890, 1893, 1895, 1896, 1897, 1903-1906, 1907-1909).

A record of all correspondence received by the treasurer listing date of receipt in each instance, by whom written, from what places, summary of contents, to whom referred, book number of property to which letter referred, and number of tax bill. Arranged alphabetically. Handwritten. Volumes average 400 pages. 15.25 x 11.25 x 1.5. Second floor, Hart Building.

1384. LIST OF VARIOUS OFFICERS OF TOWNSHIPS AND VILLAGES
1879-1883. 1 volume.
A list of township clerks, clerks of boards of elections, clerks of boards of education, treasurers of townships and villages, and ward assessors of townships. Alphabetical by townships and villages. Handwritten on printed forms. 260 pages. 15 x 8.75 x .75. Second floor, Hart Building.

1385. CLAIMS AGAINST CUYAHOGA COUNTY
1889-1902. 3 volumes. (1889-1893, 1 volume, 3; 1898-1900, 1 volume, 6; 1900-1902, 1 volume, 7).
Lists journal and page number; date of approval; name of person to whom paid; purpose, amount, and date of payment; and voucher number. Alphabetical index by claimants. Handwritten on printed forms. Volumes average 650 pages. 14.5 x 18.75 x 2. Second floor, Hart Building.

1386. LIST OF INVOICES FOR WORK IN COURTHOUSE
April 26, 1911-October 4, 1917. 1 volume.
A list of invoices for material used in the courthouse, approved by the auditor for payment by the county treasurer. Arranged alphabetically by firms. Handwritten. 200 pages. 16 x 10.5 x 1.5. Second floor, Hart Building.

1387. TREASURER'S STREET BOOK
1919. 1 volume, Cities, Townships, and Villages.
A listing directory of streets and roads, and names of taxpayers. Alphabetical by names of streets and roads. Handwritten on printed forms. 200 pages. 9 x 14 x 1.5. Second floor, Hart Building.

1388. ROAD RECORD

1902-1925. 4 volumes. (1902-1903, 1 volume; 1912-1917, 1 volume; 1918-1925, 2 volumes).

Lists number of each voucher for payment of work done, amount paid, date of payment, number of copies redeemed, rate of interest, and number of coupons outstanding and cancelled. Arranged alphabetically by roads. Handwritten. Volumes average 250 pages. 17.5 x 11.75 x 2.25. Second floor, Hart Building.

1389. RECORD OF COST INSANE INQUEST OF LUNACY

June 25, 1902-March 4, 1903. 1 volume.

A record of fees of probate judges, sheriff's, and witnesses. Chronological by dates of inquest. Handwritten on printed forms. 400 pages. 16 x 10.5 x 4. Second floor, Hart Building.

1390. RECEIPTS FOR ABSTRACT FEES

1923-1928. 1 letter box.

Receipts for money paid out by the treasurer for abstracts required on property foreclosed by the state for taxes. The payments were made to the several abstract companies after foreclosure. Arranged alphabetically by abstract companies. Handwritten on printed forms. Record discontinued after 1928. Letterbox 10 x 4 x 8. Second floor, Hart Building.

A measure was adopted in 1927 which created in each county a budget commission to consist of the auditor, treasurer, and prosecutor. The county auditor was designated secretary. The commission is required to meet annually for the purpose of adjusting rates of taxation, and fixing the amount of taxes to be levied each year; to ascertain that tax levies are properly authorized; to adjust the estimated amounts required for the general property tax for each fund, so as to bring the tax levies within the ten mill limitation; to fix the amount of proceeds of classified property tax to be distributed to the boards of public library trustees; and to fix the amount of taxes to be distributed to each township board of park commissioners, and to each municipal corporation. Minor amendments were approved in 1934, and 1935. (112 O.L. 399; 115 O. L.,pt. 2, 412; 116 O. L. 585).

1391. BUDGET COMMISSIONERS' JOURNAL
June 1911-1923. 2 volumes.

Lists budgets allowed to different townships, villages, etc., giving salaries, taxable valuations (real and personal property), and school district valuations. Arranged chronologically. Typed. Volumes average 500 pages. 17.5 x 13.5 x 2.5. June 1911-1917, 1 volume, Room 70; 1918-1923, 1 volume, Room 149, County courthouse. 1923—, see Tax Rate, number 1103.

1392. RESOLUTIONS AUTHORIZING LEVIES
1927—. Approximately 3000 in 2 file boxes.

Resolutions passed by the various political subdivisions in which the amounts of money and tax rates as determined by the budget commission are accepted, the necessary tax levies being authorized by the commission and certified to the county auditor. Alphabetically arranged by taxing districts. Handwritten and typed. Each file box 13.25 x 10.75 x 4.75. Room 149, County courthouse.

The county auditor, commissioners, and assessor constituted the first board of equalization, which was created in 1831. The board met annually for the purpose of hearing complaints, and equalizing the assessments and valuation of all real and personal property within the county. (29 O. L. 272). This act was amended in 1859 to the effect that the board be composed of the county commissioners and the county auditor. In the same session of the general assembly a separate board of equalization was created, consisting of the county auditor, county surveyor, and county commissioners. This board, in contrast to the board of complaints, did not receive complaints, but was essentially a board of assessment. Members of the board were required to meet once every six years for the purpose of passing on the returns of the district assessors, and could either raise or lower valuations. (56 O. L. 193). By amendment in 1868 this board was required to meet decennially. (65 O. L. 168). Its title was changed in 1891 to board of revision; its composition and duties, however, remained the same. (88 O. L. 399).

All boards of equalization were established in 1913. At that time the state was divided into assessment districts, in which the tax commission was authorized to direct and supervise assessments. The governor was directed to appoint two deputy state tax commissioners in each urban district who constituted a district board of assessors, for the assessment of all real and personal property. The legislature also provided for boards of complaints, each of which was to consist of three persons, to be appointed annually by the tax commission with the consent of the governor. They were given the duty of hearing all complaints relating to assessment of both real and personal property. (103 O. L. 387).

Separate boards of assessors and boards of complaints were abolished in 1915 and the county auditor, under supervision of the tax commission, became the chief assessing officer. (106 O. L. 246). The president of the board of commissioners, treasurer, prosecutor and a probate judge constituted a board for the purpose of appointing three members to a board of revision. (106 O. L. 433). In 1917 this board was abolished and the county auditor, treasurer, and the president of the board of commissioners were named the county board of revision. (107 O. L. 29).

1393. MINUTES OF BOARD OF REVISION
1915—. 5 volumes, 1-5.

A record of the final decisions rendered regarding complaints on the valuation of lands and buildings. Arranged by dates of final actions. Volumes average 400 pages. 17 x 12 x 1. Typed. Room 154, County courthouse.

1394. COMPLAINTS AS TO ASSESSMENTS OF REAL PROPERTY
1910—. Approximately 18,105 in 140 file boxes.

Complaints filed with the board of revision, listing name and address of owner, original lot number, sublot number, frontage or acreage, house number, name of street, taxing district, current assessed value, last year's assessed value, real value, decrease asked, from whom property was purchased, date of entry, price paid, amount of mortgage, amount of insurance, type of building, whether appraised at time of purchase, and amount of appraisal. Handwritten on printed forms. Each file box 9 x 4 x 14. 1910-1906, 55 file boxes, Room 72; 1917—, 85 file boxes, Room 154, County courthouse.

1395. CERTIFICATION OF UNCOLLECTIBLE PERSONAL PROPERTY TAX CHARGES
1934-1935. 2 bundles.

Lists name, year, unpaid personal taxes, penalty, grand total, and reason why uncollectible. Alphabetically arranged. Typed on printed forms. Each bundle averages approximately 150 sheets. 10 x 14 x 1. Prepared by the Treasurer's office. Room 154, County courthouse.

1396. RECORD OF THE BOARD OF REVISION AND TAX COMMISSION FINDINGS IN REFERENCE TO COMPLAINTS ON REAL ESTATE VALUES
1924-1926. 1500 pages in 6 bundles.

Findings of the State tax commission in cases appealed from local boards of revision. Filed chronologically. Handwritten on printed forms. Each bundle 13 x 10 x 4. Room 72, County courthouse.

1397. INDEX OF PERSONAL PROPERTY, COMPLAINTS, BOARD OF REVIEW
1908-1914. 1 volume.

An index of complaints, listing address; complaint number; ward number; abatement, addition, or allotment number; date of filing; and remarks on complaint. Handwritten on printed forms. 250 pages. 16 x 15 x 1.75. Attic storeroom, fourth floor, County courthouse.

1398. ACTION OF THE BOARD OF EQUALIZATION AND ASSESSMENTS

1893-1896. 7 volumes. (1893, 3 volumes; 1894, 1 volume; 1895, 2 volumes; 1896, 1 volume).

A list of abatements issued by the board of equalization and assessments upon the real estate of Cleveland, showing name of owner, subdivision, original lot or block, sublot, what part of lot, owners frontage, street, depth, total value, land value, amount abated, and corrected value for taxation. Alphabetical by owners. Handwritten on printed forms. Volumes average 110 pages. 19 x 16.5 x 1. Room 70, County courthouse.

1399. ADDITIONS BY THE BOARD OF EQUALIZATION AND ASSESSMENTS ON REAL PROPERTY

1892-1897. 1 volume.

Lists number of addition, owner's name, ward number, subdivision, original lot number, name of street, sublot number, what part of lot owned, frontage, depth, notice number, value, addition to land, addition to buildings, and value as amended. Alphabetical by names of owners. Handwritten on printed forms. 200 pages. 18.5 x 14 x 1.5. Room 70, County courthouse.

A measure was adopted in 1919 providing that in each county owing a bonded debt, there shall be a board designated as trustees of the sinking fund, to be composed of the county prosecutor, auditor and treasurer, the president of which shall be the prosecutor, and the secretary of which shall be the auditor. The chief duty of these trustees was to provide for the payment of all bonds issued by the county and the interest maturing to the holders of the bonds. The law also provided that no bonds issued by the county shall be valid in the hands of any purchaser unless recorded in the office of the trustees; that the latter shall invest all money subject to their control and federal, state, municipal, school, township or county bonds; that they shall annually certify to the county commissioners the rate of tax necessary for the payment of bonds maturing, and for payment of interest on bonded indebtedness; and that when the commissioners issue bonds, they shall first offer them to the trustees who may take any or all of them, if they have money available in the sinking fund. (108 O. L. pt. 1, 700-702).

Only minor changes have been made since the passage of the law. In 1935 the clause by recordation of bonds was repealed. (116 O. L. 443).

1400. MINUTES OF THE TRUSTEES OF THE SINKING FUND
September 1919—. 2 volumes.
A record of all meetings of the trustees of the sinking fund in chronological order. Typed. Volumes average 1000 pages. 13.25 x 18 x 3. Room 149, County courthouse.

1401. SPECIAL ASSESSMENT SINKING FUND RECORD
March 1919—. 2 volumes.
Lists premium on hand, accrued interest, surplus construction account, transfers, interest on deposits, special assessment collections, date, check number, from whom received and to whom paid, total receipts, balance, expenditures, redemption of bonds, interest on bonds, refund of assessments, and miscellaneous columns. Alphabetically arranged by improvements. Handwritten on printed forms. Volumes average 390 pages. 19 x 14 x 3. Room 149, County courthouse.

1402. RECORD OF SPECIAL ASSESSMENT BOND DISTRIBUTION
March 1919—. 2 volumes.

List expenditures, bonds redeemed, interest, check numbers, improvements, and to whom bonds were sold. Arranged alphabetically by funds, and by dates of entries. Handwritten on printed forms. Volumes average 1000 pages. 16.25 x 21.5 x 4. Room 149, County courthouse.

Under the laws of the Northwest Territory the sheriff and two members of the court of common pleas were required to be the judges of all elections for representatives in the general assembly, in their respective counties. They also appointed two poll keepers whose duty it was to aid them in preventing fraud, deceit and abuse, and in preserving order and regularity. At the close of the election, it was the election judges' duty to proclaim the person or persons who had received the highest number of votes. The sheriff and other judges of election then delivered to every such person, a certificate of his election signed with their names, and the names of the poll keepers. The last step was the transmission by the sheriff for purposes of preservation of a copy of the poll, together with the governor's writ of election, certified by himself, to the office of the secretary of the territory, and a duplicate of the poll to the clerk of the peace. (Pease, *op. cit.,* 404-414).

At the first meeting of the Ohio General Assembly in 1803, it was provided that each township constitutes an election district, and that the sheriff, fifteen days preceding an election, give public notice by proclamation that an election was to be held. On election day the electors assembled at 9 A. M., and chose by a *viva voce* vote three of their number to act as judges. These judges in turn, choose two others, to act as clerks. They were sworn in by the justice of the peace. In voting, the ballot was handed to one of the judges, who pronounced the name of the elector and entered it in the poll books. At 4 P. M. the poll books were signed by the judges, attested by the clerks, and the names were read individually by one of the judges. The second judge also read the names individually and delivered the balance to the third judge who strung them on a thread until the number of ballots equaled the number of names contained in the poll books. The clerk then entered the count opposite the candidates name in a special section of the poll books, and publicly proclaimed the results and entered them in the poll books. One poll book was sealed and taken to the clerk of common pleas court; the other was delivered to the township clerk for public inspection.

Six days later, the county clerk, assisted by one or two common pleas judges or one or two justices of peace, open the returns and made two abstracts of the votes, one abstract of the votes for governor, and the other of the votes for county officers. Both abstracts were signed by the counting officials and a copy was retained by the clerk. The original of the first abstract was sent to the Speaker of the Senate, and the original of the second to the Secretary of State. Both bore of the official seal and the certification of the clerk. The Speaker opened and published the abstract of votes received by him. (Ohio Const., Art. 2, sec. 2; 1 O. L. 76-89).

In 1809 a bill was carried which amended the method of regulating elections, requiring that the township trustees serve as judges, and the township clerks as clerks, of the election. (7 O. L. 112-125).

The election regulations were again amended in 1852 requiring the preparation of four abstracts by the clerk of courts. (50 O. L. 311-325). The following year the county commissioners were required upon presentation of a petition signed by the majority of the electors of any township, asking for a division of such township into election precincts, to issue their order for such division. (51 O. L. 1853).

The place and manor of voting were affected by an act of 1877, which authorized the councils of municipalities to divide any wards having more than 600 electors into precincts containing approximately 300 electors, and also empowered them to designate the polling place in every ward and in every precinct. The same act authorized the judges of elections, if requested by an elector, to permit one or more friends of the respective candidates, not to exceed three, to be present during the time of receiving and counting the ballots. (74 O. L. 215).

The first registration law, affecting the larger municipalities, was enacted in 1885, for the purpose of "ascertaining the citizens who shall be entitled to vote." It provided for two registration periods before each general election, and specified that alphabetical list shall be made of such registered persons, with addresses, which shall be posted conspicuously at usual place of holding elections. The registrars were appointed by the city council from the two largest political parties. It was made unlawful for persons to loiter within one hundred feet of the voting place, or within that distance attempt in any way to influence an elector in a matter of casting his vote. (82 O. L. 232-236).

A comprehensive election law was enacted a year later, again affecting only Cleveland and Cincinnati. It provided that the governor shall appoint a board of elections for each city, to consist of four electors of the municipality, not more than two of whom shall be of the same political party. Their salaries, which were to be paid by each of the cities, was set in Cleveland at $600 per year. The governor was empowered to appoint a secretary to the board whose salary of $2400 per year was also to be paid by the city. The members of the board were required to meet in the mayor's office, within ten days after their appointment and elect one of their members president. The board was empowered to appoint all registrars, judges, and clerks of election; to fix the place for holding elections; to rent suitable rooms for election purposes; to provide for necessary furniture and supplies; to issue all notices required by law; to define the boundaries of the election precincts;

and to issue all necessary rules, regulations, and instructions. The secretary of the board was required to keep a full account of the board's proceedings; file and preserve all the registers, books, maps, forms, oaths, certificates, instruments and blanks for the use or guidance of registrars, judges and clerks of elections, and the board of canvassers; to furnish officers with all the necessary supplies for election purposes; and to take charge of the ballot boxes while deposited at the office of the board. The city board of canvassers was to be composed of the board of elections and the city clerk. The law further stipulated that the poll books, formally delivered to the clerk of the common pleas court, be delivered to the city clerk and then be turned over to the board of canvassers to be canvassed by them in the office of the city clerk, not later than four days after the election. The poll book which had formerly been delivered to the township clerk for public inspection was now to be deposited with the board of elections. (83 O. L. 209-229).

A number of other significant provisions were made at this time. Not more than half of the registrars, clerks or judges were permitted to be of the same political party; registrars and judges were empowered to call upon the chief of police to arrest any individual disturbing the peace at or about the places of registration and of holding elections; political parties were given the right to designate certain persons as witnesses and challengers; and after the count had been made, the clerks and judges were required to make out a summary statement of the votes cast at the election and dispatch it in a sealed envelope to the board, simultaneously telephoning the information. They destroyed by fire the ballots so counted. (*Ibid*).

The city board of elections in any county having within its territory a city of the first class, became the county board of elections by an enactment of 1891. Thus, the Cleveland Board of Elections became the Cuyahoga County Board of Elections. (88 O. L. 468).

Earlier that year the judges and clerks were required to make out election returns and tally sheets thereof in triplicate, one copy going to the county board, one to the clerk of common pleas court, and one copy, with the poll books of the election, to be filed with the township, city, town or village clerk, as the case may be, to be preserved for one year. It also provided that the county board shall open and canvas the returns not less than five days after the election, and make and certify all abstracts required by law. (88 O. L. 452-3).

A county board of canvassers was set up in 1892, to be composed of the members of the board of elections, taking over all the duties of canvassing the votes and making returns. The rule was again changed by disposition of the poll books, one going to the board of canvassers, and the other to the clerk of common pleas court. The latter book was to be preserved for one year for the purpose of public inspection, or, upon demand, for the inspection and use of the board of canvassers. (89 O. L. 430).

The offices of state supervisors and deputy supervisors of elections were created in the same year. The secretary of state, by virtue of the duties and imposed upon him by law, was made the state supervisor. Four deputy supervisors were to be appointed by the secretary of state upon recommendation of the two dominant political parties. This provision, by the deputy supervisors, however, did not apply to Cuyahoga County. (89 O. L. 455-460). In 1900, the act providing for the appointment of deputy state supervisors was extended to Cuyahoga County and their salary was set at $500 per year. In the same session, the salary of the members of the board of elections was raised to $1000 per year. (94 O. L. 304; 94 O. L. 668).

The office of deputy state supervisor of elections, and a member of the board of elections, was abolished in 1904 in counties containing large municipalities and the duties thereof conferred upon the newly created office of the board of deputy state supervisors and inspector of elections. The Secretary of State was named state supervisor and inspector of elections. Within the same statute, the composition of the city board of canvassers was changed. It was now to be composed of the board of deputy state supervisors and inspectors of election and the city auditor. This act also provided for an annual general registration in the largest municipalities. (97 O. L. 185-241).

No major changes affecting election laws were made until 1929 when a new election code was adopted. The county board of elections was re-created, to consist of four members, and were vested with their former powers. The secretary of state was given the power to appoint such members, half of whom were to be from each of the two dominant political parties. The term of office was to be four years. The two parties were given the right to recommend members. The board was also empowered to appoint a clerk and a deputy clerk, who were to be of opposite political parties. It was further stimulated that in no event was a member of the board to receive a salary of more than $4200 a per year, and that the board in urban counties was to act as a board of registration of naturalized voters, receiving and recording any certificate of naturalization offered it. No board of canvassers was provided for, the board of elections taking over their duties.

Also contained within this code were the first real provisions against corrupt practices, specifying the purposes for which money was to be spent by or for a candidate, and the total amount to be expended by each candidate for public office. It also provided that within ten days after election, each candidate for office file an itemized and sworn statement listings such expenditures with either the secretary of state or board of elections, depending upon whether it pertains to a state, district, or county office. Intimidation by employers or by newspaper owners or editors was also outlawed. (113 O. L. 307-412).

The last significant change was made in 1931 providing that the members of the county board of elections be appointed by the secretary of state as representatives of the secretary of state. The canvassing duties of the board were increased by requiring seven different abstracts of the votes. In the same session an enactment specified that no make of voting machines shall be purchased or used in any county until it shall have been approved by the secretary of state, and that he shall appoint a board of voting machine examiners to consist of one competent election officer and two competent mechanical engineers, whose duty it shall be to examine these machines, and file written reports thereon with the secretary of state with their recommendations. (114 O. L. 579-714; 114 O. L. 701).

Registrations, Poll Lists, Tally Sheets

1403. LIST OF ELECTORS
1893—. 195 volumes. (Volumes are numbered according to year dates).
A record of name, address, ward, and precinct of all registered electors who are eligible to vote at the general election. The volumes are compiled each year. Arranged by ward and precincts. Volumes average 300 pages. 9 x 6 x 4.25. 1893-1915, 35 volumes, Room 31; 1916—, 160 volumes, Room 119, City Hall.

1404. REGISTRATION RECORD
1895—. 4 volumes. (1895-1904, 1 volume; 1904-1916, 1 volume; 1917—, 2 volumes).
Lists total registration of men and women for each ward and precinct. The recapitulation shows the total of those registered and the total vote cast for the county. In chronological order. Handwritten on printed forms. Volumes average 250 pages. 21 x 12 x 3. Room 119, City Hall.

1405. MASTER FILE OF ALL REGISTERED VOTERS
1930——. 330 cabinets.

A card record of all registered voters in Cuyahoga County, listing name and address of elector; ward number and precinct letter, whether native or naturalized, date of naturalization, name of court, and place where naturalized. Filed alphabetically. Handwritten on printed forms. Each cabinet 25 x 10 x 27.5. First floor, City Hall.

1406. PRECINCT RECORD BOOKS
1930——. 1132 volumes. (Volumes numbered according to wards and precincts).

A record of all registered electors, showing name and address, ward number and precinct letter, whether native or nationalized, date of naturalization, name of court, and place where naturalized. Indexed alphabetically by electors in each volume. Handwritten and typed on printed forms. Volumes average 200 pages. 14 x 10.5 x 3. First floor, City Hall.

1407. CERTIFICATE OF REMOVABLE STUBS
1928. 300 stub books in 1 paper box.

Each stub lists certificate number, name of elector, new and old address, precincts from which and to which removed, and date of entry. In order of certificate numbers. Handwritten on printed forms. Books average 75 pages. 7 x 9 x 1. Paper box 36 x 18 x 12. Room 16, City Hall.

1408. MILITARY REGISTRATIONS
1917. 11 volumes.

A record of the name, address, ward, and precinct of each Cuyahoga County soldier at camp during the World War who voted on local ballots sent him from this county. Arranged by wards and precinct. Volumes average 100 pages. 22 x 11 x 1. Room 31, City Hall.

1409. REGISTER OF ABSENT VOTERS' BALLOTS
1930——. 1 volume.

A record of applications for ballots made by voters absent from county during elections, showing kind of election, date, application number, name and address of applicant, name of township or village, ward and precinct, date application is given to voter, and date of return. In order of application numbers. Handwritten on printed forms. 200 pages. 14.5 x 18 x 2. Room 119, City Hall.

1410. COMPLETED TRANSFER CARDS
1934—. 16 file drawers.

Cards listing transfers of electors from one district to another, listing old and new address, the ward and precinct, and date of transfer. Filed alphabetically. Handwritten on printed forms. Each file drawer 6 x 15 x 27.5. First floor, City Hall.

1411. LIST OF CANCELLATIONS
1931—. 10 volumes.

A record of names and addresses of electors whose registrations have been cancelled, listing ward number and precinct letter of each elector. Arranged according to wards and precincts. Typed. Volumes average 400 pages. 8 x 14 x 3. First floor, City Hall.

1412. RECORD OF CANCELLED REGISTRATIONS
1934—. 84 file drawers.

Cards listing names and addresses of electors whose registrations were cancelled, date of cancellation, and reason for cancellation. Alphabetical by names of electors. Handwritten on printed forms. Each file drawer 6.5 x 10.5 x 18. First floor, City Hall.

1413. ALPHABETICAL POLL LIST FOR SIGNATURES AND ADDRESSES OF ELECTORS VOTING
1934—. 134 bins.

Lists signature and address of each elector, together with stub number of his ballot. One book is kept for each precinct at the general election; two books for each precinct at the primary elections - one for the democratic party, and the other for the republican party. Arranged alphabetically in each book. Handwritten on printed forms. Books average 140 pages. 13.5 x 8 x .25. Destroyed every two years. 1934, 42 bins, Room 31; 1935—, 92 bins, Room 122, City Hall.

1414. TALLY SHEET BOOKS
1934—. 40 bins.

A record listing total of electors voting, total number of unused ballots, number of soiled and defaced ballots, number of blank ballots, and number of disputed and invalid ballots. Arranged according to wards and precincts. Handwritten on printed forms. Volumes average five pages. 17 x 11 x .125. Destroyed every two years. Room 31, City Hall.

Abstracts of Elections

1415. ABSTRACT OF ELECTIONS
November 1893—. 65 volumes. (Volumes are labeled according to the nature of the election by dates).
Record of total votes received by candidates for office and for special questions. The grand recapitulation shows total votes received by candidate. Abstract sheets show total votes received by candidate from each ward and number of votes from each precinct. Each volume contains a marginal index by subjects. 1893-1915, handwritten; 1916—, typed. Volumes average 200 pages. 22.5 x 17 x 2. Room 119, City Hall.

1416. ELECTIONS OF SPECIAL QUESTIONS
1903—. 1 volume.
Record of all special questions put before voters, listing date of election, the question, number of voters for and against, and majority necessary for the issue to pass. Arranged by state, county, and city. Typed. 200 pages. 18 x 11 x 2. Room 119, City Hall.

1417. RECORDS OF ELECTED OF OFFICERS
1896—. 2 volumes.
A record of all officers elected in the state, county, and city, listing title of office, name of elected officer, political party, length of term, date of election, date term expires, and general remarks. Marginally indexed by state, county, and city. Typed. 150 pages. 17.5 x 10.5 x 1. Room 119, City Hall.

1418. OHIO ELECTION STATISTICS
1912; 1918. 5 volumes. (1912, 1 volume; 1918, 4 volumes).
Total vote cast in Ohio for state and Federal officers, also an abstract of the votes cast in each county. Arranged by subjects. Printed. Volumes average 150 pages. 8 x 6 x 1. Room 16, City Hall.

1419. OHIO ROSTER OF TOWNSHIP AND MUNICIPAL OFFICERS
1916-1917. 1 volume.
Record of names of township trustees as reported by county auditors, listing name of each county and township, and name of trustee and past office address. Arranged according to counties. Printed. 155 pages. 8 x 6 x 1.5. Room 16 City Hall.

Receipts and Expenditures

1420. EXPENSE STATEMENTS
1934-1936. 32 file boxes.

Notarized expense statements of candidates running for office. Arranged according to subjects and register numbers. For index see number 1421. Each file box 14 x 4.5 x 10. Destroyed every two years. Room 119, City Hall.

1421. INDEX TO EXPENSE STATEMENTS
August 1933—. 1 volume.

An alphabetical index of candidates, listing expense statement filed by candidate, office for which he ran, register number, and address. Handwritten on printed forms. 50 pages. 13.5 x 8 x .25. Room 119, City Hall.

1422. VOUCHERS
1929—. 3 bundles.

Lists name and address of corporation to whom voucher is issued. Date issued, serial number of voucher, and number of warrant. Arranged by voucher numbers. Each bundle 14 x 14.5 x 8. Room 31, City Hall.

1423. GENERAL EXPENSE BILLS
January 1934—. 4 file boxes.

Paid and unpaid bills for office supplies, service on equipment, etc. Material for each year is arranged alphabetically by name of creditor. 25.5 x 13.5 x 11. Room 119, City Hall.

1424. CASH BOOK
1906—. 2 volumes. (1906-1920, 1 volume; 1920— 1 volume).

A record of all money received by the board of elections, listing date received, name of payer, purpose, amount, and date deposited with the county treasurer. In chronological order. Handwritten on printed forms. Volumes average 100 pages. 14 x 11.5 x .75. Room 119, City Hall.

1425. BOARD OF ELECTIONS DISBURSEMENTS
1904—. 3 volumes.

A record of all money disbursed by the board of elections for payrolls, office expenses, etc., listing date of payment, name of corporation or individual person, warrant number of payment, and the amount. Chronological. Handwritten on printed forms. Volumes average 125 pages. 14.5 x 25.5 x 1.5. Room 119, City Hall.

1426. BOOTH WORKERS' PAYROLL
1922—. 42 volumes, labeled according to years.

Duplicates of the checks issued to booth workers, listing name of worker, ward and precinct in which employed, check number, and amount of check. Duplicates in each volume are in the order of check numbers. Typed on printed forms. Volumes every 250 pages. 15 x 8 x 3.5. 1922-1933, 37 volumes, Room 31; 1934—, 5 volumes, Room 119 City Hall.

1427. BOARD OF ELECTIONS' OFFICE PAYROLL
1906—. 4 volumes; 7 bundles. (1906-1914, 1 volume; 1920-1923, 2 volumes; 1924-1934, 7 bundles; 1935—, 1 volume).

A record of the yearly salaries received by the board of election officers and regular employees, listing names, positions, and amount received every half month. In chronological order. Typed on printed forms. 100 pages. 9 x 19 x 1.5. Room 119, City Hall.

1428. SPECIAL PAYROLLS
1930—. 4 volumes, 1 bundle. (1930-1934, 3 volumes, 1 bundle; 1935—, 1 volume).

Record of persons employed by the board of elections for special purposes, listing position, number of days worked, rate per day, total amount paid, and date of payment. In chronological order. Typed on printed forms. 125 pages. 9 x 19 x 1.5. Room 119, City Hall.

1429. GENERAL LEDGER
January 1913—. 4 volumes.

A record of corporations and individual persons with whom the board of elections has accounts, listing dates of charges and payments, amounts charged, amounts paid, and warrant numbers of payments. In chronological order. Handwritten on printed forms. Volumes average 250 pages. 15 x 20 x 1.5. Room 119, City Hall.

1430. LEASE BOOK
1920—. 1 volume.

A record of all land leased by the board of elections for their election booths, listing ward and precinct where the land is located, name and address of owner, period of time for which land is leased, amount of monthly rental, date of payment, and warrant number of payment. In chronological order. Handwritten on printed forms. Volumes average 300 pages. 9.5 x 13 x 2.5. Room 119, City Hall.

Board of Election Employees

1431. RECORD OF BOOTH OFFICIALS
1935—. 4 volumes.

Record of booth officials, listing address, ward and precinct, title or position, and shift assignment. Arranged according to townships, wards, and precincts. Handwritten on printed forms. Volumes average 50 pages. 15 x 24 x 1. First floor, City Hall.

1432. CERTIFICATE STUBS
1936—. 306 volumes. (Volumes are numbered according to wards and precincts).

Stubs of certificates of official assignment of election booth officers by the board of elections. Each stub list number of certificate issued to officer, his name and address, ward number and precinct letter, title, date on which he is sworn in, and his signature. Arranged by certificate numbers. Typed on printed forms. Volumes average 50 pages. 10 x 14 x 1. These stubs are destroyed annually. First floor, City Hall.

1433. ELECTION OFFICERS' APPLICATIONS
1934—. 12 file drawers.

Applications filed with the board of elections for positions as election booth officers, listing name and address of applicant, and all date realative to his fitness to serve as an official. Filed alphabetically. Handwritten on printed forms. Each file drawer 6 x 10.5 x 18. First floor, City Hall.

1434. CORRESPONDENCE
1934—. 8 letter file boxes.

All correspondence pertaining to change and transfer of election booth officers. Filed according to wards and townships. Typed. Each file box 11.5 x 12 x 3. First floor, City Hall.

Naturalization Records

1435. NATURALIZATION COURT RECORDS
1829—. 12 volumes.

List names of all persons naturalized in the courts of Cuyahoga County, nativity of each, name of court in which naturalized, date of naturalization, and serial number of petition and of certificate. Alphabetical index in each volume. Handwritten on printed forms. Volumes average 100 pages. 18.5 x 12.5 x 1.5. First floor, City Hall.

1436. NATURALIZATION RECORD FILE CARDS
1906—. 120 file boxes.

A record of all persons who have recorded their naturalization papers with the board of elections, listing date of recording; name, address, and birthplace of person; date and place of naturalization; age when naturalized; certificate number; petition number; name of wife; and name of all minor children. Filed alphabetically. Each file box 4.5 x 24 x 7. First floor, City Hall.

Maps, Atlases

1437. ATLAS OF CLEVELAND, OHIO
1906; 1911. 431 volumes. (1906, 21 volumes; 1911, 410 volumes).

The maps show the boundary lines of and the precincts within each ward. Printed. Black and white. Publisher, John Mohr and Company, Cleveland, Ohio. Volumes average 32 pages. 10 x 14 x .5. Room 16, City Hall.

1438. MAP OF CLEVELAND AND CUYAHOGA COUNTY
No dates

Showing the wards and their boundary lines in the city of Cleveland. Compiled and published by The Mountcastle Map Company, Cleveland, Ohio. Black and white. Scale, 5 inches equals one mile. Framed. 12 x 12. Room 119, City Hall.

1439. MAPS, CITY OF CLEVELAND
1921—. 1 volume.

Contains maps of all wards and precincts in the city of Cleveland. Printed. Black and white. Publisher, Wood Brothers, Cleveland Ohio. 32 pages. 9 x 14.25 x .25. Room 31, City Hall.

1440. MAPS, CITY OF CLEVELAND
1906. 3 volumes.

Contain maps of all wards and precincts in the city of Cleveland. Printed. Black and white. Publisher, Mohr and Company, Cleveland, Ohio. Volumes average 32 pages. 9 x 14.5 x .25. Room 31, City Hall.

1441. MAPS, CITY OF CLEVELAND
1911. 4 volumes.

Contain maps of all wards and precincts and the city of Cleveland. Printed. Black and white. Publisher, Mohr and Company, Volumes average 32 pages. 9 x 14.5 x .25. Room 31, City Hall.

Miscellaneous

1442. ELECTION LAWS OF THE STATE OF OHIO
1904-1917. 12 volumes. (1904, 1 volume; 1910, 1 volume; 1911, 2 volumes; 1913, 2 volumes; 1914, 1 volume; 1915, 2 volumes; 1917, 3 volumes).

Laws relating to elections and to duties of election officers. In alphabetical subject index in each volume. Printed. Volumes average 135 pages. 2 x 6 x 1. Room 16, City Hall.

1443. LEGAL OPINIONS
March 1930—. 2 volumes.

A record of the legal opinions obtained from the state, county, and city law departments concerning the legality or procedure pertaining to elections. The letters are pasted in the books. An alphabetical index in each volume. Typed on printed forms. Volumes average 100 pages. 16 x 11.5 x 4. Room 119, City Hall.

1444. FORMS PRESCRIBED BY SECRETARY OF STATE
1 volume.

Sample election forms for all official uses, including forms for the certificate of appointment of the presiding judge, for instructions to absent voters, precinct envelopes, certificates of election, etc. Contains an alphabetical index of titles of forms. Printed. 250 pages. 18 x 14.5 x 3.5. Room 119, City Hall.

1445. RECORD OF BALLOTS
1919—. 2 volumes.

Duplicates of all ballots used in the election, pasted to the sheets in the volumes. In chronological order. Printed and handwritten. Volumes average 100 pages. 21 x 19 x 5. Room 119, City Hall.

1446. STREET DIRECTORY BY PRECINCTS OF THE CITY OF CLEVELAND
1916. 43 volumes.

Lists name of each street; house numbers, in consecutive order, stating whether odd or even; ward and precinct; and streets included within each precinct. In order of names of streets. Printed. Volumes average 118 pages. 1 x 8 x .75. Room 16, City Hall.

Legislation in 1911, provided for the preservation of the natural resources within the state, by the creation, development and improvement of park districts; and authorized the appointment by the judge of probate court of a board of park commissioners, consisting of four residents of the county, to serve one, two, three, and four years respectively. (102 O. L. 459). The board appointed by virtue of this act in Cuyahoga County was known as the County Park Commission.

By amendment in 1917 the board of park commissioners was reduced to three members, appointed by the probate judge, for a term of three years. Members of the board were to serve without compensation, were required to take an oath of office, and furnish bond for faithful performance of their duties. (107 O. L. 65). The Cleveland Metropolitan Park Board was organized under the provisions of this act, relieving the county park commission of its duties.

The board thus appointed a body politic and corporate, capable of suing or being sued. The board was authorized to appoint a secretary and such other employees as were necessary in the performance of the powers conferred on it, and to keep a permanent and accurate record of all its proceedings. It has the power to acquire lands within or without the park district by purchase, gift, devise or appropriation; and by agreement with municipal authorities, may assume control of parks and park lands within the municipality. The control, development, improvement and protection of all lands are vested in the board; and the board has authority to levy tax on the abutting, adjacent, contiguous and otherwise specially benefitted lands, as well as any land within the park district. (113 O. L. 659). For the preservation of good order and protection of property the board has police power within the park district, and has the power to adopt by-laws, rules and regulations for this purpose, and to appoint police officers to carry out their enforcement. (108 O. L. 1098).

The county treasurer and county auditor are *ex officio* members of the board. The county treasurer is custodian of the funds of the board, and pays out money only upon the warrant of the county auditor.

At present the metropolitan park board comprises nine separate reservations, connected by a boulevard system. All except two of the reservations are in Cuyahoga County, covering a territory of approximately 10,200 acres, to which the board holds title. Most other property, the total cost of which was approximately $4,400,000 was purchased in the years 1920 to 1926. The acquisition of lands gradually decreased until 1933, and since then practically no acreage has been added.

1447. DEEDS
1911—. Approximately 100 in 2 metal file boxes.
Copies of deeds taken from the recorder's records, for properties which the park board anticipates acquiring. Arranged according to section numbers. Handwritten and typed. Each file box 17 x 13 x 11.5. Room 1328, Standard Building.

1448. WARRANTY DEEDS
1917—. Approximately 600 in 3 metal file boxes.
Deeds to property acquired by the metropolitan park board. Filed numerically. Typed on printed forms. Each file box 15 x 12 x 4. Room 1328, Standard Building.

1449. DEED RECORDS AND RELEASES
April 1919—. 2 volumes.
Copies of all deeds and releases for property owned by the metropolitan park board. Alphabetical index of names of former owners in each volume. Typed. Volumes average 1600 pages. 12 x 4 x 3. Room 1328, Standard Building.

1450. ABSTRACTS
1917—. Approximately 540 in 9 metal file boxes.
Abstracts of title to land acquired by the metropolitan park board. Correspondence attached to the statement of title shows amount of consideration, what kind of deed, and other information pertaining to the transaction. Arranged in order of abstract numbers. Typed on printed forms. Each file box 15 x 12 x 4. Room 1328, Standard Building.

1451. OPTIONS
1917—. Approximately 300 in 2 metal file boxes.
A record of options taken by the board, showing amount of deposit, amount of consideration, description of land, date of option, length of time good for, name and address of owner, and kind of deed. Filed numerically. Handwritten on printed forms. Each file box 15 x 12 x 4. Room 1328, Standard Building.

1452. LEASES, PERMITS, AGREEMENTS, ORDINANCES, PROMISSORY NOTES, DECLARATION OF TRUST
Approximately 100 in 1 metal file box.
Filed numerically. Typed and handwritten. File box 15 x 12 x 4. Room 1328, Standard Building.

1453. MORTGAGE RELEASES AND MORTGAGE DEEDS
1917—. Approximately 170 in 1 metal file box.

Deeds and releases of mortgages acquired by the metropolitan park board. Filed numerically. Typed and handwritten on printed forms. File box 15 x 12 x 3. Room 1328, Standard Building.

1454. CONTRACT RECORDS
1927—. 2 volumes.

A record of all contracts let by the board, showing name of contractor, estimate number, voucher number, date of contract, kind of record used and work done, location of improvement, and itemized amounts. Arranged by contract numbers. Handwritten. Volumes average 150 pages. 15 x 12 x 1. Room 1328, Standard Building.

1455. SURETY BONDS, AND INSURANCE POLICIES
1917—. Approximately 75 in 1 metal file box.

Employees' and police bonds; and insurance policies. Arranged by bond and policy numbers. Typed on printed forms. File box 15 x 12 x 4. Room 1328, Standard Building.

1456. JOURNAL OF PROCEEDINGS
May 1911—. 3 volumes.

Minutes of meetings held by the board of park commissioners, together with financial reports and statistics. Alphabetical index of subject matters in each volume. Typed. Volumes average 1400 pages. 14 x 12 x 3. Room 1328, Standard Building.

1457. JOURNAL AND LEDGER
December 1927—. 1 volume.

A cash journal, listing date of entry, name of person or firm, purpose of entry, receipt or voucher number, name of general fund charged to or credited to, special assessment fund, general expense and outlay, parks controlling accounts, account number, and amounts received or paid out. Arranged chronologically. Handwritten on printed forms. Volumes average 450 pages. 16 x 14 x 2.5. Room 1328, Standard Building.

1458. LEDGER
December 1925—. 1 volume.

Lists date of entry, the items, folio number, amounts of debits and credits, and name and address of firm or person. Arranged alphabetically by names of accounts. Handwritten on printed forms. Volumes average 250 pages. 13 x 10 x 3. Room 1328, Standard Building.

1459. VOUCHERS
1917—. Approximately 14,000 in 28 metal file boxes.

List name and address of person to whom voucher is made out, purpose of voucher, order number, voucher number, and amount. An itemized statement is attached. Arranged numerically. Typed on printed forms. Each file box 15 x 12 x 4. Room 1328, Standard Building.

1460. POLICE DAILY REPORT CARDS
1922—. Approximately 2800 in 4 metal file boxes.

Show date of report, name of park, territory covered, duration of duty, and a patrol report. Chronological. Handwritten on printed forms. Each file box 17 x 5 x 4. Room 1328, Standard Building.

1461. MAPS, TRACINGS, AND BLUEPRINTS, CUYAHOGA COUNTY
1911—. Approximately 715 maps in 143 metal file boxes.

Blueprints and tracings of property which the park board has either purchased or had under consideration. Arranged numerically. For index see number 1462. Various sizes. Room 1328, Standard Building.

1462. INDEX TO MAPS
1911—. 1 volume.

An alphabetical index of owners or subdivisions, listing corresponding map numbers. Handwritten. Volumes average 150 pages. 12 x 7 x 1.5. Room 1328, Standard Building.

1463. CORRESPONDENCE
1928—. 10 file boxes.

General correspondence of the metropolitan park board. Alphabetical by subject matters. Typed and handwritten. Each file box 27 x 13 x 11.5. Room 1328, Standard Building.

Libraries were originally treated as a part of the common school system, and in1853 the state school commissioner was empowered to purchase books and established libraries in each school district, for the use of every family within the district. (51 O. L. 447).

In 1921 the general assembly authorized the creation of a county library district in any county composed of territory in which free library service is not furnished to all its citizens. Upon the filing of a petition in probate court by twenty-five percent of the electors in the territory comprising the proposed library district, the probate judge was required to set a date for the hearing, and if he found the territory sufficiently described, he certified the proposal to the county supervisor of elections for submission to the electors of the territory at the next general election. (109 O. L. 351).

This same act provided that the management of the county library district be vested in five trustees, two of whom were to be appointed by the judges of common pleas court, and three by the county commissioners. They were to serve without compensation, but were to receive an allowance for personal expenses. They were given the power to receive real or personal property, or money; to purchase, lease, or dispose of grounds or buildings; to construct buildings; and to furnish, equip and maintain the buildings for library purposes. They submitted an annual report to the county commissioners and the state director of library service. They were required to submit a budget annually to the budget commission. (109 O. L. 351).

The act creating the county district library board was amended in 1923, providing that the petition requesting a library district be signed by only ten percent of the electors. (110 O. L. 328). In 1931 the filing of a petition by the electors was abolished and the county commissioners, upon the adoption of a resolution to provide a county library board, were permitted to file the resolution in probate court, and to be acted upon as provided in the original act. The act was further amended stipulating the appointment of seven trustees instead of five. Three members are appointed by the judges of common pleas court and four by the county commissioners. The term of office for trustees was changed to seven years. (114 O. L. 56).

1464. CATALOG FILES

1924—. 360 metal file drawers.

Cards listing all books of the library, showing whether purchase or gift, author, title, subdivision, publisher, date and number of books. Filed alphabetically both by author and title. Typed. Each drawer 3 x 5 x 18. Basement of the Cleveland Public Library, 325 Superior Avenue.

1465. ROOM INVENTORY AND STATISTICAL REPORT

1924—. 12 volumes.

Reports showing circulation, branches and all other agencies, registration, number of books on hand, whether purchased or gift, whether adult or juvenile, date, total books and grand totals. Chronological. Typed. Approximately 75 loose leaf-pages in each volume. 24 x 18 x .5. Basement of the Cleveland Public Library, 325 Superior Avenue.

1466. UNION SHELF FILES

1924—. 100 metal file drawers.

Cards list name of book, author, number, classification, date and the location of the book. Filed alphabetically. Typed. Each drawer 3 x 5 x 18. Basement of the Cleveland Public Library, 325 Superior Avenue.

In 1882 the general assembly authorized the presiding judge of common pleas court to appoint five persons annually, all of whom were to be residents of the county, and three of them were to be women, to constitute a board of visitors. It was the duty of the board, by personal visitation or otherwise, to keep themselves fully advised of the condition and management of all charitable and correctional institutions supported in whole or in part by county or municipal taxation. At the close of the term of service the board was required to prepare and file with the clerk of courts a full report of their proceedings, with any recommendations they deemed advisable. The members of the board were to serve without compensation. (79 O. L. 107).

Amendment in 1892 provided for six members instead of five, and further provided that not more than three members be of the same political affiliation. (89 O. L. 161).

In 1913 the power of appointing the county board of visitors was vested in the judge of probate court and the term was changed to three years. The annual report and recommendations of the board are now filed with the judge of probate court. Another act that same year required the judge of juvenile court to notify the board of visitors before sending a child to the reformatory. (103 O. L. 174).

1467. MINUTE BOOK
1935—. 1 volume.
Minutes of the meetings of the board of county visitors. Handwritten. 10 x 8 x .5. 50 loose-leaf pages. Office of Miss Buscha, Cleveland College.

The first mention of boards of health in Ohio law is to be found in a bill passed in 1854 entitled "an act to provide for the organization of cities and incorporated villages," and also providing for city and village boards of health for "the purpose of securing the city . . . from the evils of contagious, malignant, and infectious diseases." (52 O. L. 126).

The health problems of the county were met by over 2,000 village and city boards in the State of Ohio, until 1919, when the first comprehensive state health law was passed. This act which was amended during the same session provided that each municipality constitute a separate health district; and that the townships and villages in a county combined into a general health district. Provision was also made whereby a city and a general health district might combine for administrative purposes. (108 O. L. pt. 1, 236-251; 108 O. L. pt. 2, 1085-1093).

The law also provided that in each general health district there was to be a board of health, to consist of five members who were to serve without compensation for a term of five years, and one of whom had to be a physician. These members were to be appointed by a district advisory council to be made up of the mayor of each municipality not constituting a city health district, and the chairman of the trustees of each township. Each board was first given the duty of appointing a district health commissioner who was to be a licensed physician, and, upon his recommendation, a public health nurse, a clerk, and such additional public health nurses, physicians, and other persons as might be necessary for the proper conduct of the board's work. Each board was required to study and record the prevalence of disease within its district, to provide for prompt diagnosis and control of communicable diseases, to provide for free distribution of anti-toxin for diphtheria, and to exercise all powers and perform all duties conferred by law upon municipal boards of health. (*Ibid.,* 237-241; 1086-1089).

A great many discretionary powers were given to boards of health. They may provide for the carrying on of such laboratory work as is necessary, either by establishing a district laboratory, or by contracting with an existing one. They may also provide for the free treatment of social diseases, and may establish detention hospitals for cases of communicable diseases. The district health commissioner was also made a deputy of the state registrar of births and deaths with the duty of enforcing all laws governing the registration of births and deaths. He was also empowered to provide for the frequent inspection of all county and primaries, children's homes, workhouses, jails or other charitable, benevolent, or penal institutions in the district, including physical examination of the inmates whenever necessary. The board may also provide for the inspection at dairies, stores, restaurants, hotels, and other places where food is manufactured, handled, stored, sold, or offered for sale. (*Ibid.,* 241, 242, 244, 246; 1091).

The county board of health must estimate the amount needed for the current expenses of the next fiscal year. The aggregate amount is then apportioned among the townships and municipalities composing the health district. The board also receives state aid, which in no event, however, exceeds $1,000. The prosecutor of the county constituting a major part of the health department must act as legal advisor of the board. (*Ibid.,* 243-5; 1091).

A great deal has been done in Cuyahoga County in furtherance of the act. The Cuyahoga County Board of Health was formed in September 1920. Clinics have been established to treat school children afflicted with defects which makes their association with other children dangerous, or with proved respiratory diseases, coughs and colds. In addition, the board of health has established clinics for infant welfare, and stations for the administration of anti-toxin to combat diphtheria.

1468. MINUTE BOOK
1920—. 1 volume.

Minutes of the annual meetings of the county board of health. In chronological order. Typed. 150 pages. 11.5 x 9 x 1.25. Engineers' Building, Room 207.

1469. BIRTH RECORDS
1920—. Approximately 16,000 cards in 16 metal file boxes.

List name of child, date of birth, place of birth, maiden name of mother and full name of father, name of doctor, registration district number, and date received for record. Filed alphabetically. Typed on printed forms. Each file box 17 x 5.25 x 4.25. Engineers' Building, Room 207.

1470. DEATH RECORDS
1920—. Approximately 12,000 Cards in 12 metal file boxes.

List the name and address of deceased, cause of death, date of death, name of attending physician, registration district number, and date on which record was received. Filed alphabetically by names of deceased. Typed on printed forms. Each file box 17 x 5.25 x 4.25. Engineers' Building, Room 207.

1471. CLOSED CONTAGION CASES
1920—. Approximately 4,000 cards in 4 metal file boxes.
List name of disease, name and address of patient, age of patient, name of attending physician, date of onset, date reported, and date released. Filed alphabetically by names of patients. Typed on printed forms. Each file box 17 x 6.25 x 5. Engineers' Building, Room 207.

1472. CURRENT RECORD OF CASES OF NOTIFIABLE DISEASES REPORTED DURING THE MONTH
1920—. 2 volumes.
List; name of disease; case number; name, address, age, sex, and color of patient; name of attending physician; and date of onset of the disease. In chronological order. Handwritten on printed forms. Volumes average 225 loose-leaf pages. 20 x 14.5 x 3. Engineers' Building, Room 207.

1473. INACTIVE TUBERCULAR CASES
1920—. Approximately 2,500 cards in 2 metal file boxes.
List name and address of patient; name of county, and of municipality, village, or township; date case was reported; age, sex, color, and nationality of patient; name of dispensary; name and business address of employer; occupation of patients; length of time in county and state; name of person who referred case to board of health; date of first contact by a visiting nurse of board of health; diagnosis of case; and condition of patient. Arranged according to chart numbers. For separate index see number 1475. Typed on printed forms. Each file box 17 x 8.25 x 6.5. Engineers' Building, Room 207.

1474. ACTIVE TUBERCULAR CASES
1920—. Approximately 2,500 cards in 2 metal file boxes.
A record, listing name and address of patient; name of county and village; date reported; age, sex, color, and nationality of patient; name of dispensary; name and address of employer; occupation of patient; length of residence in county and state; diagnosis of case; and condition of patient. Arranged according to chart numbers. For index see number 1475. Typed on printed forms. Each file box 17 x 8.25 x 6.5. Engineers' Building, Room 207.

1475. TUBERCULOSIS FAMILY CHARTS

1920—. Approximately 5000 cards in 1 metal file box.

Alphabetical card index of names of tubercular patients, listing address and chart number of the tubercular family. Typed are printed forms. File box 17 x 6.25 x 5. Engineers' Building, Room 207.

1476. MONTHLY REPORTS; ANNUAL REPORTS; BIRTH AND DEATH RECORDS

1920—. Approximately 400 cards in 2 metal file boxes.

Contains nurses' reports; health reports; and reports to various department managers, together with letters and statistical information. Arranged alphabetically by subject matters. Typed. Each file box 27 x 13.5 x 11.5. Engineers' Building, Room 207.

1477. SUMMARY REPORT FOR CUYAHOGA COUNTY GENERAL HEALTH DISTRICT

1920—. 2 volumes.

A record listing district numbers and names of villages and townships in the county health district, classification of diseases, total number of reported cases, total deaths from notifiable diseases, total deaths from all causes, total deaths under one year, total registered births, and total deaths under five years. Front numerical index of districts. Handwritten on printed forms. Volumes average 200 pages. 20 x 14.5 x 3. Engineers' Building, Room 207.

1478. GENERAL CORRESPONDENCE

1920—. Approximately 1000 in 4 metal file boxes.

Correspondence relating to the operation of the county health district offices and reports listing statistical information for all townships and villages that do not have their own board of health. Filed alphabetically. Typed and handwritten. Each file box 24.5 x 16 x 11. Engineers' Building, Room 207.

The foundation of the common school system in Ohio was laid by the Continental Congress in 1785. When the original states ceded their claims to the Confederacy upon the wilderness of the Northwest, Congress provided for the survey and sale of this land, but reserved from sale one thirty-sixth of each township, amounting to 640 acres, for school purposes. (Emilius O. Randall and Daniel J. Ryan, *History of Ohio,* III, 367-396).

Both Congress in its Ordinance of 1787, and Governor St. Clair in his address to the First Territorial Legislation in 1799, declared that education should be encouraged. However, no definite provisions for education were made. Although the Constitution of 1802 reiterated these general sentiments, the general assembly did not make any concrete provisions until 1821, when the first enactment of any significance affecting education was passed. Prior to this time the general opinion prevailed that schooling destroyed the children's capacity for work. An act of 1817 had, it was true, authorized the people in townships to build schoolhouses and incorporate for educational purposes. The bill of 1821, however, went further and empowered the electors of each township to vote on the proposition of dividing the township into school districts. They could then elect a school committee, and a clerk; and the committee in turn, could appoint a collector and competent teachers. The committee was authorized to levy taxes. (*Ibid.,* 367-396; Ohio Const., 1802, Art. 8, sec. 3, 25, 27; 15 O. L. 407; 19 O. L. 54).

The office of state superintendent of schools was created in 1838, and in the same session the county auditor was made county superintendent of schools under his supervision. Each township clerk was made superintendent of schools in his township and the trustees of each incorporated township were authorized to divide the townships into school districts. Three directors were elected in each district and were empowered to assess taxes, prescribed studies, and employ teachers. The office of state superintendent of schools was abolished in 1840, and the secretary of state assumed the duties of the office by tabulation of school statistics. It was not until 1853 that the office was recreated as an elective office under the title of state commissioner of schools. Meanwhile, in 1847, the clerks of the school district in twenty-five counties, of which Cuyahoga County was one, were empowered to appoint county superintendents of schools. The district clerks were divested of this power in 1873. The elective office of state commissioner of schools was abolished in 1914 and replaced by the appointive office of superintendent of public instruction. (36 O. L. 35, 32, 23; 38 O. L. 140; 51 O. L. 447; 46 O. L. 86; 70 O. L. 239; 104 O. L. 217).

During the same session the legislature provided for county boards of education and school districts. Each county, exclusive of the territory embraced in any city school district and the territory in any village school district exempted from the supervision of the county board of education, comprised a county school district. Five members were appointed to the board for terms of one, two, three, four, and five years respectively, one member being selected each year. They were appointed by the presidents of the board of education of the various village and rural school districts within the county school districts. This board, in turn, appointed the county superintendent of schools who served for a term not to exceed three years. The county was divided into districts for administrative purposes and a district superintendent was placed in charge of each district. This plan was eliminated, and the office of district superintendent abolished in 1921. (104 O. L. 133; 109 O. L. 142).

The office of member of the county board of education was made elective in 1921, for a term of four years. In the same act provision was made for one or two more assistant county superintendents to be appointed by the county board upon recommendation of the county superintendent, for a term not to exceed three years. (109 O. L. 242).

The secretary of the board is required to keep a full record of the board's proceedings, properly indexed, in a book provided for that purpose, and it is the superintendent's duty to see that all reports required by law are made out and sent to the county auditor and the state superintendent of public instruction. (104 O. L. 133).

The objective of the law, in establishing county school districts, was to standardize educational methods and to give to the rural schools some of the advantages formally enjoyed only by schools in urban centers.

1479. TEACHERS' APPLICATIONS

1914—. Approximately 5,000 in 4 metal file drawers.
List name, address, age, sex, marital status, date by education and practical experience, and a complete history of each applicant, with photograph attached. Filed alphabetically. Handwritten on printed forms. Each file drawer 11 x 15 x 27. Engineers' Building, Room 448.

1480. TEACHERS' EXAMINATION RECORD CARDS
1914-1935. Approximately 5,000 in 3 file drawers.
List each teacher's name and address, place of birth, age, sex, and application number, name of high school, college, and normal school attended: certificate letter and number, and date of the expiration of certificate. Filed alphabetically. Handwritten on printed forms. Each file drawer 28 x 12 x 9.5. Engineers' Building, Room 448.

1481. TEACHERS' PROFESSIONAL RECORD CARDS
1914—. Approximately 5,000 in 3 file drawers.
Lists name of teacher, school district, name of school, educational and professional training, teaching experience, annual salary, and association of which the teacher is a member. Filed alphabetically. Handwritten on printed forms. Each file drawer 9.5 x 12 x 28. Engineers' Building, Room 448.

1482. COPY OF TEACHERS' CERTIFICATES
1914—. Approximately 2,500 in 3 metal file drawers.
Copies of certificates issued by the department of education of the State of Ohio, attesting that the holder is permitted to teach the subject listed on the certificate. Filed alphabetically. Handwritten on printed forms. Each file drawer 5 x 15.5 x 27. Engineers' Building, Room 448.

1483. OFFICIAL RECORD OF AGE AND SCHOOLING CERTIFICATES
1914—. Approximately 4,000 in 1 file drawer.
Lists name and address of child, date of birth, names of parents, date of issue, name of employer, nature of industry, business address, and date of renewal of certificate. Arranged alphabetically. Handwritten on printed forms. File drawer 5 x 15.5 x 27. Engineers' Building, Room 448.

1484. MINUTES OF MEETINGS OF TOWNSHIP AND VILLAGE SUPERINTENDENTS
1914-1932. 3 volumes.
In chronological order. Typed. Volumes every 400 pages. 8.5 x 11 x 2. Engineers' Building, Room 448.

1485. MINUTES OF COUNTY BOARD OF EDUCATION MEETINGS
1914—. 4 volumes.

In chronological order. Typed. Volumes average 400 pages. 8.5 x 11 x 2. Engineers' Building, Room 448.

1486. COUNTY SUPERINTENDENT'S PERIODIC REPORTS
1914-1932. Approximately 430 in 15 file boxes.

A record listing for each village and school district, the names of superintendents and principals, total enrollment of pupils in each school, enrollment for each period, aggregate number of days of attendance, number of absences, number of days due, days not due, and average daily attendance. Arranged alphabetically by townships and villages. Handwritten on printed forms. Each file box 11 x 5 x 29. Engineers' Building, Room 448.

1487. ANNUAL FINANCIAL REPORT OF COUNTY SUPERINTENDENT TO STATE DEPARTMENT OF EDUCATION
July 1, 1930—. Approximately 5 books in 1 bundle.

Complete financial reports of all township and village schools in Cuyahoga County. Alphabetical by names of villages and townships. Handwritten on printed forms. Each book (press board cover) 8.5 x 11 x .125. Engineers' Building, Room 448.

1488. ANNUAL STATISTICAL REPORT FOR EACH SCHOOL YEAR
1914—. 22 books in 1 bundle.

A record of enrollments, average aggregate attendance, number of absences, number of days during which the schools were in session, number of teachers, and buildings and equipment used. Reports arranged chronologically. Handwritten on printed forms. Each book 8.5 x 11 x .25. Engineers' Building, Room 448.

1489. SCHOOL FILES
1918—. Approximately 500 in 1 file drawer.

Contain reports of board of education, and correspondence with various villages and townships. Arranged alphabetically by names of townships and villages. Typed. File drawer 11.5 x 16 x 29. Engineers' Building, Room 448.

1490. GENERAL CORRESPONDENCE
1914—. Approximately 10,000 in 16 metal file drawers.
A record of all general correspondence of the county board of education to each township, village, or district school relating to the reports of their principles. In alphabetical order. Typed. Each file drawer 11 x 15 x 27. Engineers' Building, Room 448.

1491. PUBLISHERS' CATALOG
No dates. Approximately 500 in 1 file drawer.
List of textbooks each publisher has in stock for schools. Alphabetical by names of publishers. Printed. File drawer 11.5 x 16 x 29. Engineers' Building, Room 448.

Old age assistance, or "old age pensions" is a plan that has been almost universally adopted for the care of the aged who are dependent upon the public for support.

In Europe a great deal of legislation providing for old age pensions was approved at the end of the nineteenth century. Although Germany adopted an old age and invalidity insurance measure in 1899, the first country to provide for gratuitous support for the aged "worthy poor" was Denmark. The chief weakness of the Danish act was its failure to fix the amount of the pension. Similar plans were approved in New Zealand, Australia, France, and Great Britain at the beginning of the twentieth century. Other countries followed this trend, although old age compulsory insurance plans were more prevalent than gratuitous support. (Barbara Nachtrieb Armstrong, *Insuring the Essentials*, 403-414).

The first legislation providing for old age assistance in this country was passed in 1923, and it has only been in the last few years, during the recent depression, that a large number of old age pension plans have been adopted.

The original Ohio provisions regarding pensions for the aged were adopted by initiative on November 7, 1933. The act specified that every person of the age of 65 years or more shall, while residing in the state of Ohio, if in need, be entitled to aid, up on meeting certain requirements. The applicant must have been a citizen for 15 years, and must have resided in the state for the same period preceding the making of such applications; must have been a resident of the county for one year; must not have been an inmate of any penal or correctional institution or hospital; must not have, during the 15 year period, for a period of six months or more, deserted his or her mate, or his or her children under the age of 15 years; must not have an income in excess of $300 per year; must be unable to support himself or herself and have no husband, wife, child, or other person who is able to support him; and must not have directly or indirectly deprived himself or herself of property or income in order to qualify for aid. It was stipulated that the amount of age shall not exceed $25 per month for each person, diminished by such an amount that the total income of the recipient from any or all sources, including such aid, shall not exceed $300 per year. The same provision supply to married couples except that the amount was set at $50 per month and $600 per year. Provision was also made that in computing the income, any real or personal property (not including clothing, and personal effects), not producing any income shall be considered as 5 percent of the net value thereof. A single person could not have property valued in excess of $3,000, nor could a husband and wife have property valued in it excess of $4,000. All real or personal property with the exception of clothing, household goods, and personal effects could be required, as a condition precedent to the payment of aid, to be conveyed or transferred to the division of aid for the aged; the recipient of the aid retaining, however, a life estate as to residents but not as to income. The persons in charitable, fraternal or benevolent homes, either public or private, were treated in a different manner. The governing body of the institution was to get the reasonable cost of the maintenance of such persons and the balance of the pension, if any remains, we should go to the individual. Up on the death of any pensioner, the division of aid for the needy aged was to defray the funeral expenses to the extent of installments then accruing plus three additional installments. (115 O.L., pt. 2, 431-439).

For the purpose of administering the law, there was created in the state department of public welfare the division of aid for the aged, the chief of which is appointed by the director of public welfare with the approval of the governor. He, in turn, is authorized to appoint all necessary assistants, clerks, stenographers, and other employees subject to the approval of the director of public welfare. In each county the county commissioners constitute a board of aid for the needy aged, unless, the commissioners, by a majority vote, declined to serve in that capacity. In that case, the state director is authorized to appoint a board to consist of three or five members, to serve without compensation. The board receives and rules on all applications for pensions. The division may, however, allow or reject the findings of the board. (*Ibid.,* 434-5).

The law was changed in 1936 in order to comply with the Old Age assistance section of the Federal Social Security Act of 1935. The Federal act does not make provision for the government to pay pensions directly to individuals. Its purpose is to aid states in paying such pensions by meeting one-half the assistance if the total does not exceed $30 per month for each individual. In order to encourage acceptance of this plan on the part of the states the Federal government helps the states to meet administration costs, paying for that purpose an additional amount up to 5 percent of its regular quarterly old age assistance payments. The states may, if they wish, (Ohio does not), pay more than $30 per month for each person. The revised statute provides that the income of the single person must not exceed $360 per year, nor may that of husband and wife exceed $720 per year. One must be a resident of the state for five out of the nine years preceding the making of application and must be a citizen of the United States. One must not, however, during the ten year period prior to the making of application, for a period of six months or more have deserted his or her mate, or his or her children under the age of 15 years. Additional obligations were undertaken by the state in order to qualify for Federal aid. Any individual whose claim is rejected must be given a fair hearing; the state must make such reports and comply with the provisions as the Federal Social Security Board may from time to time institute; it must put into operation such methods of administration as are found necessary by the board for the efficient operation of the plan; it must expend the Federal money as Congress may provide; and it must turn over to the United States one-half of the state's share of the estates of the recipients of aid. All other provisions adopted by initiative in 1933 remain unchanged. (116 O. L., pt. 2, 2nd special session, H. 605; 46 U. S. C. A., sec. 301-306).

1492. ACTIVE FILES FOR AID FOR NEEDY AGED
June 1934——. 60 metal file drawers.

Contain applications for aid, investigator's summary reports and recommendations, and correspondence on each case; and the reapplication after one year, giving name and address of applicant, case number, and complete history of applicant. Arranged by case numbers. For index see number 1494. Handwritten and typed. Each file drawer 14 x 11 x 22. Marion Building, Room 219.

1493. INACTIVE FILES FOR AID FOR NEEDY AGED
June 1, 1934——. 55 metal file drawers.

A record of rejected cases and cases of applicants who had died while receiving aid. Contains applications, investigator's summary reports and recommendations, and correspondence on each case; and the reapplication after one year, giving an address of applicant, case number, and complete case history of applicant. Arranged by case numbers. For index see number 1494. Handwritten and typed. Each file drawer 1 14 x 11 x 22. Marion Building, Room 219.

1494. CARD INDEX FOR AID FOR THE NEEDY AGED
June 1, 1934——. 40 metal file drawers.

An alphabetical index of names of applicants, listing address, application number, certificate-of-aid number, date of birth, date aid was given, date of denial, date of discharge, number of persons in the immediate household receiving aid, reason for discharge or denial of aid, total period during which aid was extended and total amount paid. Handwritten and typed on printed forms. Each file drawer 4 x 6 x 12.5. Marion Building, Room 219.

In order to aid in diffusing useful and practical information on subjects relating to agriculture and home economics, and to encourage the application of such information, Congress passed an enactment in 1914, which provided for state aid for such purposes. Each state which complied with the Federal act was to be helped to the amount of $10,000 per annum. An additional annual appropriation of $4,100,000 was provided for, out of which money was to be allotted to any state, or a county or local authority within the state which would annually appropriate a sum equal to the allotment. The specific objective of the bill was to institute co-operative extension service between agricultural colleges in the several states and the United States Department of Agriculture. In the same year, the general assembly in pursuance of the Federal act, provided that such federal money, together with any money appropriated by the state, and any county or counties, be set aside and designated as "the agricultural extension fund," and be used for the extension service of the College of Agriculture of the Ohio State University. The trustees of the University were empowered to expend, in accordance with the law, all moneys in the state treasury to the credit of the agricultural fund. (38 Stat. L. 372-374, 7 U. S. C. A., secs. 341-348; 106 O. L. 357).

The trustees were authorized to appoint county extension agents, who were required to co-operate with the United States Department of Agriculture, the College of Agriculture of the Ohio State University, the Ohio Agricultural Experiment Station, and the Ohio Department of Education, for the purpose of making available to the people the services of the agencies. Extension agents act as representatives of the Ohio State University and reach the people through personal instructions, bulletins, practical demonstrations and otherwise, subject to the regulations as may be prescribed by the board of trustees of the University. It is the duty of these agents to render educational service not only in regard to agricultural production, but also in relation to economic problems including marketing, distribution, and utilization of farm products, as well as other problems relative to the farm, the home and the community.

The original state act contained a clause which required counties to raise $1,000 annually if they wished to obtain the service of the agent. This amount was to be matched by the state by an annual appropriations not to exceed $3,000. The present law, as amended in 1929, does not provide for the appropriation of state funds. Instead, it provides that the county commissioners, by unanimous consent, may appropriate an amount not to exceed $3,000 for each agent employee, to be used toward the maintenance and extension service in the county. (106 O. L. 357; 110 O. L. 357).

1495. ANNUAL REPORTS OF COUNTY AGENT
1925—. 1 file drawer.

General correspondence; extension service annual reports; reports of cashier's funds, directors' meetings; and enrollment list. Arranged according to subjects. 24.5 x 13.25 x 11.5. Typed. 2500 copies. Room 814, Public Square Building.

1496. COUNTY FARM BUREAU ORGANIZATION FILES
1930—. 1 file drawer.

Data on the general activities of the county farm bureau, their accounts, dues, co-operative buying, and marketing. Arranged alphabetically by subjects. Typed and handwritten. 500 pages. 24.5 x 13.25 x 11.5. Room 814, Public Square Building.

1497. ALL EXTENSION SERVICE ORGANIZATION
1920—. 8 file drawers.

Monthly and annual reports of the office and field work of the agricultural extension service; and general correspondence on farm management. Arranged alphabetically by subject matter. Handwritten and typed. 2500 copies. 24.5 x 13.25 x 11.5. Room 814, Public Square Building.

1498. GENERAL AGRICULTURAL EXTENSION TOPICS
1920—. 1 file drawer.

Published information on such topics as extension service news, market news service, Federal loans, current economic information and general correspondence. Arranged alphabetically by subject matter. Typed. 500 copies. 24.5 x 13.25 x 11.5. Room 814, Public Square Building.

1499. GENERAL AGRICULTURAL BULLETINS
Approximately 1918—. 18 file boxes.

Periodic issues of bulletins on miscellaneous farming subjects. Arranged according to subject matter. Printed and multigraphed. 450 copies. 5 x 9 x 14. Room 814, Public Square Building.

1500. ILLUSTRATIVE MATERIAL THROUGH WOOSTER EXPERIMENT STATION

1926—. 1 file drawer.

Charts and descriptive material from the Wooster Experiment Station. Handwritten and typed. 500 pages. 24.5 x 13.25 x 11.5. Room 814, Public Square Building.

1501. BULLETINS, PAPERS, CORRESPONDENCE

Approximately 1918—. 6 file drawers.

Publications on floriculture, home beautification, home economics, livestock, nurseries, soils, fairs, exhibits, farm co-operatives, fruit, vegetables, co-operative buying of potatoes, farm bureau news, forestry, farm engineering, farm management, fruit spray information service, agricultural legislation, United States Department of Agriculture, Ohio Department of Agriculture, Ohio Experiment Station, and Ohio Farm Bureau Federation. Arranged alphabetically. Handwritten and printed. Room 814, Public Square Building.

Governmental

Animal Shelter (Dog Warden)
http://cuyahogadogs.com/
9500 Sweet Valley Drive
Valley View OH 44125

Board of Elections
https://boe.cuyahogacounty.gov/
2925 Euclid Avenue
Cleveland OH 44115

Board of Health
http://www.ccbh.net/
5550 Venture Drive
Parma OH 44130

Clerk of Courts
https://cuyahogacounty.gov/coc
1200 Ontario Street
Cleveland OH 44113

County Commissioners
https://cuyahogacounty.gov/boards-and-commissions
2079 East 9th St. Room 8-007
Cleveland, OH 44115

Court of Appeals
https://appeals.cuyahogacounty.gov/
1 Lakeside Avenue
Cleveland OH 44113

Engineer
https://www.cuyahogacounty.gov/publicworks
2079 East Ninth Street
Cleveland, Ohio 44115

Fiscal Officer (Auditor)
https://cuyahogacounty.gov/fiscal-officer/
2079 East 9th Street
Cleveland OH 44115

Juvenile Court
https://cuyahogacounty.gov/psjs
9300 Quincy Avenue
Cleveland OH 44106

Medial Examiner
https://cuyahogacounty.gov/medical-examiner
11001 Cedar Avenue
Cleveland OH 44106

Probate Court
https://probate.cuyahogacounty.gov/contact.aspx
Probate Court of Cuyahoga County
1 Lakeside Avenue West
Cleveland, Ohio 44113

Prosecutor
https://www.ccprosecutor.us/
1200 Ontario Street, 9th Floor
Cleveland, Ohio 44113

Public Defender
https://publicdefender.cuyahogacounty.gov/
2079 East 9th Street, Suite 5-200
Cleveland Ohio 44115

Recorded Documents
https://cuyahogacounty.gov/fiscal-officer/departments/real-property
2079 East 9th Street, 4th Floor
Cleveland OH 44115

Sheriff
shcuy@cuyahogacounty.us
1215 West 3rd Street
Cleveland OH 44113

Treasurer
https://cuyahogacounty.gov/treasury
2079 East 9th Street
Cleveland OH 44115

Veterans Service
http://cuyahogavets.org/
1849 Prospect Avenue, Ground Floor
Cleveland OH 44115

Weights and Measures
https://www.cuyahogacounty.gov/consumeraffairs
2079 East 9th Street, 2nd Floor
Cleveland OH 44115

Main non-governmental

FamilySearch
https://www.familysearch.org/search/catalog
FamilySearch is a free website with digitized records. Records located for Cuyahoga County include: Auditor, Board of Elections, Common Pleas, County Commissioners, Department of Health, Probate Court, Recorder, and Supreme Court.

Cleveland Public Library
https://cpl.org/topic/genealogy/
Louis Stokes Wing
525 Superior Avenue
6th Floor Center for Local and Global History
Records for Cleveland and Cuyahoga County include city directories, telephone books, county marriage certificates, Ohio death certificates, military/war and newspaper microfilm. The map collection includes ward maps and insurance maps, high school yearbooks, voter lists, Cleveland court cases index 1837-1877, list of public office holders 1802-1891. The Center also contains research guides for African American resources. Some databases are free to Ohio library card holders.

Western Reserve Historical Society
10825 East Boulevard
Cleveland, OH
https://www.wrhs.org/
Western Reserve Historical Society, a part of the Cleveland History Center, has a large collection of information regarding Cuyahoga County. Searching the library collections with the keyword Cuyahoga gives the extensive listing for the county. Please check the website for days of operation.
In September 2023, a fire broke out in the basement of the Library Building closing the library for restoration. The Library is now open to the public Thursday, Friday and Saturdays by appointment only. (This information was taken from the Library's website: **https://www.wrhs.org/plan-visit/places-to-visit/library).**

Heritage Books by Jana Sloan Broglin: